OECD Food and Agricultural Reviews

AF706580

Innovation, Agricultural Productivity and Sustainability in Estonia

BETTER POLICIES FOR BETTER LIVES

This work is published under the responsibility of the Secretary-General of the OECD. The opinions expressed and arguments employed herein do not necessarily reflect the official views of OECD member countries.

This document, as well as any data and any map included herein, are without prejudice to the status of or sovereignty over any territory, to the delimitation of international frontiers and boundaries and to the name of any territory, city or area.

Please cite this publication as:
OECD (2018), *Innovation, Agricultural Productivity and Sustainability in Estonia*, OECD Food and Agricultural Reviews, OECD Publishing, Paris.
http://dx.doi.org/10.1787/9789264288744-en

ISBN 978-92-64-28871-3 (print)
ISBN 978-92-64-28874-4 (PDF)

Series: OECD Food and Agricultural Reviews
ISSN 2411-426X (print)
ISSN 2411-4278 (online)

The statistical data for Israel are supplied by and under the responsibility of the relevant Israeli authorities. The use of such data by the OECD is without prejudice to the status of the Golan Heights, East Jerusalem and Israeli settlements in the West Bank under the terms of international law.

Photo credits: Cover © Enno Merivee, private collection.

Corrigenda to OECD publications may be found on line at: *www.oecd.org/about/publishing/corrigenda.htm*.

© OECD 2018

You can copy, download or print OECD content for your own use, and you can include excerpts from OECD publications, databases and multimedia products in your own documents, presentations, blogs, websites and teaching materials, provided that suitable acknowledgement of OECD as source and copyright owner is given. All requests for public or commercial use and translation rights should be submitted to *rights@oecd.org*. Requests for permission to photocopy portions of this material for public or commercial use shall be addressed directly to the Copyright Clearance Center (CCC) at *info@copyright.com* or the Centre français d'exploitation du droit de copie (CFC) at *contact@cfcopies.com*.

Foreword

Innovation, Agricultural Productivity and Sustainability in Estonia is part of the OECD Food and Agricultural Reviews series. This review was undertaken at the request of the Estonian Ministry of Rural Affairs. We are particularly grateful for the support for this study from the Toomas Kevvai, Deputy Secretary General for Food Safety, Research and Development in the Estonian Ministry of Rural Affairs.

The review examines the conditions in which farms and businesses in Estonia undertake innovation in the food and agriculture sector to become more productive and environmentally sustainable. It starts with an overview of the food and agriculture sector and outlines development challenges and opportunities (Chapter 2). A wide range of policies which influence incentives for innovation are then examined: economic stability, governance and trust in institutions (Chapter 3); a favourable and predictable environment for investment (Chapter 4); capacities and public services enabling business development (Chapter 5); agricultural policy (Chapter 6) and the operation of the agricultural innovation system (Chapter 7).

Estonian policies are analysed following a framework developed by the OECD as part of its work on agricultural innovation and in response to a request from the G20 in 2012 under the Presidency of Mexico to evaluate the extent to which a wide range of policies facilitates productivity growth and sustainability in food and agriculture. The framework has been applied to Australia, Brazil, Canada, the Netherlands, Turkey and the United States and additional reviews are underway or planned.

This review was prepared by Catherine Moreddu and Laura Munro from the OECD Trade and Agricultural Directorate and in close collaboration with the Estonian Ministry of Rural Affairs under the leadership of Helena Pärenson. Karine Souvanheuane and Urszula Ziebinska provided statistical support. Martina Abderrahmane provided editorial assistance and publication support.

The review draws heavily on a comprehensive report prepared by experts from the Institute of Economics and Social Sciences of the Estonian University of Life Science, led by Ants-Hannes Viira, on behalf of the Ministry of Rural Affairs. The review also draws on OECD analysis in various economic and social policy fields and includes cross-country comparable indicators.

At the Institute of Economics and Social Sciences of the Estonian University of Life Science, Anne Põder, Kersti Aro, Katrin Kreegimäe, Helis Luik, Jelena Ariva, Katri Kall, Liis Oper, Birgit Maasing, Katrin Lemsalu, Anu-Ell Visberg, Viia Parts, Raul Omel, Mati Mõtte and Ants-Hannes Viira provided the information for Chapters 2 to 7, with contributions from Külli Kõrgesaar in translating the materials from Estonian to English.

This report has benefitted from detailed comments from Toomas Kevvai, Külli Kaare, Mai Talvik, Kristel Maidre, Reena Osolin, Sille Teiter, Katre Kirt, Eveli Naaris, Marika Ruberg, Reelika Päädam, Reno Paju, Veronika Vallner-Kranich, Ragni Koitmaa, Erkki Miller, Eike Lepmets, Merle Saaliste, Kristi Lember, Tiina Vares from the Estonian Ministry of Rural Affairs, Ants-Hannes Viira and his colleagues from the Institute of Economics and Social Sciences of the Estonian University of Life Science, and Marju Aamisepp, Eduard Matveev from the Rural Economy Research Centre as well as Eneli Viik from the Agricultural Research Centre. It has also received valuable comments from Carmel Cahill, Frank Van Tongeren, Morvarid Bagherzadeh, Olga Melyukhina, Guillaume Gruère, Jussi Lankoski, Emily Gray, Shingo Kimura and Michael Ryan of the OECD Trade and Agricultural Directorate, and Caroline Klein of the OECD Economics Department.

This review was declassified by the Working Party on Agricultural Policies and Markets in November 2017.

Table of contents

Tables

Figures

Boxes

Acronyms

AB	Agricultural Board
AIS	Agricultural Innovation System
AKIS	Agricultural Knowledge and Innovation System
ARC	Estonian Agricultural Research Centre
ARIB	Estonian Agricultural Registers and Information Board
ASTI	Agricultural Science and Technology Indicators
AWU	Annual Work Unit
BAT	Best Available Technology
BERD	Business Expenditure on R&D
CAP	Common Agricultural Policy
CC	Competence Centre
CF	Cohesion Fund
GCI	Global Competitiveness Indicators
CMO	Common Market Organisation
COP21	Paris Climate Conference
EAFRD	European Agricultural Fund for Rural Development
EAGF	European Agricultural Guarantee Fund
EB	Environmental Board
EC	European Commission
ECRI	Estonian Crop Research Institute
EDF	Estonian Development Fund
EE	Enterprise Estonia
EEA	European Economic Area
EEA	European Environment Agency
EELC	Estonian Environmental Law Centre
EERC	Estonian Environmental Research Centre
EFM	Environmentally Friendly Management
EFSA	European Food Safety Authority
EIA	Environmental impact assessments
EIP	European Innovation Partnership
EIPTTC	Estonian Intellectual Property and Technology Transfer Centre
EKKA	Estonian Quality Agency for Higher and Vocational Education
ELASA	Estonian Broadband Development Foundation
ELF	Estonian Fund for Nature
EMFF	European Maritime and Fisheries Fund
EMÜ	Estonian University of Life Science
EPO	Estonian Patent Office
ERC	Estonian Research Council
ERDF	European Regional Development Fund
ESF	European Social Fund
ESI	European Structural and Investment (fund)
ETIS	Estonian Research Information System

EU	European Union
EU15	15 member states of the European Union, which were members in 2003
EU28	28 member states of the European Union in 2015
EUSAE	European Union Structural Assistance to Estonia
FACCE-JPI	Joint Programming Initiative on Agriculture, Food Security and Climate Change
FADN	Farm Accounting Data Network
FAO	Food and Agriculture Organization
FDI	Foreign Direct Investment
FP7	Seventh Framework Programme for Research and Technological Development
GAEC	Good Agricultural and Environmental Conditions
GCI	Global Competitiveness Index
GDP	Gross Domestic Product
GEDI	Global Entrepreneurship and Development Institute
GERD	Gross domestic expenditure on R&D
GHG	Greenhouse gas
GSSE	General Services Support Estimate
ha	Hectare
HACCP	Hazard Analysis Critical Control Point
ICT	Information and Communications Technology
IP	Intellectual Property
IPP	Intellectual Property Protection
IPR	Intellectual Property Rights
IRF	Institutional Research Funding
IT	Information Technology
JPI	Joint Programming Initiatives
kg	kilogramme
km	kilometre
km/h	Kilometre per hour
LU	Livestock unit
MEAC	Ministry of Economic Affairs and Communications
MER	Ministry of Education and Research
MFN	Most-Favoured Nation
MoE	Ministry of the Environment
MoF	Ministry of Finance
MPS	Market Price Support
MRA	Ministry of Rural Affairs
N	Nitrogen
NATARC	Natural History Archives and Information Network
NGO	Non-Governmental Organisation
NIR	National Inventory Report
NRN	National Rural Network
OECD	Organisation for Economic Co-operation and Development

P	Phosphorus
PCT	Patent Co-operation Treaty
PIAAC	Programme for the International Assessment of Adult Competencies
PISA	Programme for International Student Assessment
PMR	Product Market Regulation
PO	Producers Organisation
PPP	Purchasing Power Parity
PPP	Public-Private Partnership
PRF	Personal Research Funding
R&D	Research and Development
RDF	Rural Development Foundation
RDI	Research, Development and Innovation
RDP	Rural Development Plan/Programme
RECR	Rural Economy Research Centre
SAPS	Single Area Payment Scheme
SME	Small and Medium Sized Enterprise
SMR	Statutory Management Requirements
SP	Sole proprietor
t	tonne
TBA	Tartu Biotechnology Park
TFP	Total Factor Productivity
TNA	Transitional National Aid
TRIPS	Trade-Related Aspects of Intellectual Property Rights
TSE	transmissible spongiform encephalopathy
TU	University of Tartu
TUT	Tallinn University of Technology
UAA	Utilised Agricultural Area
UN	United Nations
UNFCCC	UN Framework Convention on Climate Change
UPOV	International Union for the Protection of New Varieties of Plants
USDA	United States Department of Agriculture
VCS	Voluntary Coupled Support
VFB	Veterinary and Food Board
YFS	young farmers' scheme
WBG	World Bank Group
WEF	World Economic Forum
WGI	Worldwide Governance Indicators
WTO	World Trade Organisation

Executive summary

The Estonian agricultural sector has experienced significant growth and structural change during the last 25 years, in particular since the country joined the European Union in 2004. High growth in agricultural production and productivity was achieved with relatively limited environmental pressure, taking advantage of abundant land and water resources. Agricultural production became more diverse in response to market and policy signals, as illustrated by the development of organic production. Most productivity improvements, however, occurred in larger farms, with smaller farms often lagging behind. Moreover, the food processing sector has not invested as much and adjusted as fast as primary agriculture, and is still struggling in terms of capacity and competitiveness, thus impeding the development of new markets and new products from agriculture.

Looking forward, the agri-food sector will have to keep adjusting to changing conditions, such as higher labour costs, CAP developments, more diverse demand, and climate change, which will provide both opportunities and challenges. The need to reduce greenhouse gas emissions for example is likely to affect livestock production and grassland. Responding to demand for diversified, healthier products can be an opportunity to develop new products, and improve the competitiveness of the Estonian agro-food sector. Maintaining the recent growth rates sustainably will require further innovation and adaptation.

Agricultural policy contributed greatly to the modernisation of Estonian agriculture. Within the EU framework, Estonia's implementation of the Common Agricultural Policy (and pre-accession schemes) generally supports productive investment to acquire modern technology to increase productivity and meet EU environmental and other regulations, while limiting market distortions. Specific policy measures also encourage more environmentally-friendly practices, which contributed to positive trends in the environmental performance of agriculture. Some areas for improvement remain, however, at the local level, and climate change may pose specific challenges for the livestock sector. It is crucial for agricultural policy to continue providing a long-term vision for the sector, which recognises the need to improve environmental performance while maintaining productivity growth.

The Estonian agricultural innovation system needs to become more participatory and responsive to facilitate further sustainable productivity growth. So far, it has played an important role in facilitating the diffusion of domestic and imported technological and other innovations facilitating sustainable productivity growth. High educational achievements in the Estonian population provide a fertile ground for innovation and growth. Estonian public research is strong, including in food and agriculture, but the contribution of private firms is limited. The government plays a strong role in the governance of innovation, and the approach to innovation remains largely top-down. More active participation of stakeholders in the Estonian agricultural innovation system, and stronger collaboration between public and private actors, at the national and international levels, would make the system more responsive to needs. Better information on challenges and opportunities for the sector is essential to guide private investment and policy decisions.

The general policy and regulatory environment is mostly supportive of investment. High quality public institutions have developed clear regulations and sound programmes within the EU framework. As a small economy, joining the single market has brought high benefits from trade and investment. Moreover, the policy environment is conducive to entrepreneurship and investment, with sound macro-economic fundamentals, low regulatory barriers by OECD standards, and well-developed financial markets in particular.

Improvements in infrastructure helped the agro-food sector by connecting people to markets and providing information and services for improved productivity and cost-efficiency. Infrastructure development and maintenance continues, with significant contributions from EU structural funds. Increasingly, infrastructure investments in Estonia also aim to improve environmental sustainability through the provision of renewable energy, or the development of resource-saving technologies. Providing infrastructure and services in remote rural areas remains, however, a challenge requiring innovative solutions, including through Information and Communication Technologies (ICTs).

A serious and growing challenge for food and agriculture is to attract and retain people, all the more as rural areas face labour and skills shortages. Mechanisms are in place to help agriculture-related education and training respond to the growing demand for skilled labour, such as the monitoring of future labour needs.

Main issues and policy recommendations are outlined in the table below:

Main findings	Key recommendations
Incentives for private investment	
Access to traditional export markets has been disrupted by the Russian ban on imports.	Promote a regional approach to trade diversification in order to gain new markets for agri-food products.
Agricultural loans have a higher risk premium on markets.	Promote risk management, through financial tools.
High taxes on labour increase labour cost.	Further reduce the taxation of labour earnings to facilitate employment in food and agriculture.
Environmental taxes and charges have increased, but do not always reflect environmental damages. Fuel used in agriculture is taxed at 27% of the standard rate.	Explore the scope for using environmental and agri-environmental taxes. Reduce gradually the tax rebate for fuel used in agriculture and encourage the use of renewable energy.
Capacities and services	
Estonia has a good potential for producing biomass from agriculture and forestry.	Develop green energy, and facilitate the development of bio-based products.
The drainage system is upgraded but requires maintenance, all the more with climate change.	Facilitate cooperation among land owners and farmers to improve the maintenance of the drainage system.
Rural areas face a declining population and shortage of skills.	Efforts to attract and maintain people in rural areas could include improving infrastructure connection, and services, providing information on employment opportunities, and facilitating relocation.
The number of Estonian students is declining overall and especially in agriculture and bioeconomy.	Attract foreign students in agriculture-related topics, by offering more courses in foreign languages and adapting them to demand.
Agricultural policy	
Implementation of agricultural policy supported investment to increase productivity and meet EU environmental and other regulations, while limiting market distortions.	Continue to limit distortions and develop support targeting for specific objectives; Promote risk management and strengthen risk management tools; Phase out national complements to Direct Payments.
Despite improvements in environmental performance some local issues remain.	Strengthen efforts by providing targeted advice on sustainable technologies and practices.
COP21 engagements may impose pressure on agriculture to reduce GHG emissions	Explore options for reducing GHG emissions from agriculture, in particular grazing livestock, and facilitate farmers' adaptation and relevant research.
The competitiveness of the agri-food sector remains low.	Develop a competiveness strategy with the sector.
Stakeholders need to develop a strategy for responding to specific market demand (e.g. organic products) and for strengthening technological, organisational, and marketing innovation.	Make use of the opportunity given by the CAP to recognise Producer and Branch Organisations and support the participation of farmers or farmers' organisations in knowledge networks.

Main findings	Key recommendations
Estonia has strong Information and Communication Technologies (ICT).	Develop further ICT solutions to collect and manage data, reduce control costs and implement more targeted policies, and to improve traceability along the food chain. Explore the scope for using output-based agri-environmental measures with the help of ICT for monitoring outcomes.
Direct incentives to innovation	
The abundance of strategic documents, action plans, programmes and projects does not facilitate coherence.	Consolidate innovation and growth strategy documents to improve clarity.
The policy framework is driven by supply-side measures, with relatively little input from, or ownership by, the business community.	Better involve the private actors in policy dialogue on R&D and innovation policies at an early stage.
The approach to innovation is top-down.	Facilitate discussion among and between producers and the industry to enable them to contribute more effectively and efficiently to the agricultural innovation system.
The funding of R&D for agriculture fluctuates across programming periods and is highly dependent on short-term projects.	Improve the stability of R&D funding; Continue developing longer-term, larger scope project funding. Explore ways to complement public funding, for example from foundations or agricultural levies.
Maintaining good research infrastructure is essential for future progress and to maintain excellence and collaboration capacity at national and international levels.	Maintain and improve research infrastructure, including EU and regional networks. Explore further opportunities to share public infrastructure with the private sector.
The contribution of private companies to research is limited, in particular in the food and agricultural sector.	Identify areas where local companies and researchers could collaborate, e.g. through public-private partnerships, to develop local or niche products and innovation.
Skills for innovation in the system need to be upgraded continuously.	Encourage a diverse supply of advice that is accessible, including through ICT, and responsive to market demand, and goes beyond technical issues towards management, marketing, and sustainability improvements. Continue ensuring farm advisors are well-trained professionals with up-to-date skills.
Innovation and policy evaluation are becoming more complex and require a wealth of information.	Continue developing information systems, including market intelligence (big data) and research results

Chapter 1

Overall assessment and recommendations: Innovation for agricultural productivity and sustainability in Estonia

This chapter introduces the framework used to analyse the extent to which Estonian policies foster productivity and sustainability in the food and agriculture sector and presents an overview of findings for a wide range of policies. It also includes specific policy recommendations for each policy area reviewed.

A framework to analyse policies for innovation, productivity and sustainability in the food and agricultural sector

Improving agricultural productivity growth to meet the growing demand for food, feed, fuel and fibre will be achieved through more efficient use of natural and human resources. A wide range of policies affect the performance of the food and agriculture sector, and these need to be considered alongside agriculture-specific policies.

The framework applied in this review considers the full range of policy incentives and disincentives to innovation, structural change, natural resource use, and climate change as drivers of productivity growth and the sustainable use of resources (Figure 1.1).

This review begins with an overview of the characteristics and performance of the food and agriculture sector and the future challenges faced by this sector (Chapter 2). A wide range of policies is considered according to the main channels or incentive areas through which they affect drivers of productivity growth and environmental sustainability:

- Economic stability and trust in institutions (justice, security, property rights), which are essential to attract long-term investment in the economy (Chapter 3).
- Private investment, which in turn requires a transparent and predictable environment that balances the interests of investors and society (Chapter 4).
- Capacity building, including the provision of essential public services (Chapter 5).
- Agricultural policy, domestic and trade-related (Chapter 6).
- The agricultural innovation system (Chapter 7).

A policy area can affect productivity and sustainability drivers through more than one channel, and policies can have a positive or negative effect depending on the type and intensity of measures. This review draws on background information provided by the Institute of Economics and Social Sciences of the Estonian University of Life Science (EMÜ), recent OECD economic and innovation reviews, and internationally comparable data.

Figure 1.1. Policy drivers of innovation, productivity and sustainability in the food and agriculture sector

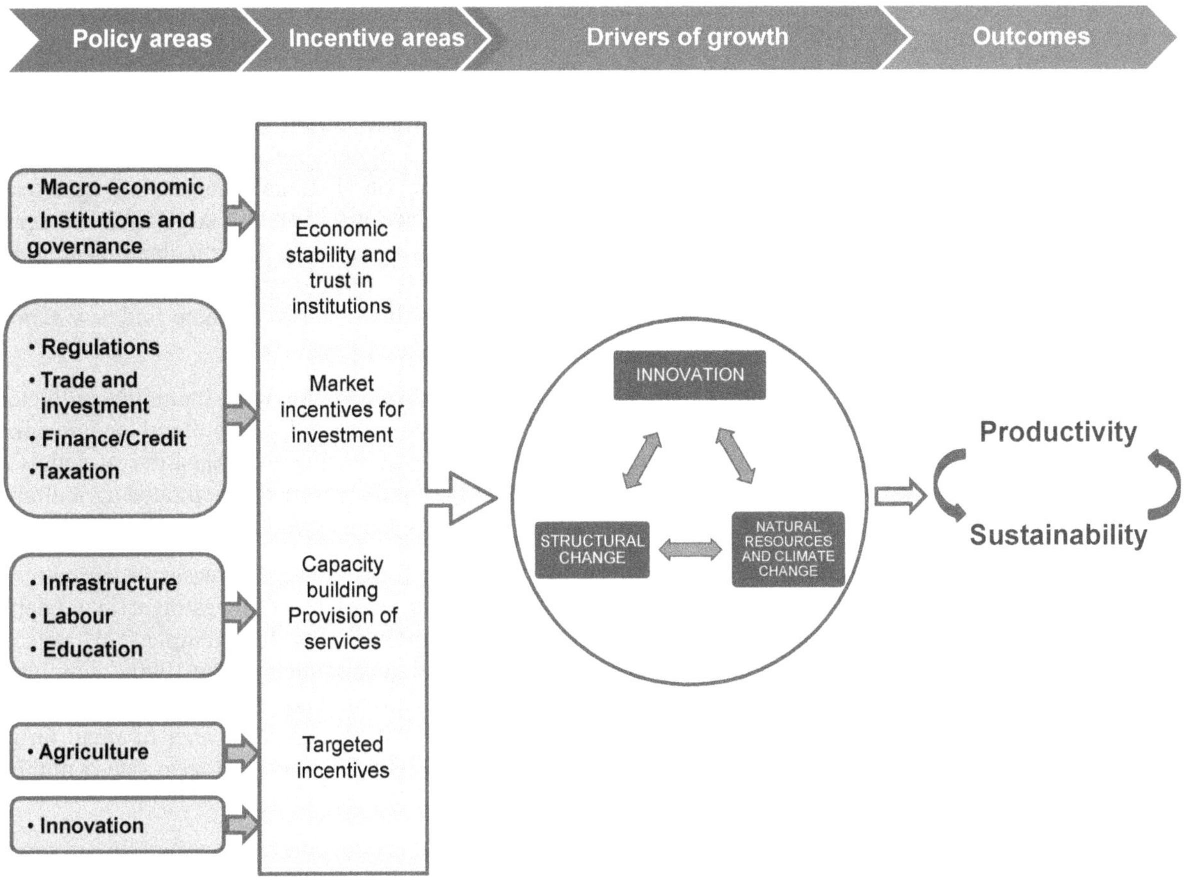

Source: OECD (2015), "Analysing Policies to improve agricultural productivity growth, sustainably: Revised framework", www.oecd.org/agriculture/policies/innovation.

Main challenges and opportunities for the Estonian food and agriculture sector

Estonia is the northernmost and smallest of the Baltic countries, which joined the European Union (EU) in 2004. The population — 1.3 million in 2015 — is relatively urban and has been decreasing since the country regained its independence in 1991, and this affects many areas of the economy, including the provision of services, the education system and labour markets.

The Estonian economy has experienced significant growth and structural changes during the last 25 years and in particular since EU accession in 2004. Gross Domestic Product (GDP) per capita has grown faster than the OECD average since 2000, but it remains 30% lower than the EU average. Estonia's economy is well integrated into global trade, and the economic, policy and regulatory environment is open to domestic and foreign direct investment (Chapters 3 and 4).

Agricultural policy and regulatory changes linked to land restitution starting in 1990 and accession to the European Union, in particular the implementation of the Common Agricultural Policy (CAP), have significantly impacted the agricultural sector. Following a contraction during the transition in the 1990s, agricultural production grew in the 2000s in response to CAP incentives to invest in agriculture, and the clarification of land property rights.

As a result of structural change in the sector and the wider economy, the share of agriculture in GDP has decreased, although not as fast as its share in employment. Compared to the EU and OECD averages, Estonia's agriculture accounts for a larger share of GDP and a lower share of employment.

Estonia's agricultural sector is dominated by milk production, but cereals, oilseeds and protein crop production has increased considerably in the last two decades. Meat production has also increased over the last two decades, though production levels have declined in the last couple of years in response to lower market prices and the outbreak of African Swine Fever (ASF).

While Estonian exports are growing, the country has a large trade deficit of agricultural and food products due to high imports of processed foods. The composition of Estonia's agro-food trade suggests the food manufacturing industry is not as developed as primary production. Estonia's imports of agro-food products are mainly for household consumption (over 70%), while the country exports a larger share of agro-food products for industrial use than the EU average. The lower processing capacity is particularly clear at the sub-sector level: Estonia is a net exporter of cereals, but a net importer of processed cereals — and a net exporter of live animals, but a net importer of meat. Strengthening the value-chain would help find new export markets and develop new products.

Estonia's agricultural sector enjoys abundant land and water resources. Arable land, including cultivated grassland and feed crop land, accounts for more than two-thirds of agricultural land. Agricultural land area has increased since EU accession, as agricultural land that was abandoned during the transition period was reclaimed to qualify for the EU single area payment scheme (SAPS). Natural resources facilitated agricultural development and could also sustain the production of biomass for energy from agriculture and forestry.

Agricultural total factor productivity (TFP) is growing fast since 2000. Strong increases in agricultural production, with more efficient input use were facilitated by economies of scale, investment in modern, including labour-saving, technologies, and seed and animal genetic improvements, for example. This reflects to some extent the catching up of the sector following the transition and uncertainties of the 1990s, stimulated by EU investment support. The large technically-efficient, input intensive and innovative farms, which dominate land use, animal numbers and production, drive TFP growth, while a large number of small farms remain. On average, farms are relatively large by EU standards and the weighted median farm size continues to increase.

The food processing sector has not adjusted as fast as agricultural production and is struggling in terms of capacity and competitiveness, as illustrated by agro-food trade flows. As the farm sector, Estonia's food processing sector is also dualistic, but large Estonian food processing companies are smaller than their foreign competitors. The dairy processing sector in particular needs to consolidate, invest in automation and increase processing efficiency to reduce costs. In the food processing sector, Estonia achieves half the EU labour productivity, as measured by value-added per annual work unit. In comparison, labour productivity in the Estonian farm sector has strongly increased since the early 1990s, but it remains 20% lower than the EU average.

Paralleling the growth in agricultural TFP and production, the use of natural resources has similarly shifted. Agricultural land area increased at a slower rate than production volume and TFP growth. Estonia's direct on-farm energy consumption and ammonia emissions also increased, raising concerns about sustainability. Eutrophication due to nutrient loads from diffuse and point sources threatens sustainable management of agricultural and water resources in certain regions. The country's phosphorus deficit has also worsened. However, higher TFP and output growth in recent years has been achieved with improvements in Estonia's nitrogen balance and lower water use, a positive trend in sustainability terms.

Environmental problems are mainly localised. Although increasing, the intensity of agriculture is relatively low and the state of eco-systems ranges from good to favourable according to the European Environment Agency. A significant share of Estonian agricultural land area is farmed under extensive and biodiversity-friendly agricultural practices, including grassland and organically-farmed area, which has almost quadrupled over the last decade. The recent development of protein crops for food and feed use also improved soil quality and thus the sustainability of agriculture. The share of land used for intensive agricultural practices is below 10%, and concerns mainly livestock farming. Moreover, some regions with fragile geological conditions need further attention in order to manage agricultural and water resources sustainably, in particular the Nitrate Vulnerable Zone in Central and North-Eastern Estonia.

Looking forward, climate change projections suggest that both grasslands and crop production may benefit from shifts in climatic conditions in the coming decades. The growing season has already begun to lengthen in recent decades, favouring the cultivation of winter crops. While such trends may continue, potential risk factors include an increase in the frequency of extreme meteorological phenomena (droughts, excessive moisture, flooding) and the spread of pests and diseases.

Overall, Estonian agriculture has seized opportunities offered by the market and policy environment, in particular EU membership, to catch up and develop further. High productivity growth, and high levels in some cases, has been achieved with relatively limited environmental issues so far. There is still scope for improvement, in particular in the smaller farms. Moreover, the sector will have to adjust to changing market, environmental, regulatory and policy conditions. The need to reduce greenhouse gas emissions for example is likely to affect livestock production and grassland. Responding to demand for diversified, healthier products can be another challenge as well as an opportunity to develop new products, and improve the competitiveness of the Estonian agro-food sector. Maintaining the recent growth rates sustainably will require further innovation and adaptation, but more careful investment, improvements along the food chain, the development of new markets and increased consideration of sustainability issues and consumer demand, as well as longer-term challenges and opportunities.

Improve further the supportive framework conditions for innovation and entrepreneurship

Macro-policies, institutions and regulations are mostly supportive of investment, but future growth depends on the ability to diversify sources of competitiveness

Macroeconomic and institutional conditions in Estonia favour innovation and entrepreneurship. Estonia is a small, competitive economy, with sound macroeconomic fundamentals, and a well-educated and flexible labour force. The fiscal space to support growth-enhancing policies is large: gross public debt as a percentage of GDP is the lowest in the OECD area and is projected to decrease in the medium term (OECD, 2017a). According to the OECD Economic Survey of Estonia (2017a), there is scope for increasing spending on measures that boost growth potential and welfare, and considering allowing a small deficit in the government budget rule in the longer term.

Even though the overall economic performance of Estonia is good, competitive advantage is still in low-cost labour or natural resources. In addition, with wage growth exceeding the productivity growth rate in recent years, the profitability of companies has declined, partly explaining low investment. In terms of business sophistication, Estonian companies do not have broad presence in the entire value chain; rather they are involved in individual steps of the value chain (OECD, 2017b). Moreover, they do not use marketing to a large extent to differentiate their products, including in the agri-food sector. To maintain long-term competitiveness, Estonia needs to diversify its sources of competitive advantage and invest along the value-chain, including in the agri-food chain.

Estonia enjoys high quality public institutions at the national level and steps have been taken to improve territorial governance. Estonia is considered as a secure country for business, with good ethical practices, independent judicial system and transparent policies. The country is recognised for the high efficiency of government spending and low burden of regulations, though Estonia has lower efficiency of the legal and judicial system for companies in settling disputes.

The decision-making process in Estonia is very transparent, but the 2011 OECD Public Governance Review (OECD, 2011) noted some drawbacks in taking account of stakeholders' opinions. In a sector with a dual structure like agriculture, a large number of actors and multiple stakeholders reflecting diverse interests poses particular challenges. But stakeholders' involvement can help improve policy relevance and effectiveness, in particular in the agricultural innovation system. Regarding governance, OECD Economic Surveys noted that there is no institution in charge of a regular assessment of productivity challenges and of monitoring policies in the field of competitiveness and that the European Council advised to set up a national productivity board. The OECD Economic Survey of Estonia (2017a) recommends establishing an independent body to advise on policies to raise productivity. Regarding the food and agricultural sector, this body could go beyond evaluation of agricultural policy to consider the whole enabling environment for the sector.

The 2011 Public Governance Review (OECD, 2011) also identified problems in territorial management and relations between different levels of government hindering efficient delivery of public services of equal quality across the territory. As part of the State reform, the abolition of county governments, the merging of some institutions, and the planned reduction in the number of municipalities, are steps to improve the situation. The 2017 OECD Environmental Performance Review of Estonia (OECD, 2017c) recommends a continuation of territorial reform to ease resource and capacity constraints. The expected improvements in the rural economy will benefit the food and agriculture sector.

The regulatory environment for entrepreneurship in Estonia is generally conducive to investment, including in food and agriculture. Reforms have eased regulatory barriers, which were overall lower than the OECD average in 2013. In particular, regulatory procedure is less complex and the administrative burden to start-up companies is lower than average, while the regulatory protection of incumbents is among the highest in the OECD area. Indicators for 2013 suggest there was considerable room for improvement in particular regarding the licences and permits system, and the reduction of entry barriers in service and network sectors (e.g. gas, electricity, water, rail, air passenger transport, road freight transport and telecoms). Significant progress has been made since, but some burden remains in environmental regulation.

Natural resources, farm inputs and food products are governed mainly by EU regulations and governance rules

Regulations on natural resources and environment in Estonia are extensive, but fragmented across multiple legal acts. This is driven in part by the increase in legislative activity — in particular, the adoption of EU regulations — during and since EU accession. For example, these laws govern the environmental monitoring system, the integrated environmental permit system and environmental liability, as well as land use, water management and biodiversity protection. Estonian regulations on the use of fertilisers have become increasingly strict in recent years. The 2017 OECD Environmental Performance Review of Estonia (OECD, 2017c) recommends to strengthen inter-ministerial co-ordination on environmental and sustainable development issues, including climate change, to better incorporate environmental concerns into strategic planning, sectoral policies and spatial planning; to encourage collaboration between local governments in all areas of their environmental competence; to consolidate legislation on natural resources and environment; and to continue developing guidelines and codes of best practices to facilitate access and understanding of regulations, and thus reduce costs and improve compliance. These actions would also facilitate enhanced sustainability and preparedness to climate change in the food and agricultural sector.

Environmental charges are also used to reduce the negative impact of economic activities on the environment. They include both natural resource use fees and pollution fees designed to decrease pollution from point sources.

Estonia also subscribes to major international and regional regulatory agreements concerning climate change and nature protection. Ensuring a clean living environment, raising the environmental awareness of the society, preservation of natural heritage and the sustainable use of natural resources is the main goal of many national and international environmental strategies, plans and agreements that Estonia has joined.

Additional incentives apply in agriculture as support is conditional on respecting regulations regarding natural resource use and protection, and the safety of food and feed products and farm inputs. This has required producers to adopt new technologies and production practices, with positive effects on productivity and sustainability.

Regulations on food safety and quality are mainly determined at the EU level and, since joining the European Union, Estonia has developed the necessary legislation and institutions to ensure compliance with regulations, including monitoring, control and information systems. This increases national and foreign consumers trust in the safety and quality attributes of Estonian agri-food products, thus facilitating access to markets and product differentiation. As the demand for products with specific attributes is growing, the government may have a role in ensuring the policy and regulatory environment facilitates the development and marketing of new products.

The Estonian economy is open to trade and investment, but further efforts could focus on removing remaining impediments and diversifying export markets

As a small economy with limited capacity to produce a large range of goods and services, Estonia is open to trade, the sum of exports and imports of goods and services representing over 150% of GDP in 2016. Since joining the European Union in 2004, it is part of the Common market. However, the common trade policy imposes higher tariffs for capital and intermediate goods than in major non-EU trading partners. Lower tariffs on intermediate goods would lower the cost of specialised inputs and machinery equipment, and thus increase the competitiveness of the agro-food sector. The composition of Estonia's agro-food trade suggests that competitive advantage is in primary production, as Estonia's imports of agro-food products are mainly for household consumption (over 70%), while the country exports a larger share of agro-food products for industrial use than the EU average. These exports are mainly to neighbouring countries, main members of the European Union and the Russian Federation, although the latter have declined since the Federation introduced an import ban in August 2014. Concerted efforts along the food chain are needed to diversify agro-food exports, both in terms of adding value and partners. Moreover, despite significant progress, trade administrative procedures, such as border agency cooperation, could be further simplified. To further facilitate trade administration, the 2017 OECD Economic Survey of Estonia (OECD, 2017a) recommends completing a one-stop shop for administrative formalities, and improving access to information on trade regulation (e.g. agreements with third countries and appeal procedures). Estonia is generally open to Foreign Direct Investment (FDI), with inwards stocks accounting for a relatively high share of GDP. Few restrictions remain, mainly related to quotas on foreign workers, but some concern the acquisition of land.

Both financial markets and agricultural policy have facilitated investment in agriculture, but better risk management will facilitate future access to loans

Financial markets are well-developed, and a diversity of banks offer services, although competition, and alternative funding sources for innovative activities, are limited. The agriculture and food sector had access to loans to fund its development. It seems, however, that credit institutions have imposed a higher risk margin on enterprises operating in the agricultural sector. One issue may be the lack of collaterals as over 60% of farm land is rented. EU payments providing an income safety net may act as collaterals to some extent. Nevertheless, the loan balance of agriculture has doubled in the past ten years, with growth slowing temporarily at the end of the 2000s because of the financial crisis. The State Rural Development Foundation facilitates access to credit to rural companies and farms, through guarantees, direct loans and loans to credit institutions.

Co-financed by the EU Common Agricultural Policy (CAP), the Estonian Rural Development Programme (RDP) supports investment in farm modernisation and the development of diversification activities, which receive a higher share of total funds than the EU average. Investment grants from the RDP are generally targeted to investments aiming to improve competitiveness and compliance with environmental, food safety and animal welfare regulations, and with conditions attached to mandatory or voluntary payments to farmers. In recent years, farmers have faced income problems, in particular in the dairy sector, leading to an increase in payment default. Promoting risk management and strengthening risk management tools, including through tax and financing tools, would help farmers manage temporary cash flow problems.

The tax system is being reformed, and will continue to favour investment, while enhancing sustainability

The Estonian tax system has been so far relatively simple with few exceptions. At 20%, the tax on corporate profit is relatively modest by OECD standards, and only applies to distributed profits. As part of the revision of the taxation system in 2017, differentiated income tax rates are introduced from 2018 in the form of lower tax rates or higher deductions for smaller incomes. Considering since July 2017 that corporate costs related to accommodation and commuting costs of employees living far way from work are not fringe benefits, and thus not taxable, is expected to facilitate the mobility of employees who live in rural areas.

While the standard corporate income tax rate is modest at 20%, companies face high taxes on labour, and when all tax sources (income, property, labour, turnover, fuel) are taken into account, the tax rate is close to 50%. This tax rate, which increases labour costs, is higher than in neighbouring countries, and thus may impede competitiveness, and favour capital investment over labour use.

There are some tax exemptions for the agriculture and food sector. Agricultural exceptions include an income tax deduction for the self-employed on the sales of self-produced unprocessed agricultural products. Two other general tax deductions help farmers manage income risk and facilitate investment: the ability to deduct income losses in one year from the business income of the following seven taxation periods, and the option to save funds in a special account for future investment.

Environmental taxes and charges have been increasing since 2005. They apply equally to food and agricultural activities. A lower excise duty applies to fuel used in agricultural activities (27% of the full rate, compared to an EU average of 6%). Implementing the full tax rate for fuel used in agriculture would lead to more efficient use of energy in the sector.

Estonia is one of the very few OECD countries that do not provide tax incentives for R&D. The exclusive corporate tax system, where profits are not taxed until their distribution, acts as an economic tax incentive to investment.

The 2017 OECD Economic Survey of Estonia (OECD, 2017a) finds that financial incentives to prevent or reduce environmental damage are too low, and recommends setting tax rates on oil shale, vehicle and energy use at a level that better reflects the environmental damage they generate.

Recommendations to improve incentives for private investment

- Promote a regional approach to trade diversification in order to gain new markets for agri-food products, drawing on regional strengths (such as clean air, extensive agriculture, or organic production).
- Promote risk management, through financial tools, to facilitate farm and agro-food firm access to loans and reduce the risk premium currently applied in the sector.
- Further reduce the taxation of labour earnings, in particular of low earnings, to reduce the costs of labour and facilitate employment in food and agriculture.
- Explore the scope for using environmental and agri-environmental taxes, including an evaluation of potential benefits for the environment (OECD, 2017c). In particular, reduce gradually the tax rebate for fuel used in agriculture to reduce the use of fossil fuels, and at the same time invest in and encourage the use of renewable energy.

Improve the capacities and services for innovation, in particular in rural areas

Infrastructure improvement continues, aiming to reduce the rural-urban gap sustainably

The main challenges for the provision of infrastructure and services in Estonia are the high concentration of the population in main urban centres (over 60% is urbanised and 40% is concentrated around the capital city), and its low density in most rural areas. There are some problems with the availability and quality of infrastructure in rural areas, where agricultural and agri-food activities are located to a large extent. In remote rural areas with sparse population, facilitating the movement of goods and services, connecting people to markets and providing information and services for improved productivity and cost-efficiency requires innovative solutions, including through Information and Communication Technologies (ICTs). Increasingly, infrastructure investments in Estonia aim to improve environmental sustainability through the provision of renewable energy, or the development of resource-saving technologies, while ensuring efficiency and stability.

Infrastructure development and maintenance in Estonia have greatly benefited from EU structural funds, which cover up to 75% or 85% of infrastructure projects. The exception is the electrical grid infrastructure, which is financed from electricity transmission charges. The overall quality of physical infrastructure in

Estonia is comparable to the average of all OECD countries, but with significant differences among the type of infrastructure and in some cases regions.

With regard to transportation modes, port infrastructure is considered by business leaders to be well developed, thus facilitating international trade. Limited capacity of air and rail transport infrastructure mainly affects passengers; this is linked to the low number of international connections, and also the low speed of passenger trains. Most main-line railways have been upgraded to enable faster speed, and renovation is progressing. The availability of faster trains is not expected to affect food and agriculture directly, although reducing commuting time will help maintain rural communities, while allowing access to job markets, and thus offering off-farm income opportunities.

The unequal quality of road infrastructure increases local transport costs. Main roads are mostly in a good or very good condition, and basic roads in a satisfactory condition, but the secondary and local roads need improvement. Estonian entrepreneurs consider the condition of local roads as the worst structural impediment for their activities. In response, the Transport Development Plan 2014-20 aims to reduce the proportion of secondary and local roads in poor and very poor condition. This could be most beneficial for the transportation of perishable agricultural and food products, and to assist labour mobility.

Improving electricity supply at reasonable cost is a serious challenge in Estonia. According to local authorities, electricity capacity upgrading, poor technical quality of the electricity supply network and excessive pricing of grid connection are the main problems. Since electricity grid connection is expensive, the use of off-grid solutions or stand-alone power systems is considered for sparsely populated regions. In this context, agricultural land and activities may provide viable opportunities for generating electricity and energy using new technologies, such as windmills and biomass conversion. Food and agricultural activities in remote areas would also benefit from a more reliable energy supply. The *Estonian National Renewable Energy Action Plan Until 2030* sets the target of 50% of the energy produced from renewable energy sources in the gross final energy consumption, and 50% in electricity consumption by 2030. It contains measures that are aimed at increasing biomass availability, taking into account other biomass users (including agriculture).

The main infrastructure challenge for agriculture in Estonia is upgrading the systems for draining land of excess water. Drainage systems cover more than half of the utilised agricultural area. Most of them are over thirty years old and need reconstruction. In terms of land improvement, upgrading drainage systems is all the more important to increase productivity sustainably that climate change may lead to an increase in precipitations in Estonia. New technologies could ensure water and energy are used in a sustainable way, improving productivity and facilitating the development of new crops.

Investment in ICT facilitates business activities and service provision

Estonia invested successfully in ICT and continues to do so. Mobile telephone subscriptions are very high and internet use relatively high (80% of individuals use internet); almost all companies use computers and almost all enterprises have broadband internet connection, including farms. Since 2010, Estonia has been rapidly developing the basic broadband infrastructure (passive optical network) with EU support. The problem lies in making high-speed broadband access to the Internet network accessible to all end users. In this area, markets fail as communications operators do not have an economic interest in connecting users in remote areas. Connection issues in sparsely populated rural areas mean that there are also problems with the accessibility of e-services for both the residents and entrepreneurs. Digital Agenda 2020 aims to address this market failure.

Growing urbanisation has led to a growing regional imbalance in the provision of public and private services. Despite the worsening of the physical accessibility and the quality of services in rural areas due to increased urbanisation, the spread of internet, improvement of computer skills and the development of public e-services have facilitated access to services in rural areas. The widespread use of electronic identification (ID) makes administration practically paper free, fast and flexible. The development of the e-government, especially the elaboration of e-services for the public sector and their application by the citizens and enterprises has so far been the strength of the national ICT policy.

ICT development and everyday use of ICT technology have enabled most farmers and food processors a very good access to information concerning market developments, technological options and weather forecasts. Improving broadband Internet services in remote areas would provide local farmers and agri-food companies with better access to inputs, technologies, advice, and consumers, allowing them to take advantage of market opportunities.

The education system is flexible and performant, but needs to be more responsive to changing skills needs

The Estonian population has access to high quality education. Governance mechanisms give schools a high level of autonomy for resource allocation. The state sets national standards and establishes principles of education funding, supervision and quality assessment. Schools in Estonia have a level of autonomy above the OECD average, including the capacity to make decisions on the curriculum and to hire and dismiss teaching staff.

The strengths of the education system include high educational attainment, interest in sciences and technology, language skills, and gender equity. In addition, costs are relatively low compared to the OECD average. The quality of the Estonian education and training system is reflected in the high scores of students and adults population in international surveys. Basic level schoolchildren are among the best performers in reading, mathematics and science, wordwide. Estonian adults perform above average levels in numeracy and functional literacy.

A main challenge for the education system is to adjust to the smaller number of students as the number of children decreases and educational rates are already quite high. Others are to improve vocational education, respond to changing skills requirements, and offer opportunities for life-long training, as discussed below.

Estonian entrepreneurs and foreign investors consider the shortage of adequately trained personnel a key challenge in the local economic development. For example, the computer skills of employees need to be improved to meet contemporary requirements. In particular, according to the OECD Programme for the International Assessment of Adult Competencies (PIAAC) survey, the problem-solving skills in technology-rich environments of the personnel at Estonian educational institutions are almost the lowest, while the frequency of computer use at work is still among the average.

Increasing the number of doctoral graduates is a real challenge for Estonian research and innovation. The number of new doctorate holders per 1 000 population in the 25-34 age group is below the EU average. Furthermore, the number of applicants to doctoral studies may decrease in the coming years, reflecting not only the population decline, but also the lack of attractiveness of academic careers because of lower wages, and the lack of demand for PhD holders in the labour markets, as there are not enough large companies in Estonia that have the need and the opportunity to recruit PhD students and specialists with a PhD.

Labour markets are flexible, but struggle to attract and retain talent, in particular in rural areas

The Estonian labour market is considered as one of the most efficient among OECD countries, mainly due to the flexible employment policy. Labour mobility facilitates structural adjustment, including farm consolidation, by assisting excess labour in farming to exploit more remunerative non-farm income and employment opportunities. However, the capacity of the labour market to attract and retain talents is limited as Estonian workers are generally well-qualified, but are offered relatively low wages and salaries. As discussed below, this is particularly acute in rural areas. As illustrated by the negative population trend, this issue affects the long-term economic and social sustainability of Estonian development.

Rural areas face labour and skills shortage

Skilled workers are difficult to find in rural areas, as the population concentrates around urban centres, where better wages and working conditions attract younger people in particular. The labour market has been evolving in the recent decade, with the share of skill-intensive positions growing and the employment structure moving towards fully-skilled jobs. In rural settlements, more people of working age have a lower level of education than in cities, and the overall employment rate is lower.

The employment rate in rural areas has increased steadily, from 54% in 2009 to 65% in 2015. But the problem lies in the lower level of education of the rural working age population, which considerably limits their competitiveness in the labour market. Estonia has initiated a number of projects to improve skills match in rural areas. A citizen initiative "Come to live in the countryside" helps people, through a website, to find jobs and housing in the countryside, as well as opportunities for entrepreneurship. The Estonian Chamber of Commerce and Industry launched a project to bring together employers and talented young people who have gone abroad to study or work. National measures, such as training for unemployed and support for starting a business can also benefit rural employment. Estonian workers take advantage of training opportunities through the formal education system to improve the adequacy of their skills set with labour market demand (see below).

The problem is worse for agriculture, with its ageing labour force, lower than average wages, and reliance on low-cost, seasonal labour. In recent years, however, the average wages in agriculture have grown faster than the national average. An increase in the average wages and a more conscious choice of profession is expected to have a positive effect on the career choice made by younger people in rural areas.

Estonian agriculture offers seasonal jobs, which could attract workers from non-EU countries given that the remuneration is relatively low for Estonians and other EU citizens. However, the terms for recruiting temporary seasonal workers from non-EU countries are very restrictive, creating competitiveness problems, in particular for horticulture, which is a very labour intensive branch of agriculture. In particular, the annual immigration quota of non-EU citizens should not exceed 0.1% of the permanent population of Estonia per annum, and until recently, employers were required to pay them a remuneration amounting to 1.24 times the Estonian average annual wage. This wage supplement is no longer required. Together with the implementation of two EU directives on entry and residence of third-country nationals widening short-term employment opportunities, and establishing a new resident permit allowing the holder to work in another EU member state, this change is expected to facilitate non-EU employment and respond to agricultural demand for workers.

Agriculture-related education and training aim to respond to the growing demand for skilled labour in food and agriculture

Policies on skills improvement and on international mobility of human resources can also help to better match labour supply with demand, and can affect innovation and knowledge transfer through exchange of skills and skilled labour.

Agricultural education and training is available in Estonia, both through higher and vocational education programmes. Meeting the growing labour market demand for agricultural specialists is, however, a challenge for the education system in a context of decreasing number of students overall, which is expected to continue in line with the Estonian low birth rate. In higher education, the number of students enrolled in agriculture has declined over the past decade, but maintained the share of the total of students in higher education. In response to growing labour market demand, the number of students in agricultural sciences at vocational level has increased in recent years.

To increase the students' motivation, study allowances are paid to students on the agriculture-related curricula in vocational education, specialisation scholarships are available for students in higher education and practical training support helps to improve practical skills.

Another challenge is to retain workers in the sector — a growing share of the university graduates of agriculture-related specialties (almost half in 2015) do not practice their profession, either because they study further or because they find employment in other sectors. This reflects the general increase in education levels, but also the fact that agriculture-related education and training provides skills that are valued in other, more attractive sectors. As a result, a significant number of positions are not filled in the agricultural and agro-food sector. Agricultural and horticultural enterprises find it difficult to find people with suitable skills, attitude and salary expectations, and prefer to re-train existing workers. They also train new workers with a non-agricultural educational background.

Overall, the share of adult learners entering vocational education is increasing, reflecting their willingness to adapt their skills to market requirements. Many of them will start their own business. Including adult learners in general and vocational education fosters better informed choices regarding the choice of their specialty, leading to a better match between the area of specialisation and the student's future professional career. For agricultural vocational education, the demand comes partly from agricultural education being a pre-condition for applying certain agricultural subsidies such as grants for young farmers.

To ensure the sufficient number of professionals entering the agricultural labour market, vocational and higher education institutions must be more effective and focused in promoting their speciality and profession in schools and in the society at large. This requires the elaboration of a more comprehensive and systematic outreach system at educational establishments. A more efficient and systematic involvement of employers and professionals of the specific field in curriculum development will help to guarantee that the knowledge and skills of graduates will take into account the future needs of the labour market and meet the expectations of professionals.

More general efforts to guide skills development include the establishment of a system to monitor and forecast labour market future skills requirements (OSKA). The system will contribute to the development of curricula, which takes into account the needs of the labour market. OSKA includes the establishment of a cooperation platform for employers and educational and training institutions. It makes a comprehensive analysis of the development opportunities and needs of different economic sectors in Estonia, and studies labour market training requirements based on various activities or professions. Training plans are developed at different levels of education and for a variety of educational institutions, including retraining, in-service training and refresher courses. The OECD Economic Survey of Estonia (OECD, 2017a) welcomes recent steps, but outlines that more needs to be done to provide career guidance leading to good job opportunities in basic education, where the quality of counselling services remains poor. The survey also recommends improving on-the-job training and apprenticeships. They can provide valuable skills in line with labour market needs, and thus improve matching quality on the labour market. The main recommendation to that effect is that Vocational Education Training (VET) institutions may allocate to companies up to 50% of the funds paid to the school for the study place.

Recommendations to improve capacities and services for innovation

- Continue to work on the last mile to improve Internet access with private providers.
- Explore the scope for diversifying sources of funding for new infrastructure and services, including through joint public and private agreements, and user fees.
- Develop green energy to increase the reliance on sustainable sources of energy, as foreseen in the Estonian National Renewable Energy Action Plan 2020, including from biomass on land currently not used for agricultural production.
- Efforts to upgrade drainage were successful, but maintenance remains an issue. Facilitate cooperation among land owners and farmers to improve the maintenance of the drainage system, and thus improve productivity, sustainably, and reduce production risk. In the light of climate warming and an increase in precipitation, it is important to support the farmers in the reconstruction and renewal of drainage systems.
- To attract and maintain people in rural areas, improve infrastructure connection, and services, and more generally living conditions, and establish long-term plans for the maintenance of those services.
- Provide information on employment opportunities, and facilitate relocation.
- Strengthen linkages between education institutions and the agri-food business community, offer practical training opportunities, and increase the financial incentives of employers to invest in lifelong learning. Monitor the effectiveness of efforts to reduce labour market imbalances may include forward looking discussion on employment and skills requirements between workers, education and employers.
- Attract foreign students in agriculture-related topics to compensate the decline in Estonian students, by offering more courses in foreign languages and adapting them to demand. Foster exchange of students among Nordic countries. Identify knowledge that Estonian students need to acquire abroad. Joint study programmes or curricula could be developed that combine both students and teachers from Nordic and Baltic and possibly other countries.

Strengthen further agricultural policy incentives targeting the adoption of sustainable technologies and practices

Agriculture policy has contributed greatly to the modernisation of Estonian agriculture, leading to high gains in productivity

The EU Common Agricultural Policy (CAP) has greatly contributed to the spectacular development of Estonian agriculture. Within the EU framework, Estonian implementation of the CAP generally supported productive investment to increase productivity and reach EU standards, while limiting market distortions.

The CAP provides most of the support to Estonian farmers. Most Pillar 1 Direct Payments are implemented as a flat-rate per-ha payment (Single Area Payment Scheme and greening payment). This suggests there is no distortion among commodities, but may reduce incentives to productive investment as illustrated by the area of agricultural land not used for production. Commodity-specific payments, which influence production choices and thus distort markets, are limited to less than 5% of the total envelope.

Payment rates are lower than in most EU member states for two main reasons: the initial national entitlement of direct payments, and the limited (or no) use of optional national complements. In addition the share of Direct Payment is particularly low by EU standards because of lower initial entitlements and part of Direct Payments being used to fund the Estonian Rural Development Programme (RDP). However, payments per ha are planned to increase with the planned convergence of payment rates within EU member states and the recent introduction of a national complement (the Transitional National Aid). This will increase farmers' income but may give them the wrong signals about the long-term competitiveness of their operations.

Cross-compliance ensures minimal requirements on sustainable farm practices covering all agricultural land. Greening has offered farmers incentives to increase the area of legumes, with beneficial effects on both productivity and sustainability. The greening requirement constraining the conversion of grass land into crop production, however, may prevent moving to more efficient activities, without significant benefits for the environment, as grassland is already abundant and a large share of land is farmed rather extensively in Estonia. For example, support for organic farming and market signals have contributed to the expansion of land farmed organically and organic production over the last decade. As organic farming expands, it would be important, however, to ensure the development is economically and environmentally sustainable.

Policies provide a range of risk management tools. Livestock producers have used the subsidised insurance scheme available to them but the size of the scheme is small. The need for more effective risk management tools should be explored in the context of future policy discussion.

The EU Rural Development framework offers further scope for targeting innovation, sustainability and competitiveness along the food chain

As part of Pillar 2 of the CAP, the Estonian RDP allows for a better targeting of national objectives. Within the EU framework, Estonian choices reflect government emphasis on investment support to primary agriculture with a view to acquire up-to-date technology and increase sustainable productivity growth. Investment support also facilitated farm consolidation and the emergence of technically efficient farms. Increasingly, it is also expected to attract a new generation of well-trained managers. As a member state, Estonia can also use some RDP measures, alone or in complement with structural funds, to fund infrastructure investment and the development of rural activities.

Within the EU framework, RDP measures can also be used to address specific gaps, for example upgrading on-farm drainage systems sustainably, adding further value along the food chain, and diversifying activities. During the 2014-20 programming period, new measures facilitate access to high quality advisory systems, and cooperation and networking activities for the development of innovative solutions to current and future challenges, such as adaptation to climate change and to regulations aiming to reduce the impact of greenhouse gas (GHG) emissions.

Estonia relies on a number of domestic policy instruments to encourage sustainable technologies and practices; preliminary evidence suggests positive impacts on agri-environmental indicators in recent years.

For instance, environmental taxes are used to encourage the efficient use of environmental resources and pollution reduction in Estonia. The CAP also offers Estonian farmers payments for voluntary agri-environmental commitments. Current support schemes are associated with several positive trends in environmental impacts (such as point source pollution, soil fertility) and the adoption of good agricultural practices.

It is crucial for agricultural policy to provide a long-term vision for the sector, which recognises the need to improve environmental performance while maintaining productivity growth. In this regard, Estonia's planning horizon is often linked to EU financial frameworks and programming cycles of seven years. There is a clear continuity in policy choices between cycles so far, within the EU framework.

The information base and analytical tools to continuously monitor progress in productivity and sustainability, evaluate agricultural and innovation policies and guide farmers' decisions should be maintained and even developed. The government has an important role to play in the collection of information, which allows for the formulation of evidence-based policy, improved through monitoring and evaluation. It is particularly important to identify the determinants of the adoption of specific types of innovation and to strengthen the capacity of farmers, or farmers' organisations, to formulate their needs, and participate in knowledge networks.

Recommendations for an agricultural policy more conducive to innovation

- Continue to develop support targeting specific objectives, including the adoption of innovative and sustainable technologies and practices, as done with transferring funds from broad-based Direct Payments to RDP measures.
- Phase out national complements to Direct Payments that were introduced recently in response to a crisis, to avoid giving the wrong signal that no adjustment is needed. Instead, promote innovation, sustainable productivity growth, risk management and strengthen risk management tools, and continue to limit the provision of coupled payments, and thus distortions in the allocation of resources, leading to sub-optimal productivity and sustainability outcomes.
- Strengthen efforts to reduce nitrate pollution in more fragile areas, and continue to address the phosphorus deficit, and ammonia emissions, by providing targeted advice on sustainable technologies and practices.
- As organic production develops, monitor environmental impacts to ensure the development is environmentally sustainable, in particular regarding the management of livestock effluents.
- Explore options for reducing GHG emissions from agriculture, in particular grazing livestock, to contribute to COP21 engagements, and facilitate farmers' adaptation and relevant research. Alternative use of grassland and land under good agricultural and environmental conditions (GAEC) for biomass could be envisaged as suggested above. More generally, raise awareness of opportunities and challenges from climate changes.
- Strengthening the value chain would help find new markets and develop new products. Help the sector identify where good commercial prospects are, and develop a competiveness strategy accordingly. This could include measures to upgrade technology, technical and management skills, and facilitate the development of high value-added chains, including in organic food. Adapt competition policy to take account of the small national market size.
- Stakeholders need to develop a strategy for responding to specific market demand (e.g. organic products, bio-based products) and for strengthening technological, organisational, and marketing innovation. Make use of the opportunity given by the CAP to recognise Producer and Branch Organisations and support the participation of farmers or farmers' organisations in knowledge networks. Use RDP to fund networking activities and knowledge flows, also to strengthen food processing and rural activities.
- Better evaluate consumers and citizens expectations towards agriculture
- Develop further Information Technology (IT) solutions to collect and manage data, reduce control costs and implement more targeted policies, and to improve traceability along the food chain. Explore the scope for using output-based agri-environmental measures with the help of ICT for monitoring outcomes.
- Strengthen further the information base and analytical capacity to monitor progress, evaluate policies and guide farmers' decisions, with specific attention to innovation adoption and environmental practices.

Foster an agricultural innovation system with stronger interactions between actors

Estonia has a strong public research system, but weak innovation in firms

The strengths of the Estonian innovation system are the conducive business environment; a government strategy integrating innovation and economic growth objectives, with investments targeting smart specialisation high-growth areas, including ICTs; a relatively strong public research system, with high public R&D expenditure and strong performance in journal publication and international cooperation; good skills base in the population, in particular young performers in science; and society's positive attitude to science and technology.

Demand side innovation policy is widely discussed, but supply-side innovation dominates with relatively little input from, or ownership by, the business community. This is particularly the case in agriculture, where the major part of innovation, as in other countries, is driven by input suppliers.

The shortcomings of the system are mainly related to low R&D and innovation in firms, partly linked to the relatively small size of Estonian companies. The most innovative companies in Estonia are the subsidiaries of foreign companies and foreign-owned companies. In particular, industry-science linkages are not strongly developed, although programmes have been implemented recently to facilitate public-private cooperation in R&D and to better connect education and skills to labour-market needs.

The government plays a strong role in governance

The strategic framework for innovation policy is clear, but there is an abundance of strategic documents, action plans, policies programmes and projects, which does not facilitate coherence. The decision has been taken to develop 18 strategies, including one for agricultural, food and fisheries growth, related to the bioeconomy (covering agriculture and forestry) and health strategies, while the overall innovation strategy will continue to cover agriculture innovation. Innovation priorities have changed between 2004-14, where the focus was on infrastructure, capacity, and entrepreneurship, and 2014-20, when horizontal innovation, risk and acceptance of innovation is emphasised. The agricultural innovation strategy, as all sectoral innovation strategies, is fully integrated into the nation-wide strategy.

Innovation policy and the impact of other policies on innovation are regularly evaluated. The evaluation of EU programmes is based on input and output indicators defined at the EU level, which describe and analyse the dynamics of the Estonian research, development and innovation system based on the framework of EU policies and objectives. Indicators have thus been used for monitoring, in particular the use of public money, but without evaluation of impact to guide public choices.

The governance and implementation of innovation policy is mainly top-down, based on a linear approach to innovation from basic research, followed by applied research and the implementation of the new practical solutions in industry and the economy. The 2017 OECD Economic Survey of Estonia (OECD, 2017a) notes that "*business representatives are not involved enough in the design of innovation policy, in particular at early stages. Regular feedback on policy instruments is organised via committees in which businesses are represented, but remains weak. Scope for changes once measures are approved should be made more flexible. A new industrial policy green paper that focuses on digitalisation of traditional industries has been initiated by the business community. This is welcome and it will be important to maintain the link with the business community while designing concrete policy measures to implement it.*" Agricultural innovation systems are characterised by a particularly large number of diverse stakeholders. This makes consensus difficult to reach although consultation mechanisms are in place. When preparing new programmes, consultation is quite active but less during implementation. More active participation of stakeholders at all stages of the innovation process would make the system more efficient and more responsive to needs.

Agricultural research is well integrated in the general system, but public actors are even more dominant

Agriculture is well-integrated in general innovation, and the agricultural innovation system shares the same strength in public research and governance. The Estonian University of life Sciences (EMÜ) carries out most agricultural-related research in Estonia, while two other universities are engaged in environmental sciences and biotechnology and food sciences, and a research institute under the Ministry of Rural Affairs is specialised into crop research. It also shares the general weakness of private research but to a much larger extent as companies lack the capacity to perform or fund research.

Public expenditures on R&D for agriculture trend upwards but fluctuate strongly

Public expenditure on agricultural research has increased since 2000, in particular as a share of agricultural value-added. There are large fluctuations, as illustrated by the EMÜ research budget, due to the dominance of project-based funding, and the dependence on EU sources, which follow seven-year programming cycles. In fact, the share of project-based research funding, including in food and agriculture sciences, is very high at about 80% of total public funding. This share is planned to decrease to ensure more stability for research institutions.

Research infrastructure has been one of the main targets of EU structural funding, following a period of underinvestment between 1990 and the mid-2000s. Since 2010, research infrastructure roadmaps guide long-term investment decisions, identifying the infrastructure items of national importance that are new or require modernisation, and updating the list every three years.

Overall, recent infrastructure investments have helped compensate previous underinvestment, but some facilities still need upgrading and further investments from EU structural funds are planned for 2014-20, representing one of the largest investment areas. By continuing to modernise R&D infrastructures, the government aims to achieve the sustainable funding and maintenance of R&D infrastructures to support their effective use and sharing (OECD, 2017a).

Collaboration between agri-food private companies and R&D institutions is limited

While Estonian agri-food companies are considered as innovative users, they have little capacity to carry out research activities and their contribution to the funding of agricultural research is estimated to be minimal (less than 1% of total expenditure). The most innovative companies are foreign-owned companies or their subsidiaries in Estonia, so research is done abroad. The most common form of collaboration is participation of representatives in steering committees and networks.

Incentives are in place to facilitate public-private collaboration. Intellectual Property Protection (IPP) is in place in Estonia and the IPP Index increased over time to reach the OECD average level. Competence centres have been recently established as an important source of collaborative innovation, but as private participation is generally from foreign companies, the focus is often on international issues as opposed to topics that can benefit the domestic agriculture sector. Three of the current six national competence centres are related to food and agriculture, as well as a regional Centre and a consortium.

Noting that the innovative capacity of Estonian firms is limited, and that collaboration between academia and businesses is too low, the 2017 OECD Economic Survey of Estonia (OECD, 2017a) recommends the Estonian government to give more weight to cooperation with the private sector when allocating funds to public R&D institutions.

International cooperation is facilitated through participation in EU research programmes, projects and networks, and incentives for research mobility such as grants and conditions favouring international experience in project allocation and nominations.

Farms and agri-food firms are innovative in a conducive environment

Innovation activities are taking place in food and drink processing industries, mainly related to upgrading of equipment and product design. Farms have also invested in modern technology allowing them to reach high technical efficiency.

Open access to knowledge, optimal knowledge circulation and transfer through the application of digital European Research Area (ERA) is a priority of the ERA concept that Estonia follows. Farmers are granted free access to the research information on the website of the Estonian Agricultural and Rural Advisory Service.

The advisory system has helped the diffusion of knowledge on technologies and practices among farms. A number of different Estonian organisations provide training and advisory services, including cooperatives, input providers, and education institutions. The Advisory Centre of RDF is currently in charge of the publically funded advisory system, providing advice to farmers and rural entrepreneurs for a minimal fee. The focus of this advice is on meeting EU regulations and conditions for receiving agricultural support.

Better information on challenges and opportunities for the sector is essential to guide private investment and policy decisions

The government has an important role to play in providing information systems needed to share information, reduce information gaps to better guide private investment decisions, monitor economic and environmental performance of the sector, identify market and policy failures, and improve policy design, implementation, monitoring and evaluation. Better information and analytical tools are also needed to monitor and evaluate the performance of the whole agricultural innovation system. Individual policies and institutes are regularly evaluated, but so far, there is no systematic mechanism in place to evaluate the agricultural innovation system and the information to do so is fragmented.

Recommendations to strengthen direct incentives to innovation

- Consolidate innovation and growth strategy documents to improve clarity, as the abundance of strategic documents, action plans, policies programmes and projects does not facilitate coherence.
- The policy framework is driven by supply-side measures, with relatively little input from, or ownership by, the business community. More involvement of the private actors in policy dialogue on R&D and innovation policies at an early stage, and facilitate networking to better reflect users' needs, and thus improve adoption.
- Facilitate discussion among and between producers and the industry to enable them to contribute more effectively and efficiently to the agricultural innovation system, including through participation in networks or formulation of demand.
- Continue improving the stability of R&D funding. The reduction in the high share of project-based funding should contribute, as well as the development of longer-term, larger scope project funding as planned for 2018. The consolidation of programmes would make them more attractive for the industry to take part.
- Focus public funds on areas generating high value-added for the Estonian sector, building on specificities, niche-markets, collaborate on more general innovation, and import other technologies. Build on local and regional assets to develop innovation and development projects, including in partnership with other countries. The principles behind the "small advanced economies" initiative could help in that regard.[1]
- Facilitate access to diverse sources of funding for research and explore ways to complement public funding, for example from foundations or agricultural levies.
- Maintain research infrastructure and improve further in areas lagging behind such as the crop sector, and focus efforts in areas where Estonia has comparative advantage, as it is essential for future progress and to maintain excellence and collaboration capacity at national and international levels. Explore further opportunities to share public infrastructure with the private sector, including foreign companies.
- Identify areas where local companies and researchers could collaborate, e.g. through public-private partnerships, to develop local or niche products and innovation. Give more weight to cooperation with the private sector when allocating funds to public R&D institutions. Encourage academics to participate in private sector innovation and research activities as a part of their curricula.

Recommendations to strengthen direct incentives to innovation (cont.)

- Explore ways to generate new (break-through) ideas to overcome current constraints, for example through demand-driven mechanisms, including to develop technologies and systems allowing for a better management of natural resources and improved resilience to risks.
- Encourage a diverse supply of advice that is accessible, including through ICT, and responsive to market demand, and goes beyond technical issues towards management, marketing, environment. Collect information on innovation practices and needs, e.g. using surveys. Provide incentives for farm managers and employees to upgrade skills (replacement, stronger link with support). Demonstrate the benefits of improved technology and practices. Focus support on advice for cross-compliance and public good aspects (e.g. promote innovative solutions to sustainability challenges, while farmers are expected to pay for private advice to support farm development.
- Continue ensuring farm advisors are well-trained professionals with up-to-date skills, by facilitating retraining and development of new skills that are needed to adapt to the new environment. Attract highly-skilled professionals in the system, using economic incentives. Encourage them to participate more actively in innovation projects, and to draw on knowledge from abroad to improve advice to Estonian farmers.
- Include activities related to knowledge and innovation in research evaluation and funding to make research more responsive to demand and facilitate adoption.
- Continue developing information systems, including market intelligence (big data) and research results, as innovation and policy evaluation become more complex and require a wealth of information. In particular, continue to monitor innovation adoption and environmental performance in surveys, in addition to economic performance, to better understand determinants and policy impact. Use and share innovative methods to reduce collection costs and improve farm and firm participation.
- Be proactive in developing indicators and tools to evaluate the performance of the agricultural innovation systems and innovation policy regularly, taking longer term effects into account, possibly in collaboration with other EU member states.

1. Small advanced economies website: http://www.smalladvancedeconomies.org/.

References

OECD (2017a), *OECD Economic Surveys: Estonia 2017*, OECD Publishing, Paris, http://dx.doi.org/10.1787/eco_surveys-est-2017-en.

OECD (2017b), "Estonia", in *OECD Science, Technology and Innovation Outlook 2016*, OECD Publishing, Paris, http://dx.doi.org/10.1787/sti_in_outlook-2016-58-en.

OECD (2017c), *OECD Environmental Performance Reviews: Estonia 2017*, OECD Publishing, Paris, http://dx.doi.org/10.1787/9789264268241-en.

OECD (2015), "Analysing Policies to improve agricultural productivity growth, sustainably: Revised framework", www.oecd.org/agriculture/policies/innovation.

OECD (2011), *Estonia: Towards a Single Government Approach*, OECD Publishing, Paris, http://dx.doi.org/10.1787/9789264104860-en.

Chapter 2

Overview of the food and agriculture situation in Estonia

This chapter describes the overall economic, social and environmental context in which the food and agriculture sector in Estonia operates, and the natural resource base upon which it relies. It provides an overview of the general geographical and economic characteristics of Estonia; outlines the share of the agri-food complex in the economy; identifies the main structural characteristics of the food and agriculture sector; provides an overview of the main food and agriculture outputs and markets; and analyses the main trends in agricultural productivity, competitiveness and sustainability.

2.1. Overview and challenges

Estonia is a Baltic country, with a favourable environment for investment, but a small domestic market (Chapters 3 and 4). Characterised by abundant land and water resources, Estonia's agricultural sector is dominated by milk production, but cereals and oilseeds production has increased considerably in the last decade. Meat production has also increased over the last two decades, though production levels have declined in the last couple of years in response to lower market prices and the outbreak of African Swine Fever (ASF).

Agricultural policy and regulatory changes linked to land restitution during the transition period starting in 1990, and EU accession in 2004, in particular the implementation of the Common Agricultural Policy (CAP), have significantly impacted the sector. Following a contraction during the transition in the 1990s, the sector expanded and grew in the 2000s in part due to the creation of agricultural land registers securing property rights. Since acceding to the European Union, agricultural land that was abandoned during the transition was also reclaimed to qualify for CAP financing (see Chapter 6 on conditions for receiving CAP support).

The sector is characterised predominantly by arable land, including cultivated grassland. Since the introduction of the EU single area payment scheme (SAPS), the area of agricultural land not used for agricultural production but maintained in good agricultural and environmental conditions (GAEC) has increased. As permanent grassland, this area is under extensive and biodiversity-friendly agricultural land use, and these areas account together for one-third of Estonian agricultural land. Moreover, Estonia's area for organic production has grown significantly due to EU support over the last decade, and part of organically-farmed land can be considered as under biodiversity-friendly practices.

The agricultural sector has a dualistic structure — with large technically-efficient, more input intensive and innovative farms, next to very small farms. This divergence can be seen both in terms of the distribution of utilised agricultural area (UAA) as well as livestock production. Estonia's food processing sector is also dualistic, and struggling in terms of capacity and competitiveness. The small domestic market is also a challenge for food processing in Estonia.

While Estonian exports are growing, the country has a large trade deficit of agricultural and food products due to high imports of processed foods. The composition of Estonia's agro-food trade suggests the food manufacturing industry is not as developed as primary production. Estonia's imports of agro-food products are mainly for household consumption, while the country exports a large share of agro-food products for industrial use. For example, Estonia is a net exporter of cereals, but a net importer of processed cereals, and a net exporter of live animals, but a net importer of meat.

Agricultural total factor productivity (TFP) has been growing rapidly since 2000. This reflects strong increases in agricultural production, with more efficient input use facilitated by economies of scale, investment in modern, labour-saving, technologies, and seed and animal genetic improvements, for example. While agricultural labour has declined steadily since 1990, labour productivity remains much lower than in EU15 countries from the North of Europe, as is the case in the food processing industry (Figure 2.15). Productivity progress is unequal across farms, with the largest operations driving sectoral performance. Thus, farm consolidation, in particular the exit of most inefficient farms, has contributed to sectoral productivity growth.

Paralleling the growth in agricultural TFP and production, the use of natural resources has similarly shifted. In particular, agricultural land area increased, but at a slower rate than production volume and TFP growth. At the same time, Estonia's direct on-farm energy consumption and ammonia emissions also increased, raising concerns about sustainability. Moreover, eutrophication due to nutrient loads from diffuse and point sources threatens sustainable management of agricultural and water resources in certain regions. The country's phosphorus deficit has also worsened. On the other hand, higher TFP and output growth in recent years has been achieved with improvements in Estonia's nitrogen balance and lower water use, a positive trend in sustainability terms.

Looking forward, climate change projections suggest that both grasslands and crop production may benefit from shifts in climatic conditions in the coming decades. The growing season has already begun to lengthen in recent decades, favouring the cultivation of winter crops. However, potential risk factors include an increase in the frequency of extreme meteorological phenomena (droughts, excessive moisture, flooding) and the spread of plant diseases, plant pests and infectious animal diseases.

The sustained production and productivity growth since 2000 reflects the catching up of the sector following the transition and uncertainties of the 1990s, stimulated by EU investment support. This has facilitated farm modernisation and upgrading of technology, in particular in dairy farms (Box 2.3) and crop farms (Box 2.4). Further efforts remain, however, to improve the productivity of smaller-scale operations, including through wider diffusion of innovation and integration in the innovation system.

Maintaining the recent agricultural growth rates sustainably will require further innovation, but more careful investment, improvements along the food chain, the development of new markets and increased consideration of sustainability issues and consumer demand, as well as longer-term challenges and opportunities.

2.2. General geographic and economic context

The Republic of Estonia, situated on the coast of the Baltic Sea, is the northernmost of the Baltic countries, and the smallest in terms of surface area. The Estonian territory comprises 45 339 km^2, of which the land surface area is 43 432 km^2. Estonia stretches 350 km from East to West and 240 km from North to South. Tallinn, the capital, is situated in Northern Estonia.

Estonia's **land and water resources** are abundant: 22% of the territory is UAA, 7% is comprised of settlements, roads and pipe-laying routes, and the rest of the territory is covered with forests (50%), marshes, bogs and shrubs. In 2013, the country had 13 million m^3 of freshwater resources. This amounts to nearly 10 000 m^3 per capita (two times higher than the EU28 average and about 20% higher than the OECD average) (Land Board, 2015; Statistics Estonia, 2016; AB, 2016; WBG, 2015).

Lying east of the Baltic Sea, Estonia's **climate** is typical for its location in the temperate zone in the Atlantic continental region. Characteristic of the boreal biogeographical region, summers are moderately warm and winters are moderately cold (the mean air temperature in July being 16-17°C and in February between -3 and -7°C). In the second half of the 20th century (especially from 1966-2010), the air temperature has risen faster than the global average. Moreover, the climate is extremely damp as annual precipitation exceeds evaporation by approximately two times.

Estonia is the smallest Baltic country in terms of **population and area**, and is relatively urban. In 2016, the population of Estonia was 1.3 million and the population density was 30 inhabitants per km^2 of land. The Estonian population decreased regularly over the period 1991-2014, as both natural increase and net migration were negative. In 2015 and 2016, net migration was slightly positive, but it is too early to say that the trend has been reversed. In 2015, nearly two-thirds of the population lived in towns and cities and just over one-third lived in rural areas. The urban-rural distribution has remained relatively constant over the past three decades.

The Estonian **economy** has grown faster than the OECD average since 2000, although it was adversely affected by the global economic crisis (Chapter 3). Economic growth in the early 2000s was driven by deepening integration with international supply chains, EU structural funds after accession in 2004, foreign direct investments and loans, fast growth in the construction and real estate sectors and the accompanying credit boom. During the global economic crisis, however, unemployment increased and internal demand was hampered by declines in investment and private consumption. However, unemployment rates were slightly above the OECD average in 2016, but below the Eurozone rate (OECD, 2016a). In 2016, GDP per capita in Estonia was 30% below the OECD average (OECD, 2017a).

2.3. The role of agriculture in the Estonian economy

The agricultural sector's contribution to Estonia's **value added** declined over the last two decades, but it rebounded to some degree in the last few years and is slightly higher than in many Northern European countries. Falling from 4.8% to 2.4% during the 2000s, the share of agriculture, hunting, forestry and fishing in Estonia's total value added increased to a peak of 3.9% in 2011 to fall again to 3.4% in 2015 and 2.9% in 2016. This share remains higher than the average of EU and OECD countries, including neighbouring EU member states except Latvia (Figure 2.1).

Employment in the Estonian agricultural sector declined faster than value-added. While 10% of the labour force was in agriculture, forestry and fishing in 1995, this share fell to 3.9% in 2015 (Figure 2.1). The share of employment in OECD countries and EU28 were only slightly higher (6% and 4.4%, respectively in 2015).

The agricultural sector is an important contributor to **trade**, though its share declined during the transition and only rebounded slightly after EU accession. As illustrated in Figure 2.1, the share of agriculture in trade in Estonia was lower compared to Denmark, Latvia and the Netherlands, but higher than the EU and OECD averages.

In terms of **natural resources**, the Estonian agricultural sector relies on a large share of land resources, but has a low share in water withdrawal (Figure 2.2). Agriculture uses less than a quarter of Estonian land, while its share in water withdrawal is the lowest among selected countries — less than 1% in 2012-15. The area of irrigated agricultural land is very small in Estonia (0.04% of agricultural land) due to the damp climate, and drainage is important.

In comparison to other Central and Eastern European countries, the intensity of agriculture is lower and the state of agro-ecosystem conditions ranges from good to favourable in Estonia (see final sections). However, certain regions in Estonia have been identified that need further attention in order to manage agricultural and water resources in a sustainable manner — in particular, the Nitrate Vulnerable Zone in Central and North-Eastern Estonia.

Figure 2.1. Share of agriculture in the economy in Estonia and selected countries, 2016

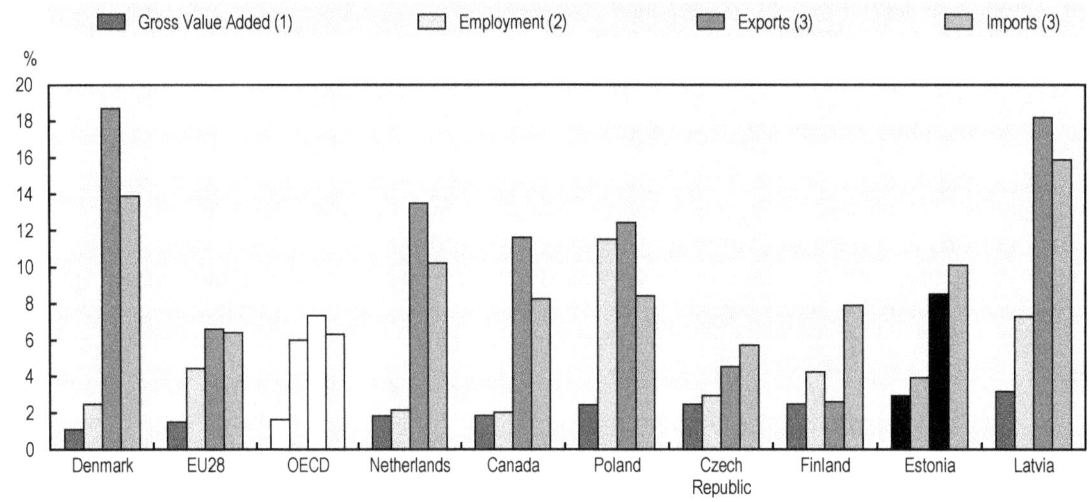

Countries are ranked according to Gross Value Added levels.

1. Value added in agriculture, hunting, forestry and fishing as a percentage of total value added.
2. Share of employed persons aged 15 years and over, in agriculture, hunting and forestry in total NACE activities. Employment data are for 2015.
3. Agro-food definition does not include fish and fish products. Agro-food codes in H0: 01, 02, 04 to 24, 3301, 3501 to 3505, 4101 to 4103, 4301, 5001 to 5003, 5101 to 5103, 5201 to 5203, 5301, 5302, 290543/44, 380910, 382360.

Source: OECD (2016b), System of National Accounts, OECD Annual Labour Force Statistics, http://data.oecd.org/; UN (2016), COMTRADE, https://comtrade.un.org/.

StatLink http://dx.doi.org/10.1787/888933653686

Figure 2.2. Share of agriculture in natural resources in Estonia and the selected countries, 2015[1]

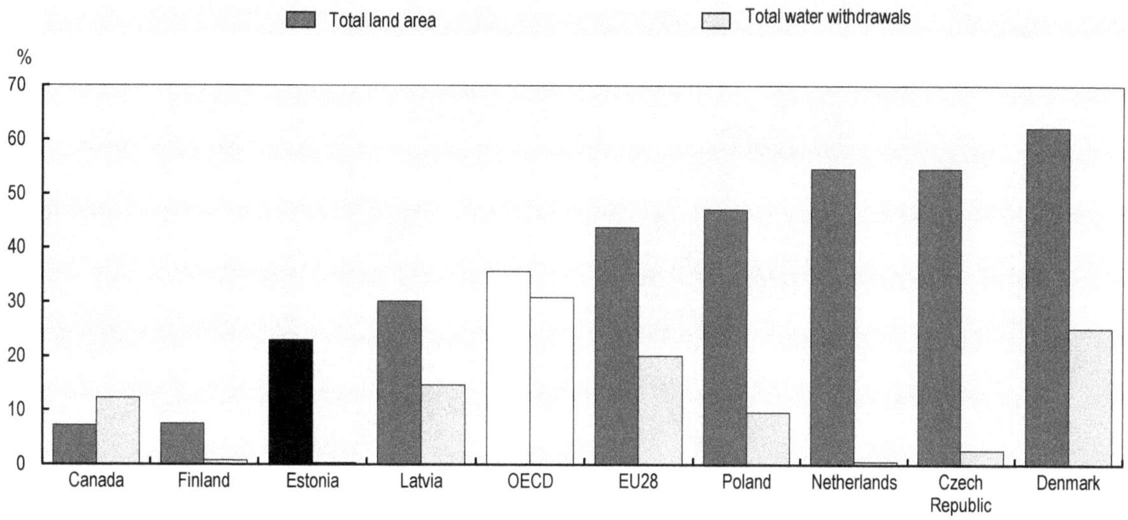

Countries are ranked according to shares of total land area.

1. 2015 or the most recent available year.

Source: FAOSTAT (2016), www.fao.org/faostat/en/; FAO (2016), AQUASTAT, www.fao.org/nr/water/aquastat/main/index.stm.

StatLink http://dx.doi.org/10.1787/888933653705

2.4. Structural characteristics of farms, and upstream and downstream industries

Land use

Estonia's **UAA** has fluctuated in recent decades, primarily due to policy shifts. During the transition period, UAA levels fell by half from about 1.4 million ha in 1993 to about 0.7 million ha in 2002. UAA then started to increase to reach 1 million ha in 2015. This is partly due to land declarations on agricultural land registers securing property rights (Seeder, 2013). In addition, after accession to the European Union, agricultural land that was abandoned during the transition period was reclaimed to qualify for CAP single area payments as agricultural land maintained in GAEC qualifies for this payment whether under production or not.

Arable land accounts for more than two-thirds of **agricultural land** in Estonia, with arable area and UAA increasing by 29% and 25% respectively over the period 2004-15 (Figure 2.3). The area of agricultural land not used for agricultural production but maintained in GAEC increased as well — its share in UAA reaching 13% in 2015, compared to 3% in 2004. Meanwhile, the share of permanent grassland in total UAA has decreased by 11 percentage points, reflecting the transition to land not used for agricultural production maintained in GAEC, and the increase in UAA (Figure 2.3).

Driven by support to organic farming, Estonia's land area under organic production has significantly increased since 2004 (Box 2.1).

Figure 2.3. Utilised agricultural area in Estonia, 2004 and 2015

1 000 ha and percentage of total utilised agricultural area (UAA)

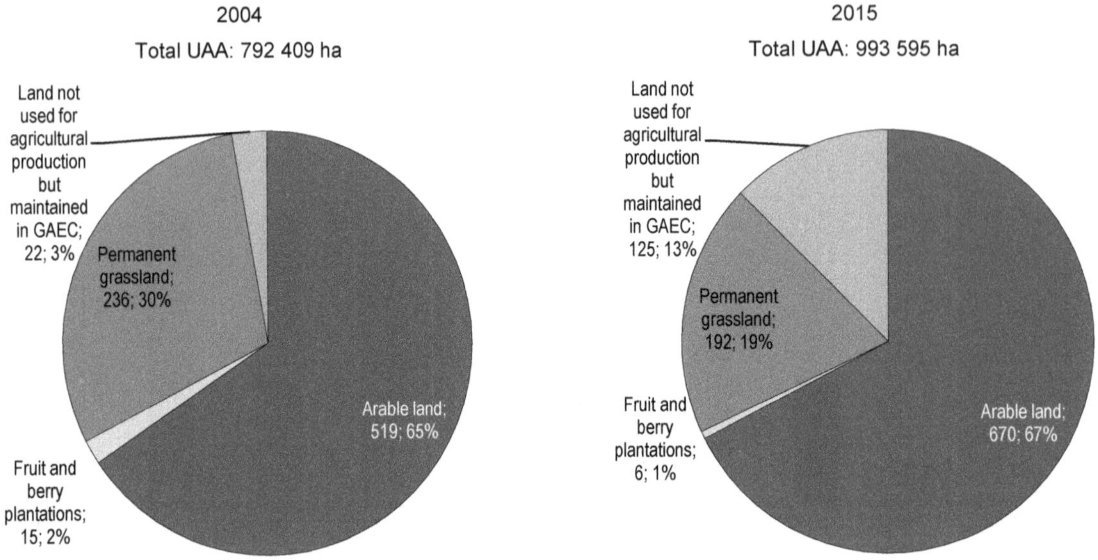

GAEC: good agricultural and environmental conditions.

Source: Statistics Estonia (2017), www.stat.ee.

StatLink http://dx.doi.org/10.1787/888933653724

Box 2.1. Organic farming in Estonia

Estonia's land area under organic production almost quadrupled from 46 000 ha in 2004 to 181 500 ha in 2016 (Figure 2.4). The average size of organic farms has also increased — from 57 ha in 2004 to 104 ha in 2016. During the same period, the number of farm enterprises engaged in organic production increased from 810 to 1 753. Organic land use in Estonia is characterised by a large share of grasslands (77% of organic agricultural land in 2015). In 2012, approximately two-thirds of organic farmers were engaged in organic livestock production (MoA, 2015). Recent years have witnessed a rise in organic processing and marketing. As of June 2017, there were 345 processors, packers, distributors and storers in the Organic Farming Register, which was 125 more than in 2014 (MRA, 2016d; AB, 2017).

Land under organic production constituted 17% of UAA in 2015. While the land productivity of organic farming has improved since 2010, yields for both crop and animal production remain lower among organic producers than those of conventional agriculture. For instance, average crop yields of organic wheat and conventional wheat in 2015 amounted to 1.7 and 4.2 tonnes per ha, respectively. During the same period, the average annual milk yields per cow in organic and conventional holdings were 6 464 and 8 266 kg (FADN, 2017a). If the share of organic production continues to increase, it will be important to increase organic productivity growth to sustain and increase further total agricultural output. At the same time, organic production has a positive impact on biodiversity indicators (such as the diversity and species composition of vascular plants in the fields and field margins; bumblebee indicators; and the diversity and abundance of nesting birds). Future efforts to promote productivity growth on organic farms will need to achieve a fine balance with environmental constraints.

The yield gap between organic and conventional production may decrease if farms in more productive areas were to adopt organic practices. The majority of organic farms in Estonia are located in regions with traditionally extensive agriculture as a result of less favourable natural conditions (Kimura and Le Thi, 2013). In 2015, the highest number of organic farms was in Võru (196) and Saare (178) counties. The largest amount of organic land was in Saare (19 251 ha) and Lääne (18 781 ha) counties — collectively comprising more than 30% of organic agricultural land. These counties are often characterised by small fields; low nutrient content and stony soils with sandy and clay texture; and a high share of semi-natural habitats on waterfront pastures and other areas with excessive moisture (MRA, 2016d; Statistics Estonia, 2017).

Box 2.1. Organic farming in Estonia (cont.)

Figure 2.4. Developments in organic farming, 1999 to 2016

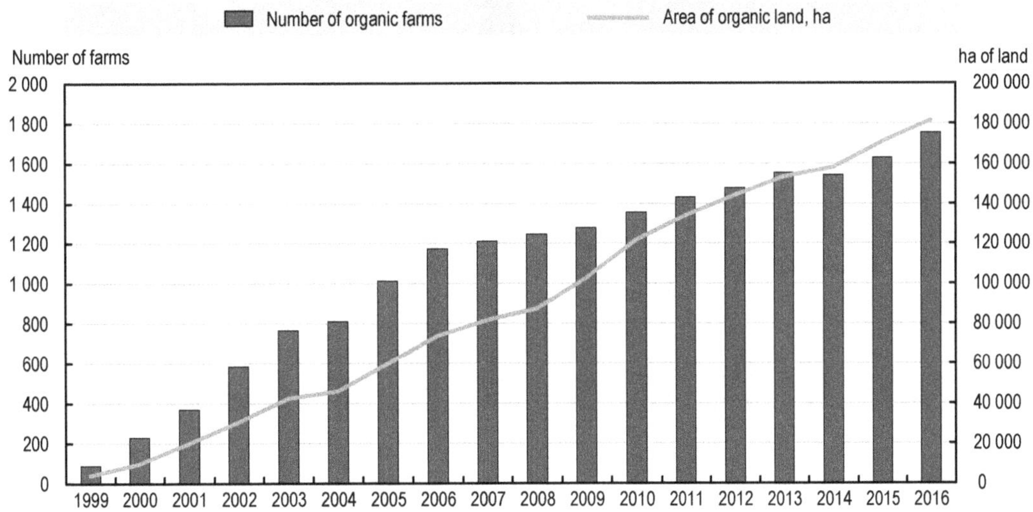

Source: EEA (2014a), MRA (2016d).

StatLink http://dx.doi.org/10.1787/888933653743

Farm structures

The **number of farms** in Estonia has fluctuated in recent decades, increasing in the 1990s due to privatisation and restitution and then decreasing in the 2000s due to consolidation and farm exit. After restoring independence, agricultural ownership and land reforms were initiated, collective and state farms were privatised, and farmsteads were restituted to the pre-war owners or their heirs. This led to a significant increase in the number of agricultural holdings — from 1 154 in 1989 to 55 748 in 2001 (Figure 2.5) (Viira et al., 2009). However, the number of farms declined in the 2000s (to 16 079 in 2016), as many of the farms established in the 1990s on reclaimed land did not prove viable (due to insufficient skills or investment). Moreover, some farms were consolidated.

Farm consolidation in the 2000s has led to an increase in average **farm size** and in the number of larger farms. The number of farms with more than 50 ha has increased substantially between 2001 and 2016, while all categories of smaller farms decreased.

Between 2000 and 2010, the mid-point farm size in crop farms[1] increased from 72 ha to 276 ha, which is higher than in France and England, but lower than in Germany and Latvia, where it reaches 472 ha (Figure 2.6.A). During the same period, the mid-point farm size of dairy farms[2] also increased from 262 to 363 Livestock Unit (LU), which is particularly high by EU standards (Figure 2.6.B).

Figure 2.5. Number of farms in Estonia, 1989 to 2016

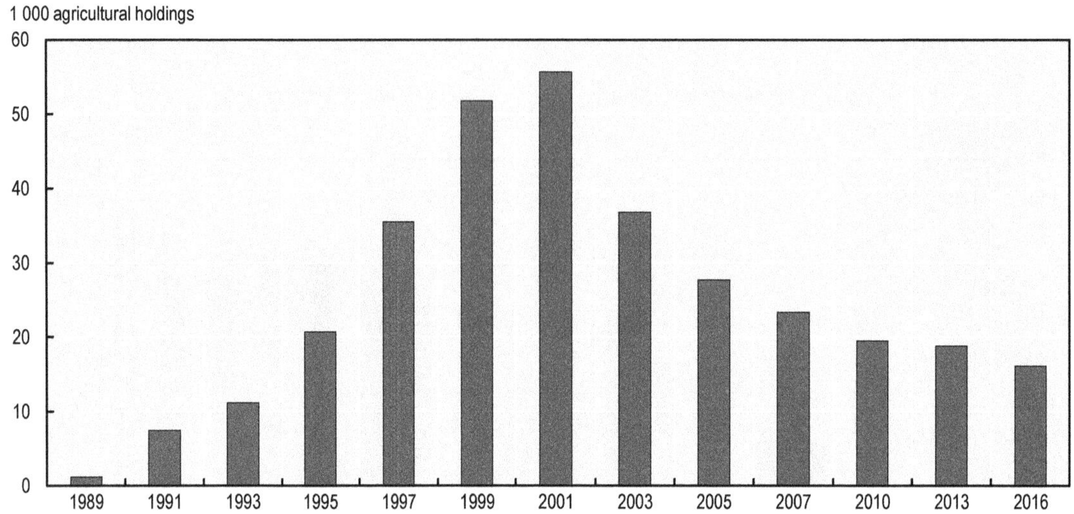

Source: Statistics Estonia (2017), [AGS406], www.stat.ee.

StatLink http://dx.doi.org/10.1787/888933653762

Figure 2.6. Developments in mid-point farm size, 2000 and 2010

A. Crop farms

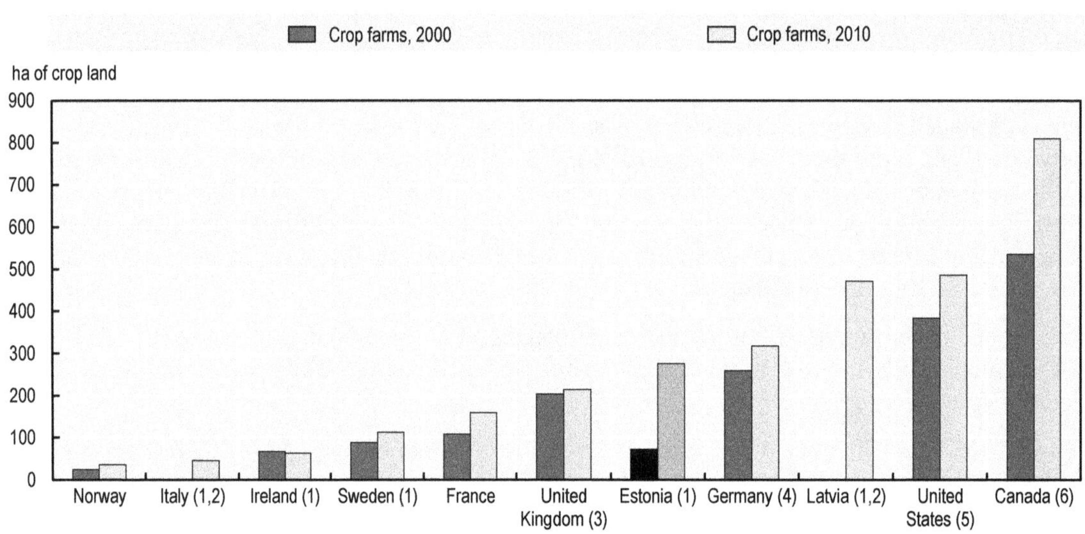

Countries are ranked according to 2010 levels.

The mid-point farm size applied to crop farms is the hectare-weighted median, which corresponds to a farm size that separates the farm size distribution into two parts: 50% of the total area of the national farmland operated by the crop farms of a larger size and the other 50% by the crop farms of smaller size than the hectare-weighted median.

1. Based on sample data.
2. For Italy and Latvia, 2000 data are not available.
3. For the United Kingdom (England), 2009 data are used for 2010.
4. For Germany, 2003 data are used for 2000.
5. For the United States, 1997 data are used for 2000 and 2012 for 2010.
6. For Canada, 2001 data are used for 2000, and 2011 for 2010.

B. Dairy farms

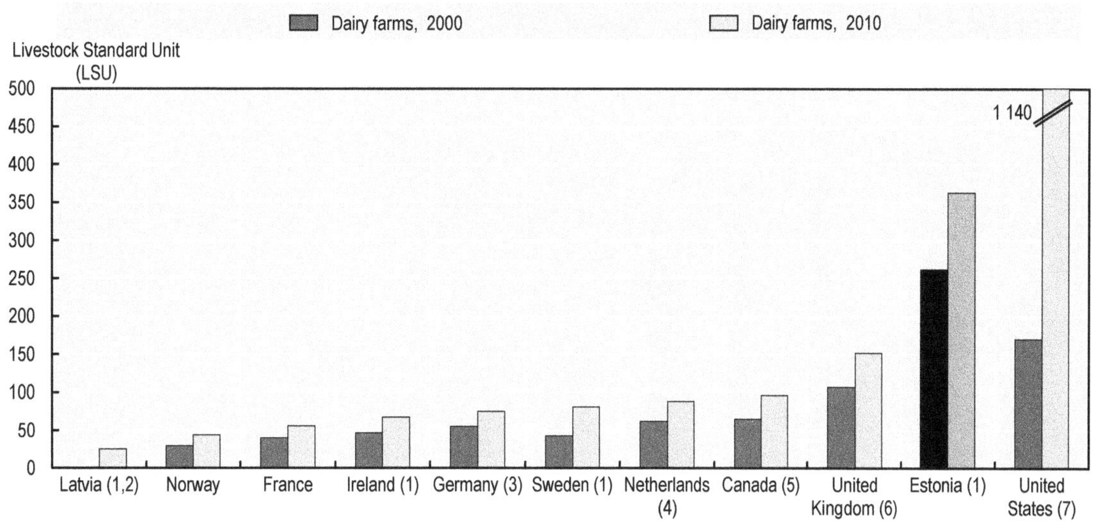

Countries are ranked according to 2010 levels.

The mid-point statistics used to measure the distribution of dairy farm size is the livestock unit-weighted median.

1. Based on sample data.
2. For Latvia, 2000 data are not available.
3. For Germany, 2003 data are used for 2000.
4. For the Netherlands, data are on all farms having cropland, dairy cows and pigs, respectively.
5. For Canada, 2001 data are used for 2000, and 2011 for 2010.
6. For the United Kingdom (England), 2009 data are used for 2010.
7. For the United States, 1997 data are used for 2000 and 2012 for 2010.

Source: Bokusheva and Kimura (2016), Tables B3 and B4, http://dx.doi.org/10.1787/5jlv81sclr35-en.

StatLink http://dx.doi.org/10.1787/888933653781

The Estonian agricultural sector is characterised by a **dualistic structure**, both in terms of the distribution of UAA as well as livestock production (Figure 2.7). In 2016, farms with less than 30 hectares (75% of holdings) managed 11% of UAA. At the same time, farms with over 1 000 hectares (1% of agricultural holdings) managed 27% of UAA, and farms with more than 300 hectares (5% of agricultural holdings) managed more than half (57%) of the UAA. The share of farms of more than 100 ha is higher than in other Baltic countries, and they operate a larger share of the UAA (almost 78%). Among selected countries in Table 2.A1.1, the Czech Republic is the only EU member state with a higher concentration of agricultural land in larger farms. Livestock production is particularly concentrated into micro (<1 ha) and large (≥500 ha) farms: 24% of total LU are in micro farms (mainly pig and poultry farms that do not have agricultural land and that have a very high livestock density), while 40% of LU are found in large farms (mainly cattle and pig farms) (Statistics Estonia, 2017).

Figure 2.7. Share of agricultural holdings and utilised agricultural area (UAA), by size class, 2016

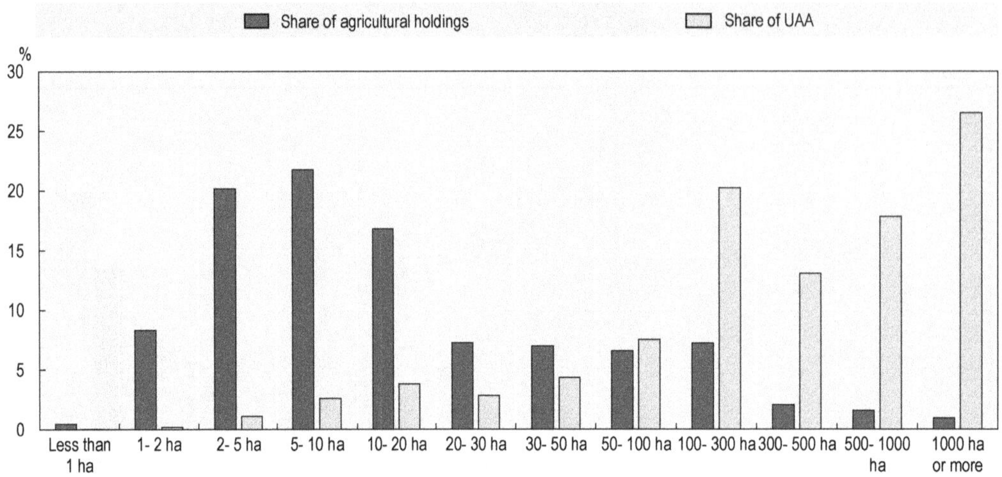

Source: Statistics Estonia (2017), [AGS420], www.stat.ee.

StatLink http://dx.doi.org/10.1787/888933653800

Farm income and wealth

The value of assets per ha of UAA is highest in the smallest and largest farm size groups, however, larger farms have higher liabilities/assets ratio, which increase pressure on their viability in the periods of low market prices. Total farm income and farm income per unpaid farm (family) labour increases with farm size. In 2015, average annual gross wage in agriculture, forestry and fishing was EUR 11 388. If this is compared to farm income per unpaid farm (family) labour in different farm types and size groups, it is clear that smallest farms are not viable if they do not have additional income sources from off-farm jobs or pensions.

Food processing sector

Similar to many other countries, the structure of Estonia's food processing sector is also dualistic. In 2014, Estonia had 10 (2%) large (≥ 250 employees) enterprises, for which gross sales comprised 32% of the aggregate gross sales of food manufacturing industry (Table 2.A1.2). The proportion of large enterprises in Estonia is similar to other observed countries. However, the share of their aggregated turnover in industry's total is smaller in Estonia, indicating that large food manufacturing enterprises in Estonia are smaller than their competitors in the selected countries. Average turnover per enterprise among large Estonian food industry companies was EUR 51 million in 2014. This figure was exceeded by large Danish and Dutch food industry enterprises (by 11 and 10 times respectively) and smaller only in Latvia.

In recent years, the number of food processing enterprises has increased by one third — from 358 in 2010 to 477 in 2014. This increase is mainly due to an increase in micro enterprises of 1-9 employees. In 2010-14, the number of food processing enterprises in size classes 50-99, 100-249 and ≥250 employees also increased.

Investment in food processing has not kept up with investment in primary agriculture. For instance, over the period 2008-15, agriculture, fishing and aquaculture invested twice as much as food and beverage manufacturers, and crop and animal production, hunting and related service activities invested 2.5 times more that manufacturers of food products (Statistics Estonia, 2017).

Recent studies investigated the competitiveness of Northern Europe dairy chains. Main findings for Estonia, presented in Box 2.2, are that the Estonian dairy processing industry achieves low total factor and labour productivity, and lacks competitiveness in the raw milk market of Baltic countries.

Box 2.2. The competitiveness of the Estonian dairy processing industry

Studying the competitiveness of Northern European dairy chains, Jansik et al. (2014) concluded that the Estonian dairy processing industry is fragmented. Since foreign investors divested in the 2000s, the industry has had one main foreign owner, a Finnish company called Valio, which is the biggest manufacturer in terms of turnover with EUR 99 million of sales revenue in 2012. The four leading companies purchased 58% of raw milk in 2012. One of the challenges for Estonian dairy processors is efficiency. The assortment of consumer products (e.g. yoghurt) in a relatively small domestic market is wide, the series are small and there are frequent shifts to new flavours, which increase costs. Authors concluded that the average annual Total Factor Productivity (TFP) growth in Estonian dairy processing industry was merely 0.3% in the period from 2000-11, compared to 0.7% in Finland, 1.5% in Latvia, 2.4% in Lithuania, but negative TFP growth in Sweden and Germany.

Viira et al. (2015) found that Estonian and Latvian dairy processing industries lack competitiveness in the raw milk market of Baltic countries. While the Estonian dairy industry processed 74.8%, and the Latvian dairy industry processed 72.0% of collected raw milk in 2014, the Lithuanian dairy industry processed 118.7% of the volume of milk collected in Lithuania, i.e. raw milk was traded from Estonia and Latvia to Lithuania. This could be explained by a lack of milk processing capacity in the Estonian dairy industry. However, in the absence of official figures, some experts state that the existing milk processing capacity in Estonia is outdated and inefficient.

The productivity of the Estonian dairy industry, measured by the quantity of processed milk per employee per year falls significantly behind productivity in the Netherlands, Germany and Ireland (Table 2.1). In addition, the production value per kg of processed milk is lower than in the Netherlands, Finland, Germany and Latvia. Viira et al. (2015) concluded that in order to increase competitiveness, the Estonian dairy industry needs to consolidate, invest in automation to achieve higher processed milk volumes per employee, and to increase the value of production per tonne of processed milk. There have been some developments since. For example, the process of acquisition of one medium-sized player by another medium-sized player started in 2017. Moreover, EUR 15 million were allocated from RDP to build a new milk processing plant owned by a cooperative of dairy farmers.

Table 2.1. Characteristics of the milk processing industry in selected countries, 2013-15

	Estonia	Latvia	Lithuania	Nether-lands	Finland	Germany	Ireland
Production value, EUR million	344.2	362.6	990.3	10 916.9	2 473.6	27 288.9	3 738.9
Number of employees	2 065	3 165	7 507	13 692	6 177	43 884	6 900
Milk processed, 1000 tonnes	545.9	571.5	1 677.4	12 442.2	2 357.0	31 816.8	6 289.1
Milk processed per employee, tonnes	264.4	180.5	223.4	908.7	381.6	725.0	911.5
Production value per employee, EUR 1 000	166.7	114.5	131.9	797.3	400.4	621.8	541.9
Production value per kg of processed milk, EUR	630.6	634.4	590.4	877.4	1 049.4	857.7	594.5

Source: Eurostat (2017) http://ec.europa.eu/eurostat/data/database.

2.5. Agricultural output and trade

Output

Estonia's agricultural output is dominated by milk production, but cereal and oilseed production is increasing at a faster rate. Milk's share in the total value of agricultural production[3] declined from 32% in 2003-05 to 29% in 2014-16 (Figure 2.8). This declining share was driven by low farm gate milk prices in 2016 as well as rising cereal and oilseed production (from 20% in 2003-05 to 34% in 2014-16). Milk production increased only 7% from 1998 to 2016, but milk collection has increased 97% as improvements in milk quality and structural changes in dairy farming sector lead to a high share of milk production reaching processing firms. Over the same period (three-year moving average), cereal production increased by 99%, mainly due to rapid growth in yields, and meat production increased by 30%. However, in 2016, meat production declined by 8% compared to 2015, mainly because of the crisis in the pig meat sector after the outbreaks of African Swine Fever (ASF) in pig farms in 2015 and 2016.

Milk production in Estonia has fluctuated over the last two decades. After regaining independence, milk production in Estonia began to decline, hitting a low threshold of 610 000 tonnes in 2003. While the number of dairy cows decreased in Estonia by 57% over 1994-2013, as milk yields increased by 132% (Figure 2.13), total milk production recovered 1994 levels in 2013. Compared to other Northern Europe countries, milk production in Estonia has demonstrated the highest growth. Milk production continued to increase in 2014, but declined in 2015 and 2016. The withdrawal of milk quotas in the EU in 2015 (which was announced in 2008) led to a 7% increase in EU production volumes from 2008 to 2014 (Viira et al., 2015). This increase in supply has had a negative impact on milk producer prices across Europe and put many milk producers under economic pressure. An import ban issued by the Russian Federation — an important export market for Estonia — in August 2014 put further pressure on Estonian milk producers. From 2014-16, Estonia's milk production declined by 3%, the number of dairy cows decreased by 10% and the average annual milk yield increased by 7%.

Figure 2.8. Developments in meat, milk and cereals production, 1998 to 2016

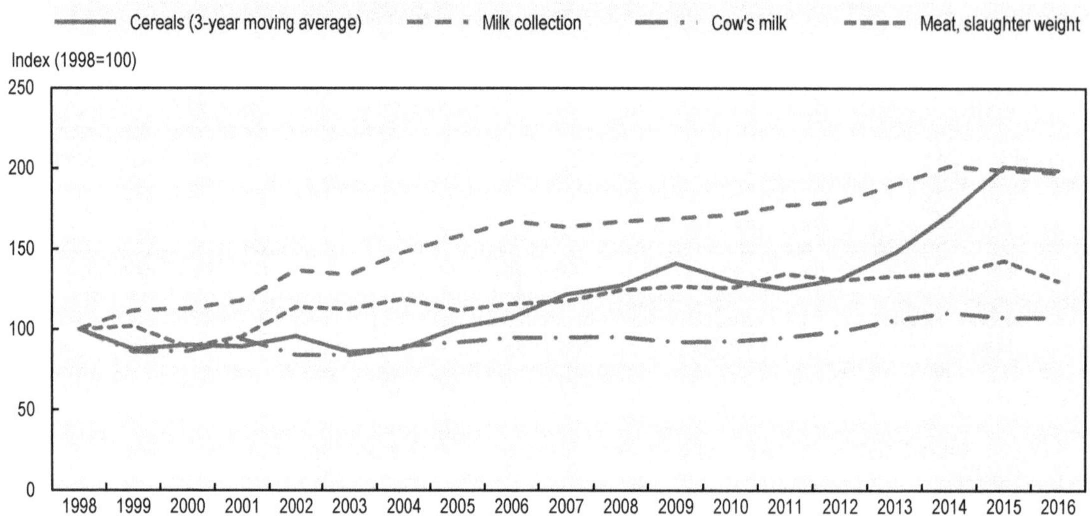

Source: Statistics Estonia (2017), [AG04, AG10, AG11], www.stat.ee.

StatLink http://dx.doi.org/10.1787/888933653819

Meat production has increased over the last two decades, by 1.5% per year on average. The highest growth rate was for poultry meat (8.3% per year) and pig meat (1.6%), while beef production declined.[4] Pig meat accounted for about 55% of all meat production in 2016, compared to 54% in 1996 and 60% in 2006. During the same period, the share of poultry meat increased from 7.3% in 1996 to 18% in 2006 and 25.3% in 2016.

Pig meat production levels have suffered in the last couple of years due to ASF outbreaks. ASF was first diagnosed among the Estonian wild boar population in September 2014. In the third quarter of 2015, the first cases of ASF were confirmed in domestic pigs. While the disease outbreak at pig farms subsided in September 2015, there have been subsequent outbreaks in 2016 and 2017. Between 2015 and 2016, around 53% of pig farmers closed down their businesses due to the spread and threat of ASF. The number of pigs kept on farms decreased by 26%, dropping from 357 900 pigs in 2014 to 265 400 in 2016. The number of pigs and pig farmers is expected to decline further, especially on the account of small-scale farmers (farms with less than 50 pigs). However, pig meat production recovered its 2011 level of 50 000 tonnes in 2015 due to the liquidation of many pig farms. In 2016 pig meat production decreased by 15% compared to 2015 (EMÜ, 2016).

Trade

Estonia has a large trade deficit of agricultural and food products due to high imports of processed foods. The annual deficit peaked to over EUR 500 million in the late 1990s, but has declined since. In 2016, the balance of trade of agricultural and food products (HS chapters 01-23) was about EUR -317 million (Table 2.2). The trade surplus was largest for cereals and dairy products. The trade balances of live animals, fish, preparations of meat and fish, animal or vegetal fats and oils and vegetable planting materials were also positive. At the same time, Estonia was a net importer of fruits, vegetables and a number of prepared food categories (e.g. meat, products of the milling industry and cereals, flour, starch or milk).

The composition of Estonia's agro-food trade suggests the food manufacturing industry is not as developed as primary production. Estonia's imports of agro-food products are mainly for household consumption (over 70%), while the country exports a larger share of agro-food products for industrial use than the EU average (Figure 2.9). The lower processing capacity is particularly clear at the sub-sector level: Estonia is a net exporter of cereals, but a net importer of processed cereals — and a net exporter of live animals, but a net importer of meat.

Table 2.2. Import and export of agricultural and food products in Estonia, 2016

	Import	Share of total imports	Export	Share of total exports	Balance
HS Chapter	Million EUR	%	Million EUR	%	Million EUR
10 Cereals	15.2	0.1	106.8	0.9	91.6
04 Dairy products, eggs, honey	72.7	0.5	141.9	1.2	69.2
01 Live animals	7.6	0.1	39.7	0.3	32.1
15 Animal or vegetable fats and oils	28.1	0.2	46.4	0.4	18.3
03 Fish	93.2	0.7	111.4	0.9	18.2
16 Preparations of meat and fish	57.1	0.4	65.6	0.6	8.6
12 Oil seeds	16.4	0.1	18.9	0.2	2.5
14 Vegetable planting materials, other vegetal products	0.2	0.0	0.4	0.0	0.3
13 Lac, gums, resins	1.6	0.0	1.1	0.0	- 0.5
05 Other animal products	4.5	0.0	4.1	0.0	- 0.5
21 Miscellaneous edible preparations	111.8	0.8	110.2	0.9	- 1.6
11 Products of milling industry	16.8	0.1	10.9	0.1	- 5.9
19 Preparations of cereals, flour, starch or milk	86.4	0.6	63.6	0.5	- 22.8
06 Live trees and plants	29.0	0.2	3.2	0.0	- 25.8
07 Vegetables	62.4	0.5	33.7	0.3	- 28.8
17 Sugars and sugar confectionery	46.4	0.3	10.8	0.1	- 35.6
18 Cocoa and cocoa preparations	62.4	0.5	19.6	0.2	- 42.8
20 Preparations of vegetables and fruits	65.9	0.5	19.0	0.2	- 46.9
09 Coffee and tea	63.5	0.5	14.8	0.1	- 48.6
23 Residues and waste from food industry	65.2	0.5	15.9	0.1	- 49.3
02 Meat	100.0	0.7	47.2	0.4	- 52.8
08 Fruit	111.6	0.8	26.3	0.2	- 85.3
22 Beverages, spirits and vinegars	277.1	2.1	166.3	1.4	- 110.8
Total	**1 394.9**	**10.3**	**1 077.6**	**9.1**	**- 317.2**

Source: Eurostat (2017), Traditional international trade database (ComExt), http://ec.europa.eu/eurostat/data/database.

Figure 2.9. Composition of agro-food trade, 2016

Intra and extra EU trade

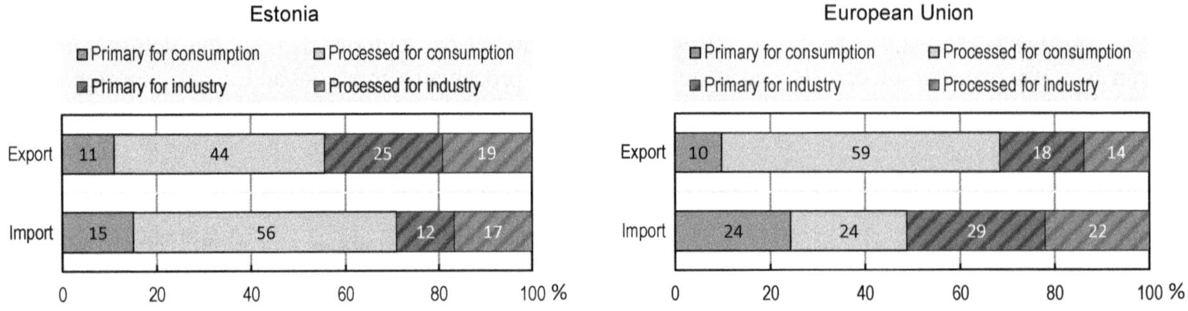

Numbers may not add up to 100 due to rounding.

Source: Eurostat (2017), Traditional international trade database (ComExt), http://ec.europa.eu/eurostat/data/database.

StatLink http://dx.doi.org/10.1787/888933653838

Estonia's trade in agricultural and food products is primarily EU-focused (Figure 2.10). In 2016, 93% of Estonian agricultural and food products originated from EU28 countries, and 74% of Estonian agricultural and food exports were exported to them. Latvia, Lithuania and Finland are the main trading partners for agricultural and food products. Other Northern European countries also account for a significant share of Estonian agricultural and food imports, and Sweden receives a significant share of Estonian agricultural and food exports. As noted previously, trade with the Russian Federation has markedly declined since the issuance of an import ban in August 2014 and approximately two-thirds of Estonian exports to Russia is comprised of drinks, alcohol and vinegar.

Figure 2.10. Estonia's main trade partners for agricultural and food products, 2016

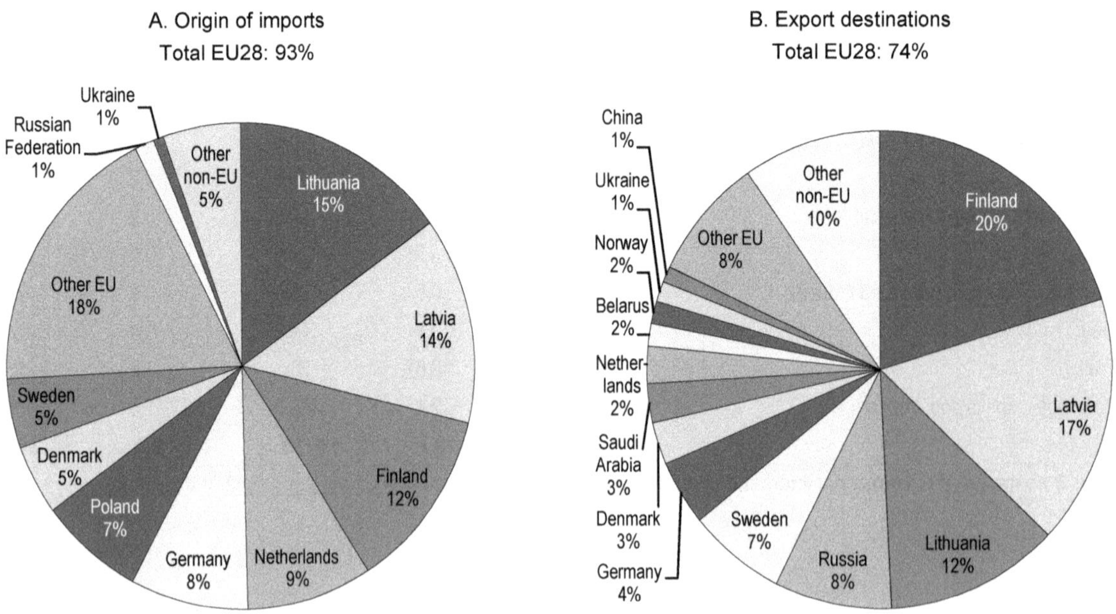

Definition of agri-food products HS 01 to 23.

Source: Eurostat (2017), Traditional international trade database (ComExt), http://ec.europa.eu/eurostat/data/database.

StatLink http://dx.doi.org/10.1787/888933653857

2.6. Trends in productivity

Total Factor Productivity

Agricultural TFP has increased strongly since 2000, following a decline in the 1990s when output levels declined more than input levels (Figure 2.11; Table 2.3). The largest declines were in the use of fertilisers and the number of animals. Machinery was the only input to increase. The reduction in agricultural labour was sustained over the period 1990-2013, leading to higher labour productivity.[5] In the early 2000s, TFP started to recover as total output levels increased in both livestock and crop production. Over the period 2000-13, the increase in output occurred while total input levels continued to decline, mainly due to lower labour and animals. Capital improvements in the 2000s have benefited Estonia's agricultural sector. Policies to stimulate investment have triggered more intensive use of intermediate inputs, the introduction of modern technology and rapid growth in knowledge.

Productivity growth in Estonia's agricultural sector has exceeded growth rates in most comparable countries and the EU average over the last decade. As illustrated in Figure 2.12, the average TFP index in Europe has experienced strong growth. However, in 2013, Estonia's TFP growth exceeded the EU average and all northern European countries excluding Denmark and the Netherlands.

Figure 2.11. Trends in the Total Factor Productivity (TFP) of Estonian primary agriculture, 1990 to 2013

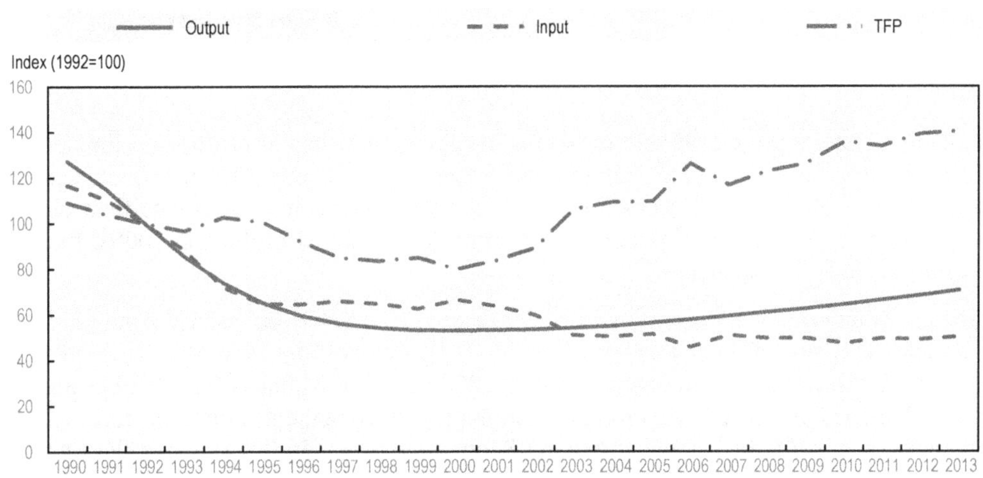

Source: USDA (2016), Economic Research Service, International Agricultural Productivity: www.ers.usda.gov/data-products/international-agricultural-productivity.aspx (accessed January 2017).

StatLink http://dx.doi.org/10.1787/888933653876

Table 2.3. Decomposition of Estonian Total Factor Productivity growth, 1991-2013

Average annual change, LN (T/ (T-1))

	Output	Labour	Land	Livestock	Machinery	Fertiliser	Feed	TFP	Total Inputs
1991-01	- 0.0885	- 0.0785	- 0.0336	- 0.1166	0.0456	- 0.2043	- 0.0312	- 0.0297	- 0.0588
2001-10	0.0223	- 0.0825	0.0017	- 0.0056	- 0.0166	0.0059	- 0.0292	0.0474	- 0.0251
2001-13	0.0246	- 0.0770	0.0052	- 0.0021	- 0.0050	0.0412	- 0.0126	0.0393	- 0.0147

Source: USDA (2016), Economic Research Service, International Agricultural Productivity, www.ers.usda.gov/data-products/international-agricultural-productivity.aspx (accessed January 2017).

Figure 2.12. Agricultural Total Factor Productivity growth, by country, 1992 and 2013

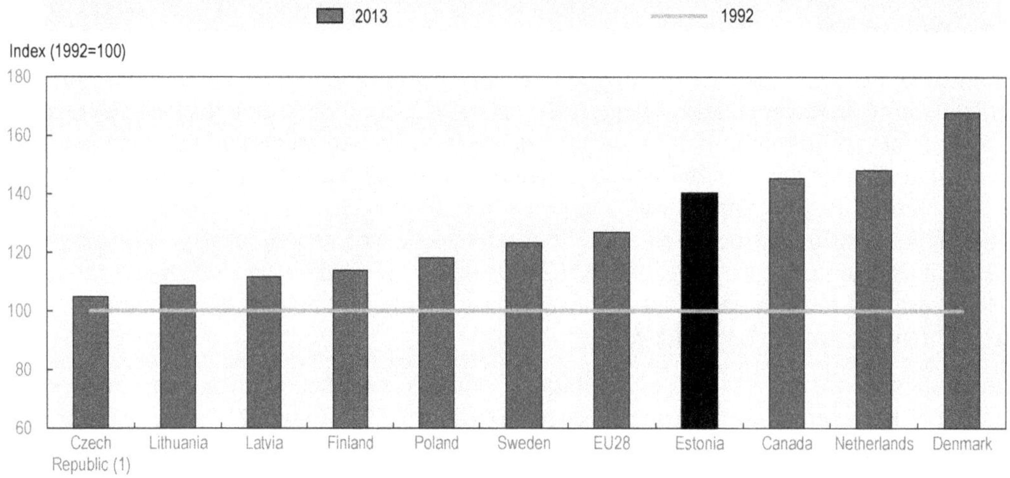

1. As data for Czech Republic are unavailable, Czechoslovakian data are used.

Source: USDA (2016), Economic Research Service, International Agricultural Productivity, www.ers.usda.gov/data-oducts/international-agricultural-productivity.aspx (accessed January 2017).

StatLink http://dx.doi.org/10.1787/888933653895

Dairy productivity

While, TFP is generally not available by sector in official statistics, it has been estimated for the dairy sector of Estonia using farm level data (Kimura and Sauer, 2015). **Dairy TFP** has fluctuated over the last decade (Figure 2.13). Following EU accession, input levels increased at a faster rate than output levels — triggering a decline in TFP in the mid-2000s. TFP partially rebounded in the late 2000s. Increases in milk yields have contributed to TFP growth.

Over the last two decades, average milk yields in Estonia have achieved faster growth rates and started to catch up the yields in many selected countries (Figure 2.14). In 1994, the average milk yield in Estonia and other member states that joined the European Union in 2004 was approximately half that in Canada, Denmark, Finland, the Netherlands and Sweden. Through technological development, improved feeding, breeding and structural change, milk yields in Estonia surpassed 8 tonnes/cow/year in 2014, above the Eastern European average and nearing the rates of Canada, Denmark, Finland, the Netherlands and Sweden. Growing fast since the recovery of milk markets (and with no quota to constrain production), Estonian milk yields are expected to reach approximately 9.5 tonnes per cow in 2017.

A first driver of productivity growth in Estonia's dairy farm sector has been **resource reallocation**. As illustrated in Figure 2.15, resource reallocation towards more productive farms stimulated productivity growth during the 2003-12 period (Kimura and Sauer, 2015). Indeed, benefiting from economies of scale, larger Estonian farms recorded higher milk yields and higher livestock density. The largest 25% farms accounted for 90% of milk production in recent years. Under this dualistic sector structure, the evolution of sector-level productivity is largely driven by improvements in a small number of large farms. As a result, the productivity difference between large and small farms increased overtime.

Figure 2.13. Evolution of Total Factor Productivity (TFP), output and input indices of Estonian dairy farm sector, 2003 to 2012

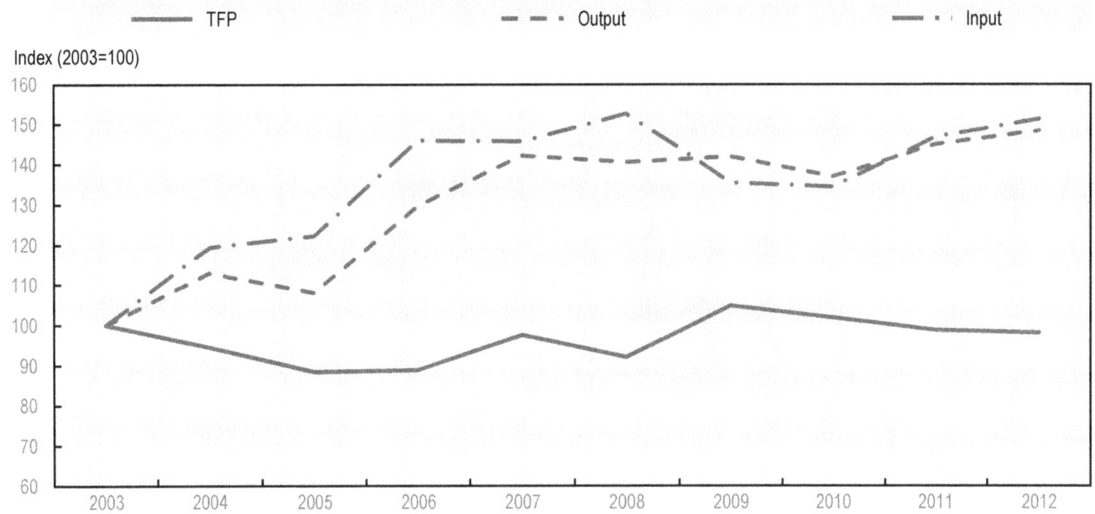

Source: Kimura and Sauer (2015), "Dynamics of dairy farm productivity growth: Cross-country comparison", http://dx.doi.org/10.1787/5jrw8ffbzf7l-en.

StatLink http://dx.doi.org/10.1787/888933653914

Figure 2.14. Developments in milk yield, 1994, 2004 and 2014

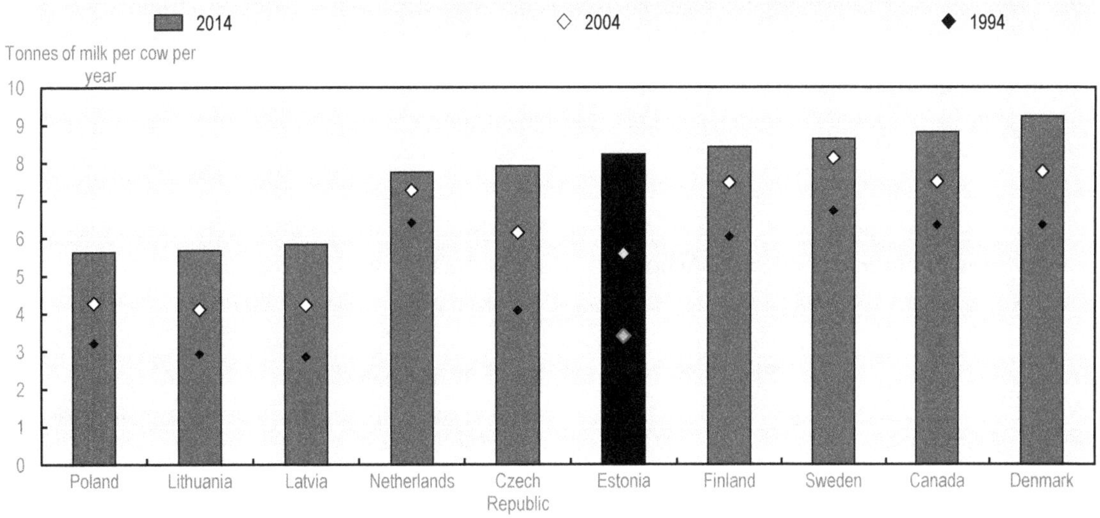

Countries are ranked according to 2014 levels.

Source: FAO Statistics Division (2016), FAOSTAT, Livestock Primary database [Milk Animals; Production; milk, whole fresh cow], www.fao.org/faostat/en/.

StatLink http://dx.doi.org/10.1787/888933653933

Figure 2.15. Decomposition of Total Factor Productivity (TFP) growth in the Estonian dairy farm sector, 2004 to 2012

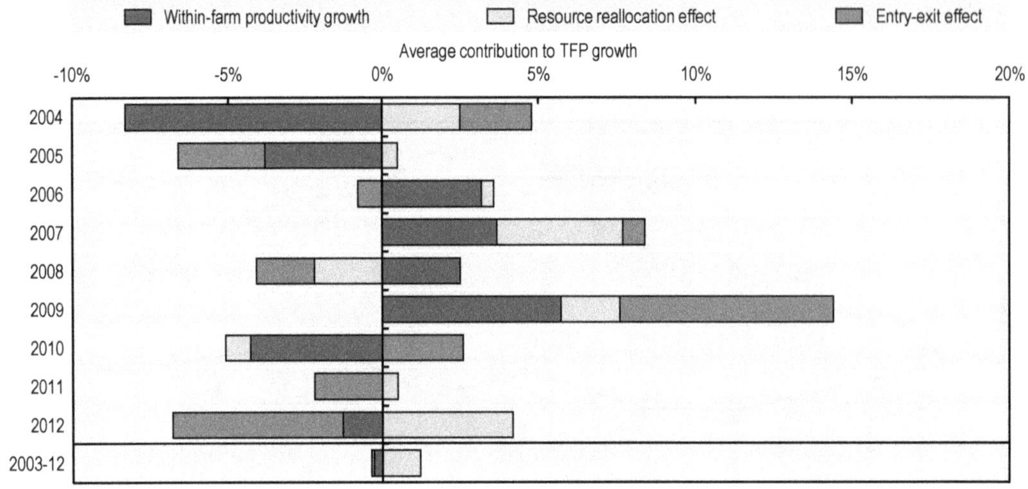

Source: Kimura and Sauer (2015), "Dynamics of dairy farm productivity growth: Cross-country comparison", http://dx.doi.org/10.1787/5jrw8ffbzf7l-en.

StatLink http://dx.doi.org/10.1787/888933653952

The **exit of inefficient farms** has also been an important driver of productivity growth in Estonia's dairy farm sector during selected years (Kimura and Sauer, 2015). In particular, due to a low milk price in 2009 and 2010, many small and less productive farms stopped producing milk and exited the market. However, exit of efficient farms from the dairy specialist category in the survey appears to have reduced productivity growth in 2011 and 2012 (Figure 2.13).

Rapid **technological change** has contributed to productivity growth in dairy farms. In line with the EU directives on agri-environmental issues and their associated investment subsidies, most feeding and milking technologies have been upgraded, and most new farms have opted for liquid manure systems since 2001 (Box 2.3).

In line with the sector-wide trends (Figure 2.14), **low labour productivity** is a key barrier to productivity growth in the dairy sector. According to Kimura and Sauer (2015), labour input per cow had a negative correlation with productivity.

Box 2.3. Estonian dairy farms' technologies

In 2013, the Institute of Economics and Social Sciences of the Estonian University of Life Sciences (EMÜ) conducted a farm survey on the *Efficiency of utilisation of the main production resources in Estonia*. The main aim was to gather information about the technologies used by dairy farms; 326 milk farms responded that had in total 366 dairy barns.

Dairy barns: Most Estonian dairy cows are in larger, more recent barns with loose housing. 67% of the barns had less than 100 places for dairy cows, but these small barns accounted for 15% of total places. Therefore 85% of places for dairy cows were in larger barns with more than 100 places. 70% of barns had tethered housing, and included 30% of the total number of places for dairy cows while the remaining 30% of barns were of the more modern loose housing type and included 70% of the places. 80% of barns with tethered housing were for less than 100 cows and most of them were constructed before 2001. 70% of the loose housing barns had space for more than 100 cows and most of these were constructed after 2001.

Milking technologies: 38% of the dairy barns had pipeline milking system, and 30% bucket milking; 26% had milking parlour or carousel, and 6% had automated milking system (robots). Despite the high share of barns with pipeline and bucket milking (68%), the share of cows milked with these technologies is quite small (26%). It means that 74% of cows are milked with up-to-date milking technologies. The pipeline and bucket milking systems are more widespread in smaller and older barns, in which the average number of dairy cows is 53. Contemporary milking systems are widespread in bigger and new barns: the average number of dairy cows in barns with milking parlours or carousels is 323; and 256 in the robot milking barns. New barns (constructed after 2001) usually have milking parlours or robots.

Box 2.3. Estonian dairy farms' technologies (cont.)

Feeding of dairy cows: the two main feeding systems are total mixed ration (TMR) feeding (22% of the farms) and regular feeding (78%) with unlimited roughage and rationed concentrates. In smaller barns, usually regular feeding is used, while the larger barns use the TMR technology.

Grazing: whether dairy cows can graze or not depends on the herd size and used technologies. Considering the large proportion of small farms, it is evident that in most of the farms (52%, average 46 places for dairy cows per barn) cows are grazed 24 hours per day during the grazing period. In 25% of the farms (average 107 places for dairy cows in the barn), cows graze only in daytime during the grazing period. In 21% of the farms (average 377 places for dairy cows), cows do not graze and are fed with silage all year round. In 2% of the farms (average 390 places for dairy cows), cows are not grazed but during the summer, fresh cut grass is fed to dairy cows. In 77% of farms, cows grazed during the grazing period, and in 23% of the farms, cows were kept indoors the whole year round.

Manure: in 64% of barns, a solid manure system was used. Most of these barns were older and smaller, and not reconstructed. New or renovated barns (25% of all barns) usually have liquid manure system. 10% of barns use combined system — both solid and liquid manure. Manure is usually used in the farm. Manure application technology depends on the size of the farm and type of manure. Smaller farms use broadcast spreader or spray-based slurry spreading, larger farms use various manure application technologies that enable to inject manure into the soil immediately.

In Estonia, the rapid technological change in dairy farms started in 2001. Since then, most of the barns that are built are uninsulated (cold), feeding and milking technologies are upgraded, and manure systems are changed to liquid systems. These changes have been in line with the EU directives related to the agri-environment and have been supported through CAP funding.

Source: EMÜ (2013a); Luik and Viira (2016).

Crop yields

Notwithstanding a low base level in the early 1990s, Estonia's barley and **wheat yields** have achieved the highest growth rates among selected countries over the last two decades. From 1992-94 to 2012-14, they increased by 111% and 98% respectively, followed closely by Lithuania and Latvia, while rye yields increased most in Latvia, almost twice as much as in Estonia and Lithuania (Figure 2.16). Despite these increases, Baltic countries still achieve relatively low yields compared to the Netherlands, Denmark, Sweden and the Czech Republic. With its northernmost location, Estonia's crop yields are close to those in Finland, but wheat yields are lower than in Southern neighbours.

Figure 2.16. Developments in cereal yields, 1992-94, 2002-04 and 2012-14

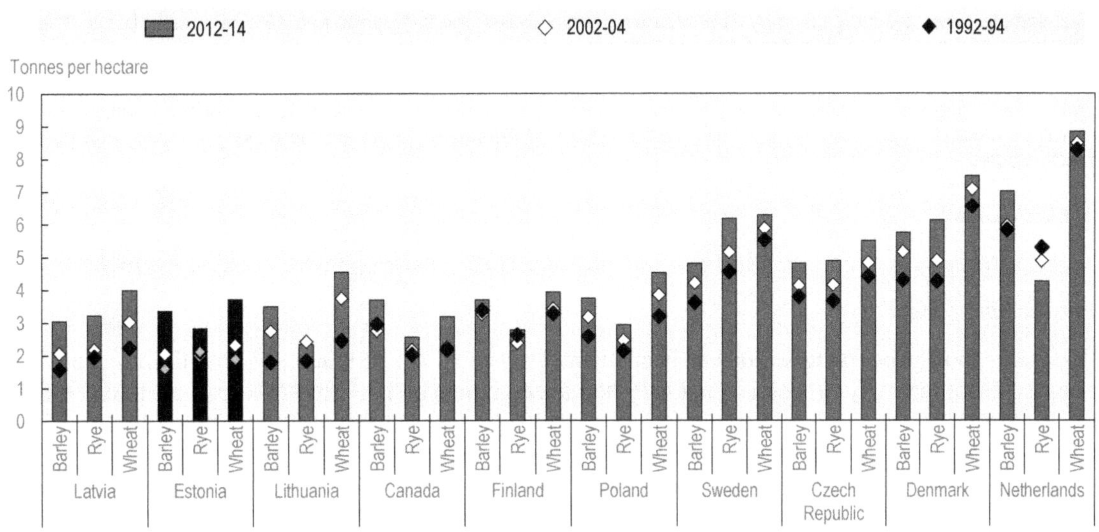

Countries are ranked according to barley 2012-14 levels.
All cereals harvested for dry grains.

Source: FAO Statistics Division (2016), FAOSTAT, Crops database [Production, Area harvested], www.fao.org/faostat/en/.

StatLink http://dx.doi.org/10.1787/888933653971

Box 2.4. Estonian crop farms' technologies

In 2013, the Institute of Economics and Social Sciences of the Estonian University of Life Sciences (EMÜ) conducted a farm survey on the Efficiency of utilisation of the main production resources in Estonia. The main aim was to gather information about the technologies used by crop farms. 333 crop farms responded. Farms were divided into three size groups, by agricultural land use: <100 ha (small); 100-399.9 ha (medium); ≥400 ha (large). The survey included 141 smaller farms (42%), 137 medium farms (41%) and 55 larger farms (17%).

The surveyed farms used various precision farming techniques, mainly in relation to crop protection (36%), sowing (30%) and fertiliser application (29%). For tillage and grain harvesting precision farming techniques were used less often, 11% in both cases. Precision farming techniques were more often applied in larger farms — 67% in crop protection, 55% in fertiliser application and 45% in sowing — but less in smaller and medium farms — respectively 26% and 34% in crop protection, 19% and 19% in fertiliser application and 26% and 28% in sowing.

Among precision farming techniques, assisted steering systems were the most widespread (30% of the respondents). Other options were used less frequently: precision crop management (12%); geomapping (9%); variable rate technology (ability to adapt parameters on a machine to apply, for instance, seed or fertiliser according to the exact variations in plant growth, or soil nutrients and type) (5%); measuring soil parameters (e.g. nutrients and moisture) at precise points (3%).

Among the larger farms 67% used precision steering systems and 31% geomapping of crop quantity and quality. Thus, operators of larger farms have adopted innovative technologies more often than those of smaller and medium sized farms.

Direct seeding and combined seeding, that help mimise tilling and costs, have become more widespread.

Table.2.4. Adoption of technology in crop farms, 2013

Farm size	Direct seeding	Combined seeding (seeds + fertiliser)	Combined seeding (seeds + fertilisers + soil tillage equipment)	Seed drill	Seed drill with soil tillage equipment
<100 ha	11%	50%	9%	28%	8%
100-400 ha	24%	35%	23%	18%	17%
>400 ha	18%	13%	29%	29%	29%
Total	**17%**	**38%**	**18%**	**24%**	**15%**

Source: EMÜ (2013a).

Larger and medium farms used more often seeding in combination with tillage equipment, while smaller farms used more often seeding without combined tillage equipment.

Soil samples were regularly taken by 85% of larger farms, 75% of medium farms and 49% of smaller farms. This indicates that larger farms had more information about the soil condition.

The respondents were also asked about their plans for adopting new technologies. Over half of the respondents intended to adopt minimised tilling and precision farming techniques. About three-quarters intended to start using certified seeds. Direct seeding will be more likely adopted by larger and medium farms, while smaller farms are more likely to continue using ploughing-based technologies.

Source: EMÜ (2013a).

Food processing productivity

Estonia's **food processing** sector has been characterised by low productivity growth in recent years. For instance, the Estonian dairy processing industry had average annual TFP growth of merely 0.3% in the 2000-11 period (Box 2.2). As a result, Estonia's dairy industry processed only 75% of the volume of raw milk collected in 2014, whereas Lithuania's dairy industry processed 119% of the milk collected in Lithuania. In other words, raw milk was traded from Estonia to Lithuania — indicating a lack of competitiveness in milk processing (Viira et al., 2015).

A first barrier to productivity growth in the food processing sector is lack of investment and **low labour productivity.** In 2014, value added at factor cost per employed person was EUR 23 300 (Figure 2.17). While Estonia exceeded the Latvian, Lithuanian and Czech Republic's figures, it is almost on par with the performance of food manufacturers in Poland. Compared to Scandinavian countries, value added per employed person in the Estonian food industry is approximately three times lower. While labour productivity in the food processing sector is higher than in agriculture in Estonia, the labour productivity gap between the two is low compared to other countries (e.g. the Netherlands, Poland, Sweden, EU28) shown in Figure 2.17.[6]

Lower levels of **automation** also constrain productivity growth for the Estonian food processing industry. For instance, as outlined in Box 2.3, automation is an important barrier to the development of Estonia's milk processing industry: some experts have highlighted that current equipment is outdated and inefficient. Investing in automation would help to achieve higher processed milk volume per employee (Viira et al., 2015). The industry fragmentation also limits productivity growth.

Figure 2.17. Labour productivity in food manufacturing companies and farms, selected countries, 2015

Value added per work unit (1, 2)

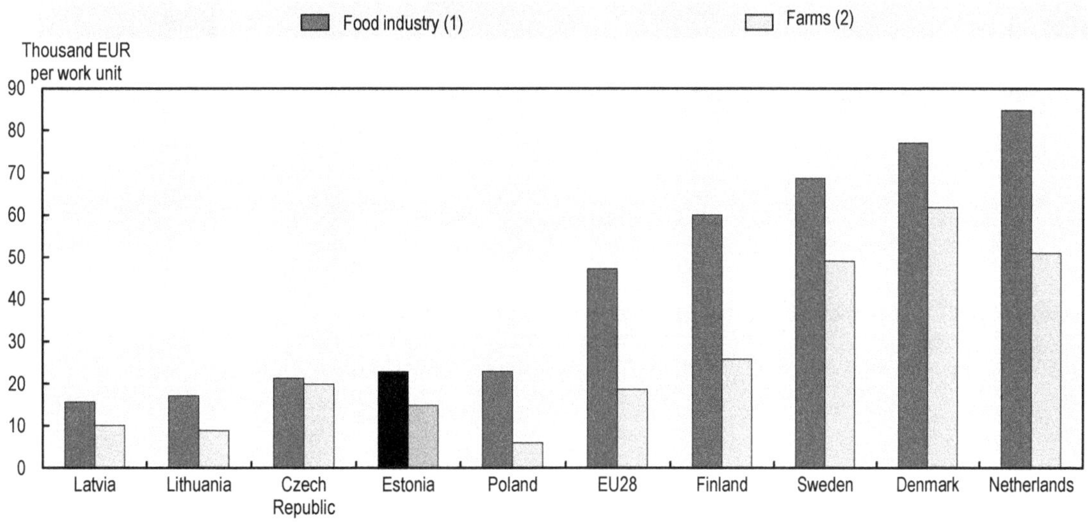

Countries are ranked according to food industry levels.

1. Value added at factor costs, EUR 1 000 per employee.
2. Farm net value added, EUR 1 000 per Annual Work Unit (AWU).

Source: Eurostat (2017) [sbs_sc_sca_r2] http://ec.europa.eu/eurostat/data/database, FADN (2017b), http://ec.europa.eu/agriculture/rica/database/database_en.cfm.

StatLink http://dx.doi.org/10.1787/888933653990

2.7. Trends in natural resource use and the state of the environment

Over the last decade, Estonia's TFP growth paralleled increases in certain agri-environmental pressures but decoupled from trends in others (Figure 2.18 and Table 2.A1.3). In particular, Estonia's production volume increased at a faster rate than agricultural land area due to TFP growth, among other factors. Over the same period, the OECD and EU15 maintained agricultural production levels, while reducing agricultural land area. Estonia's growth in TFP, production volume and land area also surpassed the trends in the Netherlands, Canada, the Czech Republic, Denmark, Finland, Latvia and Poland.

Over the same period, total direct on-farm energy consumption increased, at a rate surpassed only by Canada and Latvia, but the increase was lower than that of agricultural production, indicating more efficient energy use. This upward trend could be due to the shift in production from small, labour-intensive farms to larger, capital-intensive farms. Ammonia emissions increased at a faster rate than all other comparator countries, in spite of a decline in the number of dairy cows. Moreover, Estonia's phosphorus deficit increased, while phosphorus surpluses in the OECD, EU and several comparator countries declined at faster rates. At the same time, a decoupling can be seen between TFP growth and Estonia's nitrogen balance: Estonia's nitrogen surplus per ha decreased, at a faster rate than the OECD average and a slightly lower rate than the EU15 and EU28. Estonia's agricultural water abstraction is very low.[7] The rest of this section discusses these and other environmental trends in more detail.

Figure 2.18. Developments of environmental indicators for agriculture, Estonia, OECD and European Union, 2002-04 to 2012-14

Average annual percent change 2002-04 to 2012-14, or nearest available period

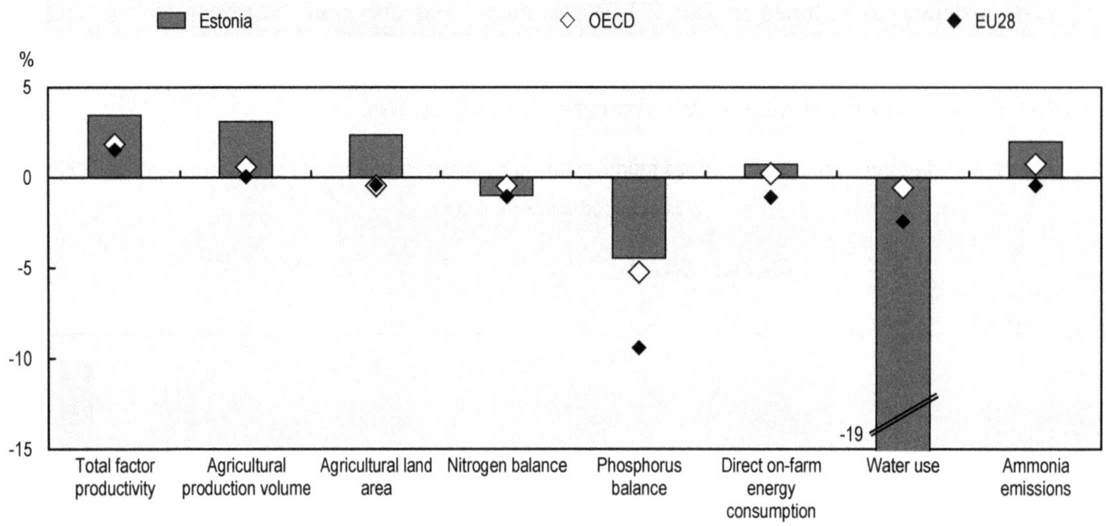

Source: OECD (2017b), Agri-environmental Indicators, www.oecd.org/tad/sustainable-agriculture/agri-environmentalindicators.htm ; USDA (2016), Economic Research Service Agricultural Productivity Database for Total Factor Productivity, www.ers.usda.gov/data-oducts/international-agricultural-productivity.aspx.

StatLink http://dx.doi.org/10.1787/888933654009

Inputs

Over the last decade, Estonia's **Nitrogen (N) balance** per ha of agricultural land was positive but declined at a faster rate than many comparative countries — a positive direction for sustainability (Figure 2.19). From 2004 to 2012, the N balance fell significantly, from 36 to 22 kg/ha in Estonia. During the same period, the N balance fell from 64 to 59 in the EU15 and 67 to 65 in the OECD area. The improvement in N balance in Estonia is mainly due to the higher productivity of crops: crop production increased faster than fertiliser use. Some improvement also occurs in livestock as manure application is stable, while animal production increases (Figure 2.8).

Estonia's Phosphorus (P) deficit has increased in recent years. From 2004 to 2013, Estonia's **P balance** fell from -5.0 to -8.0. During the same period, the P surplus of many comparator countries was reduced; for instance, the EU15 balance fell from 7.8 to 5.5 and the OECD average fell from 6.0 to 3.0. Higher crop production per fertiliser use due to policy shifts since EU accession as well as a declining number of agricultural animals (and thus a reduction in manure production, Box 2.3) may be contributing to Estonia's growing deficit. In the long term, such trends may lead to a decline in both soil fertility and productivity growth.

Certain support schemes may be exacerbating the P deficit. For enterprises benefiting only from the Single Area Payment Scheme (SAPS), the average P balance was negative in only 2 out of 11 years from 2004 to 2014. For enterprises receiving support from the agri-environmental management scheme, the average P balance was negative in 8 out of 11 years. For organic farms the P balance was negative for all 11 years. While only a correlation, this trend raises concern that the P deficit may further increase as the area under organic farms and farms supported from the agri-environmentally friendly management scheme continues to expand (ARC, 2016; ELF, 2016).

Figure 2.19. Nitrogen and phosphorus balance[1] in Estonia, 2004 to 2014

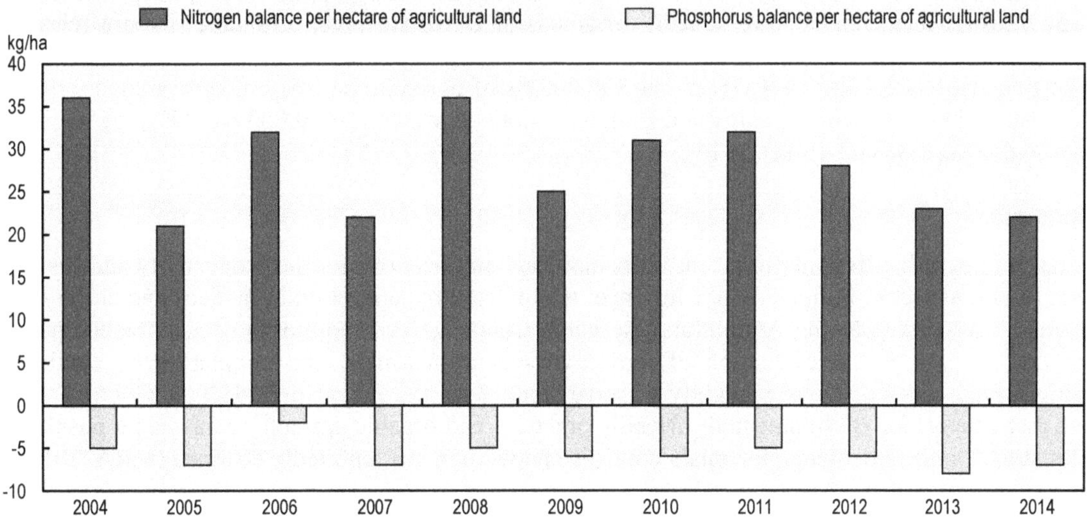

1. The gross nitrogen (phosphorus) balance (surplus or deficit) calculates the difference between the nitrogen (phosphorus) inputs entering a farming system (i.e. mainly livestock manure and fertilisers) and the nitrogen (phosphorus) outputs leaving the system (i.e. the uptake of nitrogen/phosphorus for crop and pasture production). Here, balance (surplus or deficit) expressed as kg nitrogen per hectare of total agricultural land.

Source: OECD (2017b), Agri-environmental Indicators, www.oecd.org/tad/sustainable-agriculture/agri-environmentalindicators.htm.

StatLink http://dx.doi.org/10.1787/888933654028

Estonian **pesticide** sales have rebounded from low levels in the 1990s, but remain well below sales in most other EU and OECD countries. From 2011 to 2013, Estonia's pesticide sales increased from 0.49 to 0.59 kg of active ingredient/ha.[8] During the same period, the EU28 average was four times higher, but declining (from 2.11 to 2.02 kg/ha). Meanwhile, the OECD average increased from 0.86 to 0.89 kg/ha (FAOSTAT, 2016).

Sustainability issues may also vary according to farm size. As illustrated in Table 2.A1.4, larger farms (>100 ha) have higher average wheat yields, but also have higher intensity of fertilisers and pesticide sales per ha. On the other hand, smaller farms (<100 ha) appear to achieve higher average wheat yield per EUR spent on fertilisers and pesticides.

Water

The majority of Estonia's abundant water resources are in good status, but pressures from nutrient use and other sources threaten **water quality** in certain regions. Groundwater resources are estimated at 4 000 million m³/year. Internal renewable surface water resources are estimated at 11 712 million m³/year in 2013 (FAO, 2016). More than 90% of Estonia's groundwater — and 70% of Estonia's surface water bodies — have good ecological and chemical status. However, eutrophication due to nutrient loads from diffuse and point sources threatens sustainable management of agricultural and water resources in certain regions — in particular, the Nitrate Vulnerable Zone in Central and North-Eastern Estonia (OECD, 2017c).

Water use in agriculture draws primarily on surface water and has decreased in recent decades. In 2014, total water withdrawal was estimated at 1 720 million m³. Around 88% of total water withdrawal was withdrawn from surface water, 3% from groundwater and 9% from mining water (FAO, 2016). Less than 5 million m³ (0.3%) of total water withdrawal was withdrawn for agricultural purposes (including irrigation, livestock watering and cleaning, forestry and aquaculture). From 2000 to 2014, water use in Estonian agriculture decreased on average by 5% annually. This decrease is due in great part to a decline in certain forms of agricultural production – such as the area under orchards and berry gardens and the number of farm animals. Over the same period, average water use has also declined in Canada and the OECD area.

In terms of **water-related infrastructure**, irrigation use is minimal and declining but drainage is growing in importance. Falling from 3 680 ha in 1995, the total area equipped for irrigation was estimated at only 458 ha (of which 326 ha were actually irrigated) in 2010. However, drainage is more relevant: it is estimated, that without drainage about half of the land for agricultural production would suffer from waterlogging (EMÜ, 2013b). In 1975, about 390 000 ha of agricultural land were drained. In 1995, about 732 400 ha, or almost 85% of the cultivated land, were drained, of which 650 000 ha (89%) are equipped with subsurface drainage systems (FAO, 2016).

Biodiversity

Trends in agro-**biodiversity** in recent years may have implications for the productivity and sustainability of the agricultural sector. Pollinators, for instance, are affected by agricultural practices and at the same time affect yields. According to the Agricultural Research Centre (ARC) monitoring of bumblebee populations carried out as part of the evaluation of agri-environment measures, the population of bumblebees in agricultural landscapes displays a slightly positive trend over the recent period 2009-16 (ARC, 2017). It appears that support for environmentally-friendly practices and organic agriculture has had a positive impact on pollinators. On the other hand, Estonia's honeybee population has reportedly declined (MRA, 2016b).

The farmland bird index is another indicator of agrobiodiversity, which has been monitored since 1983 in Estonia. As is the case across Europe, the index for Estonia has a declining trend – the index value (based on 2000=100) was 75.4 in 2015, with significant annual variations. The number and status of birds is the highest in organic farming areas. This is probably caused by the prohibition of mineral fertilisers and synthetic pesticides, thereby increasing the birds' food supply. Another important reason is the larger share of grasslands in organic land use. Extensively-managed grasslands offer a more permanent population site for bird. At the same time, no significant differences can be seen between areas applying support for agri-environmentally friendly management schemes or only for Single Area Payment Scheme support (ARC, 2016).

Ammonia

Estonia achieved a significant decline in **Ammonia** (NH_3) emissions in the 1990s, but rising emissions in the 2000s raise concerns for sustainability. From 11 108 tonnes in 1995, ammonia emissions fell to 9 058 tonnes in 1999 due to a decrease in the number of livestock (EMÜ, 2008). Ammonia emissions then increased over the last decade (to 13 042 tonnes in 2014), while the number of cows decreased and milk production increased (FAOSTAT, 2016).

As in most countries, agriculture is the primary source of ammonia emissions in Estonia (accounting for 94% in 2012-13). Livestock breeding contributes 69%, and the use of N fertilisers contributes 25%. Other major sources of pollution include road transport, the production of fertilisers and the burning of firewood in households (EEA, 2014b).

Greenhouse Gas emissions

Following the energy sector (which produced 89% of total Greenhouse Gas (GHG) emissions in 2014), Estonia's agricultural sector is the second largest contributor (producing 1 318 thousand tonnes of CO_2 equivalent, or 6% of total GHG emissions (Estonian NIR, 2015). The main agricultural GHG emissions in Estonia are CH_4 emissions from enteric fermentation of domestic livestock and direct N_2O emissions from agricultural soils. N_2O emissions from manure management systems, indirect N_2O emissions from agricultural soils, and CO_2 emissions from liming and urea application to agricultural soils also contribute.

Agricultural GHG emissions declined significantly in the 1990s as the sector contracted, but have experienced positive growth over the last decade as the sector expanded and input use increased. From 1990-92 to 2000-02, agricultural GHG emissions in CO_2 eq. decreased in Estonia on average 8% annually – much faster than in other selected countries (Figure 2.20). However, from 2002-04 to 2012-14, agricultural emissions increased by an annual average of nearly 2%. During the same period, Latvia experienced a similar increase, but emissions experienced close to zero or negative growth in all other selected countries.

Notwithstanding, low-income EU member states are not obliged (for now) to reduce emissions in sectors excluded from the emissions trading system such as agriculture. Rather, by 2020, the increase of emissions in such countries should not exceed 11% of 2005 emissions (Government Office, 2014; MRA, 2013c; MoE, 2016).

As agriculture intensifies due to continued EU support, agricultural GHG emissions are likely to increase without further measures. As crop production expands, it is important to ensure that crops are not cultivated on peat and eroded soils, which could enhance GHG emissions (since the intensification of agriculture and the expansion of agricultural land will induce the application of mineral fertilisers, which, in turn, will result in increased direct and indirect nitrous oxide (N_2O) emissions from agricultural lands) (MoE, 2013a). Moreover, more efficient livestock practices will be needed to increase production while meeting EU targets for reductions in GHG emissions.

Figure 2.20. Average annual percentage change of GHG emissions from agriculture, 1990-92 to 2000-02 and 2002-04 to 2012-14

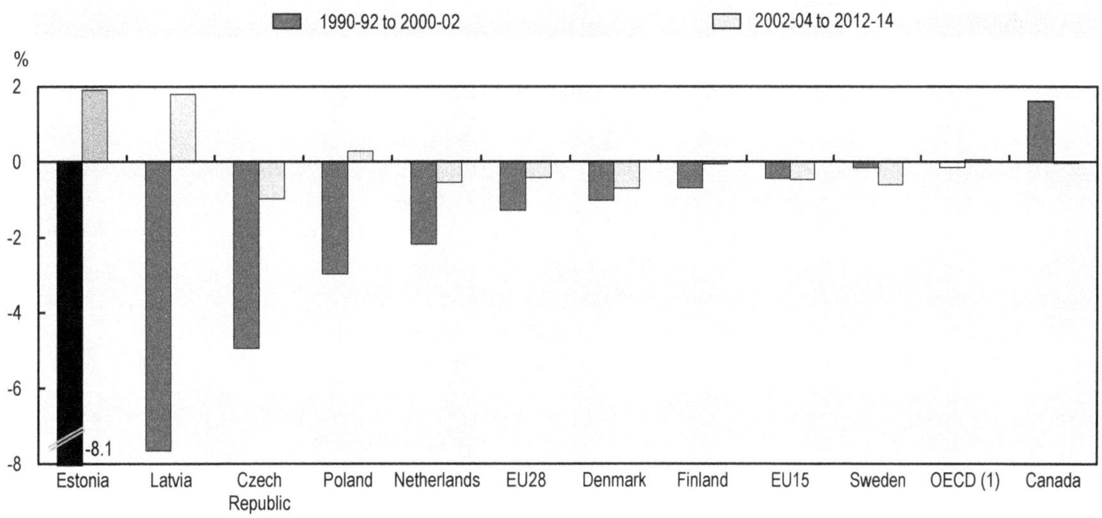

Countries are ranked according to (1990-92 to 2000-02) levels.
1. OECD total, excluding Chile, Israel and Mexico.
Source: UNFCCC (2016), http://unfccc.int/ghg_data/items/4133.php.

StatLink http://dx.doi.org/10.1787/888933654047

Climate change

Over the past 50 years, the growing season in Estonia has become considerably longer. From 1965 to 2013, the overall vegetation period (t>5°C) and the active growing season (t>10°C) in Estonia increased by an average of three weeks — primarily due to the earlier occurrence of the last spring frost. This shift was the largest in South-Eastern Estonia, and less pronounced in North-Eastern Estonia (ETKI, 2015). This shift has contributed to the expansion of permanent grasslands and favoured the cultivation of winter crops.

Several shifts in **climate conditions** in the coming decades may further affect the Estonian agricultural sector (ETKI, 2015). Compared to the reference period 1971-2000, the air temperature in Estonia is projected to increase 2.0°C (RCP4.5 scenario) to 2.6°C (RCP8.5 scenario) during the period 2041-70 and 2.7°C to 4.3°C during the period 2071-2100. According to RCP4.5 (RCP8.5), average annual precipitation is also projected to rise by 10% (14%) in the period 2041-70 and 16% (19%) in the period 2071-2100. Moreover, extreme precipitation (more than 30 mm per day) is expected to increase, though the probability of occurrence is very low in every season except summer. RCP4.5 and RCP8.5 scenarios also project a significant decrease in snow cover by the end of the century. Furthermore, average wind speed is expected to increase (in the range from 3-18%) in winter and partly also in spring, triggering an increase in the number of cyclones moving from the Atlantic to Estonia (Estonian National Climate Change Adaptation Strategy and Implementation Plan).

Shifts in Estonia's **water** supply may also affect the agricultural sector. Sea-level rise may increase the risk of flooding in coastal areas (with valuable semi-natural coastal meadows (habitats) and grazed and managed pastures, which have historically adapted to flooding) and the destruction of port and harbour structures. Several valuable natural ecosystems may also be threatened, encompassing both marine and mainland ecosystems. Inland water may also be affected, as climate change may induce significant changes in the hydrological cycle. It is possible that the four main hydrological periods will be replaced by two, which means a fundamental change in the hydrological regime. As a consequence, the levels of inland water bodies may become lower than at present and more evenly distributed (in addition to spring floods, also autumn floods), potentially affecting land use. Compared to the baseline, climate change will have a favourable effect on river management in connection with the convergence of the seasonal distribution of run-offs. However, it may induce significant changes in the hydrological regime of near-groundwater layer because freshet infiltration into groundwater may increase by 20% to 40% due to the shortening and warming of the winter period. Owing to climate change, the ratio of the total groundwater recharge to surface runoff is projected to increase from 30% to 40% (EEA, 2014b; MoE, 2013b, MoE 2016; EMÜ, 2015). These hydrological changes could affect land use, its productivity and resilience to water related events.

Such changes in Estonia's environment and climatic conditions are expected to generate both positive and negative impacts for crop and livestock production. Taking into consideration the latitude of Estonia, the positive effects of climate change for **grasslands** will probably dominate at first. In particular, the increase in temperature and in the volume of precipitation will benefit grassland productivity (a rise in the average annual temperature by 1°C may improve the dry matter harvest of perennial forage crops by as much as 0.2 t/ha). The growing period will be lengthened and a higher number of cuttings will be available from grasslands (three times instead of the two in the last few years). In addition, the development and growth of grasses may accelerate and the suitable time for harvest may shift to an earlier period. This will ensure better fodder for livestock in summer and winter.

The estimated rise in temperature may also benefit **crop production**. In particular, it may enable Estonia to grow new, heat-loving crops and/or crops with longer growing cycles (ETKI, 2015). In the vegetation period, more heat than is necessary for the growth and development of plants will accumulate. The development of arable crops will quicken and the vegetation period will shorten (the optimal sowing period will shift forward by 4-11 days on average, and in order to achieve the maximum harvest the entire vegetation period should be lengthened by 10-30 days on average). This will increase the efficiency of arable land and will disperse the workload of agricultural producers. The lengthened vegetation period will additionally allow for the growing of new plant species and varieties in Estonia.

Several **potential risk factors** for the agricultural sector may also be exacerbated by climate change. In particular, grazed grasslands will be more sensitive than mown meadows to droughts brought about by climate warming. Yields may also be reduced by an increase in the frequency of extraordinary meteorological phenomena (droughts, excessive moisture, flooding etc.).[9] One of the greatest threats of climate change to Estonia would be the accelerated sea-level rise brought about by thermal expansion and the melting of glaciers, ice sheet and ice cap, which could trigger flooding along the coastline and extensive low-lying coastal areas of Estonia (MoE, 2013b). Lastly, the spread of plant diseases, plant pests and infectious animal diseases may increase with climate change.

2.8. Summary

- Estonia, situated on the coast of the Baltic Sea, is the northernmost of the Baltic countries, and the smallest in terms of surface area. Characterised by abundant land and water resources, the agricultural sector has expanded in the last two decades, although its contribution to a growing economy remains small.

- Estonia's **utilised agricultural area** (UAA) has fluctuated in recent decades, primarily due to policy shifts. After accession to the EU, agricultural land that was abandoned during the transition was reclaimed to qualify for CAP financing.
- The **type of agricultural land** in Estonia is predominantly — and increasingly — arable land. The area of agricultural land not used for agricultural production but maintained in good agricultural and environmental conditions (GAEC) has increased as well in recent years.
- Estonia's area for **organic production** has significantly increased. Driven by EU support to organic farming over the last decade, Estonia's land area under organic production has increased nearly four times. Organic production now constitutes 18% of UAA in 2015. However, part of organic production is sold to conventional processors.
- Significant restructuring has occurred in recent decades, resulting in a **dualistic structure** with large technically-efficient, more input intensive and innovative farms, as well as very small farms. This divergence can be seen both in terms of the distribution of UAA as well as livestock production. Similar to many other countries, the structure of Estonia's food processing sector is also dualistic.
- Estonia's **agricultural output** growth has been rapid since the EU accession. Agricultural output is dominated by milk production, but cereals and oilseeds production is increasing at a faster rate. Meat production has also increased over the last two decades, though production levels have suffered in the last couple of years due to African Swine Fever (ASF).
- While Estonian exports are growing, the country has a large **trade** deficit of agricultural and food products due to high imports of processed foods. Estonia's imports of agro-food products are mainly for household consumption, while the country exports a larger share of agro-food products for industrial use, suggesting the food processing industry is not as developed as primary production.
- The small size of Estonia's food processing companies and low labour productivity limit total factor productivity (TFP) growth and competitiveness.
- **Agricultural TFP** has increased strongly since 2000, following declines in the two previous decades. While low labour productivity has constrained productivity growth, capital improvements in the 2000s have benefited Estonia's agricultural sector. Policies to stimulate investment have facilitated the introduction of modern technology and rapid growth in knowledge.
- Growth in agricultural TFP and production volume has paralleled changes in the use of **natural resources** in Estonia over the last decade. In particular, agricultural land area increased, but at a slower rate than production volume and TFP growth. Direct on-farm energy consumption also increased. Furthermore, ammonia emissions increased at a higher rate than all other comparator countries. Moreover, eutrophication due to nutrient loads from diffuse and point sources threatens sustainable management of agricultural and water resources in certain regions. Furthermore, Estonia's phosphorus deficit increased — a growing concern for soil conditions. At the same time, a decoupling has occurred between TFP growth and Estonia's nitrogen balance and water use — both positive signs for the sustainability of the sector.
- Over the past 50 years, the growing season has become considerably longer in Estonia, contributing to the expansion of permanent grasslands and favouring the cultivation of winter crops. **Climate change** projections suggest that several shifts in the coming decades may further affect the Estonian agricultural sector, benefiting both grasslands and crop production. However, potential risk factors include an increase in the frequency of extreme meteorological phenomena (droughts, excessive moisture, flooding) and the spread of plant diseases, plant pests and infectious animal diseases.

Notes

1. The mid-point farm size applied to crop farms is the hectare-weighted median, which corresponds to a farm size that separates the farm size distribution into two parts: 50% of the total area of the national farmland operated by the crop farms of a larger size and the other 50% by the crop farms of smaller size than the hectare-weighted median.

2. The mid-point statistics used to measure the distribution of dairy farm size is the livestock unit-weighted median.

3. Excluding subsides on products and other subsidies on production.

4. While total beef production has declined, the quality of meat has changed. While in the 1990s beef was produced as a by-product of milk production (from culled cows and young bulls), after the EU accession, the number of beef cattle has increased significantly, from 9 400 in 2004 to 66 238 in 2016 (Vaan, 2016).

5. During the 1990s, the number of persons employed in agriculture, forestry and hunting decreased by 76%, from 161 400 in 1990 to 39 200 in 2000. This was the result of the transition from collective and state farms to private farms. Since 2000, farm employment has declined by 36% to 25 000 in 2016 as investments into modern equipment and technologies have increased labour productivity. At the same time, the number of small farms has decreased markedly since 2001.

6. The labour productivity indicators of food industry (value added at factor costs per employed person) and farms (net value added per Annual Work Unit, AWU) are not directly comparable, but here it assumed that they are acceptable proxies for the current comparison.

7. Statistics show a decline in water abstraction between 2002-04 and 2012-14 because data for 2002-04 include fish farming and data for 2012-14 do not.

8. Due to a change in methodology, data for earlier years is not available.

9. Higher temperatures have a particularly adverse effect on the yield of cereals and rapeseed. Rapeseed is particularly sensitive to high temperatures during seed development. Higher temperatures are often combined with drought, which further enhances the yield loss. The yields of winter cereals can also be affected by temperature fluctuations in autumn and winter, both excessively warm and excessively cold winters may act upon the yield. Long and warm autumns impair cold hardening in sowings. The scenarios for a typical winter in case of climate warming foresee more frequent changes between warm and cold periods during the winter, whereas alternations between cold and thaw and close to zero temperatures when it freezes at night and thaws during the daytime, increase, which significantly impairs wintering and increases the risk of frost damage. Data from national comparative trials and long-term complex experiments conducted at Kuusiku suggest that high temperatures during heading and booting, drought or excess water before and after sowing and drought before booting reduces the yields of spring cereals (barley, oats, wheat) (ETKI, 2015).

References

AB (Agricultural Board) (2016), Organic plant production, www.pma.agri.ee/index.php?id=104&sub=128&sub2=296&sub3=297 (accessed 9 April 2016).

AB (2017), Mahepõllumajanduse register [Organic Farming Register] www.pma.agri.ee/index.php?id=104&sub=128&sub2=319 (accessed 29.06.2017).

ARC (Agricultural Research Centre) (2016), MAK keskkonnaalaste tegevuste püsihindamine: Ülevaade hindamisest [MAK environmental activities ongoing evaluation: Overview of the evaluation], http://pmk.agri.ee/pkt/index.php?valik=2012&keel=1&template=mak_sisu.html (accessed 30 January 2016).

ARC (2017). keskkonnaalaste tegevuste püsihindamine [ongoing evaluation of environmental activities], Agricultural Monitoring Office, http://pmk.agri.ee/mak/hindamisvaldkonnad/elurikkus/ (accessed September 2017).

Bokusheva, R. and S. Kimura (2016), "Cross-Country Comparison of Farm Size Distribution", *OECD Food, Agriculture and Fisheries Papers*, No. 94, OECD Publishing, Paris. http://dx.doi.org/10.1787/5jlv81sclr35-en.

EEA (Environment Agency) (2014a), Share of total organic crop area out of total Utilised Agricultural Area, www.eea.europa.eu/data-and-maps/daviz/share-of-total-organic-crop-area (accessed 29 June 2016)

EEA (2014b), Eesti tuleviku kliimastsenaariumid aastani 2100 [Estonia's future climate scenarios for the year 2100], www.envir.ee/sites/default/files/kliimastsenaariumid_kaur_aruanne_ver190815.pdf (accessed 11 April 2016).

ELF (2016), Põllumees puhastab vett: Fosfori indeks [Farmer purifies water: Phosphorus index], Eestimaa Looduse Fond (ELF) [Estonian Fund for Nature (ELF)], http://elfond.ee/images/fosfori_indeks_1.pdf (accessed 13 June 2016).

EMÜ (2016), Ülevaade seakasvtussektorist [Overview of the pig sector] http://ms.emu.ee/userfiles/instituudid/ms/MSI%20failid/Uuringud/%C3%9Clevaade_seakasvatussektorist_aruanne_28_11_2016_FINAL.pdf (accessed 29 June 2017).

EMÜ (2015), Climate change adaptation strategy and measures for thematic fields of natural environment and bioeconomy: BioClim, http://pk.emu.ee/en/structure/landscapemanagement/projects/bioclim/project/ (accessed 9 April 04 2016).

EMÜ (2013a), Farm survey "Efficiency of utilisation of the main production resources in Estonia", unpublished data.

EMÜ (2013b), Maatulundusmaa sihtotstarbega katastriüksuste tegeliku kasutamise ning võimalike meetmete välja selgitamine põllu- ja metsamajanduse taristu arendamiseks kuni aastani 2020 - Töövõtuleping nr 94 lõpparuanne [Profit yielding land for cadastral units: Actual use and possible measures, clarification of the infrastructure of agriculture and forestry development until 2020 - Final Report on Contract No 94], Report for the Ministry of Agriculture, Tartu, https://www.agri.ee/sites/default/files/public/Leping-94_LOPP_aruanne__2013_.pdf.

EMÜ (2008), Keskkonnakaitse majandushoobade rakendamise vajadus ja võimalused Eesti põllumajanduses – Eesti Maaülikool, Majandus- ja sotsiaalinstituut [Environmental protection and the need for the implementation of economic opportunities for agriculture, Estonia, Estonian University of Life Sciences, Economic and Social Research Institute], www.envir.ee/sites/default/files/elfinder/article_files/keskkonnakaitsemajandushoovadpollumajanduses05.04.2008_0.pdf (accessed 22 June 2016).

Estonian NIR (2015), Greenhouse gas emissions in Estonia 1990-2013, National inventory report, United Nations Framework Convention on Climate Change, http://unfccc.int/files/national_reports/annex_i_ghg_inventories/national_inventories_submissions/application/zip/est-2015-nir-02nov15.zip (accessed 9 April 2016).

ETKI (2015), Kliimamuutuste mõju põllukultuuridele [Climate change impact on crops], Eesti Taimekasvatuse Instituut, (www.pikk.ee/upload/files/684_7_kliimamuutused_LISA1.pdf) (accessed 7 July 2016).

Eurostat (2017), on-line database, http://ec.europa.eu/eurostat/data/database.

FADN (2017a), Standard results of Estonian FADN farms, online database, http://maainfo.ee/standardtulemused/ (accessed 14 June 2017).

FADN (2017b), FADN Public Database, http://ec.europa.eu/agriculture/rica/database/database_en.cfm (accessed 5 June 2017).

FADN (2016), Standard results of Estonian FADN farms, online database, http://maainfo.ee/standardtulemused/ (accessed 5 June 2016).

FAOSTAT (2016), on-line database, www.fao.org/faostat/en/.

FAO (2016), AQUASTAT, www.fao.org/nr/aquastat/.

Government Office (2014), National Reform Programme "ESTONIA 2020", https://riigikantselei.ee/sites/default/files/riigikantselei/strateegiaburoo/eesti2020/estonia_2020_nrp2014_en.pdf (accessed 28 January 2016).

Jansik, C., X. Irz, and N. Kuosmanen (2014), Competitiveness of Northern European dairy chains, MTT Agrifood Research Finland. Economic Research. Publications 116, https://portal.mtt.fi/portal/page/portal/mtt/mtt/julkaisut/Dairy%20chain%20competitiveness%20MTT%202014%20final%20version.pdf.

Kimura, S. and J. Sauer (2015), "Dynamics of dairy farm productivity growth: Cross-country comparison", *OECD Food, Agriculture and Fisheries Papers*, No. 87, OECD Publishing, Paris, http://dx.doi.org/10.1787/5jrw8ffbzf7l-en.

Kimura, S. and C. Le Thi (2013), "Cross Country Analysis of Farm Economic Performance", *OECD Food, Agriculture and Fisheries Papers*, No. 60, OECD Publishing, http://dx.doi.org/10.1787/5k46ds9ljxkj-en.

Land Board (2015), Maa-amet on täpsustanud Eesti haldusüksuste piire ja pindala [The Land Board has specified boundaries of Estonian administrative units and the area], www.maaamet.ee/index.php?page_id=1&lang_id=1&news_id=1179&no_cache=1459155134 (accessed 9 April 2016).

Luik, H., and A.-H. Viira (2016), "Söötmis-, lüpsi-ja sõnnikusüsteemid Eesti piimakarjalautades - Feeding, Milking and Manure Systems in Estonian Dairy Barns", *Journal of Agricultural Science*, Vol. 2, XXVII, pp. 92–107.

MoA (2015a) Estonian Rural Development Plan (ERDP) for 2014–2020, Ministry of Agriculture, www.agri.ee/sites/default/files/content/arengukavad/mak-2014/mak-2014-v14-2015-01-27.odt (accessed 29 May 2016)

MoE (2016), Kliimapoliitika põhialused aastani 2050: Põllumajanduse valdkonna mõjude hindamine [Climate Policy Fundamentals for 2050: Impact assessment in the field of agriculture], http://envir.ee/sites/default/files/kpp_pillumajanduse_mijude_hindamise_seletuskiri_18.03.pdf (accessed 9 April 2016).

MoE (2015), *Fifth National Report to the Convention of Biological Diversity*, Ministry of Environment, Tallinn, www.cbd.int/doc/world/ee/ee-nr-04-en.pdf.

MoE (2013a), Eesti võimalused liikumaks konkurentsivõimelise madala süsinikuga majanduse suunas aastaks 2050: Lõppraport [Estonia's opportunities to move towards a competitive low-carbon economy by 2050: Final Report], www.envir.ee/sites/default/files/loppraport_2050.pdf (accessed 9 April 2016).

MoE (2013b), Estonia's sixth national communication, Under the United Nations Framework Convention on Climate Change, www.envir.ee/sites/default/files/elfinder/article_files/kliimaaruanne_en.pdf (accessed 9 April 2016).

MRA (2016a). Interview with Ministry of Rural Affairs, Estonia June 2016.

MRA (2016b), Estonian Rural Development Plan 2014-2020, www.agri.ee/et/eesmargid-tegevused/eesti-maaelu-arengukava-mak-2014-2020 (accessed 29 January 2016).

MRA (2016c), Toiduainetööstus [Food and Drink Industry]. www.agri.ee/et/eesmargid-tegevused/pollumajandus-ja-toiduturg/ulevaated/toiduainetoostus (accessed 30 January 2016).

MRA (2016d). Mahepõllumajandus Eestis. Organic Farming in Estonia. 2015. – Ministry of Rural Affairs. www.maheklubi.ee/upload/Editor/Mahepollumajandus_Eestis_2015_kujundus_loplik_trykki.pdf (accessed 5 June 2016).

MRA (2013c), Põllumajandussektoris kliimamuutuste leevendamise ja kliimamuutustega kohanemise tegevuskava 2012 – 2020 [Action plan for mitigation of and adaptation to climate change 2012-2020], http://www.agri.ee/sites/default/files/public/juurkataloog/ARENDUSTEGEVUS/kliimamuutused-tegevuskava-2012-2020.pdf (accessed 8 May 2016).

OECD (2017a), Country Statistical profile, http://data.oecd.org/ (accessed 3 April 2017).

OECD (2017b), Agri-environmental Indicators, www.oecd.org/tad/sustainable-agriculture/agri-environmentalindicators.htm.

OECD (2017c), *OECD Environmental Performance Reviews: Estonia 2017*, OECD Publishing, Paris, http://dx.doi.org/10.1787/9789264268241-en.

OECD (2016a), *OECD Economic Outlook, Volume 2016 Issue 2*, OECD Publishing, Paris, http://dx.doi.org/10.1787/eco_outlook-v2016-2-en.

OECD (2016b), System of National Accounts, http://data.oecd.org/.

Seeder, H-V. (2013), "Ettekanne 01.11.2013 maakonverentsil, Põllumajandusmaa väärtus ja kasutamise perspektiivid", Põllumajandusministeerium ["Presentation on agricultural use value and prospects", Ministry of Agriculture], www.slideshare.net/pollumajandusministeerium/pllumajandusmaa-vrtus-ja-tulevik (accessed 30 June 2016)

Statistics Estonia (2017), Economic and labour market trends, Tallinn, www.stat.ee/publication-download-pdf?publication_id=44115.

Statistics Estonia (2016a), *Minifacts about Estonia 2016,* www.stat.ee/277649 (accessed 4 June 2016).

Statistics Estonia (2016b), Online statistical database, www.stat.ee (accessed 11 February 2016).

UN (2016), COMTRADE, https://comtrade.un.org/.

UNFCCC (2016), http://unfccc.int/ghg_data/items/4133.php.

USDA (2016), Economic Research Service, International Agricultural Productivity, www.ers.usda.gov/data-products/international-agricultural-productivity.aspx (accessed January 2017).

Vaan, A. (2016), Lihaveisekasvatus 2015 [Beef cattle raising in 2015] (accessed 29 June 2017).

Viira, A.-H., R. Omel, R. Värnik, H. Luik, B. Maasing, and R. Põldaru (2015), "Competitiveness of the Estonian dairy sector, 1994–2014", *Agraarteadus: Journal of Agricultural Science*, Vol. 24, No. 2, pp. 84–104.

Viira, A.-H., A. Põder, and R. Värnik (2009), "20 years of transition- institutional reforms and the adaptation of production in Estonian agriculture", *Agrarwirtschaft*, Vol. 58, No. 7, pp. 286–295.

WBG (World Bank Group) (2016), World Development Indicators 2015, http://data.worldbank.org/products/wdi (accessed 27 June 2017).

Annex 2.A1. Background tables

Table 2.A1.1. Structure of agricultural holdings in selected countries, 2013

		Farm size group, ha								
		0 ha	<2	2-4.9	5-9.9	10-19.9	20-29.9	30-49.9	50-99.9	≥100
Czech Republic	Holdings	1.1	10.3	7.2	18.8	17.6	9.0	9.0	9.4	17.6
	UAA	0.0	0.1	0.2	1.0	1.8	1.6	2.6	4.9	87.8
Denmark	Holdings	3.7	0.8	2.2	20.0	17.7	10.2	11.2	13.9	20.3
	UAA	0.0	0.0	0.1	2.1	3.8	3.7	6.4	14.8	69.0
Estonia	**Holdings**	**2.2**	**9.2**	**21.6**	**20.7**	**17.4**	**7.3**	**6.2**	**6.0**	**9.3**
	UAA	**0.0**	**0.3**	**1.4**	**3.0**	**5.0**	**3.6**	**4.8**	**8.4**	**73.5**
Latvia	Holdings	1.3	21.6	19.7	19.7	19.3	6.5	5.1	3.3	3.5
	UAA	0.0	0.8	2.9	6.2	11.7	6.9	8.5	10.0	53.1
Lithuania	Holdings	0.0	14.1	39.1	22.4	11.7	3.8	3.2	3.0	2.7
	UAA	0.0	1.3	7.5	9.4	9.8	5.5	7.5	12.4	46.6
Netherlands	Holdings	2.5	10.3	14.6	13.9	14.9	10.2	16.3	13.8	3.5
	UAA	0.0	0.4	1.8	3.7	7.9	9.3	23.3	33.6	20.0
Poland	Holdings	0.5	22.8	31.1	21.6	14.6	4.3	2.8	1.4	0.8
	UAA	0.0	3.0	10.0	15.1	20.0	10.4	10.6	9.7	21.1
Finland	Holdings	0.3	1.6	3.5	11.3	20.2	15.1	20.1	19.4	8.5
	UAA	0.0	0.0	0.3	2.0	7.2	8.9	18.7	32.1	30.9
Sweden	Holdings	0.9	1.1	9.5	23.5	20.3	9.9	10.8	12.2	12.0
	UAA	0.0	0.0	0.9	3.7	6.4	5.4	9.3	19.1	55.2

UAA: Utilised Agricultural Area.

Source: Eurostat (2017), [ef_kvaareg], http://ec.europa.eu/eurostat/data/database.

Table 2.A1.2. Structure of the food processing industry in selected countries, 2015

Share of enterprises and turnover of various size classes in the total food industry, and average turnover per size class

		Size group, number of employees				
		0-9 persons	10-19 persons	20-49 persons	50-249 persons	≥250 persons
Czech Republic	Enterprises, %	82.3	6.5	6.0	4.3	0.9
	Turnover, %	3.6	3.3	9.7	43.1	40.3
	Turnover per enterprise, EUR million	0.1	0.7	2.4	14.8	69.0
Denmark	Enterprises, %	57.3	21.7	10.6	8.4	2.1
	Turnover, %	2.4	2.4	6.0	23.1	66.2
	Turnover per enterprise, EUR million	0.7	1.9	9.5	46.6	542.8
Estonia	**Enterprises, %**	**66.5**	**10.9**	**10.9**	**10.0**	**1.8**
	Turnover, %	**4.2**	**4.1**	**10.1**	**51.1**	**30.5**
	Turnover per enterprise, EUR million	**0.2**	**1.1**	**2.6**	**14.4**	**47.3**
Latvia	Enterprises, %	69.7	9.0	10.3	9.2	1.7
	Turnover, %	3.3	2.7	12.2	49.2	32.6
	Turnover per enterprise, EUR million	0.1	0.5	1.7	7.9	28.2
Lithuania	Enterprises, %	71.7	9.8	8.9	7.5	2.1
	Turnover, %	1.4	1.9	7.4	25.3	64.0
	Turnover per enterprise, EUR million	0.0	0.4	1.9	7.6	68.7
Netherlands	Enterprises, %	77.6	9.5	6.3	5.5	1.1
	Turnover, %	3.1	2.5	7.1	32.9	54.4
	Turnover per enterprise, EUR million	0.5	3.0	13.1	70.4	558.1
Poland	Enterprises, %	70.7	9.8	9.8	7.8	1.9
	Turnover, %	4.9	2.9	7.5	28.9	55.7
	Turnover per enterprise, EUR million	0.2	1.0	2.6	12.8	102.0
Finland	Enterprises, %	76.0	9.2	8.6	5.2	1.0
	Turnover, %	3.7	3.3	10.0	26.6	56.3
	Turnover per enterprise, EUR million	0.3	2.0	6.5	28.8	305.4
Sweden[1]	Enterprises, %	81.7	8.2	6.1	3.3	0.8
	Turnover, %	5.4	4.4	9.1	32.8	48.2
	Turnover per enterprise, EUR million	0.3	2.4	6.6	45.1	281.8

1. 2014.

Source: Eurostat (2017), [sbs_sc_sca_r2], NACE Rev2, C10, http://ec.europa.eu/eurostat/data/database (accessed in October 2017).

Table 2.A1.3. Developments of environmental indicators for agriculture in selected countries, 2002-04 to 2012-14

Average annual percent change 2002-04 to 2012-14, or nearest available period

	Total factor productivity	Agricultural production volume	Agricultural land area	Nitrogen balance	Phosphorus balance	Direct on-farm energy consumption	Water use	Ammonia emissions
	Index (1992=100)	Index (2004-06 =100)	thousand hectares	kg per hectare	kg per hectare	thousand tonnes of oil equivalent	million m^3	thousand tonnes
	2002-04 to 2011-13	2002-04 to 2012-14	2002-04 to 2012-14	2004-06 to 2011-13	2004-06 to 2011-13	2002-04 to 2012-14	1999-2001 to 2009-11	2002-04 to 2012-14
Canada	1.74	1.91	-0.33	1.87	-15.69	5.72	..	-0.03
Czech Republic	..	-0.45	-0.11	1.43	..	0.40	11.26	-1.52
Denmark	2.11	0.32	-0.14	-3.62	-6.79	-0.72	3.39	-2.19
Estonia	**3.44**	**3.08**	**2.34**	**-0.99**	**-4.46**	**0.72**	**-19.37**	**1.99**
Finland	1.66	-0.16	0.11	-1.44	-7.68	-0.19	..	-0.09
Latvia	2.62	3.08	1.50	6.06	2.64	2.38	-1.08	1.09
Netherlands	2.73	1.35	-0.52	-3.53	-15.89	-0.43	8.56	-2.34
Poland	1.34	0.77	-1.29	0.95	-5.28	-1.87	0.87	-0.17
EU28	0.40	15.06	-0.72	0.72	-1.11	-0.19	0.69	-100.00
OECD	1.43	2.37	-3.62	-0.99	-1.07	-1.44	-1.26	0.32

..: Not available.

Source: OECD (2017), Agri-environmental Indicators, www.oecd.org/tad/sustainable-agriculture/agri-environmentalindicators.htm; USDA (2016), Economic Research Service Agricultural Productivity Database for Total Factor Productivity, www.ers.usda.gov/data-oducts/international-agricultural-productivity.aspx.

Table 2.A1.4. Some farm sustainability indicators in Estonia, by farm type and size class, 2015

Farm type	Farm size group, ha				Total
	0-<40	40-<100	100-<400	> 400	
Field crops					
Use of fertilisers, EUR/ha of UAA	54	65	111	155	125
Use of crop protection, EUR/ha of UAA	15	20	43	50	43
Wheat yield, kg/ha	3 181	3 918	4 440	5 235	4 795
Ratio of wheat yield to costs of fertilisers and crop protection, kg/EUR	45.9	46.0	28.8	25.6	28.6
Assets, EUR/ha	3 739	1 505	1 688	1 814	1 841
Liabilities/assets, %	9.6	15.3	28.7	38.4	30.2
Farm net income, EUR	6 905	9 429	27 631	43 680	16 750
Farm income per unpaid farm labour, EUR/AWU	12 722	11 925	33 279	125 323	25 222
Milk					
Use of fertilisers, EUR/ha of UAA	4	4	31	77	60
Use of crop protection, EUR/ha of UAA	1	1	8	21	16
Livestock density, LU/ha of UAA	0.70	0.53	0.63	0.54	0.56
Wheat yield, kg/ha	3 180	3 752	4 672	5 165	5 056
Ratio of wheat yield to costs of fertilisers and crop protection, kg/EUR	637.8	885.0	118.5	52.7	66.3
Milk yield, kg/cow	7 400	7 200	7 571	9 007	8 511
Assets, EUR/ha	4 503	2 910	2 762	2 897	2 952
Liabilities/assets, %	33.8	29.4	32.9	44.8	40.9
Farm net income, EUR	764	5 653	-3 391	-19 511	946
Farm income per unpaid farm labour, EUR/AWU	712	4 870	-4 046	-154 040	-995
Other grazing livestock					
Livestock density, LU/ha of UAA	0.39	0.37	0.33	0.39	0.36
Milk yield, kg/cow	4 867	5 599	5 958	5 201	5 516
Assets, EUR/ha	2 206	1 525	1 277	1 123	1 431
Liabilities/assets, %	1.4	13.2	33.6	21.8	19.7
Farm net income, EUR	2 758	8 693	7 987	20 947	5 917
Farm income per unpaid farm labour, EUR/AWU	2 906	8 449	7 367	25 962	5 958
Mixed					
Use of fertilisers, EUR/ha of UAA	3	21	54	141	90
Use of crop protection, EUR/ha of UAA	1	7	17	46	29
Livestock density, LU/ha of UAA	0.17	0.22	0.21	0.37	0.28
Wheat yield, kg/ha	2 191	3 097	3 710	5 241	4 673
Ratio of wheat yield to costs of fertilisers and crop protection, kg/EUR	587.0	113.4	51.8	28.0	39.4
Milk yield, kg/cow	3 203	5 257	6 541	8 754	8 205
Assets, EUR/ha	4 127	1 827	1 676	2 617	2 461
Liabilities/assets, %	2.2	14.6	32.9	42.2	30.6
Farm net income, EUR	5 301	3 157	27 322	1 668	7 294
Farm income per unpaid farm labour, EUR/AWU	6 557	3 450	26 641	4 762	8 770

UAA: Utilised Agricultural Area; AWU: Annual Work Unit; LU Livestock Unit.
Source: FADN (2016), www.maainfo.ee/standardtulemused/.

Chapter 3

Economic stability and quality of institutions in Estonia

This chapter gives an overview of the performance of the overall economy, macroeconomic developments and challenges, and the governance and institutions.

3.1. Macro-economic policy environment

At the broadest level, stable and sound macroeconomic policies, leading to high growth and low and stable inflation rates, play an important role in setting a favourable environment for investment in farms or agri-food firms seeking to introduce new products, to adopt new production methods, or to undertake organisational changes that can lead to higher productivity growth and more sustainable use of natural resources. Assessment of the country's overall growth and growth potential in the short- to medium-term has implications for sector specific prospects as well. In some circumstances, macroeconomic policies and their impacts can contribute to implicit and perhaps unintended biases for or against the food and agriculture system.

Overall economic performance and medium term prospects for growth

Fast economic growth in Estonia during the last 25 years has caused significant structural changes. The competitiveness of Estonian goods and services both in domestic and international markets has changed, as well as the structure of foreign trade. Regaining independence in 1991 and the integration of the Estonian economy into the World economy, the accession to the European Union in 2004, and the recent financial crisis have been the main drivers behind the dynamics of competitiveness of the Estonian economy.

Estonia is a small country of only 1.3 million inhabitants, with open investment laws, and a balanced state budget. Since joining the European Union in 2004, it is part of the common market. Openness to international trade and investment started after regaining independence in 1991. According to the Wall Street Journal and the Heritage Foundation's Index of Economic Freedom, Estonia ranks as one of the freest economies in the world, being 9th among 178 countries in 2016 (Miller and Kim, 2016). In the Fraser Institute's "Economic Freedom of the World: 2015 Annual Report", the economic freedom scoreboard ranks Estonia 22nd among 157 countries (Gwartney et al., 2015).

According to the OECD better life index Estonia has made progress over the last decade in terms of improving the quality of life of its citizens, however, there are still only a few aspects of well-being where Estonia is performing well compared to industrialised countries. Estonia is performing above the OECD average in education and skills, environmental quality, and work-life balance, but below average in housing, jobs and earnings, subjective well-being, personal security, income and wealth, health status, and civic engagement.

Since the 1990s, growth in the Estonian economy has been considerable (Table 3.1). During the period 2001-07, the growth of GDP was very high making Estonia one of the fastest growing economies in Europe. Following the global financial crisis, the Estonian economy experienced a sharp contraction of output in 2008-09. The downturn of the economy was reinforced by the domestic credit boom in the construction sector and by pro-cyclical fiscal policy (OECD, 2011a, 2012, 2015a).

In recent years, economic growth has been disappointing, but it accelerated in 2017 (OECD, 2017a). According to the Bank of Estonia (2015), potential growth in 2015-16 has been below expectations for long-term growth for structural reasons, for example the decline in exports to traditional partners such as Finland and the Russian Federation, and the difficulty to find other export markets in the short term. In addition, a lower growth rate was also associated with a low investment rate compared to previous years. The OECD economic outlook from June 2017 projects higher GDP growth of 2.6% in 2017[1] and 3.1% 2018 (Table 3.1), helped by stronger investment in the public and private sectors. Higher public investment will partly reflect higher disbursement of EU structural funds in mid-programming period (OECD, 2017a). At the same time, consumption will remain strong, supported by accommodative tax measures (OECD, 2017b). In the longer term, the population decline and the slower productivity growth are the main factors behind a potential decrease in economic growth.

Table 3.1. Estonia's key indicators of macroeconomic policy, 1995 to 2018

	2000	2005	2008	2009	2010	2011	2012	2013	2014	2015	2016	2017e	2018e
Real GDP growth, %	9.8	9.1	-5.0	-14.2	1.7	7.5	4.3	1.6	2.7	1.5	1.7	2.6	3.1
General government financial balance[1]	-0.1	1.1	-2.7	-2.2	0.2	1.2	-0.3	-0.2	0.7	0.1	0.3	-0.4	-0.7
Current account balance[1]	-5.4	-8.7	-8.7	2.5	1.8	1.3	-2.0	-0.4	0.9	2.2	2.7	1.8	1.3
Exchange rate, EUR per USD[2]	1.08	0.80	0.68	0.72	0.76	0.72	0.78	0.75	0.75	0.90	0.90	0.92	0.91
Consumer price index, harmonised, index 2010	0.7	0.8	1.0	1.0	1.0	1.1	1.1	1.1	1.1	1.1	1.1	1.2	1.2
Unemployment rate, %[3]	14.6	8.0	5.5	13.6	16.7	12.3	10.0	8.6	7.4	6.2	6.8	7.6	8.4
Labour productivity, index 2010	0.7	0.9	1.0	0.9	1.0	1.0	1.0	1.0	1.1	1.0	1.1	1.1	1.1

e: OECD Economic Outlook estimate.

1. As a percentage of Gross Domestic Product (GDP).
2. Period average.
3. End of year, as a percentage of total labour force.

Source: OECD (2017b), *OECD Economic Outlook, Volume 2017 Issue 1*, http://dx.doi.org/10.1787/eco_outlook-v2017-1-en.

Inflation has been low since 2000, but is projected to increase fast at around 3% according to the OECD economic outlook from June 2017, not least because excise tax rates and wage growth is expected to push it up (OECD, 2017b).

Statistically, the situation in the labour market also improved in the mid-2010s, but this is partially due to new regulations on the employees' registry since mid-2014, which have reduced undeclared work. The wage growth has exceeded productivity growth. Therefore, the profitability of companies has declined, which is one reason behind low investments by companies (MoF, 2015a). The labour market has tightened and shortages of skilled labour have started to appear in some sectors like agriculture. According to the OECD economic outlook from June 2017, growing tensions in the labour market will maintain wage growth above productivity growth. As a result, firms will hire less and unemployment will increase, reaching 8.4% of the labour force in 2018 (Table 3.1).

The general government financial balance was positive over 2014-16 due to increased tax receipts and dividends from the financial sector. It is projected to be slightly negative in 2017 and 2018, as public investment is expected to rise, notably in infrastructure, health care and education (Table 3.1). This increase is appropriate given Estonia's robust public finances and spending needs (OECD, 2017b). Estonia's general government gross debt — below 10% of GDP in recent years[2] — is the lowest in the OECD area. Current account surplus reached a height of 2.7% of GDP in 2016, but is expected to decrease in 2017 and 2018 (Table 3.1).

Estonia is a member of the Eurozone, as it adopted the euro in 2011. Comparing the trade structure of Estonia with exchange rate development, there are two groups of trading partners: countries from continental Europe who have floating currencies against the euro; and other countries using the US dollar. While the euro has weakened against the US dollar, it has strengthened against the currencies of non-EUR continental trading partners. As estimated by the Bank of Estonia (2016), the composition of the Estonian export markets implies that the depreciation of the euro against the dollar has little impact on trade while the nominal effective exchange rates have strengthened over all foreign partners combined.

Main components of global competitiveness

In terms of overall competitiveness, the World Economic Forum (WEF) Global Competitiveness Indicators (GCI) for 2016-17 ranks Estonia 30th among 140 countries. Figure 3.1 compares Estonia's score in the different components (pillars) of CGI with the OECD average, while the section below discusses rankings. Estonia is considered an innovation driven economy. The macroeconomic environment, rising to 12th rank in 2016/17 (3rd pillar), and labour market efficiency (7th pillar), for which it takes 15th place, contribute strongly to the overall good performance. However, Estonia lacks in market size and business sophistication (WEF, 2016).

Figure 3.1. Global Competiveness Index: All components, 2016-17

Scale 1 to 7 (best)

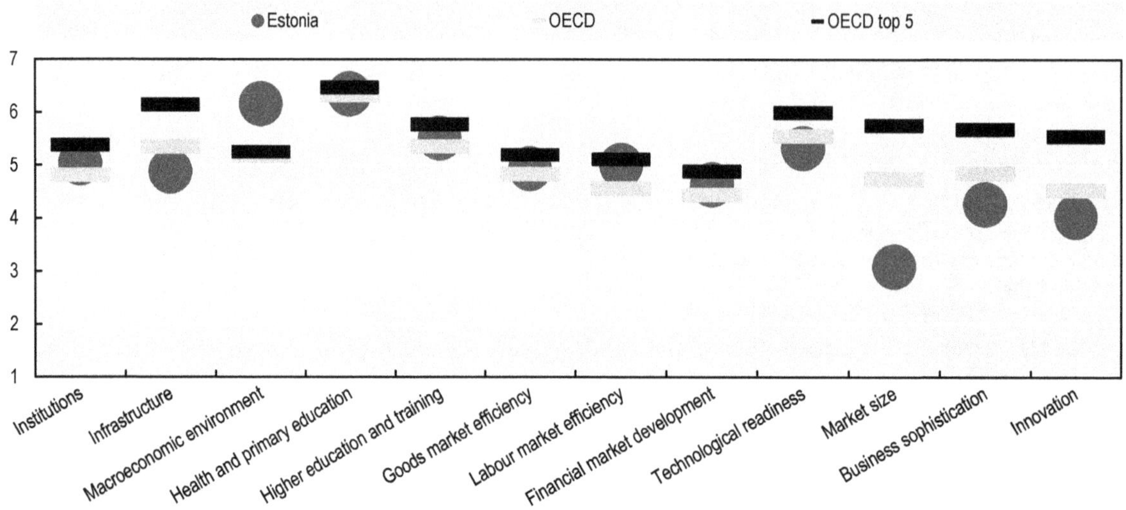

OECD top 5 refers to the average of the scores for the top 5 performers among OECD countries for the overall index (Switzerland, United States, Germany, Netherlands, and Japan).

Indices for EU28 and OECD are the simple average of member-country indices.

Source: World Economic Forum (2016), http://reports.weforum.org/global-competitiveness-index/.

StatLink http://dx.doi.org/10.1787/888933654066

Estonian companies rank 44th in business sophistication and 28th in innovation. In business sophistication, companies are not successful in having a broad presence in the entire value chain; rather they are involved in individual steps of the value chain. Moreover, they are not very successful in using marketing to differentiate their products. The nature of competitive advantage in the Estonian economy is still in low-cost labour or natural resources (WEF, 2016). With regard to technological innovation, two issues stand out: the availability of scientists and engineers for companies (rank 45), and the level of government procurement for advanced technology products (rank 49).

The macroeconomic environment component of CGI consists of indicators, which are considered important for business and are significant for the overall competitiveness of a country. On a 7-point scale Estonia scores 6.2, only slightly behind the OECD top 5 (Figure 3.2). This good score reflects low inflation (though the reasons behind the low levels of inflation do not stem from competitiveness but more from continuing recession in the economy and imported inflation), low levels of government debt — Estonia ranks 5th in government debt as a % of GDP according to the 2016/17 CGI — and a positive account balance (WEF, 2016).

Figure 3.2. Global Competiveness Index: Macroeconomic environment, 2016-17

Scale 1 to 7 (best)

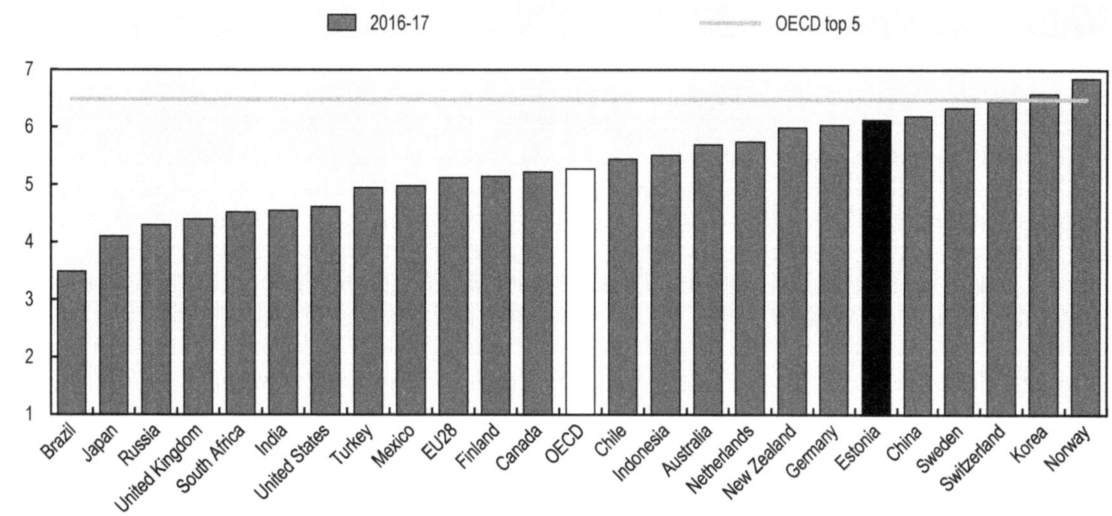

OECD top 5 refers to the average of the scores for the top 5 performers among OECD countries (Norway, Korea, Switzerland, Sweden and Luxembourg).

Indices for EU28 and OECD are the simple average of member-country indices.

Source: World Economic Forum (2016), http://reports.weforum.org/global-competitiveness-index/.

StatLink http://dx.doi.org/10.1787/888933654085

Both public and private institutions are considered very well developed and very reliable with combined ranking 23rd. The quality of infrastructure has a slightly weaker position (rank 33). The biggest disadvantage is in air transportation where both the quality of air transport infrastructure and the availability of airlines are very low. In addition, the quality of roads is low. Estonia ranks very high only in the maritime transport infrastructure (Chapter 5).

Estonia's educational system is considered to be of high quality (Chapter 5). Health and primary education (4th pillar), and higher education and training (5th pillar), support competitiveness and are ranked very high (12 and 18 respectively). Financial market development (8th pillar) is also considered very high (rank 22), especially the trustworthiness and confidence of the financial market. Both goods and labour markets (ranking 20th and 15th, respectively) are very efficient.

The Global Entrepreneurship and Development Institute (GEDI) with the Estonian Development Fund (EDF) carried out a survey in 2014, to analyse and identify the problems of entrepreneurial performance. Estonia was ranked 21st (among 120 countries) in the global ranking of entrepreneurship ecosystems, which is high compared to its GDP per capita. The most important obstacles to entrepreneurial performance were found to be innovation, finance, attitudes towards, and skills for, entrepreneurship (GEDI, 2014).

Government measures for promoting economic growth and jobs

In the National Reform Programme "Estonia 2020", approved in 2011, the two main objectives for 2015-20 to improve competitiveness were: 1) increasing the productivity, and 2) enhancing employment. In the programme, the main focus is on education and employment, with an emphasis on the integration of long-term and young unemployed people in the labour market, and on the development of their skills (Government Office, 2014).

Strategic planning in Estonia is governed by the State Budget Act and by Government Regulation No. 302 dated 13 December 2005, which states the types of strategic plans developed by the ministries. Development plans are divided into two broader categories: 1) sectoral plans, which are typically coordinated by the responsible ministry, and 2) organisation-based development plans that include the area of a ministry or government.

3.2. Governance and institutions

Good governance systems and high-quality institutions provide economic actors with the assurance that the government is accountable, transparent and predictable. They are a fundamental pre-condition both to encourage public and private investment in the economy and to enable those investments to achieve the intended benefits, both for investors and the host country. Moreover, governance systems play an important role in addressing market failure, influencing the behaviour of firms in terms of investment and compliance to regulations, as well as the efficient functioning of farm input and output markets. Finally, how the environment and natural resources are part of the institutional framework and public decision making is important in the capacity for designing efficient and acceptable policy tools (OECD, 2015b).

Transparency, clarity and predictability of governance rules, institutions and regulatory process

Since 1991, Estonia has transformed from a centrally-planned economy to a market economy. During the transformation process, the government followed a policy of openness to world markets and maintaining a balanced budget and a low level of government debt. As the 2011 OECD Public Government review recognises, Estonia has developed all the necessary functions and apparatus of a modern state. However, there are a number of challenges starting with continuing economic slowdown, worsening demographical situation and growing regional disparities. The policy of openness has improved competitiveness, but has also made the economy more vulnerable to external shocks. Nevertheless, the OECD review states that the Government of Estonia has been quite effective in state building and becoming a model for small open economies (OECD, 2011b).

An important conclusion from the OECD analysis is that in the post-crisis period, Estonia has shown good progress in developing further a single government approach with stronger administration from the Cabinet of ministers, constrained financial management and stronger governance and accountability frameworks. Nevertheless, there is strong evidence of the importance of informal networks and practices (OECD, 2011b).

The quality of public institutions is considered to be very good according to the World Bank's Worldwide Governance Indicators (WGI). The WGI define governance as the traditions and institutions by which authority in a country is exercised. WGI measures six broad aspects of governance: voice and accountability, political stability, government effectiveness, regulatory quality, rule of law and control of corruption. Voice and accountability indicates how citizens are able to participate in selecting their government, freedom of expression and association, and a free media. This is an area where Estonia ranks very high, slightly below the OECD average. The lowest percentile rank is in political stability and the highest in regulatory quality (Table 3.2).

Table 3.2. World Bank's Worldwide Governance Indicators for Estonia, 2015

Percentile rank (0 to 100)

	Estonia	High income (OECD) countries
Voice and accountability	85	87
Political stability	66	74
Government effectiveness	83	88
Regulatory quality	93	87
Rule of law	87	88
Control of corruption	87	85

Source: World Bank (2016), World Bank's Worldwide Governance Indicators, http://info.worldbank.org/governance/wgi/.

According to WEF GCI, Estonia ranks very high in the quality of public institutions (Figure 3.3). Estonia scores above the OECD average in all categories of public sector quality, and performs very well in security, reflecting a very low level of organised crime (rank 10), business costs of terrorism (rank 12), crime and violence (rank 21). In ethics and corruption, the overall rank is 28, showing that illegal diversion of public funds, irregular payments and bribes are not common. However, Estonia is lagging somewhat behind in public opinion about ethical standards of politicians. Concerning undue influence, Estonia is also well considered (rank 18), meaning that the judicial system is independent from influences of the government, individuals, or companies, and that government officials show little favouritism when deciding upon policies and contracts. Government efficiency ranks 23 meaning a high efficiency of government spending and a low burden of government regulations, though Estonia is less efficient in the legal and judicial system for companies in settling disputes. The overall rank of Estonia in the quality of public institutions is 23 (WEF, 2016).

Figure 3.3. Global Competitiveness Index: Quality of public institutions, 2016-17

Scale 1 to 7 (best)

A. Total index, international comparison

B. Index of quality of public institutions by component

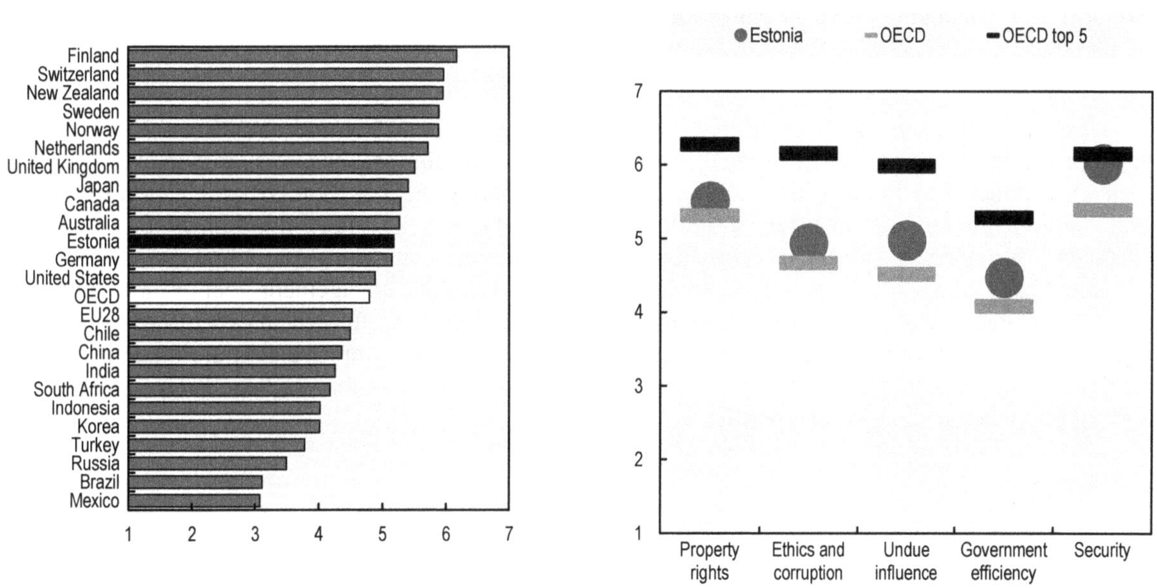

Indexes for EU-28 and OECD represent simple averages of member-country indexes.

OECD top 5 refers to the average of the scores for the top 5 performers among OECD countries (Finland, Switzerland, New Zealand, Sweden and Norway).

Property rights refers to the average of the indices Property rights and Intellectual property rights. Ethics and corruption refers to the average of the indices: Diversion of public funds, Public trust in politicians and Irregular payments. Undue influence refers to the average of the indices for: Judicial independence and Favouritism in decisions of governmental officials. Government efficiency refers to the average of the indices for Wastefulness of government spending, Burden of government regulation, Efficiency of legal framework in settling disputes, Efficiency of legal framework in challenging regulations and Transparency of government policymaking. Security refers to the average of the indices for: Business costs of terrorism, Business costs of crime and violence, Organized crime and Reliability of police services.

Source: World Economic Forum (2016), http://reports.weforum.org/global-competitiveness-index/.

StatLink http://dx.doi.org/10.1787/888933654104

According to GCI scores, property rights, including financial assets and intellectual property rights are well protected. Based on business opinion surveys, Estonia ranks 25 in property rights protection, and has a higher score than the OECD average (WEF, 2016).

The 2011 OECD Public Governance review shows that national and sub-national administrative structures, problems in territorial management and relations between different levels of government hinder efficient delivery of public services of equal quality across the territory. However, the relatively even distribution of the working-age population across the territory is an advantage for the territorial balance of competitiveness (OECD, 2011b). The State reform subsequently abolished a layer of local government and merged some institutions in an effort to solve these problems. The government is carrying out a territorial reform aimed at significantly reducing the number of municipalities by 2018, which would help alleviate resource and capacity constraints (OECD, 2017c).

Environmental and natural resources concerns in institutions and the decision-making process

An example of natural concerns in institutions and the decision-making process is the project aiming to improve environmentally sound public procurements (MoE, 2014). In 2009, a four-year programme called "Better Use of Environmental Management in the Public Sector" was initiated by the Ministry of the Environment (MoE). The following programme covering 2014-20 was targeted on improving environmentally sound public procurements. It included training for government officials to enhance understanding and build new knowledge on environmental issues. These programmes originated from the EU initiative, Eco-Management and Auditing Scheme, developed by the European Commission and implemented by several countries, and used in public sector institutions. An environmental management plan for 2012-20 was developed in Estonia to improve measures for environmental management.

Mechanisms for ensuring policy coherence and transparency

According to the 2011 OECD Public Governance Review, the decision-making process in Estonia is very transparent, but there are still some drawbacks in taking account stakeholders opinions (OECD, 2011b). A survey conducted by Praxis (2010) shows that the main barriers to stakeholder participation with the state public administration are: insufficient preliminary information; too short timeframes for commenting; insufficient resources to divert to participating; and too time-consuming participation. OECD (2011b) concludes that Estonia has been successful in achieving stakeholder engagement goals in a relatively short period, but suggests that the engagement activities should be developed further, in order to make stakeholder engagement as effective as possible. Important suggestions for further improvement are made in embedding stakeholder engagement into the culture of the public administration so that its benefits are identified at all levels of public administration and politics.

3.3. Summary

- Estonia is a small country open to investment, with sound macroeconomic fundamentals, including a balanced state budget and low government debts following a sustainable fiscal strategy initiated in the 1990s.
- Due to a continuing economic slowdown of the main trade partners, especially in Finland and the Russian Federation, the demand for Estonia's goods and services has been low. Economic growth has been based on domestic consumption in recent years.
- The nature of competitive advantage is still in low-cost labour or natural resources. However, the wage growth has exceeded productivity growth in recent years. As a result, the profitability of companies has declined, partly explaining low investments.
- In terms of global competitiveness, Estonia ranks 30th among 140 countries. Estonia is considered by business leaders as an innovation driven economy, with a sound macroeconomic environment and high labour market efficiency. Even though the overall performance is very good, Estonia lacks in market size and business sophistication.
- In terms of business sophistication, Estonian companies do not have broad presence in the entire value chain; rather they are involved in individual steps of the value chain. Moreover, they are not using marketing to differentiate their products to a large extent, including in the agri-food sector.

- Estonia enjoys high quality public institutions and is considered as a secure country for business, with good ethical practices, an independent judicial system and transparent policies. Government efficiency is recognised for the high efficiency of spending and low burden of regulations, though Estonia is less efficient in the legal and judicial system for companies in settling disputes.

Notes

1. In revised OECD projections, growth will be expected to be above 3% in 2017.
2. General government gross debt according to the Maastricht definition is below 10%.

References

Bank of Estonia (2016), *Estonian Competitiveness Report*, www.eestipank.ee/en/publication/estonian-competitiveness-report/2016/estonian-competitiveness-report-2016 (accessed 29 March 2016).

Bank of Estonia (2015), *Estonian Economy and Monetary Policy* No. 2/2015, www.eestipank.ee/en/publication/estonian-economy-and-monetary-policy/2015/estonian-economy-and-monetary-policy-22015 (accessed 29 March 2016).

GEDI (Global Entrepreneurship and Development Institute) (2014), Estonia Regional Facilitation Report: Towards a More Entrepreneurial Estonia, http://thegedi.org/estonia-regional-facilitation-report/ (accessed 11 April 2016).

Gwartney, J., R. Lawson, and J. Hall (2015), *Economic Freedom of the World: 2015 Annual Report*, Fraser Institute, digital copy available from www.fraserinstitute.org and www.freetheworld.com (accessed 29 March 2016).

Government Office (2014), National Reform Programme "ESTONIA 2020", https://riigikantselei.ee/sites/default/files/riigikantselei/strateegiaburoo/eesti2020/estonia_2020_nrp2014_en.pdf (accessed 28 January 2016).

Miller, T. and A.B. Kim (2016), The 2016 Index of Economic Freedom, The Heritage Foundation and The Wall Street Journal, Washington, DC and New York, NY, www.heritage.org/Index/Default.aspx (accessed 29 March 2016).

MoE (2014), Improving environmentally sound public procurements, www.envir.ee/en/improving-environmentally-sound-public-procurements (accessed 31 January 2016).

MoF (2015), *Riigi eelarvestrateegia 2016-2019* [State budget strategy], www.fin.ee/riigi-eelarvestrateegia (accessed 31 January 2016).

OECD (2017a), *OECD Economic Surveys: Estonia 2017*, OECD Publishing, Paris, http://dx.doi.org/10.1787/eco_surveys-est-2017-en.

OECD (2017b), *OECD Economic Outlook, Volume 2017 Issue 1: Preliminary version*, OECD Publishing, Paris. DOI: http://dx.doi.org/10.1787/eco_outlook-v2017-1-en.

OECD (2017c), *OECD Environmental Performance Reviews: Estonia 2017*, OECD Publishing, Paris, http://dx.doi.org/10.1787/9789264268241-en.

OECD (2016), Better Life Index, www.oecdbetterlifeindex.org/countries/estonia/ (accessed 29 March 2016).

OECD (2015a), *OECD Economic Surveys: Estonia 2015*, OECD Publishing, Paris, http://dx.doi.org/10.1787/eco_surveys-est-2015-en.

OECD (2015b), "Analysing Policies to improve agricultural productivity growth, sustainably: Revised framework", www.oecd.org/tad/agricultural-policies/Analysing-policies-improve-agricultural-productivity-growth-sustainably-december-2014.pdf.

OECD (2012), *OECD Economic Surveys: Estonia 2012*, OECD Publishing, Paris, http://dx.doi.org/10.1787/eco_surveys-est-2012-en.

OECD (2011a), *OECD Economic Surveys: Estonia 2011*, OECD Publishing, Paris, http://dx.doi.org/10.1787/eco_surveys-est-2011-en.

OECD (2011b), *Estonia: Towards a Single Government Approach*, OECD Publishing, Paris, http://dx.doi.org/10.1787/9789264104860-en.

Praxis (2010), "Survey of Engagement in Estonian Government Agencies", presentation of Survey results, Praxis Centre for Policy Studies, Tallinn.

World Bank (2016), World Bank's Worldwide Governance Indicators, http://info.worldbank.org/governance/wgi/.

WEF (World Economic Forum) (2016), The Global Competitiveness Report 2016-2017, Geneva, http://reports.weforum.org/global-competitiveness-index/.

Chapter 4

General incentives for investments in Estonia

This chapter reviews general incentives for firm-level investments, stemming from regulations governing entrepreneurship, access to natural resources and products and processes, and policies related to trade, investment, finance and taxation.

4.1. Regulatory environment

4.1.1. Regulatory environment for entrepreneurship

The overall regulatory environment establishes basic conditions within which all firms, including farms, input suppliers, and food companies, operate and make investment decisions. Competitive conditions in domestic markets, including low barriers to entry and exit, can encourage innovation and productivity growth, including through their impact on structural change. Regulations may also enable or impede knowledge and technology transfer directly, contributing to more or less innovation, including in sustainability-enhancing technologies (OECD, 2015).

The Estonian Entrepreneurship Growth Strategy for 2014-20[1] points out that the regulatory environment for entrepreneurship in Estonia is generally business-friendly with still considerable room for improvement. The strategy sets two main objectives: 1) to increase productivity per employed person to 80% of the EU average; and 2) to raise the employment rate in the age group 20–64 to 76%. Closely linked with other development plans, the strategy targets mainly innovation and entrepreneurship and focuses on growth areas and enterprises with strongest economic importance.

Recognising the legal and regulatory environment is essential to growth in firms. Legislators and governments in Estonia have always given priority to policies that will improve the business environment in order to benefit from tax revenues and the jobs created by attracting foreign investors.

According to the overall OECD Product Market Regulation (PMR) indicator, which measures key regulations influencing business in the areas of state control, barriers to entrepreneurship, and barriers to trade and investment, Estonian regulations impose a low, and decreasing level of restrictions. In the scale from 0 to 6, with a higher number indicating more restrictions, Estonia's overall score of 1.29 in 2013 is lower than the OECD and EU averages (Figure 4.1.A). The PMR shows that Estonia's regulations in the areas of state control and barriers to entrepreneurship are less restrictive than the OECD average. However, while the PMR indicator considers regulations impose low barriers to trade and investment, they appear higher than on average in the OECD area (Figure 4.1.B).

The state has largely disengaged from business ownership and exercises little control over business enterprises, as reflected by the PMR indicator measuring state control. In 2015, there were 25 solely state-owned companies of limited scope.[2] Only two of these companies are connected to the agri-food sector, namely Vireen Ltd.,[3] which collects and recycles perished farm animals and animal by-products of the meat industry, and the Estonian Livestock Performance Recording Ltd established in 2015.[4] According to the PMR indicator, however, government involvement in network sectors (gas, electricity, water, rail, air passenger transport, road freight transport and telecoms) is more important in Estonia than in the EU or OECD averages (OECD, 2014b).

Figure 4.1. OECD Integrated Product Market Regulation (PMR) Indicator, 2008 and 2013

Scale from 0 (least) to 6 (most) restrictive

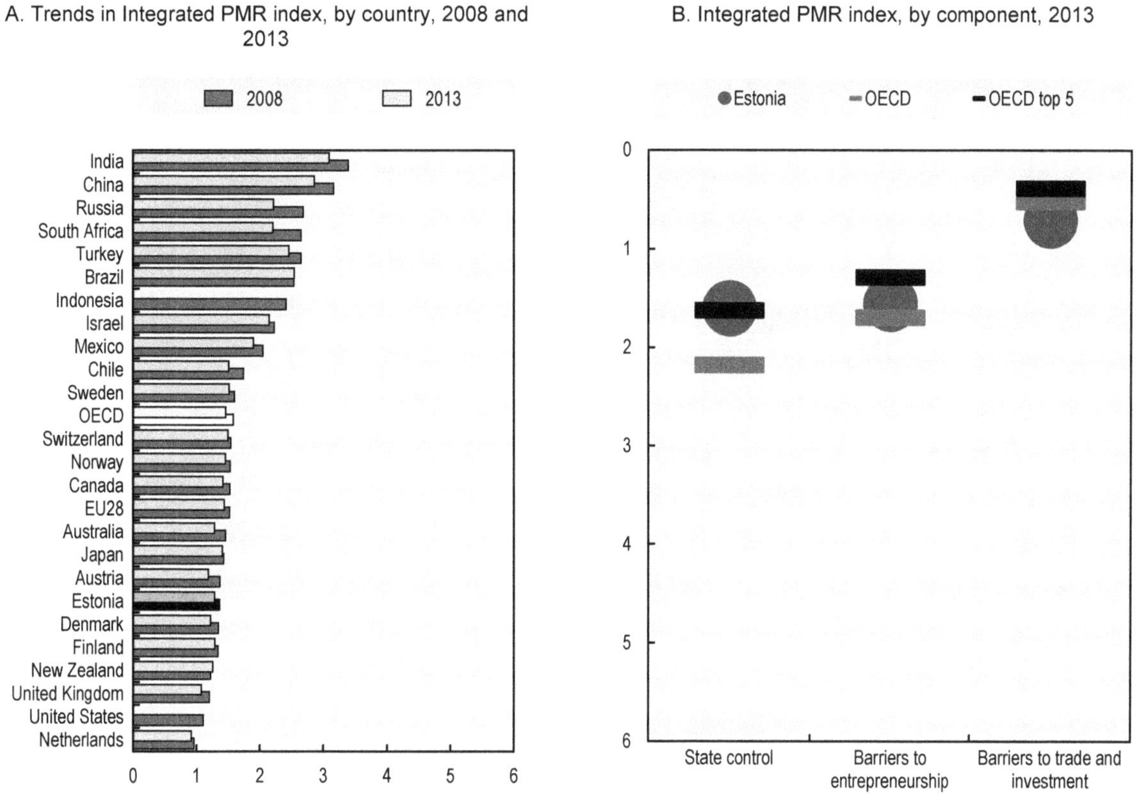

Countries are ranked according to 2008 levels.
Indices for EU28 and OECD are the simple average of member-country indices.
For Indonesia and United States, 2013 data are not available.

OECD top 5 refers to the average of the scores for the top five performers among OECD countries (Sweden, United Kingdom, United States, Austria and Denmark), with US data referring to 2008.

OECD Product Market Regulation (PMR) indicators measure key regulations in the areas of state control, barriers to entrepreneurship, and barriers to trade and investment.

Source: OECD (2014b), OECD Product Market Regulation Database, 2014, www.oecd.org/economy/pmr.

StatLink http://dx.doi.org/10.1787/888933654123

There are very few barriers to starting and running a business in Estonia. Foreign investors and local entrepreneurs have equal rights and obligations, and do not face any restrictions to start a business in Estonia. According to the PMR barriers to entrepreneurship indicator, Estonia is among the least restrictive OECD countries (Figure 4.1.B).

There has been a significant decline in barriers to entrepreneurship in Estonia between 2008 and 2013 (Figure 4.2.A). Estonia has witnessed considerable decline in barriers in network sectors, legal barriers to entry and in communication and simplification of rules/procedures. However, Estonia still lagged behind the OECD top 5 performers in some areas, indicating scope for further improvement. These included regulatory barriers in the service sector, administrative burdens for corporations and access to licenses and permits. Significant progress has been made since, but some burden remains in environmental regulation.

Figure 4.2. OECD Product Market Regulation (PMR) Indicator: Barriers to entrepreneurship

Scale from 0 (least) to 6 (most) restrictive

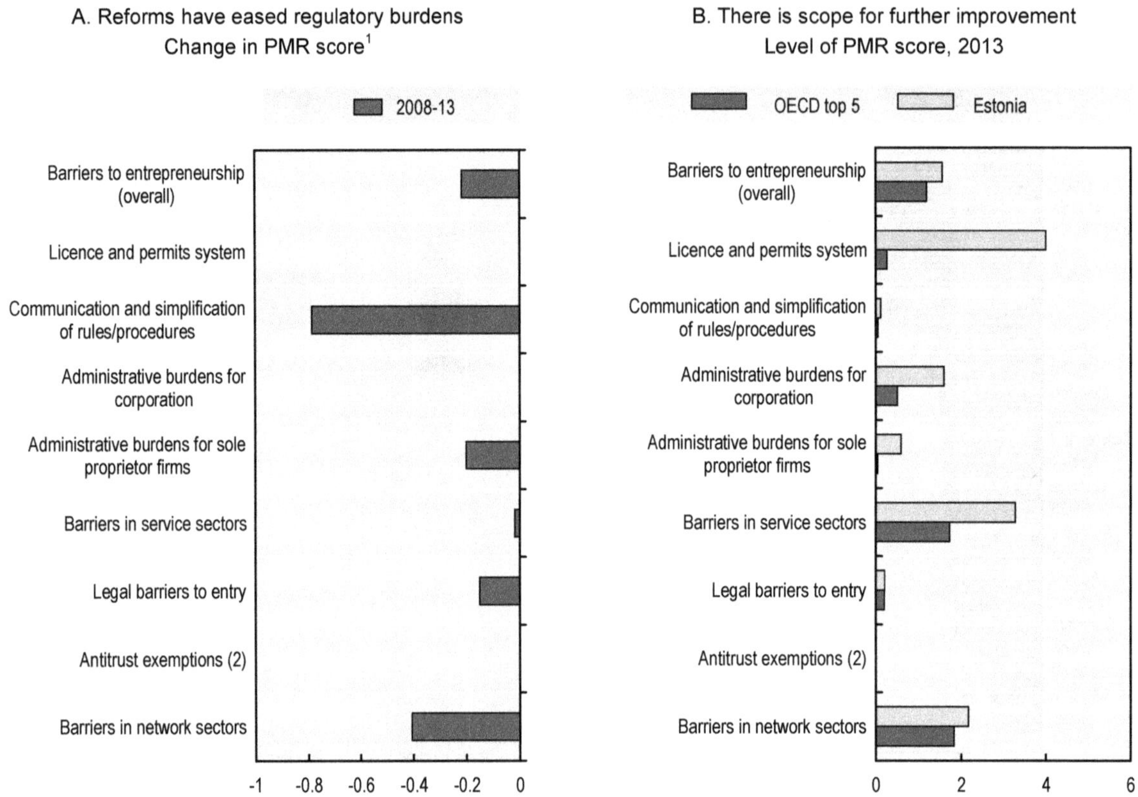

1. There was no change in the indicator for licence and permits system, administrative burdens and antitrust exemptions in 2008-13.
2. For antitrust exemptions the PMR scores are zero.

Source: Koske et al. (2015), "The 2013 update of the OECD's database on product market regulation: Policy insights for OECD and non-OECD countries", http://dx.doi.org/10.1787/5js3f5d3n2vl-en.

StatLink http://dx.doi.org/10.1787/888933654142

Table 4.1. Estonia's ranking in World Bank's Ease of Doing Business, 2017

	Rank (out of 190 economies)
Overall rank	**12**
Ranking by specific regulatory area	
Starting a business	14
Dealing with construction permits	9
Getting electricity	38
Registering property	6
Getting credit	32
Protecting minority investors	53
Paying taxes	21
Trading across borders	17
Enforcing contracts	11
Resolving insolvency	42

Source: World Bank (2017), *Doing Business 2017*, www.doingbusiness.org.

Competition policy in Estonia is generally in compliance with EU principles. Supervision in the fields of competition, electricity, natural gas, district heating, postal services, water and railways and dispute settlement regarding airport fees is performed by the Estonian Competition Authority.[5] Estonia is one of the few countries in the European Union, where the anti-competitive agreements, so-called cartels, are processed in criminal proceedings.[6]

4.1.2. Regulations on natural resources

Regulations on natural resources are central to ensuring the long-term sustainable use of natural resources and in large part determine access to and use of land, water and biodiversity resources. They also impose limits on the impact of industrial and agricultural activities on the state of the natural resource (e.g. water pollution, soil degradation, greenhouse gas emissions). The design of natural resources and environmental policies is important in terms of their incentives for innovation and sustainable productivity growth (OECD, 2014a).

Estonian regulations are designed to help reach the country's **objectives** to ensure a clean living environment, raise environmental awareness of society and preserve the sustainable use of natural resources. The framework for environmental protection and the sustainable use of the environment was established in the Estonian Environmental Strategy 2030, which sets the long-term objectives for waste, residual pollution and pollution load, water, mineral resources, energy, transportation, forestry, fisheries, hunting and maintaining landscape and biodiversity. One of the aims of the national development strategy Sustainable Estonia 21 (SE21) is the achievement and maintenance of the ecological balance[7] (SE21). Moreover, Estonia subscribes to the Seventh EU Environment Action Programme (EAP) "Living well, within the limits of our planet" (MoE, 2016a; MoE, 2016b). This section reviews regulations set out to achieve the aims of these and other policies and programmes.

Governance of regulations on natural resources and the environment

Regulations on natural resources and environment in Estonia are **extensive, but fragmented** across multiple legal acts. This is driven in part by the increase in legislative acts – in particular, the adoption of EU regulations — during and since EU accession. The General Part of the Environmental Code Act — which came into force in 2014 and 2015 — developed a unified base for some acts in environmental law. In addition to the direct legal acts on environment and resource use, the Environmental Strategy 2030, the National Strategy on Sustainable Development "Sustainable Estonia 21", the Estonian Rural Development Plan for 2014-20, the National Reform Programme "Estonia 2020", thematic and regional action-plans include requirements concerning environmental impacts. The principles of the environmental legal acts are sustainable development, effective management of natural resources, and prevention and avoidance of environmental damages.

The main act regulating **environmental supervision** in Estonia is the Environmental Supervision Act. Environmental supervision involves control over the use of natural resources and products, the legality of the operations dealing with them and the factors influencing the environment. The main supervisory agency is the Environmental Inspectorate, though local municipalities are involved in some instances. During environmental supervision, supervisory authorities are permitted to perform control operations and prescribe injunctions (EELC, 2016).

Environmental impact assessments (EIA) are carried out in Estonia when planning an activity with significant environmental impact. The regulation of EIA is stipulated by the EU directive 2001/42/EC and the actions with significant environmental impact are listed in the Environmental Impact Assessment and Environmental Management System Act (EIAEM). While EIA is obligatory for some actions, the permission-granter has to weigh the necessity for EIA in other cases. A strategic environmental assessment (SEA) is also carried out during the compilation of strategic planning documents (for instance, in land use planning and development plans) (EELC, 2016).

Impact assessments in other policy areas also inform the design of environmental standards and regulations, though the lack of harmonisation across indicators collected impedes their effectiveness. In addition to assessing environmental impacts, assessments focus on: 1) social and demographic impacts; 2) impacts on the economy; 3) security and international relations; 4) regional development; 5) administrative burden on institutions. Impact assessments of rural development policy, for instance, conduct *ex-ante*, midterm and *ex-post* policy assessments in accordance with EU guidelines and include agri-environmental measures among others. A diverse range of indicators is collected for these assessments, but is not co-ordinated. In recognition of the need for a harmonised approach to environmental impact assessment (MoE, 2012), the government plans to develop a unified and representative data network on natural resources and environment by 2020.

Estonia's **environmental monitoring** system — which includes extensive observation and analysis of the state of the environment and the factors affecting it (Box 4.1) — is governed by several international legislative instruments. In particular, key instruments include the Agreement between the European Community and the Republic of Estonia on the Participation of the Republic of Estonia in the European Environment Agency (EEA), the Ratification Act of the European Environmental Information and Observation Network (EIONET), and the European Union INSPIRE Directive 2007/2/EC governing the establishment of EC spatial data infrastructure. Environmental monitoring is also governed by the Estonian Environmental Monitoring Act, and — as per the Public Information Act — the data obtained in the course of monitoring is made available on the Environmental Registry website (EELC, 2016).

Box 4.1. Monitoring of agri-environmental indicators in Estonia

Monitoring of agri-environmental issues is conducted by several agricultural institutions in Estonia. For instance, information about national agri-environmental indicators is gathered by Statistics Estonia.

The Ministry of the Environment (MoE) is responsible for a number of national environmental and nature protection issues related to agri-environmental monitoring. This includes fulfilling tasks related to land and databases containing spatial data; organising the use, protection, re-production and accounting for natural resources; ensuring radiation protection; performing tasks related to mitigation of effects of climate change; environmental supervision; meteorological observations, nature and marine research; geological, cartographic and geodetic operations; maintenance of land cadastre; organising the use of external tools for environmental protection; as well as compiling strategic documents and draft legislation. Moreover, the Environmental Board (EB) — which falls within the MoE — seeks to preserve a realistic balance between the use and protection of natural resources. One of its most important tasks in the field of nature conservation is gathering the data it needs to make decisions, including for the organisation of inventories and monitoring. The Information System for Environmental Permits holds digital data about six major fields: water, waste, mining, air, complex and climate.

As part of its activities related to food and farm product safety, the Agricultural Board covers areas that affect the environment such as land improvement, plant protection products and fertilisers (Box 4.3).

The Estonian Agricultural Research Centre (ARC) conducts field and laboratory tests, which concern mainly food and farm input safety, but also the environment, such as soil contamination, and fertiliser and pesticide evaluation. It also has competency in evaluation of agri-environment measures. It prepares fertiliser and lime consumption cards, carries out research in the field of good agricultural practices and agricultural chemistry.

Environmental liability is governed by several international and Estonian legal acts.[8] Environmental liability in the strict sense applies to three types of damage – soil, water and biodiversity. According to the regulation, a person who causes damage must promptly implement preventive measures. In the event of damage, the perpetrator must work in cooperation with the Environmental Agency to work out the remedies, or to compensate for remedies or for the corresponding costs, as well as to implement preventive measures to limit the extent of the damage. If the person has acted in accordance with a permit issued or made use of a technique in which the probability of occurrence of the injury was not foreseeable, it is exempted from the application of the measures. If the party causing the damage cannot be ascertained, or he refuses preventive or remedial action, or is exempted from this obligation, the implementation of the right to reparation lies with the Environmental Agency (EELC, 2016).

Estonia also has an **integrated environmental permit system** to assess and reduce the impact of productive activities (for example, intensive livestock production) that can negatively impact various environmental elements (including water, soil, air, and waste production, among others). This mechanism requires enterprises over the threshold capacities (including farms with over 2 000 pigs; over 40 000 poultry; and over 400 dairy cows) to obtain integrated environmental permits (RT I, 11.06.2013, 19). The conditions and restrictions assigned by the permit must include use of the best available technology (BAT) — for instance, for the determination of emission limit (RT I, 03.12.2015, 7). Estonia's integrated environmental permits are regulated by the Industrial Emissions Act, which in turn is compiled according to the directive 2010/75/EU issued by the European Parliament and Council. Moreover, integrated pollution prevention and control is regulated by the EU Parliament and Council directive 2008/1/EU, as well as by the Environmental Impact Assessment and Environmental Management System Act in Estonia (EELC, 2016).

As for other sectors, agriculture is subject to EU regulations related to the protection of natural resources, which set minimum sustainability conditions for farm practices. While farmers are expected to respect regulations as any other citizen, the EU Common Agricultural Policy (CAP) provides additional incentives for farmers to comply with those regulations (and those related to the safety of food, feed and farm inputs), as well as to adopt more environmentally-friendly practices (Box 6.1). Other CAP incentives for the adoption of more environmentally-friendly practices are discussed in Chapter 6.

Land use and soil

Regulations on **land use** are covered by several legal acts. In particular, land use is regulated by the Planning Act, Land Cadastre Act, Land Consolidation Act and Nature Conservation Act, among others. Moreover, access to agricultural and forestland is regulated through Restrictions on Acquisition of Immovables Act.

A range of agricultural policies and regulations also cover **soil protection**. The Earth's Crust Act, Land Improvement Act and the Plant Protection Act are key in this regard. For instance, such acts oblige agricultural producers to keep field records with information of used plant nutrients. Moreover, recipients of agri-environmental subsidies are required to regularly monitor the acidity of soil, exchangeable phosphorus (P), potassium (K), and organic carbon contents (EEIC, 2013). Yet, management and protection of soils in Estonia remains difficult due to spatial variation in soil properties. As a result, only 46% of Estonian soils have a very good fertility potential and good environmental protection value (EEIC, 2013).

Water

Water management and protection regulation is aligned with both EU and regional regulations. Estonia's Water Act, which regulates water use and protection, the relations between the landowners and the users of water, as well as the use of public water bodies and water bodies designated for public use, is elaborated in accordance with the EU Water Framework Directive (2000/60/EC); Marine Strategy Framework Directive (2008/56/EC); Urban Waste Water Treatment Directive (91/271/EEC); and Nitrates Directive (91/676/EEC). In addition, agreements within the Convention on the Protection of the Marine Environment of the Baltic Sea Area and the Baltic Sea Action Plan also form the basis of water protection regulations in Estonia.

Water usage for production purposes is charged depending on the water layer used. Charges for abstraction of surface water range from EUR 1.55 to EUR 38.34 per 1 000 cubic metres, depending on the purpose of usage. Charges for water from aquifers range from EUR 30.65 (Quaternary period aquifer) to EUR 191.7 per 1 000 cubic meters (potable quality water from the Cambrian-Vendian period aquifers for technological purposes, except for production of foodstuffs). The specific provision for agriculture and fisheries is that charges are not imposed for irrigation of agricultural land (incl. greenhouses) and for fish farming purposes. However, as the irrigation is used mainly by private households in home gardens and by horticultural farms, the share of irrigation water in total water abstraction is minimal (RT I, 17.12.2015, 44).

Nitrates

Estonian regulations on **usage of organic fertilisers** have become increasingly strict in recent years, in response to encouragement from the European Commission (OECD, 2017a). According to the Estonian Water Act[9] applying during 2014-17, the amount of Nitrogen and Phosphorus in organic fertilisers — including the manure left by grazing animals — must be limited to 170 kg and 25 kg[10] per hectare of fertilised land, respectively. Fertiliser application on the soil surface is also prohibited for land with a slope of more than

10%. On fields that are not covered with plants, organic fertilisers must be mixed into the soil within 48 hours (within 24 hours as of January 2021). Moreover, fertilisation of natural grasslands is prohibited — except for the manure left by grazing animals. Lastly, manure storage requirements are also stipulated. For instance, animal barns for more than 10 livestock units (LU) (more than 5 LU as of January 2023) should have manure storage for solid and/or liquid manure depending on the manure type. Storage space must be sufficient for storing manure during eight months. Producers who have less than 10 LU can temporarily store their solid manure on watertight ground near the barn if protected from rainfall (RT I, 06.01.2016, 14). The timing of mineral and organic fertiliser application is also regulated based on weather and soil conditions.[11]

While the aforementioned regulations incentivise agricultural producers to improve the usage of organic fertilisers, **poor market conditions** are hindering shifts to newer technologies that are more efficient in terms of nitrogen losses. According to a recent farm survey, the majority of dairy farmers with liquid manure systems use trailing hose applications or broadcasting systems with mixing into soil. Even in larger dairy farm groups (>100 cows), the share of trailing hose and broadcasting systems used is still high. Contractors are also employed for slurry injection — in order to shorten the application period and fulfil environmental requirements.

Nitrate Vulnerable Zones (NVZ) are also protected in Estonia by government decree, though pollution levels in these zones continue to increase. In 2003, an NVZ was established in the Pandivere and Adavere-Põltsamaa region.[12] The area (3 250 km^2) was determined based on ground and surface water vulnerability related to geological characteristics and intensity of agricultural production in the region. The restrictions and duties of this NVZ are corrected every fourth year based on the results of periodic monitoring exercises (MoE, 2016c). Moreover, fertilisation and land use for agricultural production are subject to certain restrictions[13] in this region (RT I, 06.01.2016, 14). However, the groundwater nitrate levels in the Pandivere and Adavere regions have grown steadily. Moreover, the water in some wells has become undrinkable due to high nitrate levels, suggesting that the existing requirements are not sufficient.

Biodiversity

Biodiversity and nature protection are covered by several normative documents, programmes and regulations. Nature protection is based on two directives: the EU Habitats Directive (Council Directive 92/43/EEC on the conservation of natural habitats and of wild fauna and flora) and the Birds Directive (Council Directive 79/409/EEC on the conservation of wild birds). The principles of these directives are integrated into the Estonian Nature Conservation Act. Overall development issues for nature conservation in Estonia are also specified in the Nature Conservation Development Plan 2020, which is in accordance with the global and EU biodiversity strategies as well as the national level strategies on environment and sustainable development. The Natura 2000 network of protected areas — designed to fulfil the objectives of the EU habitats and bird directives — includes 542 natural areas and 66 bird areas protected by the Nature Conservation Act. In total, 22% of Estonia's territory is currently under protection (EEIC, 2015), highlighting the far-reaching potential of these programmes and regulations. Nonetheless, as discussed in Section 2.2, Estonia's biodiversity indicators, which are based on the number of birds, have deteriorated in recent years, highlighting the need for further efforts in the regional context.

International agreements

Estonia also subscribes to major international and regional regulatory agreements concerning **climate change**. Key international agreements include the United Nations (UN) Climate Change Framework Convention and the Kyoto Protocol. Estonia has also supported objectives set at the 2015 Paris Climate Conference (COP21) to conclude a global climate agreement in order to avoid irreversible temperature rise and climate change (MoE Climate). As a low-income member of the European Union, Estonia contributes to achieving the objectives of the 2020 climate and energy package, and 2030 climate and energy framework. As noted previously, Estonia is not required to reduce emissions in sectors excluded from the emissions trading system such as agriculture. Rather, by 2020, the increase of emissions should not exceed 11% of 2005 emissions (Government Office, 2014; MoE, 2016d).

The main aims of Estonian environmental policy are also in line with international agreements related to **nature protection**. In particular, many objectives align with the Ramsar Convention, the Bern Convention, CITES or the Washington Convention, the Rio de Janeiro Convention on Biological Diversity, and agreements related to the Bonn Convention — EUROBATS and AEWA, HELCOM, IUCN, IWC (MoE Nature conservation). In addition, many of Estonia's policy objectives come from the following international multilateral agreements:

- Conventions regarding the protection of seas and sea pollution;
- Conventions regarding the protection of internal waters;
- Fisheries' conventions;
- Conventions regarding hazardous waste;
- Conventions on nature conservation;
- Conventions regarding the prevention and avoidance of atmosphere pollution;
- Conventions regulating nuclear issues;
- Stockholm Convention on Persistent Organic Pollutants;
- The horizontal conventions on the environment: Aarhus Convention and Espoo Convention (MoE International co-operation).

The Estonian Nature Conservation Development Plan 2020 has also been developed in accordance with a number of international and national strategic documents. Such strategies include the Convention on Biological Diversity and the Global Biodiversity Strategy and the respective EU Biodiversity Strategy, the Estonian national sustainable development strategy Sustainable Estonia 21, the Estonian Environmental Strategy 2030 and the Estonian Rural Development Plan 2007-2013. The Estonian Nature Conservation Development Plan 2020 is a strategic document for the development of the areas related to nature protection and the use of nature. Its objectives include raising environmental awareness and nature valorisation, preserving species, maintaining a favourable habitat for species and for biodiversity and ensuring the sustainable use of natural resources by following an ecosystem approach. The Nature Conservation Development Plan identifies base level indicators in 2011 and targets for 2020 (Table 4.A1.1) (MoE, 2012).

4.1.3. Regulations on products and processes

Regulations on products and processes aim to protect human, animal and plant health and can also impact on natural resource use. Environmental and health related regulations can boost innovation by building consumer and societal trust in the safety and sustainability of new products or processes, but unnecessary or dis-proportionate regulations can stifle innovation and technological developments (OECD, 2014a).

Establishment and enforcement of regulations and private standards related to products and processes

Since Estonia is a member of the European Union, regulations on products and processes, ensuring food safety and quality, are mainly determined at the EU level, while implementation is at the national level. EU regulations cover farm practices as well as food and input safety.

Food safety issues, policies and actions cover the entire food chain, from the environment, production, processing and delivery to food processing, preparation and consumption (WHO, 2015). The EU food policy includes, inter alia, important food and feed safety and food hygiene regulations (EU, 2016). Primary and feed producers need to comply with food and feed safety requirements (unless produced for their own use). Food and feed safety issues are part of the cross-compliance system for receiving EU CAP payments (Box 6.1).

Food safety requirements are set out in the **Food Act,** the **Feed Act**, and different regulations under the Ministry of Rural Affairs (MRA). The **Fertilisers Act** provides the requirements for fertilisers and their handling to ensure that fertilisers do not pose a threat to human and animal life and health or to property or the environment, and that fertilisers have a favourable effect on plants and plant products. The **Plant Protection Act** lays down the requirements for plant health and plant protection products that guarantee the safety of plant protection products to human and animal health and to the environment, as well as the requirements for plant protection equipment, and the grounds and scope of state supervision.

The general principles and requirements are laid down in the food law and in the Regulation (EC) No 178/2002 of the European Parliament. MRA is in charge of food safety standards and legislation. It also exercises in-country control and monitoring of the food chain. In order to ensure food safety, MRA develops legislation related to food hygiene, food additives and contaminants and labelling, food contact materials and articles, novel foods and genetically modified organisms[14] and other food groups or participates in the development of this legislation in the EU decision-making process. In addition, MRA is responsible for the communication related to the international food standards programme *Codex Alimentarius* in Estonia and coordinates cooperation with the European Food Safety Authority (EFSA), the European Commission and the food supervisory authorities of the EU member states (MRA, 2016a).

At the state level the legislation regulates the provision of veterinary services and the work of authorised veterinarians; animal health; animal protection; food inspection; organic farming (Box 4.2); veterinary medicinal products; CAP in Estonia; alcohol surveillance; farm animal breeding; feed control; supervisory fees and state fees, as well as administrative and misdemeanour proceedings (Box 4.3). Directly applicable EU legislation include those on animal health; animal protection; breeding of farm animals; food control; market organisation; international trade and organic farming (VFB).

Box 4.2. Organic farming regulation

Organic farming in Estonia is regulated by the EU Organic Farming Regulation (EC) No. 834/2007 (that regulates organic production and the labelling of organic products) and implementing legislation. The regulation clearly defines the aims, principles and general rules of organic production. The common basic principles laid down in the EU Organic Farming Regulation are directly applicable to Estonia. Moreover, at the national level, organic farming is regulated by the Estonian Organic Farming Act that establishes the requirements for operating in the areas not subject to the EU regulation, the scope and rules for national surveillance in organic farming and the provisions concerning the liability of farmers for non-compliance and the ordinances associated with it:

- Basic regulation for keeping the Organic Farming Register;
- Procedure for seeking approval for operating in in the organic sector;
- Requirements for organic production;
- Codes of the authorities exercising supervision over the persons employed in the organic sector;
- Standard description of the label referring to organic production methods and the procedure for using the label.

The terms "öko" and "mahe", which are both legally acceptable terms in Estonian for "organic" and their derivatives may be used in labelling or promoting organic products, if at least 95% by weight of the ingredients of agricultural origin are organic. The products must have been grown on converted land or come from animals that have gone through the conversion period. The qualifying product must bear the EU organic logo, origin marking and the code of the supervisory authority. Depending on the origin of the raw material, the labelling must include indication of the place where the agricultural raw materials of the product were farmed: 'Estonian Agriculture', 'EU Agriculture', 'non-EU Agriculture', 'EU/non-EU Agriculture'. In addition, the Estonian organic eco-label can be used, which indicates that the product is manufactured and inspected in Estonia and meets the requirements set out in the Organic Farming Act. Eco-labelled products must be produced in compliance with the requirements and they may be marketed only under state supervision. All companies engaged in organic farming are checked regularly at least once a year. All organic companies are listed in the Organic Farming Register, which is available on the website of the Agricultural Board. The company must pay the state fee for registration, certification (approval) and surveillance activities. The supervision of organic farm production is the responsibility of the Agricultural Board, while food and feed processing, marketing (including importing) and catering is the responsibility of the Veterinary and Food Board (VFB). New eco labels are now available for restaurants and catering, which include as a criteria the percentage of organic raw materials used.

Source: MRA (2016b), www.agri.ee/en/objectives-activities/organic-farming.

To ensure biosafety, general measures of food storage requirements are set down. Special requirements apply to the handling and labelling of frozen food. Microbiological requirements have been established to assess food quality and the extent of food contamination. The reduction of anti-microbial resistance in ensuring food safety is gaining more and more importance. The content of food additives, flavourings, contaminants and food enzymes in food, as well as the application of materials and articles in contact with food, their application in accordance to the permissible standards and the relevance of processing methods are monitored closely in order to ensure chemical safety. Alcohol management, placing foods for particular nutritional use on the market, the safety of genetically modified foods, cross-compliance of enriched food, the use of food additives and placing novel foods on the market are regulated by both national and EU legislations (VFB, 2016).

Assessment of regulatory impacts when developing new and reviewing existing regulations

In order to shape political decisions in agricultural and food industry, MRA subscribes applied research. The results of the R&D activities financed by MRA (including animal health, welfare and breeding and collecting and maintaining genetic resources) help to improve the knowledge base and raise the level of employability, provide necessary guidance for successful management and science-based applications. To guarantee a high level of Estonian agricultural research, MRA strengthens local cooperation, promotes innovation, implements the European Innovation Partnership (EIP) programme, participates in research councils and committees and cooperates with other countries (MRA, 2016c).

Implementation of product and process safety regulation in food and agriculture

Conditions for farmers to receive most CAP support also include the respect of food, feed and farm input safety regulations (Box 6.1).

All food-related companies have to comply with the general food safety principles to ensure food safety. The responsibility for ensuring food safety lies with food business operators, who must determine the stages in food handling which are significant from the food safety perspective, monitor them and register the results in accordance with the Food Act and the European Parliament and Council Regulation No 852/2004. Food business operators must be familiar with the requirements and Hazard Analysis Critical Control Point (HACCP) principles. To ensure the compliance with the hygiene requirements and to make self-checks, the self-regulation operators may use guidelines, which are prepared at the EU level, by a local professional association or some other interested party (MRA, 2016a).

Box 4.3. Monitoring of the safety of food, feed and farm inputs

The Agricultural Board's areas of activity include land improvement, plant protection, plant health, plant variety rights, seed and plant propagating materials, organic farming, fertilisers and horticultural products. The board organises the surveillance of plant health, plant protection products, seed and vegetative propagation material and organic plant production.

The Estonian Agricultural Research Centre (ARC) conducts field and laboratory tests (pesticide residues and other contaminants in plant materials and in soils, plant pest diagnoses, agrochemical analyses of soil and fertilisers, microbiological analyses of plant production, seed quality testing etc.). The organisation has competency in different areas: soils, seeds, fertilisers, feeding stuffs, grain and grain products, plant product quality and safety analysis, identification of plant diseases and pests, and evaluation of agri-environment measures. It prepares fertiliser and lime consumption cards, carries out research in the field of good agricultural practices and agricultural chemistry

Source: ARC (2016), Estonian Agricultural Board, http://pmk.agri.ee.

In order to help farmers and food businesses to jointly develop new products, processes and technologies, the state informs the producers about the applicable requirements, laws and their amendments, introduces the specificities of EU membership and support measures and supports the collaboration between the primary producers and the processing industry in the agricultural sector and promotes innovation (MRA, 2016c). For example, in September 2016, the Estonian food industry introduced the "Good practice of the application of the concept of 'whole grain products', which defines the whole grain standard and formulates which products may be described as 'whole grain products'. In the case of bakery products, at least 50% of the ingredients must be whole grain, in the case of whole grain pasta and extruded whole-grain products, 100% of the cereal ingredients used in the manufacture must be whole grain. Transition to good practice will take place gradually, and the food industry is expected to comply by the end of 2017.

In general, changes in agricultural production and food processing related legislation will lead to new production conditions that call for adaption, which in turn stimulate the development and introduction of new technologies and production practices.

4.2. Trade and investment policy

Trade can facilitate the flow of goods, capital, technology, knowledge and people needed to innovate. Openness to trade and capital flows is conducive to innovation as it provides a larger market for innovators, reinforces competition, increases access to new technologies, ideas and processes, including from foreign direct investment (FDI) and related technological spill-overs, and facilitates cross-country collaboration. Trade and investment openness can influence innovation throughout the food supply chain, from input suppliers to food service and retail firms. Input and output markets that operate effectively can foster productivity growth. Trade and investment openness can also facilitate the development of market mechanisms to foster more environmentally sustainable production (OECD, 2014a).

In Estonia, the organisation of foreign trade policy is divided between different ministries. Industrial products trading policies are mostly managed by the Ministry of Economic Affairs and Communications (MEAC). The co-ordination of common foreign trade policy in general is managed by the Ministry of Foreign Affairs; Customs and taxation issues are managed by the Ministry of Finance; and agricultural products trading policies and related sanitary and phytosanitary measures are managed by the MRA.

Trade policy and EU accession

Estonia became a member of the WTO in 1999. Since becoming a member state of the European Union on 1 May 2004, Estonia is a member of the WTO as an EU member state, and is included in the WTO Trade Policy Reviews of the European Union. Before EU accession, Estonian policy towards foreign trade and investments can be described as unilaterally open. Due to the nature of macroeconomic reforms carried on at the beginning of 1990s, Estonia became one of the countries with the most liberal trade policy. All tariffs and quantitative restrictions were abolished. Estonia is now part of the EU common market and applies common trade policy.

The impact of EU accession on Estonian trade, in particular agro-food trade has been thoroughly analysed *ex-ante*. Varblane and Toming (2002) pointed out that EU accession would change the Estonian trade policy regime radically and that agro-food trade would be the most affected, as the free trade agreement Estonia had with the European Union prior to accession did not include agricultural and food products. While Estonia did not apply any tariffs on imports originating from the European Union, Estonian exports of agricultural and processed food products to the European Union were restricted by tariffs and quotas. EU accession thus granted Estonia free access to the EU agricultural and food products market. When Estonia implemented common tariffs and all non-tariff barriers against third countries, protection increased, but there was also trade creation, as the EU food market opened to Estonian exporters. Varblane and Toming (2002) found in a partial equilibrium framework that trade diversion had already taken place before accession as Estonia had already implemented limited tariffs on food products against third countries since 2000. They estimated that 75% of imports from third countries had been partly driven out by the imports from EU member states and from countries with free trade agreements with the European Union.

Another aspect of Estonia's EU accession concerned bilateral and regional trade agreements. Estonia had bilateral trade agreements with 25 countries and regional free trade agreements with the Baltic countries. The trade agreement with Ukraine was the most affected by Estonia's EU accession. Today, all the bilateral and regional trade agreements concluded by the EU are implemented in Estonia.

Trade openness

Estonia is a small open economy with limited capacity to produce a large range of goods and services, and thus depends on foreign trade. Together with trade policy, this makes Estonia one of the most open economies in the world, openness to trade being the value of total merchandise trade (the sum of exports and imports of goods and services) measured as a share of gross domestic product (GDP) in PPP. Merchandise trade as a percentage of GDP increased from 100% in 1995 to 156% in 2000. In 2005, the year of EU accession, merchandise trade was 129% of GDP and started to decline during the crisis years. The lowest value was 99% in 2009, however in 2011 and 2012, the openness to trade was again higher at about 150% (WITS, 2017).

Efficiency and effectiveness of customs and border procedures

Level of protection in Estonian foreign trade is described by EU common tariffs. Most favoured nation (MFN) tariff rates applied on agricultural goods are on average higher than those on capital goods and industrial goods (Figure 4.3). Moreover, EU tariffs on capital goods and intermediate goods are on average higher than in major non-EU trading partners. This raises the cost of specialised inputs and machineries, and thus reduces the competitiveness of the agri-food sector.

Figure 4.3. Import tariffs for industrial and agricultural goods, 2015 or latest available year

Simple average MFN applied tariff rates[1]

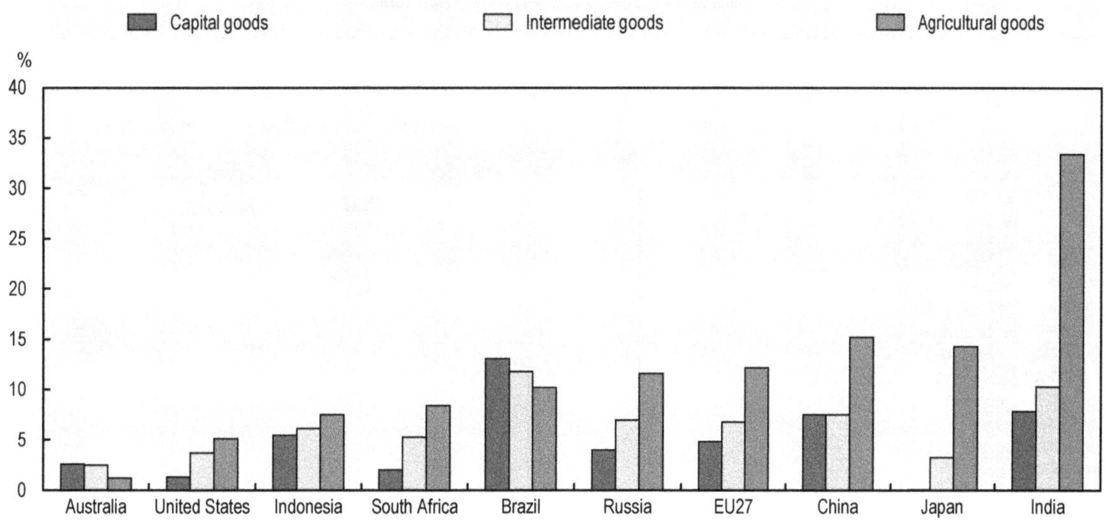

MFN: Most Favoured Nation.

1. Tariff rates for agricultural products include both ad valorem duties and specific duties in ad valorem equivalent, while tariff rates for agricultural products only include ad valorem duties.

Countries are ranked according to Agricultural goods levels.

Source: UNCTAD Trade Analysis Information System (TRAINS) (for non-agricultural products) and World Tariff Profiles, 2014 (for agricultural products). WITS (2017), World Integrated Trade Solution, http://wits.worldbank.org/.

StatLink http://dx.doi.org/10.1787/888933654161

During the OECD accession process, Estonia participated in a Review of Market Openness with the OECD Trade Committee (OECD, 2011). This review included an evaluation of domestic regulations directly or indirectly distorting or facilitating international competition, leading to suggestions to improve the domestic regulatory framework for international trade and investment liberalisation. The market openness review pointed out that Estonia applied an active infrastructure for regulatory transparency. The principle of non-discrimination is highly supported under the regulatory framework and particularly in the area of investment policy.

OECD PMR indicators evaluate regulatory restrictions to trade and investments, considering tariffs, differential treatment of foreign suppliers, barriers to foreign direct investment and barriers to trade facilitation. According to the index for 2013, regulatory restrictions to trade and investment in Estonia are limited — the score is less than one on a scale zero to six, but they are slightly more restrictive (score 0.71) than the OECD average (0.52) (Figure 4.4). Restrictions to Foreign Direct Investment (FDI) are among the lowest in OECD indicating that Estonia is open for foreign investors and both foreign and local investors are treated equally. In terms of differential treatment of foreign suppliers, Estonia is more restrictive than the OECD average level. According to Estonia's index of regulatory restrictions to trade, the differential treatment of foreign suppliers refers to limited situations where there are shortcomings when business practices are perceived to restrict competition in Estonia, namely in the cases when foreign firms need to redress. According to the index of regulatory restrictions to trade, foreign firms have difficulties to have redress through trade policy bodies and private rights of action. But when business practices are perceived to restrict competition, foreign firms can have redress through competition agencies and regulatory authorities.

Compared to the OECD average, Estonia is more restrictive in setting barriers to trade facilitation. In the PMR indicators, barriers to trade facilitation refer to the extent to which the country uses internationally harmonised standards and certification procedures, and Mutual Recognition Agreements (MRAs) with at least one other country.

Figure 4.4. OECD Product Market Regulation (PMR) Indicator: Regulatory restrictions to trade and investment, 2008 and 2013

Scale from 0 (least) to 6 (most) restrictive

A. Index of regulatory restrictions to trade, international comparison, 2008 and 2013

B. Index of regulatory restrictions to trade by principle components, 2013

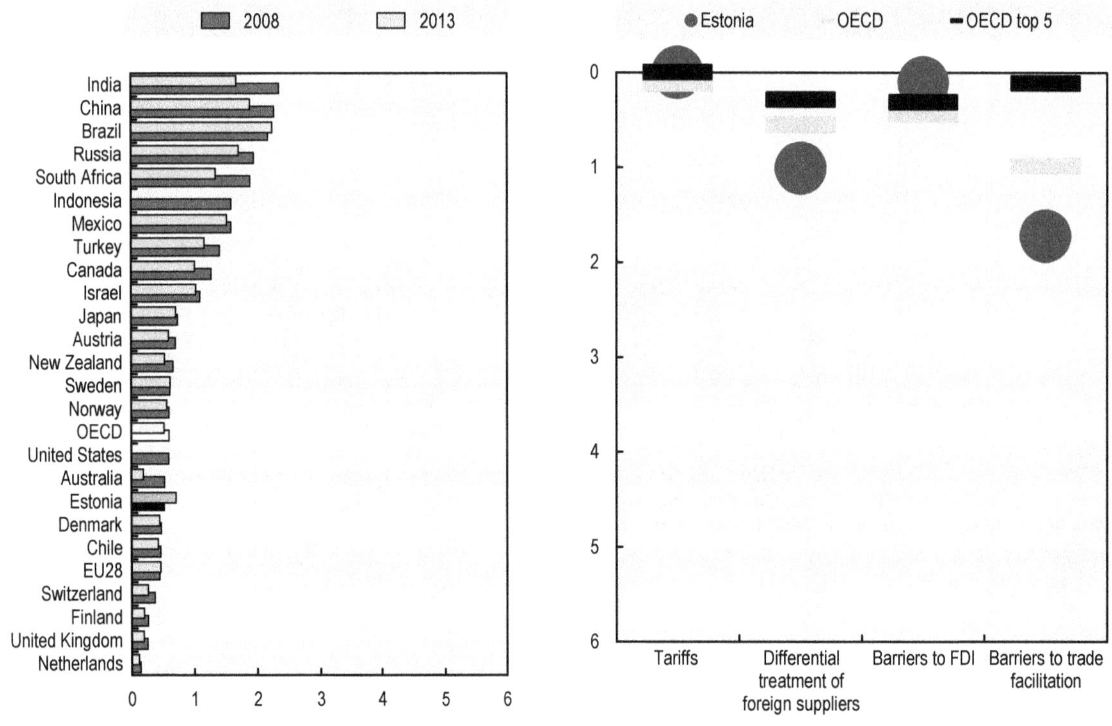

Countries are ranked according to 2008 levels.
Indices for EU28 and OECD are the simple average of member-country indices.

OECD top 5 refers to the average of the scores for the top five performers among OECD countries (Netherlands, Belgium, Australia, United Kingdom and Finland).

Barriers to trade facilitation refer to the extent to which the country uses internationally harmonised standards and certification procedures, and Mutual Recognition Agreements (MRAs) with at least one other country. Tariff index is based on an average of effectively applied tariff, scaled within a range between 0 and 6 points, whereby a tariff below 3% is attributed zero points and a tariff above 19.6%, 6 points.

Source: OECD (2014b), Product Market Regulation Database, www.oecd.org/economy/pmr.

StatLink http://dx.doi.org/10.1787/888933654180

Other OECD trade facilitation performance indicators cover different types of procedures performed in borders (Figure 4.5). In all procedures, Estonia obtains high scores, at or above the OECD average. Relative to other procedures, there is still scope for improvement in external and internal border agency cooperation, and relative to other countries in involvement with the trade community. The strongest points concern appeal procedures and governance and impartiality. Compared to the 2015 version of OECD trade facilitation indicators, Estonia made significant progress in all procedures, in particular formality procedures and border agency cooperation, although some of the improvement reflects better question design.

Figure 4.5. OECD Trade Facilitation Indicators: Estonia's performance, 2017

Scale from 0 (least) to 2 (best) performance

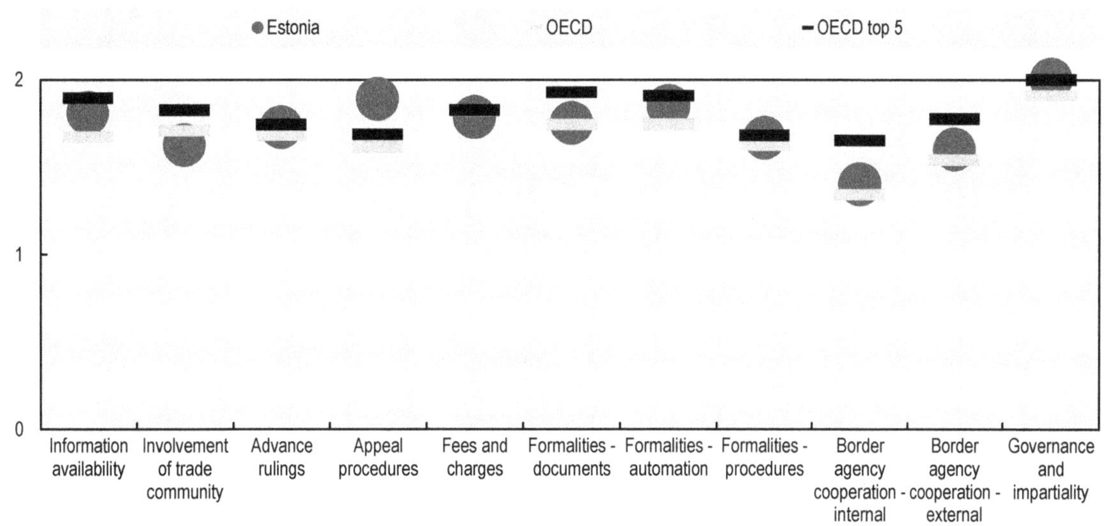

OECD top 5 refers to The Netherlands, United States, Korea, Norway and France.

Source: OECD (2017b), Trade Facilitation Indicators, www.oecd.org/trade/facilitation/indicators.htm.

StatLink http://dx.doi.org/10.1787/888933654199

FDI regulations

While the government generally does not control FDI, there are few restrictions concerning certain sectors, which apply to foreign ownership by applying ownership responsibilities. The FDI Regulatory restrictiveness index measured by the OECD describes Estonia as one of the countries with least restrictions to FDI (Figure 4.6). The scale of the index varies form 0 (least restrictive) to 1 (most restrictive). FDI restrictiveness index for Estonia in 2014 was 0.018, which is lower than the OECD average (0.069) and the EU average (0.097). For FDI in agriculture and food sectors, indices are very small and well below OECD and EU average levels, indicating very low level of restrictions. Some restrictions remain, however, for agriculture concerning land.[15] However, these do not apply to citizens of Estonia or another country which is a contracting party to the European Economic Area (EEA) Agreement or a member state of the OECD, which have the right to acquire agricultural or forest land without restrictions.

Liberal economic policy and openness have made Estonia an attractive destination of FDI. Total FDI inwards stocks are down to 75% of GDP in 2015, compared to 80% in 2005. This is much higher than the OECD average but less than in Ireland or the Netherlands (Figure 4.7).

In the 1990s, most of FDI was made through the privatisation process, but gradually the emphasis shifted on investments into other enterprises and establishing new companies. After the completion of privatisation, the structure of inward FDI has changed. The dominant forms of FDI are the acquisition of Estonian enterprises by foreign investors and the re-investment of profits by subsidiaries of foreign companies.

Figure 4.6. OECD Foreign Direct Investment (FDI) Regulatory Restrictiveness Index, 2016

Scale from 0 (least) to 1 (most) restrictive

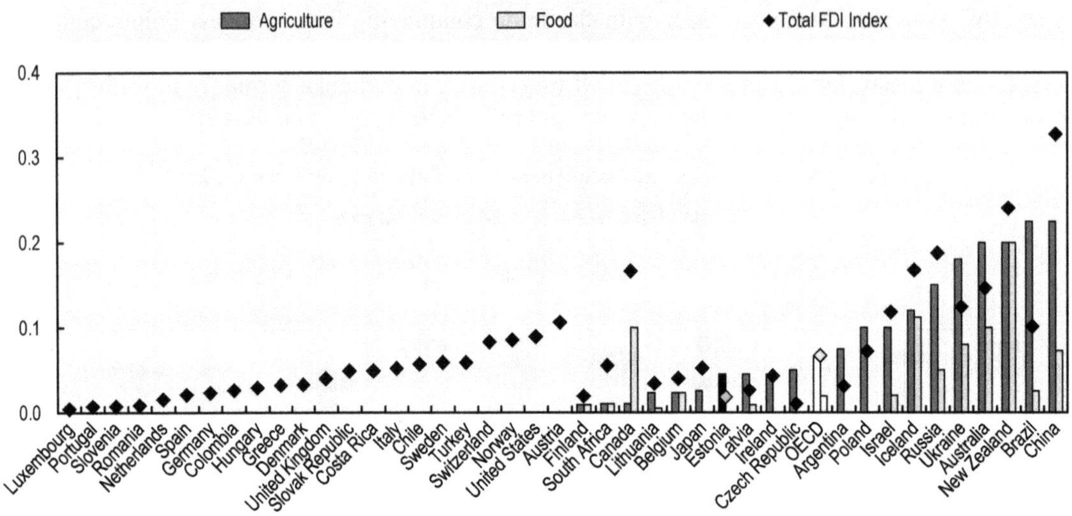

Countries are ranked according to Agriculture levels.

Indices for OECD are the simple average of member-country indices.Four types of measures are covered by the FDI Restrictiveness Index: 1) foreign equity restrictions, 2) screening and prior approval requirements, 3) rules for key personnel, and 4) other restrictions on the operation of foreign enterprises.

Source: OECD (2017c), "OECD FDI Regulatory Restrictiveness Index", OECD FDI Statistics (database), www.oecd.org/investment/fdiindex.htm.

StatLink http://dx.doi.org/10.1787/888933654218

Figure 4.7. Total FDI inward stocks, 2005 and 2016[1]

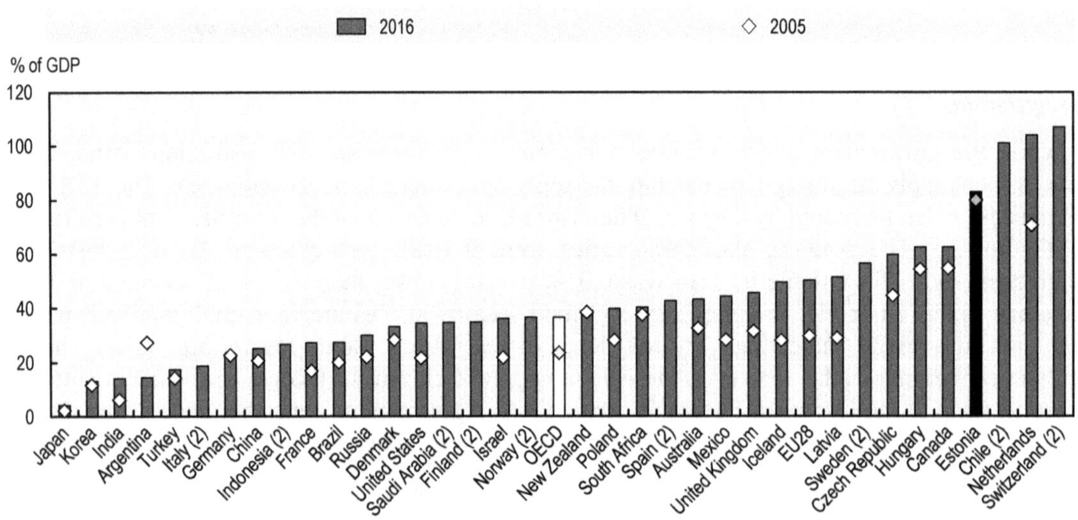

Countries are ranked according to 2016 levels.

1. 2016 or latest available year.

2. For Chile, Finland, Indonesia, Italy, Norway, Saudi Arabia, Spain, Sweden and Switzerland, 2005 data are not available.

Source: OECD (2017d), International Direct Investment Statistics, http://dotstat.oecd.org/?lang=en.

StatLink http://dx.doi.org/10.1787/888933654237

4.3. Finance policy

Efficient financial markets are one key to enable balanced development of any economy and society. Access to financial services can be limited or unequal across regions and firms when financial markets fail or when risks are too high. Policies that improve the functioning of financial markets can facilitate productivity enhancing investments in agriculture and farm size growth. Policies may also facilitate access to funding for sustainability enhancing investments. Low cost loans and venture capital can also be an important source of funding for innovative firms with high growth sectors potential (OECD, 2015).

Financial market development

According to WEF GCI, Estonia ranks higher than the OECD average in financial market developments (Figure 4.8.A). The mean aggregated results for Estonia are slightly higher than the OECD average and significantly higher than the EU28 average.

The analysis of the index components shows that the lowest score is given to the availability of loans and venture capital, but ranking was still higher than the OECD average (Figure 4.8.B). The only component below the OECD average is financing though local equity markets. As everywhere else in Europe, banks have been the main sources of financing for Estonian entrepreneurs. The entrepreneurs are not aware of the various possibilities for attracting equity capital, and so far, there are still virtually no opportunities for equity exposures. Estonian companies are relatively small and therefore comparatively little public information is available, which does not make the companies particularly attractive to external investors. Also, companies do not want to relinquish control over their businesses. A survey conducted among Estonian farmers at the end of 2015 revealed that 71.5% of entrepreneurs were not ready to transfer parts of their company or the company shares to other parties, justifying this with the reluctance to lose control over their company.

Compared to other countries, the legal rights index indicator is ranked relatively high. The legal rights index measures the degree to which collateral and bankruptcy laws protect the rights of borrowers and lenders and thus facilitates lending. Over the past five years, scores for all the index components have gone up, the largest increase being for the availability of loans and access to venture capital (WEF, 2016).

The loan balance (in current prices) granted by credit institutions to companies operating in agriculture, forestry and fishing has doubled over the past ten years. In 2009-11 the loan balance increased slowly, but by the end of 2012, the indicator was 25% higher than in 2011 (Figure 4.9). The loan balance of companies operating in agriculture, forestry and fishing constituted 5.6% of the total loan balance as of the end of 2016 (in 2005 the share was 3.8%). In relative terms, the balance of loans granted to the agricultural sector has increased in the last decade, but since 2014 it has remained fairly stable.

In Estonia, there are nine credit institutions and seven branches of foreign credit institutions, functioning with an operating licence, but two of these credit institutions — Swedbank and SEB Bank hold the biggest market share of the loan capital granted to the agriculture sector. Loans to the agricultural sector granted by Swedbank make up about 27.5% of the market share of this sector. The same figure for SEB Bank is 34%. In recent years, a number of other credit providers have entered the credit market, but the interest rates offered by these credit providers are considerably higher (starting from 8%).

The interest rates on long-term loans reached a peak in 2008, after which the rate began to decline and the average interest rate by fields of activity dropped to 3% from the end of 2013 (Figure 4.10). A general decline in the interest rates was brought about by a slump in Euribor rates. From 2010-14, the interest rate on loans in the agricultural sector was comparable to or even lower than the average interest rate across all sectors, but since 2015, higher interest rates on loans to the agricultural sector could be observed. In connection with a decline in agricultural producer prices, the financial solvency of agricultural enterprises has remained low and, therefore, banks have become more conservative, and all credit seekers do not get a positive response. Decrease in solvency increases exposure to the credit risk, which, in turn, brings about a rise in interest margins. In other words, credit institutions have imposed a higher risk margin on enterprises operating in the agricultural sector.

Figure 4.8. Global Competiveness Index: Financial market development, 2016-17

Scale 1 to 7 (best)

A. Total index of financial market development, by country

B. Index of financial market developments, by component

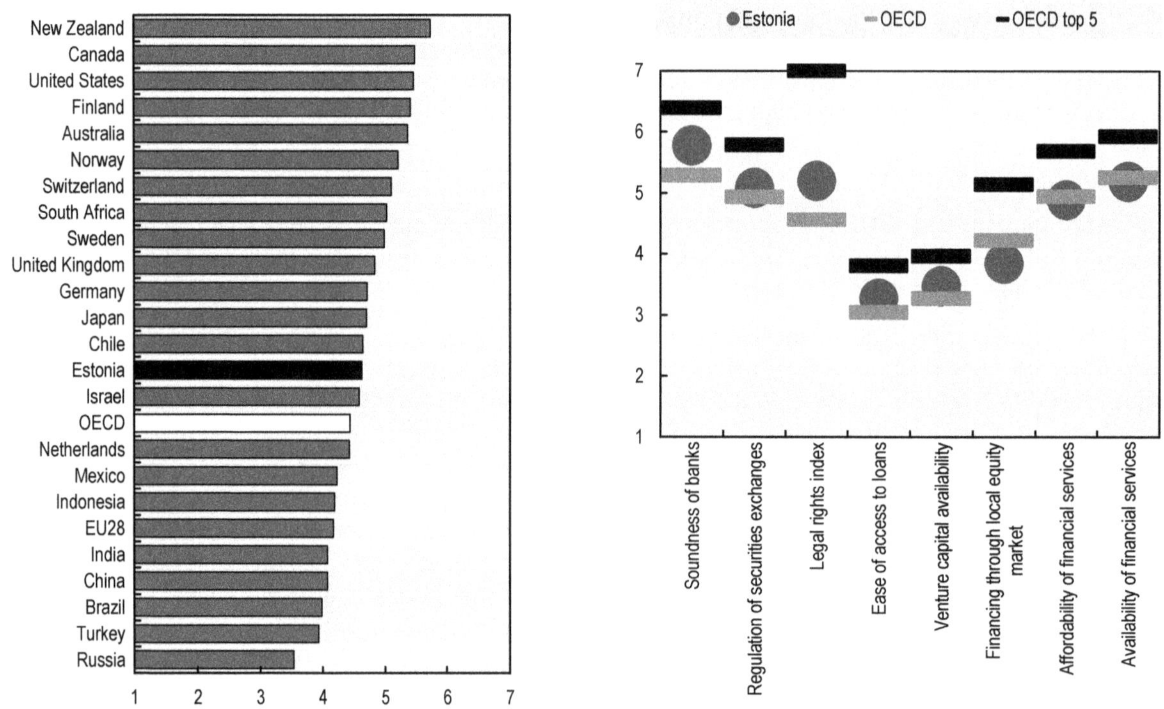

Indices for EU28 and OECD are the simple average of member-country indices.

Top 5 refers to the average of the scores for the top 5 performers among OECD countries (New Zealand, Canada, United States, Finland and Australia).

The Legal rights index is scored on a scale from 1 to 10 based on calculations by the WEF from the World Bank–International Finance Corporation's Doing Business 2013.

Source: World Economic Forum (2016), The Global Competitiveness Report 2016-2017: Full data Edition, http://reports.weforum.org/global-competitiveness-index/.

StatLink http://dx.doi.org/10.1787/888933654256

Figure 4.9. Loan balance of companies operating in agriculture, forestry and fishing, 2006-16

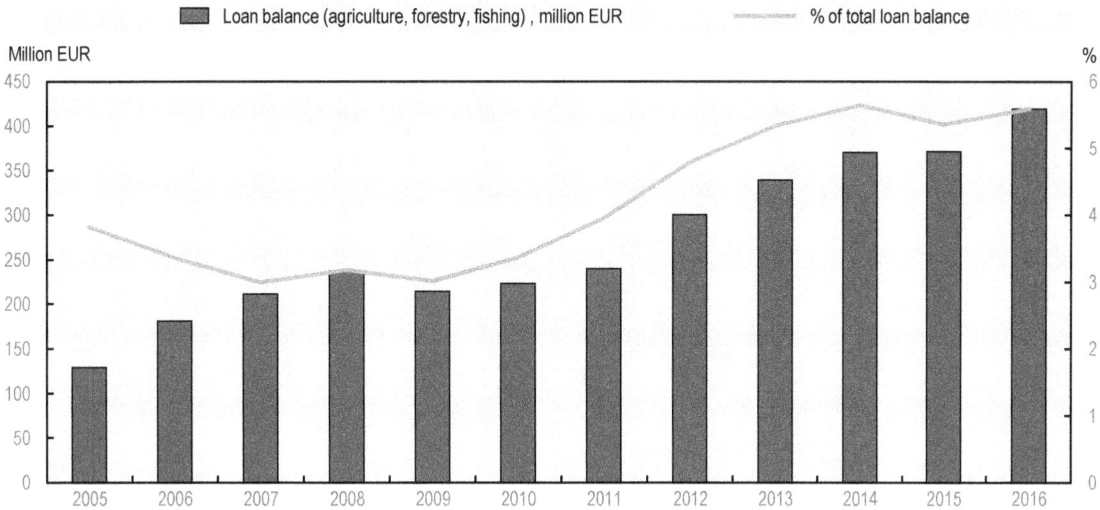

Source: Bank of Estonia (2017), http://statistika.eestipank.ee/?lng=et#listMenu/1057/treeMenu/FINANTSSEKTOR/147/650 (accessed June 2017).

StatLink http://dx.doi.org/10.1787/888933654275

A survey conducted by Krediidiinfo Ltd. pointed out that in 2015, the proportion of corporate payment defaults in the fields of agriculture, forestry and fishing increased from 4.3% to 4.8%. At the beginning of 2016, the average amount of payment default was the highest in the agricultural sector as well. Bank representatives are closely monitoring the cash flows in the companies and, if necessary, a grace period is allowed. Compared with cereal and vegetable producers, milk producers currently face income problems, making debt repayment difficult; for example at the beginning of 2016, nearly a quarter of the loan portfolios in the dairy sector held by Swedbank had been granted a period of grace. In comparison, it should be stated that in 2013 there were very few applications for grace periods.

Figure 4.10. Interest rates on loans by fields of activity in 2006-16

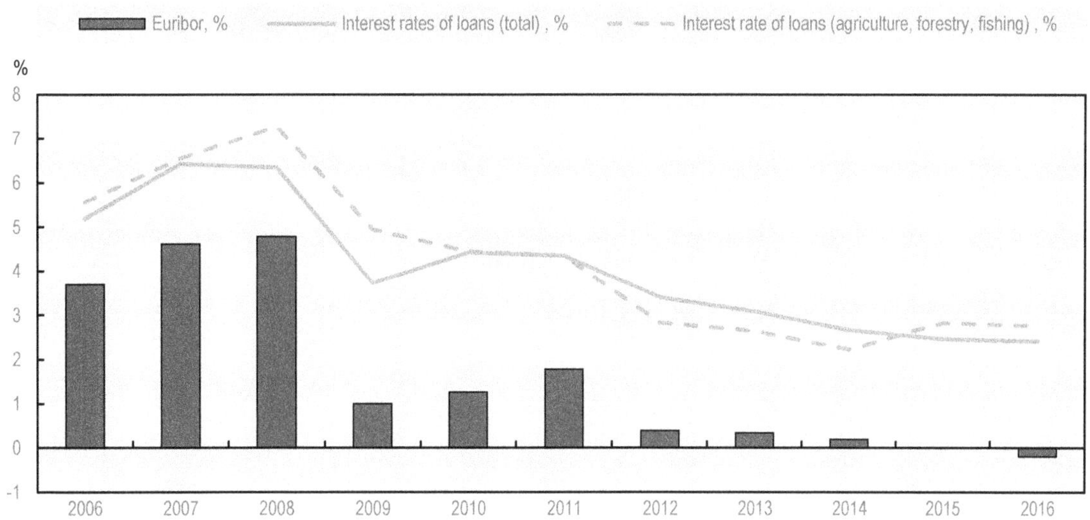

Source: Bank of Estonia (2017), http://statistika.eestipank.ee/?lng=en#listMenu/1811/treeMenu/FINANTSSEKTOR/147/979 (accessed June 2017).

StatLink http://dx.doi.org/10.1787/888933654294

Access of food and agricultural firms to credit and finance

The European Commission monitors Developments in SMEs' access to finance through the joint European Commission/European Central Bank Survey on the Access to Finance of Enterprises (SAFE). The results of the SAFE Analytical report 2015 show what sources of funding are considered the most important by Estonian small and medium-sized firms. The results are compared to the average EU28 results (Figure 4.11).

Figure 4.11. Sources of external financing of SMEs, 2015

Percentage of all respondents

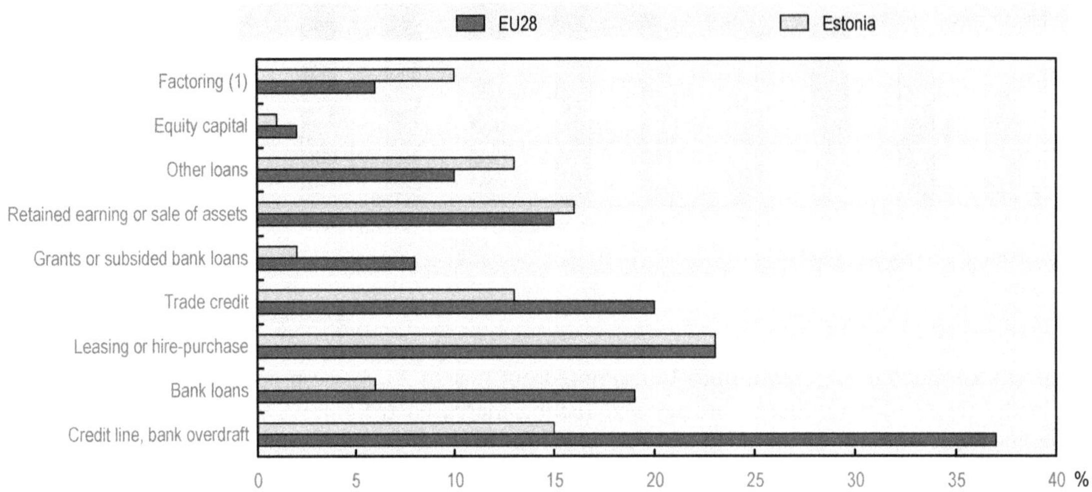

Figures refer to the following question: "Are the following sources of financing relevant to your enterprise, i.e. have you used them in the past or considered using them in the future?"

1. Factoring refers to selling invoices to a factoring company, which gets the debt and collects it, making a profit by paying less cash to the company selling the debt than the face value of the invoice.

Source: SAFE (2015), Survey on the access to finance of enterprises (SAFE) Analytical Report 2015. www.ecb.europa.eu/stats/ecb_surveys/safe/html/index.en.html.

StatLink http://dx.doi.org/10.1787/888933654313

Figure 4.12 gives an overview of the factors that are likely to become an obstacle to seeking financing. Slightly more than a third of the respondents do not face any obstacles in finding financing, while over 10% of the companies consider no access to financing their biggest problem. Insufficient guarantee is considered to be a limiting factor in obtaining financing both in Estonia as well as in other EU countries. But in Estonia interest rates are not considered so high that they would limit financing, i.e. high interest rates were seldom marked off as factors hampering financing.

Figure 4.12. The factors limiting the access to future financing, 2015

Percentage of all respondents

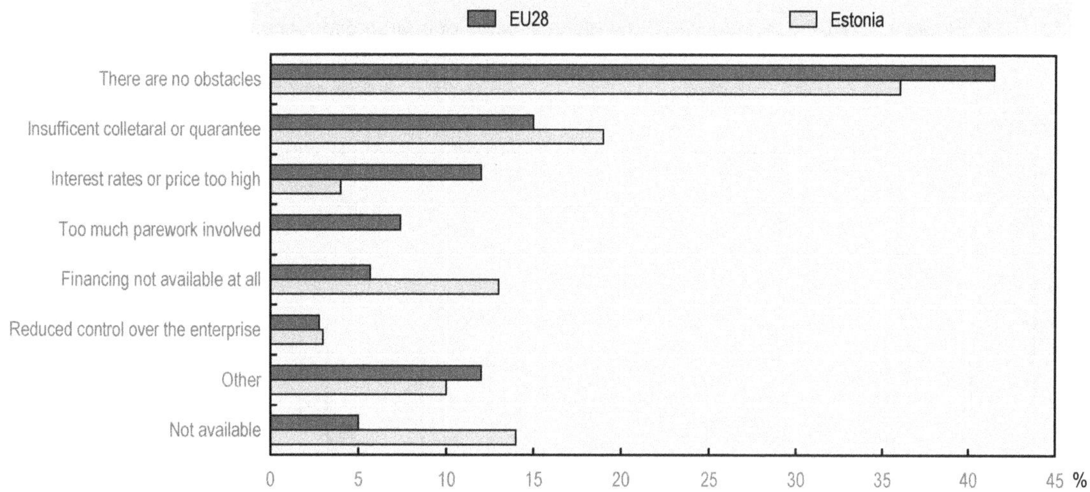

Figures refer to the following question: "What do you see as the most important limiting factor to get this financing?"
Source: SAFE (2015), Survey on the access to finance of enterprises (SAFE) Analytical Report 2015, www.ecb.europa.eu/stats/ecb_surveys/safe/html/index.en.html.

StatLink http://dx.doi.org/10.1787/888933654332

Government programmes to improve access to finance

Rural enterprises in Estonia have access to a variety of financial services with the mediation of the Rural Development Foundation (RDF). RDF is a foundation founded by the state whose goal is to support and stimulate entrepreneurship in rural areas by providing the rural enterprises and farms opportunities for accessing financial capital (guarantees, direct loans, loans to credit institutions).

RDF issues guarantees for the debt obligations of entrepreneurs (such as loan and leasing). This is expected to ensure a better access to credit facilities by increasing the credit worthiness of the borrower (which can be reduced by insufficient or illiquid collateral (underlying assets), high risk start-ups, changing the area of activity, absence of earlier borrowing experience or unclear reliability) (RDF). In 2016, RDF issued guarantees to a total of 352 enterprises, the majority (82%) of which were micro-enterprises. The rest were small and medium-sized companies. The volume of guarantees provided by the RDF has multiplied over the decade (Figure 4.13). The ratio of guarantee portfolios to guaranteed loans in the period under review was slightly above 50%.

In 2016, agricultural enterprises held the largest share of guarantee contracts (34.4%). Industrial enterprises located in rural areas ranked the second (16.7%) (including the food industry by 4.3%) and the rest of guarantee contracts belonged to other activities such as construction (3.0%), renewable energy (6.4%) and forestry.

RDF provides both direct loans to businesses and loans through a credit institution. Loans through credit institutions are meant for commercial and non-profit sectors, both for long- and short-term investments. The loans are earmarked. In 2015, direct loans to agricultural enterprises constituted 35.7%, and loans through credit institutions accounted for a bit more than 10% of the total volume of loans. Loans to agricultural enterprises formed nearly half of the total loan volume. Nearly 20% of the loans went to the renewable energy sector and fisheries received 12.4% of the lending volume.

Due to the reform of the budget, in the new EU budgetary period from 2021 onwards, the support to entrepreneurs is likely to decline significantly or disappear altogether. Having acknowledged the situation, the state is seeking ways to reduce risks so that the situation of 2009-10 would not be repeated, when the banks lost the ability, interest and willingness to lend money to enterprises. Consequently, the government is working on reducing the dependence of rural entrepreneurs on investment grants.

Figure 4.13. RDF guarantees and the residual value of guaranteed loans, 2006 to 2016

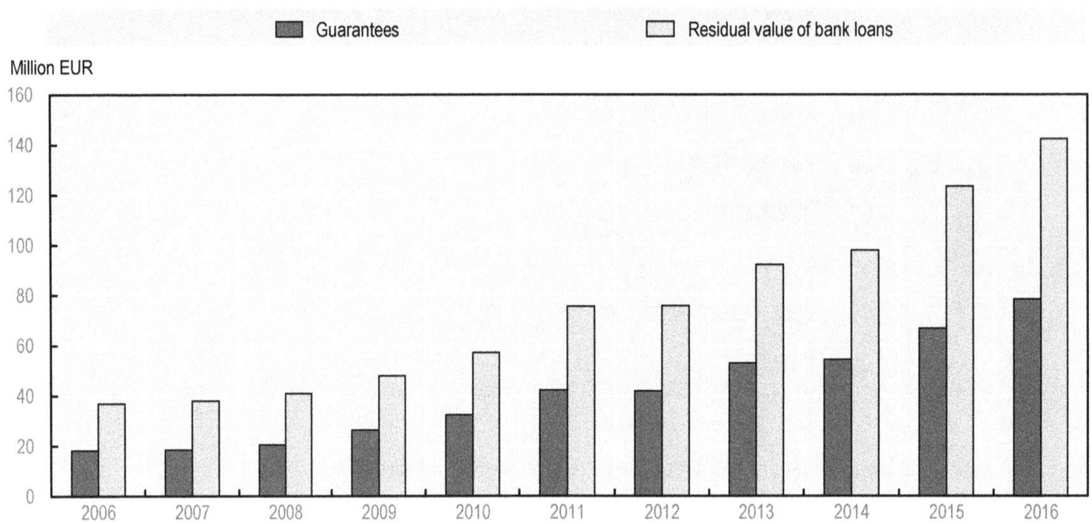

Source: Rural Development Foundation (2017), www.mes.ee.

StatLink http://dx.doi.org/10.1787/888933654351

Starting from 2016, the RDF under a contract with the MRA will issue loans (growth loans and long-term investment loans) and collaterals to the entrepreneurs in agriculture, food industry and in rural and collateral. The RDF funds are allocated from the measures of the Estonian RDP 2014-20 and their total volume is EUR 36 million. The measure is expected to improve the access of the food sector and rural entrepreneurs to capital and allow the necessary investments for which financing is otherwise difficult to find at the market.

The RDF and the Government of the Republic of Estonia are considering launching a commercial organisation in cooperation with farmers to provide alternative financial services to producers in the agricultural and fishery sectors, which would contribute to the diversification of the funding possibilities for businesses. One of the alternative financial services under consideration is property sale and leaseback that is directed at producers. Another initiative, regarding mutual insurance associations, is currently under public consultation.

Investment support for agricultural and agri-food firms

The Estonian RDP 2014-20 supports farmers in making investments into tangible assets, which will help modernise production and increase productivity, promote joint economic activity, build and upgrade environmental-friendly agricultural and livestock facilities and produce bioenergy for their company's use (Chapter 6). The specific objectives of the measures are, first and foremost, building and upgrading environmentally friendly agriculture and livestock facilities and ensuring the security of an environmentally friendly energy supply to agricultural businesses. As a rule, support is co-financed by the EU and the Estonian budgets, and constitutes up to 40% of the eligible investment cost, but only 30% for the purchase of tractors. The support rate is up to 5% higher if the support is applied by a young entrepreneur aged up to 40 years of age, or by a group of farmers.

4.4. Tax policy

Tax policy affects innovation, productivity and sustainability in many ways: it affects the decision of firms and households to save or invest in physical and human capital, and thus the adoption of innovation; it raises government revenues, which can then finance public services, including those enabling innovation such as education and skills, R&D, and strategic infrastructure; it can also be used to provide direct incentives, for example preferential tax treatment to investments in private R&D or to young innovative companies. In addition to its economy-wide impacts, tax policy influences the conduct, structure and behaviour of farms, input suppliers and food companies. Taxes on income, property and land and capital transfer, may affect structural change, while differential tax rates on specific activities (polluting or environmental friendly), resources, or input use may affect sustainability.

Overview of the Estonian tax system

In Estonia, the objective of the government's tax policy is to shift part of the tax burden from income taxation to the taxation of consumption, use of natural resources and the pollution of the environment. At the same time, the government has been trying to keep the tax system simple and transparent with as few exceptions as possible. In 2017, however, differentiated income tax rates were introduced. In recent years there have been no surveys studying the achievement of the fiscal policy objectives carried out.

The Estonian social security system is financed by a social tax imposed on employers and sole proprietors (self-employed persons) and by the state. The social tax rate was 33% of the gross salary and entrepreneurial income of sole proprietors in 2016. There are specificities to collecting social taxes from sole proprietors' income and emoluments fringe benefits payable to the employed. The employer pays the unemployment insurance benefit (the rate is 0.8% over 2015-18), which is classified as employers' charges, on the emoluments payable to the employed.

Customs duty is collected on the basis of EU Regulations (Council Regulation 2913/92/ EEC and Commission Regulation 2454/93/EEC).

Alcohol, tobacco, fuel and electricity are taxed in Estonia pursuant to the relevant EU directives. As an exception, a reduced rate of excise duty on beer is applied to small producers, and in agriculture and commercial fishing, discount rates are used on specially marked diesel fuel. The Packaging Excise Duty act applies in Estonia.

As to property (or wealth) taxation, Estonia applies taxes on land and on heavy goods vehicles. In addition to environmental taxes (excise duties on fuel and electricity, heavy goods vehicle tax and packaging excise), various other environmental charges have been introduced.

The contribution of environmental taxes and charges to the tax revenues and social security contributions increased over the period 2004-14 from 6.9% in 2004 to about 8% in 2014 (OECD, 2017f). This is higher than the OECD average, which decreased from 5.8% in 2004 to 5.2% in 2014.. Investments in the environment are mostly encouraged by the EU support programmes and the possibility to substitute the obligation to pay the pollution tax for making investments in environmental protection measures.

Tax provisions for farms or agriculture related businesses

Farms and agri-food firms are generally subject to the same taxation regime as the rest of the economy. There are differences in the taxation of the return on sales of self-produced unprocessed agricultural products, of land used in agricultural production, and reduced excise duty rates for agricultural producers and small producers of beer.

The Estonian tax system distinguishes companies (public limited company, private limited company, limited partnership, general partnership or cooperative) and sole proprietors or self-employed persons (SP). As of 1 January 2016, 8 195 companies (4.6% of the total registered companies) and 10 417 SPs (33.0% of the total registered SPs) were registered in the fields of agriculture, hunting and fishing. In both cases, the income tax rate is 20% since 2015, but there are different provisions for calculating taxable income (Box 4.4). In 2017, the government introduced differentiated tax rates.

Box 4.4. Taxation of self-employed person's income

Since 2015, the personal income tax rate for taxable income, including business income, is 20%. A **basic exemption** applies for resident individuals in Estonia. It amounted to EUR 2 160 per year in 2017.

A basic exemption for total income of EUR 6 000 per year (EUR 500 per month) applies from 2018, and additional exemptions for pensions and employee injury compensation were abolished. If the annual income is under EUR 14 400, the exemption is EUR 6 000 per year. If the annual income is between EUR 14 400 and EUR 25 200, the exemption is reduced according to the formula: 6000–6000/10800*(actual income 14 400). If the annual income is higher than EUR 25 200, the tax exemption is zero.

Other deductions can be made to gross revenue to calculate taxable income:

- It was decided in 2016 that from 2017, **low-paid employees** working full-time would be able to apply for a **refund**, which would be established by the state budget for the year on the basis the estimated subsistence minimum and the minimum monthly wage. The 2016 Budget Act established a refund rate of EUR 228 for 2017.[1] This applied only to taxation of income for 2016 as the regulation was abolished later in 2017.
- A SP can deduct up to EUR 2 877 from the income received from the **disposal of self-produced unprocessed agricultural products** minus the documented business expenses. Cleaning, sorting, cutting, drying, cooling and packaging of agricultural products is not considered processing.
- SPs have the opportunity to postpone their social and income tax payment without limitation in time by using a **special account**, collecting, for example, money for major investments. The special account is opened in a credit institution. The interest on the special account is taxed as business income.
- In case the business related expenses exceed the business income, the difference may be deducted from the business income of the following **seven taxation periods**.
- Entertainment and **representation expenses** for the catering, accommodation, transport or cultural services rendered to business partners or guests may amount to 2% of the deductibles corrected gross revenue.
- In case the business assets are transferred from one SP to another or to another company, which will continue its activities, the SP may, together with the assets, also transfer the carryforward amount of the costs and balance of the special account on a tax-free basis.
- The law that will reduce the maximum social tax burden of SPs and simplify their taxation was still processed in the parliament at the end of 2017, and is planned to be enforced at the beginning of 2018.

1. 2016 State Budget Act § 2, article 7, item 6.

One tax deduction on the sales of self-produced unprocessed agricultural products is specific to agriculture. In 2015, the supplementary deduction for SP amounted to EUR 2.5 million (MoF as of 26 May 2016), constituting 0.3% of the value of agricultural output. While some post-harvest activities are included, this provision may act as a disincentive to further on-farm processing.

Two other general provisions may help farmers manage income risk and facilitate investment. First, income losses in one year may be deducted from the business income of the following seven taxation periods, thus reducing income variability over time. Second, a special account can be opened in a credit institution to save money for future investment. The money set-aside in the year can be deducted from the taxable income, but interest gains are taxed as income every year. Special accounts are not widely used. In 2016, only 4.0% of the 32 701 SPs submitting their annual tax return and reporting business income stated some movement in the special account. This may be due to the complexity of accounting for the changes in the special accounts over different periods of taxation.

Social tax contributions for SPs are not handled as for corporate companies. As a rule, the annual social tax (rate 33%) paid by a SP per year should be higher than the monthly rate established in the Social Tax Act (EUR 430 in 2017) and multiplied by twelve, but there are a number of exceptions. The maximum social tax liability of a SP is calculated on the basis of the 15-fold (since 2018, ten-fold) amount of minimum monthly wage rates in the tax period (EUR 470 in 2017).

Similarly, SPs and companies are subject to different treatment as regards social taxes: SPs receive benefits (sickness and pension insurance) and there is a maximum limit for the social tax they pay, whereas a company pays the social tax, there is no maximum limit and the employees receive the benefits.

From 2018, the new law on simplified taxation of entrepreneurial income will be enforced (the law was accepted on 19 June 2017). This allows physical persons to open an entrepreneurial account and earn entrepreneurial income from selling services and goods without the need to register him- or herself as SP. The tax on entrepreneurial income is paid from the entrepreneurial account. The tax rate on entrepreneurial income is 20% if the entrepreneurial income is less than EUR 25 000 per year. The amounts exceeding this sum will be taxed at a 40% tax rate. The tax on entrepreneurial income includes components of income tax, social tax and mandatory pension insurance. If the paid social tax component is lower than the minimum monthly social tax amount set by the regulation, then the person is not entitled to public health insurance.

Taxes on corporate income

The income tax rate is 20% (as of 2015), and the taxable sum (dividends or previously listed objects) is first divided by 0.86 and then multiplied by the tax rate. Maximum tax-free levels are set for gifts and donations and representation expenses. The taxation of dividends will change from 2018. If the paid dividends are less than or equal to the average paid dividends of the previous three years, the tax rate is 14%. If the company is a resident, from 2018 it has to pay income tax on the loans given to its shareholders, if the circumstances indicate that it could be considered as a hidden dividend.

The corporate income tax system introduced in 2000 exempts all undistributed corporate profits regardless of companies' field of operation: companies are subject to corporate income tax only in respect of dividends, or on other payments made to capital holders from equity. During a calendar year, corporate income tax is levied on 1) fringe benefits and the social security tax imposed on them; 2) gifts and donations; 3) representation expenses; 4) dividends and other profit distributions; and 5) expenses and payments not related to business.

Since 1 July 2017, a number of corporate costs are not considered fringe benefits and are not taxed accordingly. They include accommodation costs of the employees that live far away (over than 50 km) from the workplace, and their commuting costs (for using private vehicle) if they cannot cover the distance with public transport at reasonable time and cost. In principle these provisions should to improve the mobility of employees that live in rural areas. There will be also changes made in taxation of passenger cars owned by companies and used partly for private purposes. This places Estonia in the lower range of rates in OECD countries in 2017, as Finland and Central European countries (Figure 4.14).

Figure 4.14. Total corporate income tax rate, 2017[1]

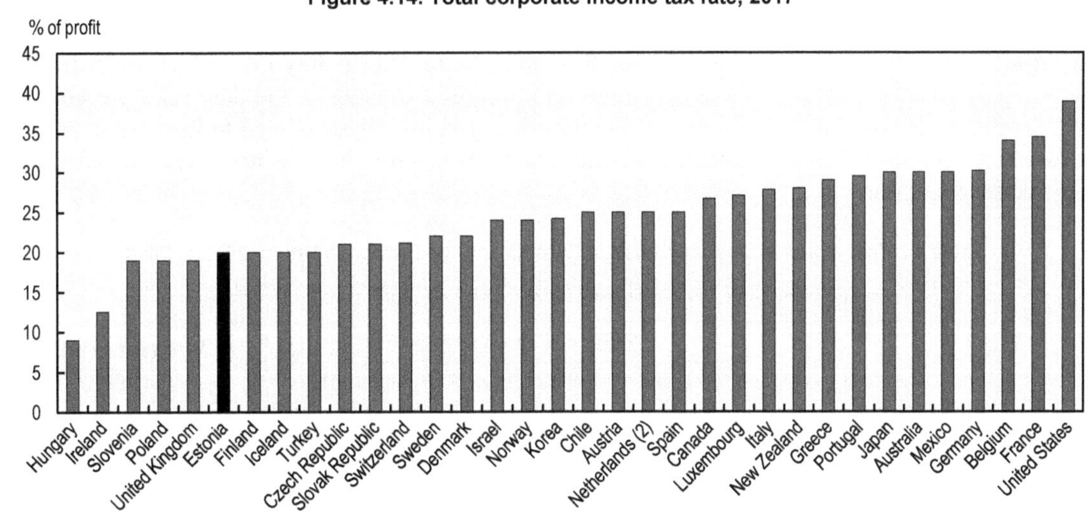

1. Basic combined central and sub-central (statutory) corporate income tax rate given by the adjusted central government rate plus the sub-central rate.
2. Netherlands: applies to taxable income over EUR 200 000.

Source: OECD (2017e), OECD Tax Database, www.oecd.org/tax/tax-policy/tax-database.htm.

StatLink http://dx.doi.org/10.1787/888933654370

Property taxes

The share of property taxes is very low in Estonia, with very few special conditions for farmers. The tax on land is a state level tax, which accrues entirely to the budget of the local governments. The tax is paid by the land owner, in some cases, the land user (if entered in the Land Register or the lessee of public land). The amount of land tax is obtained by multiplying the assessed value of land by the land tax rate. The assessed value of land is determined by the regular evaluation procedure through mass land evaluation and on the basis of market information. The land tax is imposed on land only, without taking account of the value of the buildings, forests, plants and other accessories. The land tax rates are imposed by national Land tax Act, but the applicable tax rate is established by the local government council within the set out range.

The land tax rate is set by local governments and generally ranges between 0.1% and 2.5% of the taxable value of land annually. As an exception, the rate of land tax for areas under cultivation used for the production of agricultural products is 0.1-2.0% of the assessed value of the land annually. The land tax burden of agricultural producers may vary across regions. The information from the Estonian Tax and Customs Board shows that the tax rate most widely used by local authorities for the production of agricultural products and for natural grasslands is 2%. The average land tax in 2014 amounted to EUR 2.37 per ha, whereas the mean land tax for areas under cultivation for agricultural products and natural grasslands was 1.24% of the assessed value of the land determined in the regular evaluation (Pedaste, 2015). Thus, it can be stated that agricultural land is subject to a lower tax rate.

A heavy goods vehicles tax is levied on lorries with a maximum authorised weight or gross laden weight of not less than 12 tonnes that are registered in the traffic register or road trains composed of lorries and one or more trailers with a maximum authorised weight or gross laden weight of not less than 12 tonnes whereas the lorries are registered in the traffic register. The tax is paid by natural persons residing in Estonia on a temporary or permanent basis, who are the owners or users of the heavy goods vehicles and have been entered in the traffic register, as well as legal persons registered in Estonia. Heavy goods vehicles are taxed based on the maximum authorised weight, number of axles and the type of suspension of the driving axle of the truck.

Reduced fuel excise duty for diesel fuel for specific purposes

Pursuant to the Fiscal Marking of Liquid Fuel Act of 1 January 2015, fiscal marking applies to diesel fuel that is intended to be used in machinery, tractors and non-road mobile machinery used for agricultural purposes and in drying facilities that are used to dry agricultural produce; and in commercial fishing. The value of fiscal benefits used in agricultural machinery, tractors and mobile machinery, and agricultural drying kilns increased in recent years, reflecting the growth in the general excise duty rate, which users for specific purpose pay only 27%. Diesel fuel excise duty rates and proposed changes in the duty rates are presented in Table 4.2. While the excise duty rate for diesel fuel used in agriculture is scheduled to increase over 2016-18, it remains a fixed proportion of the general rate, and much lower, providing disincentives for farmers to use practices that save on diesel use.

Table 4.2. Diesel fuel excise duty rates in Estonia and the European Union, 2016 to 2018

Actual rates in 2016, proposed rates for 2017 and 2018, EUR per 1 000 litres

	Excise duty rate in Estonia			Minimum rate in the European Union in 2016
	From 2016	From 2017	From 2018	
Diesel fuel	448	493	493	330
Diesel fuel for specific purposes	121	133	133	21
Rate of duty for pecific purpose as a percentage of the general rate	27%	27%	27%	6%

Source: MoF (2017), www.rahandusministeerium.ee/et/maksu-ja-tollipoliitika/aktsiisid.

Reduced excise duty rates for individual small breweries

The rate of excise duty on beer produced by small breweries whose production volumes do not exceed 6 000 hectolitres per calendar year is half of the regular rate of excise duty (Table 4.3). The exemption of excise duty for small breweries amounted to EUR 0.2 million in 2015, and was projected to increase as the gap between the two rates widens.

Table 4.3. Excise duty rates on beer in Estonia and the European Union, 2017 and 2018

EUR per 1% volume of ethanol in 100 litres

Volume of production, in litres	Duty rate in Estonia, in EUR			Minimum excise duty rate in the European Union
	1.02.2017	1.07.2017	1.02.2018	
> 600 000	9.13	15.52	18.26	1.87
< 600 000	4.565	7.76	9.13	1.87

Source: MoF (2017), www.rahandusministeerium.ee/et/maksu-ja-tollipoliitika/aktsiisid.

Packaging Excise

Excise duty on packaging is imposed on all packaging brought to the Estonian market. Excise duty on packaging filled in Estonia shall be paid by the person, who brings the packaged goods to the Estonian market for the first time and makes these available for distribution and use. Full exemption from excise duty is granted to:

- beverage packaging, to which the deposit has been assigned and whereof at least 85% of every class of packaging material is recovered;
- metallic beverage packaging, whereof at least 40% is recovered
- other packaging, that is recovered to the provided rate.

From 2012 agricultural plastic (bale plastic wrap, silage cover, tunnel plastic, plastic mesh and plastic twine) is not subject to packaging excise. The company, which sells packaged goods to the end user or consumer is obliged to collect the farm plastics waste from the agricultural producer without any possible additional administrative burden. Pursuant to the Packaging Act, as of 1 January 2009, the company selling packaged goods shall be obligated to partly recover the packaging material annually.

The payer of excise duty has the right to transfer its recycling and excise obligations to an accredited recovery organisation. Exemption from excise duty on packaging is applied on the entrepreneurs whose packaging amounts are small and the mass of plastic packaging does not exceed 25 kg in a quarter, and packaging of other material 50 kg in a quarter. Upon imposing excise duty on packaging, first and foremost, the actual results of recovery are taken into account. The payer of excise duty that has failed to meet the rates of recovery has to pay excise duty for the deficit quantity of packaging.

Impacts of tax arrangements on the environment

Environmental charges and fees

Estonia's Environmental Charges Act specifies environmental charges for the right to use certain environmental resources. In particular, the Act lays out taxes for "environmental use" including: 1) regeneration cutting of forest stands; 2) extraction of mineral resources; 3) water abstraction; 4) fishing; 5) hunting; 6) emission of pollutants into the ambient air, water bodies, groundwater or soil; and 7) waste disposal by way of depositing in landfills or other activities that result in the discharge of waste into the environment.

Environmental charges are divided into two categories: natural resource charges and pollution charges. Natural resource charges are paid at the rates established on the basis of this Act. The situation, place of use, quality and deficiency of the reserves of natural resources, the environmental hazards of the manner of use and the need to protect other natural resources are taken into account upon establishment of charge rates. The pollution charge is paid at the established pollution charge rates. The sensitivity to pollution of the emission site, the hazardousness of the pollutant and the use of the best possible technology are taken into account to determine the charge rates.

Agricultural producers who have been granted the following permits are subject to environmental charges:

- integrated environmental permit (including the water abstraction permit and ambient air pollution permit);
- water abstraction permit for the right to abstract water;
- water permit for the right to discharge waste water into any receiving water body;
- ambient air pollution permit (Heinma 2014).

In 2013, the pollution charges from agriculture, forestry and fishing activities amounted to EUR 458 000 and fees for use of natural resources to EUR 1 847 000, whereas in food and beverage industry pollution charges amounted to EUR 279 000 and fees for the use of natural resource to EUR 504 000 (Statistics Estonia, 2016).

The Ecological Tax Reform, launched in Estonia in 2005, provided for an increase in environmental fees, and the environmental charges have been consistently on the rise since the beginning of the reform. Estonian statistics classifies environmental charges as environmental taxes. The environmental taxes laid down in the tax laws are fuel excise duty, heavy goods vehicles tax and packaging excise duty. The structure of environmental taxes and charges is different from the one in use in the rest of the European Union – the share of transport taxes in environmental taxes is the smallest. Estonia has not imposed such wide-spread transport taxes that have been established in other EU member states, as annually paid car fee and toll on roads.

Impact of environmental taxes and charges

According to survey data from 2000 to 2010, a number of impacts of environmental taxes and charges can be seen (Sustainable Estonia Institute, 2013):

- the impact of the ambient air pollution taxes on the reduction of the emissions of pollutants from a stationary source or on the quality of the ambient air in Estonia is low;
- the impact of mineral extraction fees aimed to motivate companies to mine and use mineral resources in a more efficient way is weak or there is no effect at all, because the changes in mining volumes and losses occur regardless of the increase in the pollution tax rates;
- special water abstraction charges have generally increased, but trends in the amounts of water used vary by abstraction and fields of use, and the correlation with elevated environmental charges could not be established;
- the respondents stressed that, as compared to environmental charges, direct environmental requirements, which set the criteria for obtaining licenses and rates for fines, as well as the need to save resources for cost saving purposes, are far more powerful motivators.

Moreover, Arus (2016) suggests that the impact of pollution tax levels on pollutant emissions in Estonia varies. Based on the period 2008-13, Arus finds that air pollution charges as a whole have not led to a marked decrease in pollutant emissions, while the government received higher tax revenue. Quite the opposite rings true for the water pollution taxes: increasing tax rates have reduced pollutant emissions. Waste pollution charge rates have risen more slowly than the reduction in the quantities of waste, resulting in a decrease in pollution tax revenues to the public sector.

Overall tax impact on investment

When all taxes are taken into account, the total tax rate on profit is close to 50% in Estonia (Figure 4.15).[16] This high rate, which is close to that found in many OECD countries, is mainly due to labour taxes and social contributions. As a result, Estonia is 108th among 138 countries (World Economic Forum, 2016).

Respondents to the World Economic Forum Executive Opinion Survey 2016 (WEF, 2016) identify tax rates on profit as the most problematic factors for doing business in Estonia. As to the effect of taxation on the incentives to invest, Estonia was ranked 15th and the effect of taxation on incentives to work 47th among the 140 countries (WEF, 2015).

Figure 4.15. Total corporate tax rate as a percentage of profit, 2015

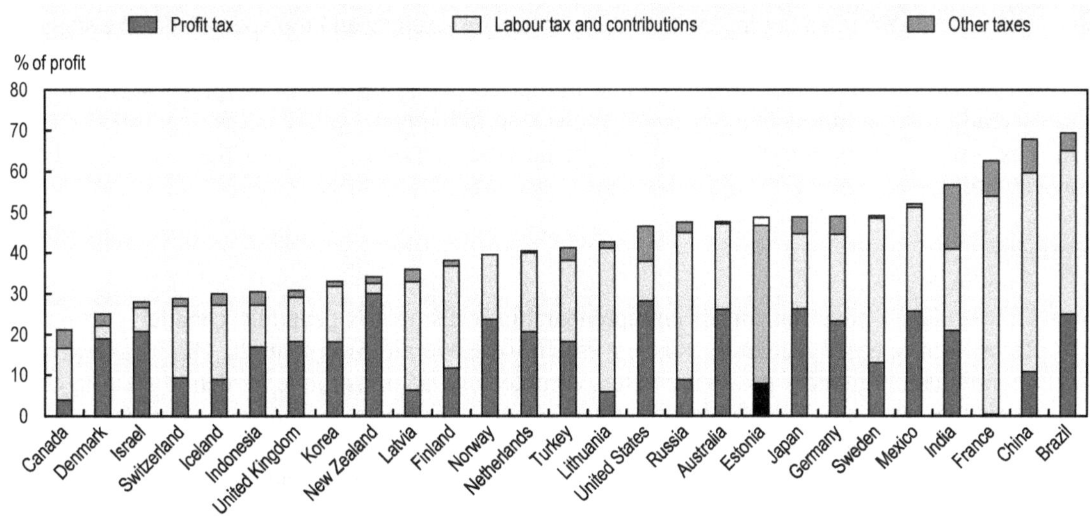

The evaluation uses a concept of a "case study company" defined on the basis of a set of criteria, including the legal form of business (limited liability), start date of operation (January 2012), geographic location (country's one or two largest business cities), origin of ownership (100% owned by domestic natural persons), type of activity (general industrial and commercial), size (own capital amount, number of employed, turnover, etc.). The total tax rate is the sum of taxes and contributions payable after accounting for allowable deductions and exceptions related to commercial profit of businesses before all taxes borne. The groups of taxes covered include: profit or corporate income tax; employer's social contributions and labour taxes; property taxes; turnover taxes and other (such as municipal fees and vehicle and fuel taxes).

Source: World Bank Group and PwC (2017), Paying Taxes 2017 - The Global Picture, PwC, World Bank and IFC, www.doingbusiness.org/data.

StatLink http://dx.doi.org/10.1787/888933654389

Tax incentives to support R&D

Estonia does not provide any tax rebates to research and development (R&D). In 2014 it was one of the two EU member states in this case, the other being Germany (OECD, 2014a). The Estonian tax system favours capital investments, but it stimulates the volumes of external funding and does not contribute to attracting higher value-added investments (innovation, knowledge-based and higher-productivity investments) to Estonia. Investments in intellectual property and creating 'smart jobs' still call for greater attention from the tax policy point of view (MEAC, 2014).

The creation of tax incentives for R&D has been discussed in Estonia for nearly a decade. An analysis of tax incentives to promote research and development in Estonia, conducted in 2009 by KPMG Baltics LLC, PRAXIS Centre for Policy Studies and Karsten Staehr (PhD) (2009), suggested to:

- Reduce the income tax rate for R&D employees to 10%.
- Reduce the social tax rate to 15% for R&D employees.

- Exempt from the social tax any monthly income in excess of either EUR 500, EUR 400 or EUR 300.

For the social tax, two possible alternatives were envisaged:

- Cap the social tax at EUR 1 000 in absolute value (meaning EUR 3 000 salary with 33% social tax rate) for imported R&D employees, who spend three years in Estonia. After three years, the social tax is 33%.
- Exempt any annual income in excess of double of the annual average wage (EUR 17 256).

Some of the suggestions are being discussed. For example, the exemption from the social tax of any monthly income in excess of EUR 500 is currently in the process for adoption. Teder (2014) pointed out that as the aim is to enhance knowledge-based Estonian economy, tax incentives could be applied for research intensive enterprises to ensure a net increase in salary to top researchers and top specialists. The suggested tax incentives included reducing the personal income tax and the social tax. With regard to tax breaks, the Minister of Finance (in 2014) was of the opinion that at corporate tax level enterprises were enjoying tax reductions already and the introduction of tax incentives on individuals would call for control exerted by the Estonian Tax and Customs Board to identify whether the activities fall into the category of research development or not.

4.5. Summary

- The regulatory environment for entrepreneurship in Estonia is generally conducive to investment. Reforms have eased regulatory barriers, which were overall lower than the OECD average in 2013. In particular, regulatory procedure is less complex and administrative burden to start-up companies lower than average. The regulatory protection of incumbents is among the highest in the OECD area. There is, however, still considerable room for improvement, in particular in licences and permits system, and the reduction of entry barriers in service and network sectors. (e.g. gas, electricity, water, rail, air passenger transport, road freight transport and telecoms).
- Regulations on natural resources and environment in Estonia are extensive, but fragmented across multiple legal acts. This is driven in part by the increase in legislative acts – in particular, the adoption of EU regulations – during and since EU accession. For example, these laws govern the environmental monitoring system, the integrated environmental permit system and environmental liability, as well as land use, water management and biodiversity protection. Estonian regulations on usage of organic fertilisers have become increasingly strict in recent years.
- Estonia also subscribes to major international and regional regulatory agreements concerning climate change and nature protection. Ensuring a clean living environment, raising the environmental awareness of the society, preservation of natural heritage and the sustainable use of natural resources is the main goal of many national and international environmental strategies, plans and agreements that Estonia has joined.
- Regulations on food safety and quality are mainly determined at the EU level and, since joining the European Union, Estonia has developed the necessary legislation and institutions to ensure compliance with regulations, including monitoring, control and information systems.
- EU support is conditional on the respect of regulations regarding natural resource use and protection, and the safety of food and feed products and farm inputs. This has required producers to adopt new technologies and production practices.
- Estonia is a small, open economy. Since joining the European Union in 2004, it is part of the EU single market. The common trade policy thus applies, which imposes higher tariff for capital and intermediate goods than in major EU trading partners. Trade facilitation could improve in some areas, such as advance rulings, formalities procedure and border agency cooperation. Estonia is

generally open to Foreign Direct Investment (FDI), with inwards stocks accounting for a relatively high share of GDP. Few restrictions remain, some concerning the acquisition of land.

- Financial markets are well developed, and a diversity of Banks offer services. The agriculture and food sector had access to loans to fund its development. It seems, however that credit institutions have imposed a higher risk margin on enterprises operating in the agricultural sector. The loan balance of agriculture has doubled in the past ten years, with growth slowing temporarily at the end of the 2000s. The state Rural Development Foundation facilitates access to credit to rural companies and farms, through guarantees, direct loans and loans to credit institutions. With EU co-financing, the Estonian Rural Development Plan (RDP) support investment in farm modernisation and the development of diversification activities, which receives a higher share of total funds than the EU average. In recent years, farmers have faced income problems, in particular in the dairy sector, leading to an increase in payment default.
- The government's goal is to shift the tax burden from income to consumption, use of natural resources and pollution of the environment. This is expected to foster investment, while improving sustainability. The government also envisages the possibility to impose excise duties on energy drinks.
- The government has so far attempted to keep the system simple and transparent with as few exceptions and differences as possible. As a result, there are few tax exemptions for the agriculture and food sector, including a tax deduction on the sales of self-produced unprocessed agricultural products. While some post-harvest activities are included, this provision may act as a disincentive to further on-farm processing.
- Two other general tax deductions may help farmers manage income risk and facilitate investment: the ability to deduct income losses in one year from the business income of the following seven taxation periods, and the option to save funds in a special account for future investment.
- Environmental taxes and charges have been increasing since 2005. They apply equally to food and agricultural activities. A lower excise duty applies to fuel used in agricultural activities (27% of the full rate, compared to an EU average of 6%). It increased in 2017 in the same proportion as the full rate, but will remain constant in 2018. Overall, the impact of environmental taxes has been varied.
- While the 20% income tax is relatively moderate by OECD standards, and thus favours investment, when all tax sources (income, property, labour, turnover, fuel) are taken into account, the tax rate is close to 50%, as in Germany and Sweden.
- Estonia is one of the very few OECD countries that do not provide tax incentives for R&D. The corporate tax system, where profits are not taxed until their distribution, acts as an economic tax incentive to investment.
- The new government that took office in November 2016 initiated several tax reforms. Some were implemented in 2017, others will be enforced in 2018. The main changes concern the introduction of progressivity in income tax, taxation of passenger cars owned by companies, and taxation of entrepreneurial income.

Notes

1. Estonian Entrepreneurship Growth Strategy for 2014-20, http://kasvustrateegia.mkm.ee/index_eng.html.
2. See list of state-owned companies at: www.eesti.ee/eng/contacts/riigi_osalusega_ariuhingud_2.
3. Vireen Ltd website: www.vireen.ee/Home_500.htm.
4. Estonian Livestock Performance Recording Ltd website: www.jkkeskus.ee/jkk/en.html.

5. Competition authority website: www.konkurentsiamet.ee/?lang=en.

6. Regulations for business in the web site of the Estonian Chamber of Commerce and Industry: www.koda.ee/en/services/business-environment/regulations-for-business/.

7. Defined as a harmonious and balanced management of natural resources.

8. International acts include the Council of Europe Convention on Civil Liability for environmental damage caused by hazardous activities and the European Union directive of the European Parliament and Council Directive 2004/35/EC on environmental liability for preventing and remedying of environmental damages. Estonian legal instruments include the Environmental Liability Act, the Additional List of habitat and species in the sense of the Environmental Liability Act and the risk of environmental damage and the list of data about the risk of environmental damage.

9. Water Act: www.riigiteataja.ee/en/eli/512012017001/ consolidated from 1994.

10. On the average of five consecutive years.

11. Fertilisation is currently not allowed from the 1 December to 20 March. From the 1st to the 30th of November, organic fertiliser application on fields with plant cover is only allowed if incorporated into soil within 48 hours. As of January 2021, liquid organic fertilisers must be injected into the soil after the 20th of September on fields with winter plant cover (RT I, 06.01.2016, 14).

12. See map of NVZ at: www.arcgis.com/home/item.html?id=e9addece02ad465181fca9a0fb47d62d.

13. For instance, at least 30% of arable land should have winter crop cover from 1 November to 31 March. Moreover, in areas with unprotected groundwater and a soil depth of up to 2 metres, and in karst funnel areas, spreading of nitrogen with mineral fertilisers can be limited to 100 kg per year per hectare of arable land; stocking density can be limited to 1.5 animal units per hectare and usage of waste water sediment can be restricted with the Order of Protection (RT I, 29.04.2014, 6). Furthermore, in areas surrounding springs and karst funnels, in a range of 50 metres from the boundary of the water or from the edge of a funnel, it is prohibited to use fertilisers, plant protection agents and to keep manure in a manure stack, if the Order of Protection will not state otherwise.

14. As of 1 September 2016 no enterprises have submitted the VFB any applications for entering the market with novel food and GM food and feedstuffs (ECCI, 2016).

15. The Restrictions on Acquisition of Immovables Act provides the restrictions on the acquisition of fixed assets used as profit yielding land arising from public interest and the restrictions on the acquisition of fixed assets arising from national security reasons.

16. This indicator includes the corporate income tax, the dividend tax, employer's social security contributions and labour taxes, property taxes, waste collection taxes, vehicle taxes, tolls and other taxes imposed on the model business in the second year of operation are taken into account towards calculating the total tax rate (%) of profit.

References

ARC (Agricultural Research Centre) (2016), http://pmk.agri.ee.

Arus, I. (2016), Saastetasumäärade dünaamika mõju saasteainete heitkogustele ning valitsussektori keskkonnamaksude laekumisele Eestis aastatel 2008-2013 [The Effect of the Dynamics of Pollution Charge Rates on the Emissions of Pollutants and Government Environmental Tax Collected in Estonia from 2008 to 2013], Eesti Maaülikool, bakalaureusetöö [Estonian University of Life Sciences, Bachelor's], https://dspace.emu.ee/xmlui/handle/10492/2733.

Bank of Estonia (2017), http://statistika.eestipank.ee/?lng=et#listMenu/1057/treeMenu/FINANTSSEKTOR/147/650 (accessed June 2017).

ECCI (Estonian Chamber of Commerce and Industry) (2016), Toiduseaduse ja söödaseaduse muutmise seaduseelnõu väljatöötamise kavatsus [Intent on a draft law amending the Food Act and Feedingstuffs Act], www.koda.ee/public/VTK.docx (accessed 1 November 2016).

EEIC (2015), Kaitstava territooriumi pindala Eestis 31.12.2015 seisuga [Area of protected territory as of 31.12.2015], http://loodus.keskkonnainfo.ee/avalik/el_fil/kaitstav_territ31122015.htm (accessed 4 June 2016).

EEIC (Estonian Environment Agency) (2013), Estonian Environmental Review 2013, www.keskkonnaagentuur.ee/et/review2013 (accessed 4 June 2016).

EELC (2016), Estonian Environmental Law Centre. www.k6k.ee/en (accessed 4 June 2016).

EU (2016), Food safety in the EU. – European Union (EU), https://europa.eu/european-union/topics/food-safety_en (accessed 7 October 2016).

Government Office (2014), National Reform Programme "ESTONIA 2020", https://riigikantselei.ee/sites/default/files/riigikantselei/strateegiaburoo/eesti2020/estonia_2020_nrp2014_en.pdf (accessed 28 January 2016).

Heinma, K. (2014), Saastetasud põllumajandussektoris [ECs in the agricultural sector], http://emu2014.lapub.ee/userfiles/TLTT2014/Kaupo_Heinma.pdf (accessed 31 May 2016).

KPMG Baltics AS, PRAXIS Center for Policy Studies, and Karsten Staehr (Ph.D) (2009), *An Analysis of Tax Incentives to Promote Research and Development,* www.mkm.ee/sites/default/files/ta-maksuuuring-2010-01.pdf (accessed 5 November 2016).

Koske, I., et al. (2015), "The 2013 update of the OECD's database on product market regulation: Policy insights for OECD and non-OECD countries", *OECD Economics Department Working Papers*, No. 1200, OECD Publishing, Paris, http://dx.doi.org/10.1787/5js3f5d3n2vl-en.

MEAC (2014), Made in Estonia 3.0, www.mkm.ee/sites/default/files/mie_3.0_english_version.pdf.

MoE (Ministry of the Environment) (2016a), Strategy and development, Ministry of the Environment, www.envir.ee/en/news-goals-activities/strategy-and-development (accessed 1 June 2016).

MoE (2016b), Management of the environment – Ministry of the Environment, www.envir.ee/en/management-environment (accessed 1 June 2016).

MoE (2016c), Põllumajandus ja veekaitse [Agriculture and Water Protection], www.envir.ee/et/nitraaditundlik-ala (accessed 4 June 2016)

MoE (2016d), Kliimapoliitika põhialused aastani 2050: Põllumajanduse valdkonna mõjude hindamine [Climate Policy Fundamentals for 2050: The agricultural area of impact assessment], http://envir.ee/sites/default/files/kpp_pillumajanduse_mijude_hindamise_seletuskiri_18.03.pdf (accessed 9 April 2016).

MoE (2012), Looduskaitse arengukava aastani 2020 [Nature Conservation Development Plan 2020], www.envir.ee/sites/default/files/lak_lop.pdf (accessed 4 June 2016).

MoF (Ministry of Finance) (2017), www.rahandusministeerium.ee/et/maksu-ja-tollipoliitika/aktsiisid.

MRA (2016a), Food safety, www.agri.ee/en/objectives-activities/food-safety.

MRA (2016b), Organic farming, www.agri.ee/en/objectives-activities/organic-farming.

MRA (2016c), Research, development and advice, www.agri.ee/en/objectives-activities/research-development-and-advice.

OECD (2017a), *OECD Environmental Performance Reviews: Estonia 2017*, OECD Publishing, Paris, http://dx.doi.org/10.1787/9789264268241-en.

OECD (2017b), *Trade Facilitation Indicators.* www.oecd.org/trade/facilitation/indicators.htm (accessed July 2017).

OECD (2017c), "OECD FDI Regulatory Restrictiveness Index", *OECD FDI Statistics (database)*, www.oecd.org/investment/fdiindex.htm (accessed June 2017).

OECD (2017d), International Direct Investment Statistics, http://dotstat.oecd.org/?lang=en (accessed 3 July 2017).

OECD (2017e), Tax Database, www.oecd.org/tax/tax-policy/tax-database.htm (accessed June 2017).

OECD (2017f), Green Growth Indicators, http://dotstat.oecd.org/?lang=en (accessed October 2017).

OECD (2015), "Analysing Policies to improve agricultural productivity growth, sustainably: Revised framework", www.oecd.org/tad/agricultural-policies/Analysing-policies-improve-agricultural-productivity-growth-sustainably-december-2014.pdf.

OECD (2014a), Product Market Regulation Database, 2014, www.oecd.org/economy/pmr.

OECD (2014b), Measuring Tax Support for R&D and Innovation, www.oecd.org/sti/rd-tax-incentive-indicators.htm (accessed 13 March 2017).

OECD (2011), *Enhancing market openness, intellectual property rights, and compliance through regulatory reform in Estonia*, OECD, www.oecd.org/tad/tradedev/48262981.pdf.

RT I, 06.01.2016, 14. Veeseadus. www.riigiteataja.ee/akt/VeeS, www.riigiteataja.ee/akt/126042016006 (accessed 3 June 2016).

RT I, 03.12.2015, 7. Tööstusheite seadus [Industrial Emission Law], www.riigiteataja.ee/akt/103122015007 (accessed 9 June 2016).

RT I, 17.12.2015, 44, Keskkonnatasude seadus [Environmental Charges Act], www.riigiteataja.ee/akt/117122015044 (accessed 2 June 2016).

RT I, 11.06.2013, 19. Alltegevusvaldkondade loetelu ning künnisvõimsused, mille korral on käitise tegevuse jaoks nõutav kompleksluba [Subactivities the list of threshold values, which are required for the operation of an installation integrated permit], www.riigiteataja.ee/akt/111062013019 (accessed 6 June 2016).

Rural Development Foundation (2017), www.mes.ee.

SAFE (2015), Survey on the access to finance of enterprises (SAFE) Analytical Report 2015, www.ecb.europa.eu/stats/ecb_surveys/safe/html/index.en.html.

Statistics Estonia (2016), Online statistical database: www.stat.ee (accessed 11 February 2016).

Sustainable Estonia Institute (2013), *Environmental Charges Impact Analysis*, Stockholm Environment Institute Tallinn Centre in collaboration with the Centre for Applied Social Sciences (CASS) of the University of Tartu.

Teder, A. (2014), Eesti vajab maksusüsteemi muutust [Estonia's tax system needs change], http://arvamus.postimees.ee/2815252/allan-teder-eesti-vajab-maksususteemi-muutust (accessed 5 November 2016).

Varblane, U. and K. Toming (2002), "The Impact of EU-Accession on the Estonian Trade with Food Products — Partial Equilibrium Approach", *The 10th Annual International Conference Business and Economic Development in Central and Eastern Europe: Implications for Economic Integration into Wider Europe*, Brno, pp. 485–490.

VFB (2016), Veterinary and Food Board, www.vet.agri.ee/?op=body&id=315 (accessed 20 May 2016).

World Bank (2017), *Doing Business 2017: Measuring Regulatory Quality and Efficiency*, www.doingbusiness.org/.

World Bank Group and PwC (2017), *Paying Taxes 2017 - The Global Picture*, PwC, World Bank and IFC. www.doingbusiness.org/data.

World Economic Forum (2016), *The Global Competitiveness Report 2016-2017: Full data Edition*, Geneva, http://reports.weforum.org/global-competitiveness-index/.

World Economic Forum (2015), *The Global Competitiveness Report 201-2016: Full data Edition*, Geneva, http://www3.weforum.org/docs/gcr/2015-2016/Global_Competitiveness_Report_2015-2016.pdf.

WHO (2015), Toiduohutus WHO Euroopa regioonis. Faktileht – World Health Organisation (WHO). [online] http://ee.euro.who.int/2015WHD_Faktileht.pdf (accessed 7 October 2016)

WITS (2017), World Integrated Trade Solution, http://wits.worldbank.org/.

Annex 4.A1. Background table

Table 4.A1.1. The indicators of the Estonian Nature Conservation Development Plan 2020

Indicators	Base level in 2011	Target level by 2020
Goal 1. People are familiar with, appreciate and conserve nature and know how use their knowledge in their everyday lives.		
Percentage of people in Estonia who regard their daily behaviour as environmentally aware	22%	35%
Number of nature education programmes taught in schools and nursery schools	270	340
Number of people who have completed an environmental education programme	133 000	Level achieved: 145 000 by 2014 and 175 000 by 2020
Number of disciplines incorporated into a conservation research programme	0	6
Number of visitors to nature trails	1.55 million	1.75 million
Goal 2. The favourable conservation status of species and habitats and diversity of landscapes is ensured, habitats function as a coherent ecological network.		
Number of species of the Habitats Directive with improved conservation status	Favourable status: 23, Inadequate status: 41, Bad status: 7, Unknown status: 25 species	The conservation status of 28 species has improved, the status of all species is known
Percentage of species in a good conservation status among the species of the Birds Directive	65%	80%
Number of species with appropriate conservation guidelines	45	155
Number of new invasive alien species in Estonia per year	2...3	0...1
Area of maintained semi-natural communities	25 000 ha	45 000 ha
Percentage of strictly protected typologically representative forests in total forest land	8.7%	10%
Area of mire communities with a restored natural water regime	100 ha	10 000 ha
Number of habitat types endangered at the European level whose conservation status has improved	Favourable status: 25, Inadequate status: 21, Bad status: 9, Unknown status: 5 habitat types	Conservation status of 14 habitat types (incl. their ecological coherence) has improved, the status assessment of all habitat types is known
Number of monitored species and habitat types	Monitored species of the Habitats Directive: 74, Monitored species of the Birds Directive: 120, Monitored habitat types: 26, Monitored Category I species: 54	Monitored species of the Habitats Directive: 96, Monitored species of the Birds Directive: 221, Monitored habitat types: 60, All Category I species are being monitored
Number of indicator species indicating the coherence of the ecological network	0	15
Goal 3. Long-term sustainability of natural resources, and the preconditions for this, are ensured and the principles of the ecosystem approach are followed in the use of natural resources.		
Number of habitat type groups (mires, forests, meadows, etc.) whose ecosystem services have been assessed	0	6
Area of rehabilitated cut-over peatlands	0 ha	1 000 ha
Size of selected game populations	Wolf: 200, Lynx: 700	Wolf: 200, Lynx: 700
Share of fish stocks in a good status in the total stocks of economically important fish species	41%	60%
Number of functioning ecoducts and small game tunnels	Ecoducts: 0, Small game tunnels: 10	Ecoducts: 4, Small game tunnels: 20

Source: MoE (2012), www.envir.ee/sites/default/files/lak_lop.pdf.

Chapter 5

Capacity building and public services in Estonia

Capacity building, including provision of essential public services, is one of the main channels or incentive areas to support innovation and sustainable development. This chapter concerns three relevant policy areas: infrastructure and rural development policy; labour market policy; and education and skills policy.

5.1. Infrastructure and rural development policy

Investments in physical and knowledge infrastructures, from Information and Communications Technology (ICT) to transportation facilities, are important for overall growth and development. They are vital to the delivery of, and access to, important services and play a critical role in linking farmers and related businesses to markets, reducing food waste, boosting agriculture productivity, raising profits, and encouraging investment in innovative techniques and products. Productive and profitable enterprises may have higher incentives to invest in sustainable practices that yield long-term benefits.

Broader rural development measures also affect sustainable agricultural development and structural adjustment. Increased off-farm income and employment opportunities mitigate farm household income risks, facilitate farm investment, and enable a wider range of farm production choices. Improved rural services, from banking to ICT, are important to ensure needed connectivity to suppliers, customers, and collaborators. Rural policy can also attract innovative upstream and downstream industries, with possible spill-over effects locally. By reducing inequalities in economic development and access to services across regions, rural development policies improve the diffusion of innovation (OECD, 2015).

In a country like Estonia, where the density of population is low and the population is concentrated in main urban centres, the provision of infrastructure and services presents specific challenges. In remote rural areas with sparse population in particular, connecting people to markets and providing information and services requires innovative solutions.

Quality of physical infrastructure

According to the World Economic Forum's Global Competitiveness Report (WEF, 2016), the business community considers the quality of the overall transport infrastructure in Estonia close to the average of OECD countries (Figure 5.1.A). There are, however, large differences between means of transport and within each transport network. The quality of the port infrastructure ranks highest, with a quality close to the OECD top 5 average. But the quality of railroad and air transport infrastructures ranks very low. The small number of connections between Estonia and Europe and other continents, as well as the constantly varying destinations, possibly explain the low score of the air transport infrastructure. While the impact on the Estonian agri-food sector is likely to be limited, better international connections could help strengthen international business with other continents, including in the agri-food sector, and raise awareness of Estonian products abroad.

Rail transport also suffers from the scarcity of international connections and the limited speed of passenger train traffic. While most main-line railways have been upgraded to enable passenger trains to run at up to 120 kilometres per hour (km/h), the renovation is still incomplete with some sections remaining where trains cannot go faster than 80 or 100 km/h. The situation is, however, improving gradually. Although passenger trains purchased in 2013 can reach up to 160 km/h, the current railway infrastructure in Estonia is not ready for such high speeds (MEAC, 2013a). Higher speed would reduce travel times and shorten the distance between rural regions and consumers or tourists. Higher capacity would be needed to respond to the growing number of passengers on some lines, such as Tallinn-Tartu. However, the fleet of trains is currently too small to increase the frequency of trains or the number of carriages per train, when needed. More frequent and faster trains would increase opportunities for diversified marketing of agri-food products and tourism activities.

The business community considers the overall road infrastructure in Estonia to be below the OECD average, reflecting problems with the availability and quality of infrastructure, especially in rural areas. A 2013 government report on a road network development plan for 2014-2020 (MEAC, 2013a) acknowledges that while main roads are mostly in a good or very good condition, basic roads in a satisfactory condition, the secondary and local roads are in a rather poor condition. In 2015, 68.2% of the national roads (main, basic and secondary roads) were paved (Road Administration, 2016). The rest of the state roads are gravel or earth roads. Local roads (except streets) are mostly unpaved, or light-surfaced roads (MEAC, 2013a). The low quality of roads is related to the scarcity of funding.

The business community considers the overall electricity and telephony infrastructure in Estonia to be among the OECD average, but very unequal across components (Figure 5.1.B). On the one hand, with 1.6 mobile telephone subscriptions per person, Estonia has the highest score in the OECD area. Internet use is relatively widespread: 80% of individuals use internet, compared to 81% in high income OECD countries. On the other hand, the number of fixed telephone lines per inhabitant is below the OECD average, and the quality of electricity supply ranks below the OECD average, although it enjoys a relatively high score.

Figure 5.1. Global Competitiveness Index: Quality of infrastructure, 2016-17

Scale 1 to 7 (best)

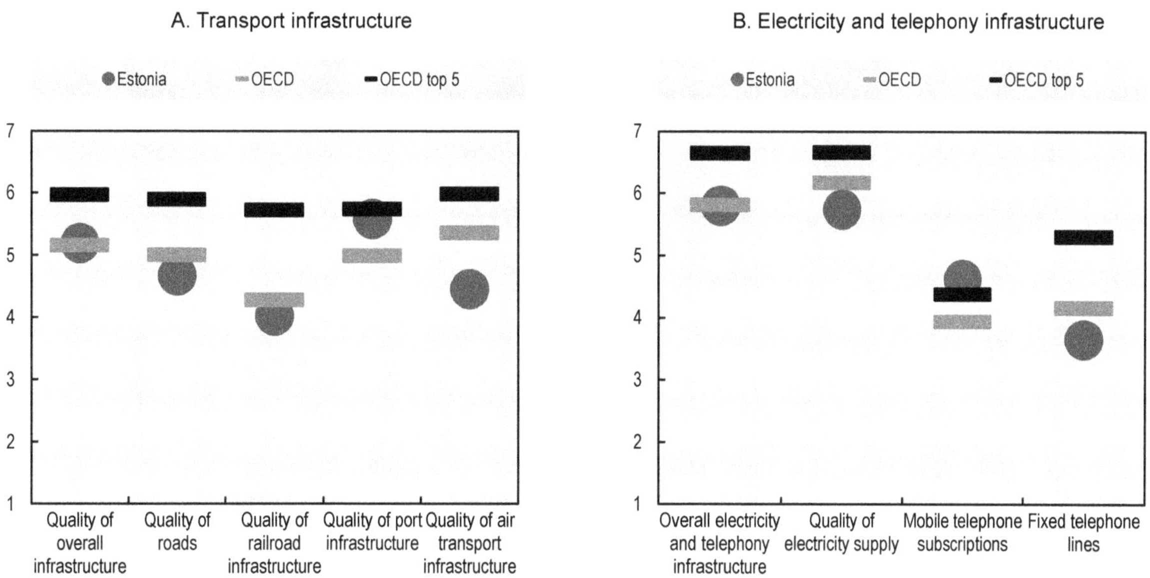

OECD top 5 refers to the average of the scores for the top 5 performers among OECD countries (Netherlands, Japan, France, United States and Germany).

The OECD index is the simple average of member-country indices.

OECD top 5 refers to the average of the scores for the top 5 performers among OECD countries (Switzerland, Luxembourg, Austria, United Kingdom and Japan).

Source: World Economic Forum (2016), *The Global Competitiveness Report 2016-2017: Full data Edition*, Geneva 2016. http://reports.weforum.org/global-competitiveness-index/.

StatLink http://dx.doi.org/10.1787/888933654408

Almost all companies use computers and almost all have broadband Internet connection (Figure 5.2). In 2005, the share of companies using computers and broadband Internet access in the agricultural sector was slightly lower than in other sectors, but by 2016 these differences became non-existent. In the manufacturing industry (including the food industry), the use of computers and fixed broadband access has always been higher than the average of all sectors. In 2016, 79% of agricultural enterprises had Digital Subscriber Line (DSL) technology (ADSL, SDSL, etc.) installed, which enables to provide high-speed internet services over a telephone line. Almost 45% of agricultural enterprises had available a rate of information transfer of 10-30 Megabits per second (Mbit/s), and about 40% a rate of up to 10 Mbit/s. The websites of agricultural enterprises included product catalogues or price lists (99%), as well as information about job vacancies (17%), and links or references to the company's social media profile (15%).

Figure 5.2. Share of companies with computers and a broadband Internet connection, 2005 and 2016

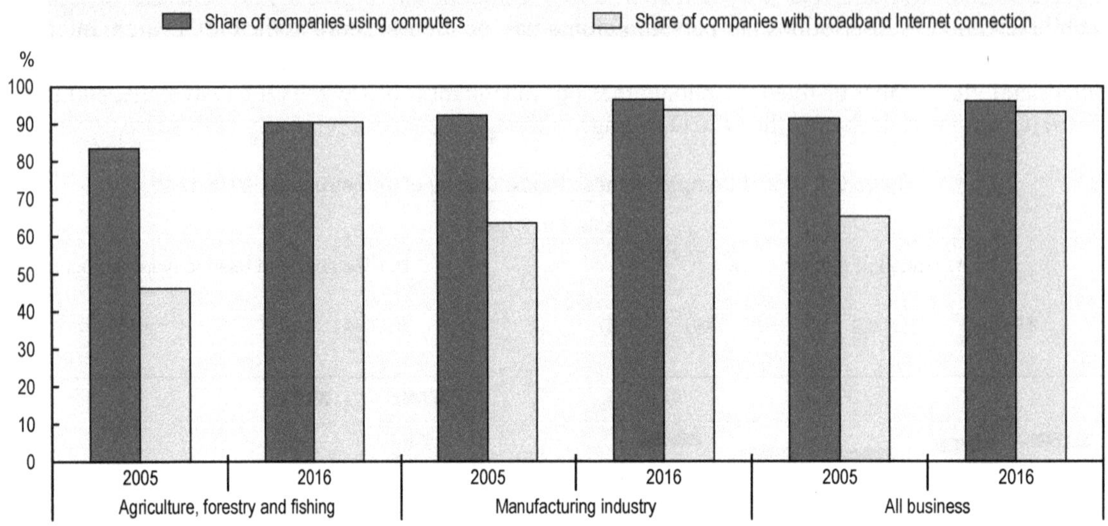

Source: Statistics Estonia (2017), [IT004], www.stat.ee/en.

StatLink http://dx.doi.org/10.1787/888933654427

Since 2010, Estonia has been rapidly developing the basic broadband infrastructure (passive optical network) with EU support with a view that around 98% of residences and businesses are within 1.5 km of the nearest connection point (MEAC, 2013a). By winter 2017, 4 162 km of EstWin broadband network had been installed (ELASA, 2017). This has contributed to the development of 4G Internet and will support the development of 5G Internet in the future. However, the development of basic broadband infrastructure has not significantly increased the number of users. In Estonia, people are using fast and ultra-fast Internet through fixed network. The problem is that communications operators do not have an economic interest in developing local high-speed broadband access for all end users. In order to achieve broader access, the government plan was to develop a Network based on contemporary fibre optic cables connecting the broadband network to the end users in sparsely populated areas with a limited number of end users (see funding section). As of autumn 2016, only 10% of the fibre optic capacity of basic broadband infrastructure was exploited (it is possible to use Optical Carrier (OC)24 or OC48 throughout the entire passive optical network). Telecommunications companies investing in the development of mobile Internet and offering their clients 4G Internet have benefited the most from the development of the basic broadband network. It is not an equivalent replacement for cable connections, but has still offered a partial solution to the problem (National Audit Office, 2014).

ICT development and everyday use of ICT technology have enabled most farmers and food processors to have very good access to information concerning market developments, technological options and weather forecasts. For example, one of the services on offer is field-based weather forecast, which enables the farmers to plan their fieldwork according to the weather conditions and thus increase their operational efficiency (Vitalfields). Farmers also receive a lot of information (on the equipment, technology, etc.) from vendors and distributors. Information on market developments can be obtained from seminars and panels organised by producer organisations. Improving broadband Internet services in remote areas would provide local farmers and agri-food companies with better access to inputs, technologies, advice, and consumers, allowing them to take advantage of market opportunities.

The electricity and gas supply interconnections in Estonia are, first and foremost, linked with the connections with the Russian Federation, other Baltic countries and Finland (only electrical connection). Connections with the other EU member states are not available (MEAC, 2013a). There are no nuclear power plants in Estonia, and 85% of the electricity is produced from oil shale. Some small islands like Ruhnu and Naissaare are not connected to the electricity grid, and rely on off-grid solutions such as a renewable power plant, a storage battery and an inverter that changes the direct current (DC) power to alternative current (AC) energy. The electricity network company is considering expanding the same solution to sparsely populated areas to reduce costs (Timm, 2016). In this context, agricultural land and activities may provide viable opportunities for generating electricity and energy, such as windmills.

While rural users consider the condition of local roads to be the main deficiency of rural infrastructure, rural entrepreneurs and local authorities also consider the electricity supply to be inadequate and that capacity needs upgrading (Box 5.1).

Box 5.1. Technical infrastructure through the eyes of rural entrepreneurs and local authorities

A well-developed infrastructure in rural areas helps to compensate for the distance between rural areas and major attraction centres. Entrepreneurs consider the availability (with sufficient capacity) and fault tolerance of the energy, availability and quality (speed) of communications infrastructure, water quality and the state of the roads, the most essential factors of the business environment.

The condition of infrastructure in rural areas of Estonia varies considerably. Entrepreneurs rank the condition of local roads as the worst of the technical infrastructure elements. The representatives of the processing industry estimated the condition of roads to be better than the entrepreneurs from the primary sector.

According to local authorities, the biggest problem is the poor technical quality of the electricity supply network and the excessive pricing of grid connection and electricity capacity upgrading. The state of the roads and the availability of adequate electric power supply was rated the worst by the entrepreneurs in South Estonia.

Source: EMÜ (2012), The study, "The situation of rural enterprises, their development trends and the need to support", Final report, Tartu.

Regarding agricultural-specific infrastructure, land improvement directly affects farm productivity and sustainability. Estonia is located in a temperate climate zone, where the amount of precipitation significantly exceeds total evaporation. Humid climate, flat terrain, unevenly distributed natural hydrological network and soils with poor permeability contribute to widespread paludification. As a result, land needs to be drained to improve productivity and 55% of the utilised agricultural area (UAA) is covered by land drainage systems. Most of the drainage systems are over thirty years old and need reconstruction. In 2005, 26% of the draining systems were in poor condition. EU support for investment in land improvements received over the period 2004-13 allowed the reconstruction of about 15%, and the renovation of about 25%, of the drainage systems in need of repair on agricultural land. Support for the reconstruction and renewal of land drainage systems is continued over the programming period 2014-20. According to the Register of Land Improvement Systems, irrigated areas make up 0.03% of the total agricultural land in Estonia. The construction of combined drainage irrigation systems (double-duty systems) is gaining more and more popularity. Such systems secure a sufficient amount of water for plants in dry periods, ensuring at the same time that water is not wasted (MRA, 2016a). They are thus expected to further improve productivity of agriculture, sustainably.

Priorities for infrastructure development

The priorities for the development of infrastructure are reflected in a number of development documents, for which the preparation and implementation is primarily the responsibility of the MEAC. All documents are, to a greater or lesser extent, related to the development of agricultural and food sectors. The development and reconstruction of the technical infrastructure in Estonia are carried out in line with the environmental legislation, and development plans pursue both efficiency and environmental sustainability. As summarised in Box 5.2, infrastructure development plans aim to respond to identified needs such as the improvement of secondary roads, more reliable and diversified energy sources, and more operational ICT connections reaching end-users. Development plans for energy in particular offer opportunities for agriculture to contribute to renewable energy supply and use.

Box 5.2. Estonian priorities for infrastructure development

The **Estonian Transport Development Plan 2014-20**, adopted in 2013, highlights efficiency and environmental sustainability. It emphasises the maintenance of the conditions of main roads and the improvement of secondary and side roads (including paving all major state gravel roads, where frequency exceeds 50 cars a day, by 2030). Reducing car use in towns, increasing the number of train connections and train speed, increasing traffic safety, and raising the share of economic vehicles and cars running on renewable energy are considered as the highest priorities. The main alternative type of fuel would include biomethane produced from domestic waste or biomass, and compressed gas (MEAC, 2016).

Digital Agenda 2020 for Estonia is the key instrument in the field of ICT. The development plan provides guidance for creating a well-operating national ICT environment. The main goals include an ICT structure that fosters economic growth, national development and the welfare of its population, increased number of jobs with higher added value, improved international competitiveness and a higher quality of life, smarter governance and increased awareness of e-governance in the world (MEAC, 2013b).

The **Estonian National Development Plan of the Energy Sector Until 2020** was established to guide the development of agricultural and food sector as well as other sectors. The principal goal of the Plan is to make energy production more environmentally-friendly and the energy portfolio more diversified (MEAC, 2013c). The Plan includes the **Estonian National Renewable Energy Action Plan Until 2020**, which endeavours to reach a level where the energy produced from renewable energy sources would account for 25% of the gross final energy consumption (MEAC, 2010). The same document contains measures that are aimed at increasing biomass availability, taking into account other biomass users (including agriculture).

The **Estonian Energy Sector Development Plan Until 2018** is linked to the Energy Sector National Development Plan and its objective is to ensure a consistent and sustainable supply of electricity at a justified price in Estonia. At present, the MEAC is working on the elaboration of a new Estonian National Development Plan of the Energy Sector Until 2030, which is aimed at ensuring an energy supply that is available to consumers at a reasonable price and effort, with an acceptable environmental impact, while observing the terms and conditions established in the long-term energy and climate policy of the EU. The most beneficial economic competitiveness aspects must be observed for the purposes of the implementation of the National Development Plan of the Energy Sector Until 2030. The new plan also drafts the benchmarks for renewable energy, energy efficiency operational programmes and the vision for the renovation of buildings (MEAC, 2016).

Funding of infrastructure development

Infrastructure development in Estonia relies heavily on EU funding. Since joining the European Union, the following EU Structural Funds have contributed to the development of transport infrastructure:

- The Cohesion Fund (CF) is used to finance major transport and environmental infrastructure projects that cost over EUR 10 million. In the transport sector, grants covering up to 85% of the total project costs are available for roads, which belong to the pan-European transport network TEN-T (Road Administration, 2016).
- The European Regional Development Fund (ERDF) supports infrastructure projects that contribute significantly to innovation, telecommunications, environment, energy economy and transport (EUSAE, 2016). In infrastructure projects, the EU contribution rate is 75% of the project cost, plus 25% of the national co-financing.

In Estonia, PPPs are generally not used for road construction. An analysis of the application of PPP in road construction, conducted in 2011, concluded that considering the size of Estonia, it is cheaper for the government to invest in road construction directly than do it within the framework of PPP.

Energy operators are granted support for the application of renewable energy sources on the basis of the Electricity Market Act, liquid fuel producers on the basis of the Alcohol, Tobacco, Fuel and Electricity Excise Duty Act, and in district heating economy from the ERDF, as well as from other sources. Electricity infrastructure is financed from electricity transmission fees or tariffs (MEAC, 2010).

During the period 2012-20 investments in port infrastructure are expected to account for more than half of the total cost of maritime activities (EUR 534 million). The investments are co-financed by EU funds, including the European Maritime and Fisheries Fund (MEAC, 2012).

High-speed broadband access and greater usability is supported by the ERDF, the European Agricultural Fund for Rural Development (EAFRD), and by the state, in areas such as South Estonia where the construction of access networks to broadband telecommunications network is not profitable for operators.

The Estonian Rural Development Programme (RDP) 2014-20 allows funding access to broadband telecommunications networks. Such investments are eligible in the framework of the LEADER programme and other investment measures targeted at agricultural producers and food processers. As part of different *ad hoc* investments, the Estonian RDP 2014-20 can also be used to fund electric, water supply and sewerage systems and connect users to these systems. In the case of investment measures targeted at agricultural producers and food processers, investments are eligible expenses (MRA, 2016a).

Cost and management of services

Regarding transport infrastructure, road use is free of charge in Estonia. Different levels of government are responsible for road construction and maintenance depending on the type of road. Rail users pay when they use the service. A state company manages the services and the development of railways infrastructure.

Electricity is primarily distributed by one network operator, whose operations and service costs are under the state control (Electricity Distribution, 2016). Fees for the connection to the electricity network for business customers depend largely on the chosen amperage and on the distance of the consumption point from the nearest substation. The results of the survey have shown that the most problematic issue for companies in rural areas is the electricity network connection fee and the high cost for increasing the capacity. Local authorities believe this cost can become a major obstacle to the development of companies (Box 5.1). Natural gas is mainly consumed by industrial companies and distributed by a distribution system operator, whose activities and service fees (including connection fees) are under the state control.

The operations of public water and sanitation service suppliers are managed at the municipal level. Connection fees to the public water supply and sewerage systems are established by the local council that has the power to impose a capping rate on the connection fee. The water company is responsible for calculating the connection fee to public water and sewerage systems. Service suppliers may also offer a connection to the systems at a preferential rate if the construction and restoration of these systems has been funded by the EU Cohesion Fund.

Public services in rural areas

Estonia is highly urbanised: 63% of the population lives in urban areas, of which 40% is concentrated in the capital city and its suburbs. This has led to growing regional imbalance with public and private services aggregated around regional centres, while accessibility to rural areas and services in rural municipality and county centres worsened. At the same time, with the spread of Internet, the improvement of computer skills and the development of public e-services, the volume of some public services has decreased.

Estonia stands out for the use of electronic ID, which can make administration practically paper free, fast and flexible. The development of the e-government, especially the elaboration of e-services for the public sector and their application by citizens and enterprises has so far been the strength of the national ICT policy. It includes distributed services-based architecture, web-based/online services, and orientation towards e-services. The basic or service infrastructure of the state information system (X-way, public key infrastructure, e-ID, document exchange centre, information gateway eesti.ee) has over the years supported the development of public services quickly and flexibly through ICT solutions (MEAC, 2013a). This has the potential to reduce the rural-urban gap and increase the accessibility of e-services for both the residents and entrepreneurs in rural areas, but as noted above, problems remain with modern Internet connection in sparsely populated rural areas and Digital Agenda 2020 aims to tackle this market failure.

Non-governmental organisations (NGOs) and local authorities in Estonia co-operate to offer public services to the population. The public services most delegated to the NGOs are in the fields of culture, leisure, sports and the promotion of regional life (Uus et al., 2014). It is a new phenomenon in rural areas for community members to offer community services for a nominal charge.

5.2. Labour market policy

Labour market policy influences employment composition and labour mobility, in particular by facilitating (or discouraging) labour to adapt to new circumstances. It can play an important role in facilitating structural adjustment, including farm consolidation, by assisting excess labour in farming to exploit more remunerative non-farm income and employment opportunities. Policies on skills improvement and on international mobility of human resources can also help to better match labour supply with demand, and can affect innovation and knowledge transfer through exchange of skills and skilled labour. Structural adjustment allowing younger and better educated farmers to enter the sector, and skills improvement policies are expected to improve the adoption of sustainable practices (OECD, 2015).

Labour market legislation

Estonia is the only Baltic state, where employment protection was significantly relaxed in the last decade. The 2009 Employment Contracts Act (Soosaar, 2015) aimed to increase employment flexibility, with labour regulation allowing the parties to agree on the conditions of industrial relations that would recognise the needs and interests of the contracting parties in the best possible way. At the same time, the act aimed to ensure the protection of the social partners by laying down the minimum conditions. The implementation of the 2009 Act allowed employers to cut salaries or leave them unchanged in the changing economic environment, which supports the view that wages are flexible (Masso et al., 2013).

The new law allows employers to manage the risks associated with the costs of training staff by concluding an agreement for the reimbursement of training expenditure. According to statistics, the proportion of employees involved in formal education and professional training has, however, not changed in conjunction with the changes in business environment after the adoption of the Act. The Act also reorganised the regulation of working time with the purpose of protecting the workers' health. However, the proportion of employees working overtime, as well as the average amount of weekly overtime, has remained the same.

Figure 5.3. OECD Indicators of Employment Protection Legislation, 2013

Index from 0 (least) to 6 (most) restrictive

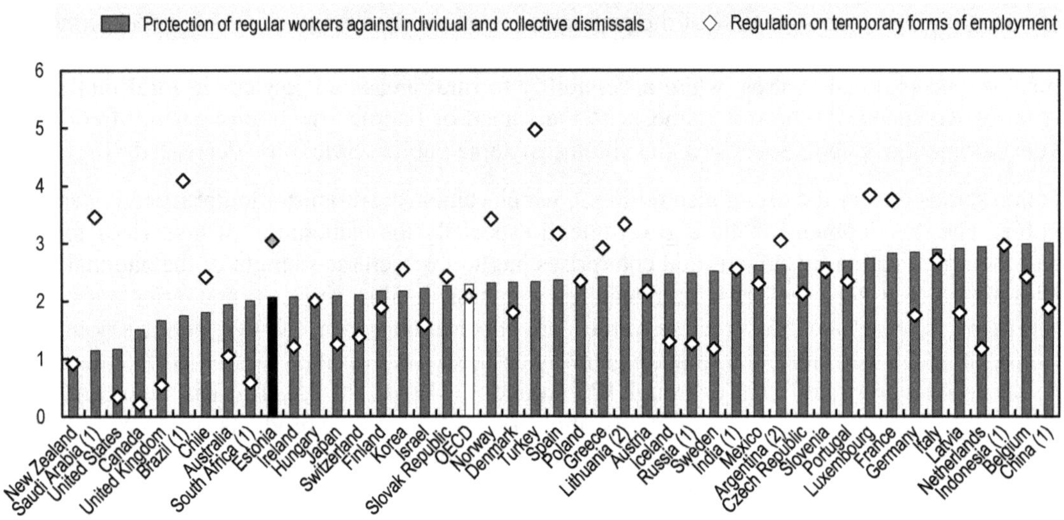

Countries are ranked according to "Protection of regular workers against individual and collective dismissals" levels.

1. Data for Brazil, China, India, Indonesia, Russian Federation, Saudi Arabia and South Africa refer to year 2012.
2. Data for Argentina and Lithuania refer to year 2014.

Source: OECD (2016a), Employment Protection Database. www.oecd.org/employment/protection.

StatLink http://dx.doi.org/10.1787/888933654446

While Estonian legislation does not overly protect regular workers against dismissal compared to the OECD average, the regulation on temporary forms of employment is one of the most protective in Europe, after Luxembourg, France, Spain and Lithuania (Figure 5.3). Among Estonia's neighbours, the regulations in Finland, Sweden and Latvia give much more flexibility to employers regarding temporary forms of employment, thus facilitating the use of seasonal labour much needed in agriculture.

Labour market efficiency

Most employers in Estonia see the labour market as flexible. In spring 2014, the Bank of Estonia and TNS Emor carried out a survey of Estonian employers on how Estonia adjusts to economic changes in comparison to other countries, how flexible is wage-setting in Estonia, and what is the effect of the major labour market reforms passed during the crisis. One of the objectives of the survey was to identify the barriers to the recruitment of new employees. The biggest barrier to recruitment was the shortage of qualified labour, which was considered serious by 90% of the employers. High labour taxes and high wages were also considered as significant obstacles to recruitment. But only 36% of employers considered the costs of firing and hiring to be a barrier (Soosaar, 2015).

According to the WEF Global Competitiveness Index, business leaders rank the Estonian labour market among the most efficient of OECD countries, below the United States, Canada or Norway, but slightly above Sweden and the Netherlands (Figure 5.4A). This overall evaluation hides differences in performance by components of labour market efficiency (Figure 5.4B). In summary, the Estonian labour market stands out primarily by the flexibility of wage determination and employment practices, and a high proportion of women in the labour market. The main weakness is the low capacity to retain and attract talents, which has social consequences and affects the long-term competitiveness of the economy. The extent to which taxation reduces the incentive to work is considered as lower than the OECD average, but the Estonian score is low, indicating the effect is significant.

Figure 5.4. Global Competitiveness Index: Labour market efficiency, 2016-17

Scale 1 to 7 (best)

A. Total Index of labour market efficiency, by country

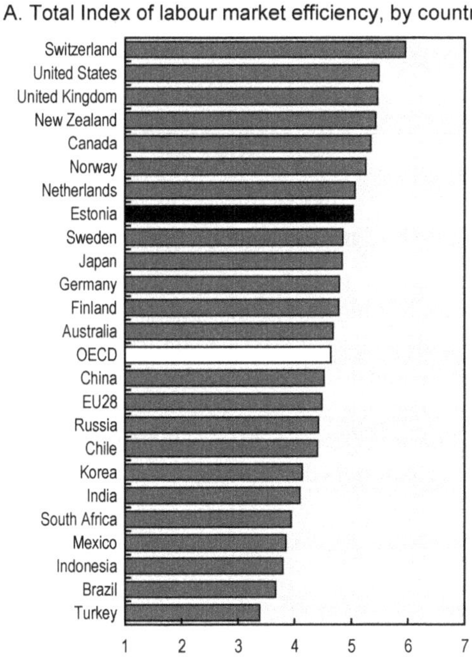

B. Estonia's Index of labour market efficiency by component

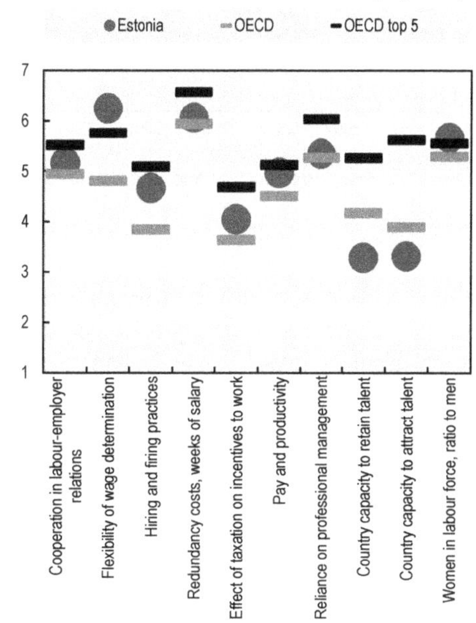

Indices for EU28 and OECD are the simple average of member-country indices.

OECD top 5 refers to the average of the scores for the top 5 performers among OECD countries (Switzerland, United States, United Kingdom, New Zealand and Canada).

Source: World Economic Forum (2016), *The Global Competitiveness Report 2016-2017: Full data Edition*, Geneva 2016. http://reports.weforum.org/global-competitiveness-index/.

StatLink http://dx.doi.org/10.1787/888933654465

Business leaders consider the extent to which labour costs are related to productivity is slightly above the OECD average, but as the pressure on salaries is growing rapidly, and wages have increased faster than productivity, this indicator is expected to deteriorate in the future. If labour productivity does not increase as fast, the competitiveness of companies decreases and economic growth slows down (Mertsina and Jänes, 2012). A sharp increase in the unit labour cost may create unemployment as companies absorb high unit costs by reducing the number of staff. At the same time, while cheap labour attracts new companies, it does not provide incentives to technology-intensive investments and the creation of smart jobs, and may delay innovation.

Estonia's unit labour costs[1] more than tripled since 2000, with a sharp increase over the period 2006-08, reflecting the overall rapid growth of the economy. Unit labour costs in Estonia have increased faster than labour productivity during the period 2012-16 (Figure 5.5). The decrease in labour productivity, however, is related to labour in Estonia being cheaper than in neighbouring countries. Box 5.3 illustrates developments in unit labour costs and labour productivity in Estonia and partner countries since 2000.

Figure 5.5. Annual change in labour productivity and unit labour costs in Estonia, 2001 to 2016

% change in real terms compared to previous year

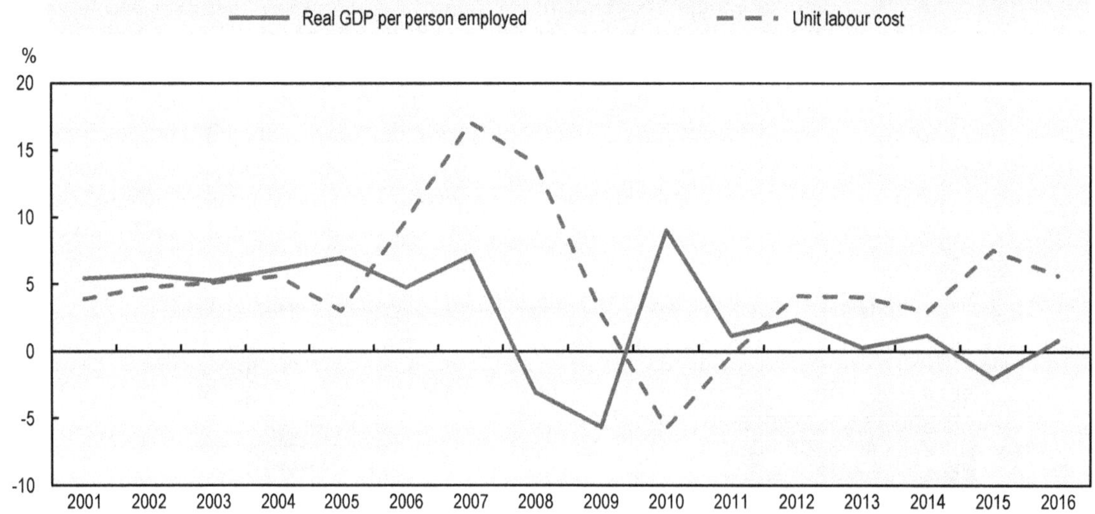

Source: OECD (2017a), Productivity and unit labour cost by main economic activity (ISIC Rev 4), http://dotstat.oecd.org/?lang=en.

StatLink http://dx.doi.org/10.1787/888933654484

Labour costs moved at the same pace across all fields of activity between 2001 and 2014. The average gross monthly wage has generally followed an upward trend, and although there was a slight setback in 2009, the average monthly gross wages began to rise in 2010 and increased to EUR 1 146 by 2016 (Figure 5.6). Wages in agriculture, forestry, and fishing have remained below average gross wages in the economy, but the gap has narrowed as they represented 82% of the average in 2008 and 92% in 2016. This suggests that the difference between the labour productivity in agriculture and the economy is decreasing.

Figure 5.6. Estonian average monthly wages, all economy and agriculture, forestry and fishery, 2008 to 2016

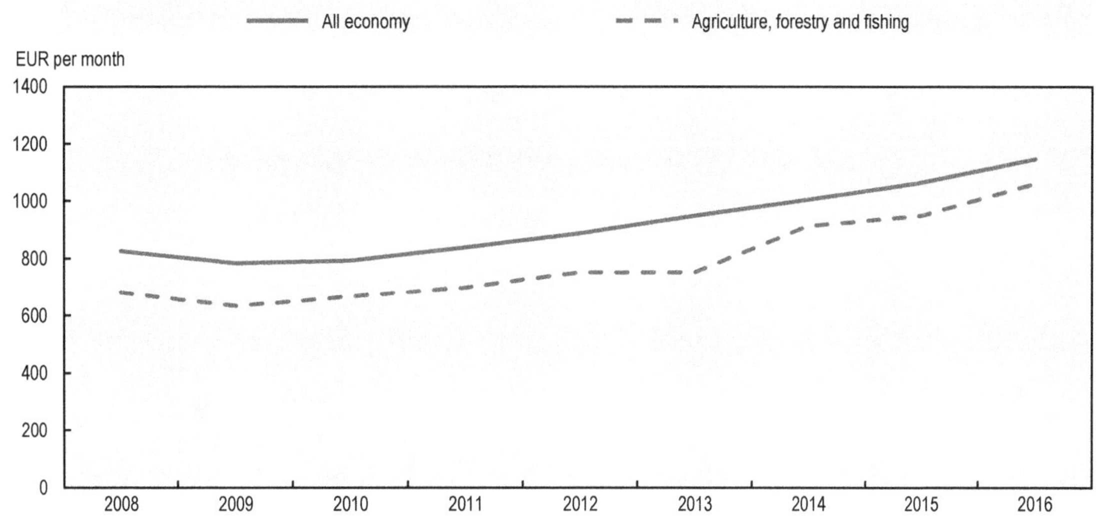

Source: Statistics Estonia (2017), [PA5211], www.stat.ee.

StatLink http://dx.doi.org/10.1787/888933654503

Box 5.3. Cross-country developments in labour costs and productivity

Labour productivity in Estonia, as measured by GDP per worked hour, has increased steadily — doubling since EU accession in 2004 and tripling during the period 2000-16. It reached around USD 30 of GDP per hour worked in 2012 and continued to increase to USD 34 in 2016, as in Poland, and Lithuania, but it remains lower than in older members of the OECD and the European Union (Figure 5.7).

Figure 5.7. GDP per hour worked in selected countries, selected years

USD, current prices PPP

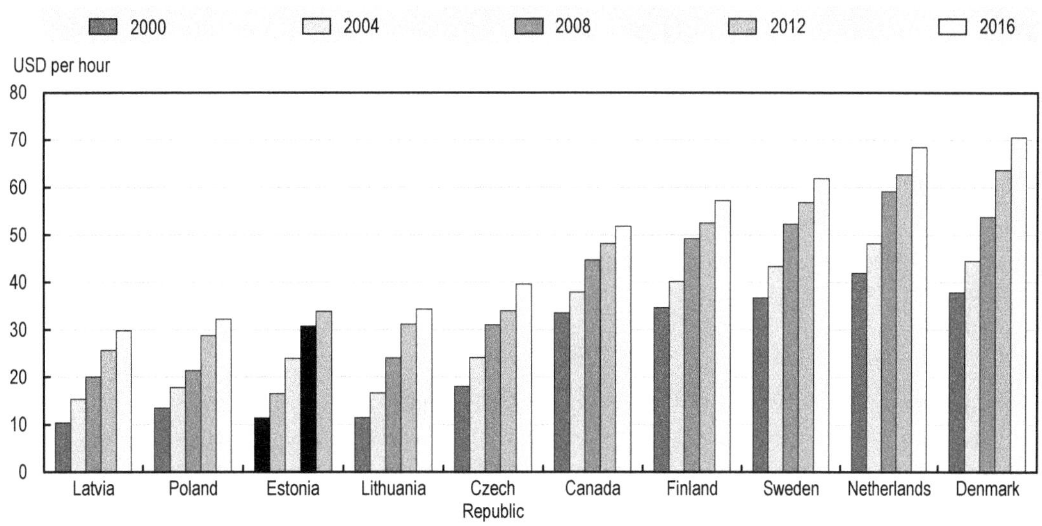

Countries are ranked according to 2016 levels.

Source: OECD (2017a), Productivity statistics, http://dotstat.oecd.org/?lang=en (accessed 30 June 2017).

StatLink http://dx.doi.org/10.1787/888933654522

Box 5.3. Cross-country developments in labour costs and productivity (cont.)

Unit labour costs also increased during the period 2000-16 in Estonia, faster than in other Baltic countries, and faster than labour productivity in Estonia. They almost quadrupled since 2000 and were multiplied by 2.5 since EU accession in 2004 to reach about EUR 11 per hour in 2016 (Figure 5.8). Estonia's unit labour costs are similar to those in the Czech Republic and higher than those in Latvia, Lithuania and Poland. However, they remain much lower than in Scandinavian countries or the Netherlands.

Figure 5.8. Hourly labour cost in selected countries, selected years

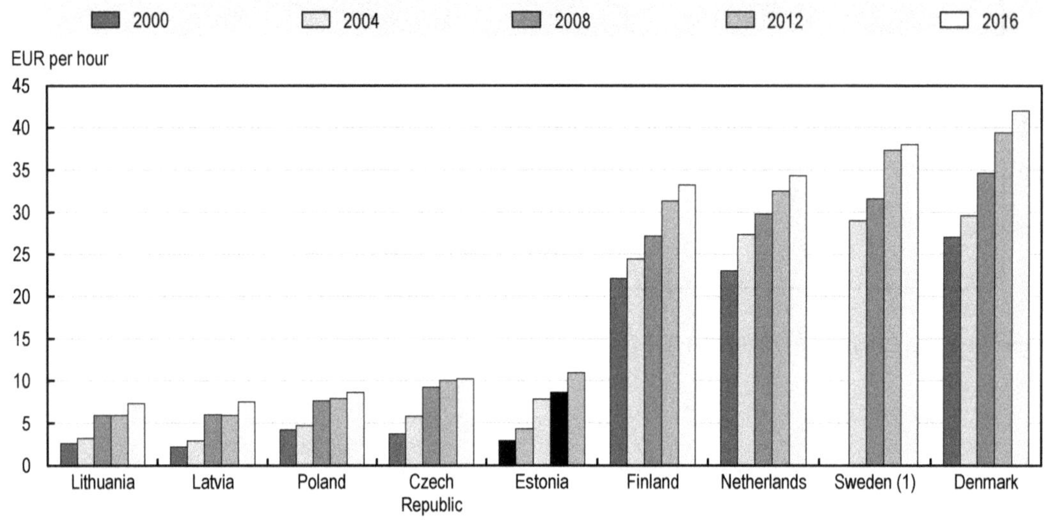

Countries are ranked according to 2016 levels.
1. For Sweden, 2000 data are not available.

Source: Eurostat (2017), Labour cost levels by NACE Rev. 2 activity, http://ec.europa.eu/eurostat/data/database (accessed 30 June 2017).

StatLink http://dx.doi.org/10.1787/888933654541

The annual growth in Estonia's unit labour cost varied during the period 2000-16. It was steady at about 5% before EU accession, and increased sharply over the period 2006-08, peaking to 17% in 2007. This peak was also registered in Latvia, to an even larger extent, but not in other Nordic countries. After a period of negative or slow growth, annual growth in Estonia's unit labour costs stabilised after 2012 around 4-6%, most years.

Initiatives to create new jobs and assist labour adjustment

A number of programmes and projects are in place to facilitate labour adjustment in a more flexible environment. The Unemployment Insurance Fund encourages job creation and training for better participation in employment. For example, programmes offer training sessions for unemployed registered with the Unemployment Insurance Fund. Financial aid, of up to EUR 4 474 in 2016, is also available for start-up companies (Unemployment Insurance Fund, 2016).

Efforts are also made to attract skilled workers. For example, the Estonian Chamber of Commerce and Industry launched the "Bringing talent home" project in 2010, which endeavours to bring together employers in Estonia with talented young people who have gone abroad to study or work (Bringing talent home, 2016). In response to the difficulty of finding skilled workforce in rural areas, a citizen initiative "Come to live in the countryside" was launched. The initiative has a website that helps to find jobs and housing in the countryside, as well as opportunities for entrepreneurship. Estonian workers also take advantage of training opportunities through the formal education system to improve the adequacy of their skills set with labour market demand (see below).

Labour supply in rural areas

Estonian rural areas face labour shortages as the Estonian population is concentrated in urban areas, emigration slows down but continues,[2] and the state policy does not favour the recruitment of temporary work force from third countries. As it offers lower than national average wages, agriculture has specific difficulties attracting hired labour, in particular for seasonal tasks. Compared with other EU member states, Estonian wages are also in the low range so the scope for attracting immigrants from the European Economic Area (EEA) is limited.

Migrant workers from third countries could fill the gap but they are subject to strict rules and regulations. As a rule, third country nationals must seek a residence permit to enter the labour market in Estonia. An annual immigration quota that should not exceed 0.1% of the permanent population of Estonia per annum is set for aliens immigrating to Estonia (Aliens Act § 113). For this purpose, permission must be granted by the Estonian Unemployment Insurance Fund and a wage criterion fulfilled. This criterion requires the employer to pay a remuneration amounting to 1.24 times the average annual wage published by Statistics Estonia (Recruiting from abroad, 2016). As a result, the share of immigrant population employed in agriculture is only 1-2%, according to Statistics Estonia.

Horticultural producers, who face labour shortages during the harvest season, have been most active in arguing against the present migration conditions, which are currently forcing employers to pay migrant workers in Estonia a higher salary than seasonal workers for example in Finland. In strawberry cultivation alone, it would be possible in the peak season to offer a temporary assignment to an additional 200 temporary employees (Gardening people, 2014).

Since May 2016, however, the Government has started to take steps to abate the law. Namely, the government approved and sent to Parliament a draft decision which obliges employers to pay foreign workers wages equal to at least the average salary in Estonia. As the wage coefficient for third-country workers coming to work in Estonia has been reduced from 1.24 to 1.0 since January 2017 the situation with seasonal workers in agriculture is expected to relax, and labour market demands will be more easily met.

In addition, two EU directives will be amended into national law:[3]

- **Directive 2014/36/EU** of the European Parliament and the Council of the European Union **on establishing uniform conditions of entry and stay of third-country nationals for the purpose of employment as seasonal workers.** The directive contributes to widening the short-term employment opportunities of third-country nationals and extending the maximum duration of short-term work from six to nine months a year. It also allows foreigners temporarily staying in Estonia to be granted a long-term visa of up to one year, with the possibility of requesting an extension for short-term employment. Foreigners staying in the country with a short-term visa are granted the right to use job matching services.
- **Directive 2014/66/EU of the European Parliament and of the Council establishes the conditions of entry and residence of third-country nationals in the framework of an intra-corporate transfer from a third country to the EU country.** A new type of residence permit — an intra-corporate transferee permit — **will be established in the Aliens Act and allows the holder of this** permit from one EU member country to work in another member country. The permit will be valid for a maximum of three years in the case of managers and specialists and one year for trainee employees.

5.3. Education and skills policy

Education policy affects innovation in at least three ways: a high level of general and scientific education facilitates acceptance of technological innovation by society at large; innovation systems require well-educated researchers, teachers, extension officers, and producers to develop relevant innovations; it is generally easier for farmers and business operators with higher education and skills to adopt some technological innovations. Continuous skills development (training, re-training) is essential to improve the matching of skills demand, in an evolving agri-food sector, which needs to adopt productivity and environmentally enhancing technologies and practices (OECD, 2015).

The Estonian education system is performing rather well, with governance mechanisms facilitating adaptation. The quality of education and training is considered slightly above the OECD average, for a lower public and private cost. The supply of education is very high, all the more as student numbers decrease reflecting lower birth rates. Educational attainment has been traditionally high and is among the highest in the OECD area, with a growing share of the population reaching tertiary education. The younger generations, however, do not seem to do as well as their elders in terms of reaching secondary education. The need for retraining is visible in the increasing share of adults in education, taking advantage of educational and training programmes and opportunities.

The general education system

Governance and funding

Estonia's education system includes basic and secondary schools, vocational educational institutions, institutions of professional education, universities, and continuing education institutions. Agricultural education is integrated into the general system and available at vocational and higher levels. Some institutions within the general system are specialised in agriculture-related fields of science (see agricultural education sub-section below).

The management of the education system is organised by the Parliament, the Government, the Ministry of Education and Research (MER) and the local authorities in accordance with their statutory competences. The governance of the education system is shared between central and local authorities, and schools have a high level of autonomy for resource allocation. The state sets national standards and establishes principles of education funding, supervision and quality assessment. Early childhood education and care is managed by local authorities, and most decisions in lower secondary education are taken at the school level (OECD, 2016c).

Schools in Estonia have a level of autonomy above the OECD average, including the capacity to make decisions on the curriculum and to hire and dismiss teaching staff. Lower secondary teachers are required to have five years of initial teacher training, including a mandatory teaching practicum, and follow continuous professional development. Primary and secondary teachers have below-average class sizes and teaching time. Their salaries are lower than the OECD average, despite a significant increase since 2000. However, the teaching profession is more valued in society than in other countries. Teacher appraisal is used for career advancement and to some extent to determine the need for professional development, but there is currently no appraisal system for school leaders. A system-level assessment of the education system is carried out yearly by the MER (OECD, 2016c).

Public expenditure on educational institutions as a percentage of GDP and annual expenditure by institutions on education per student are well below the OECD average. Education in Estonia is mainly financed by the government. While state funds cover 93% of the expenditure on basic, secondary and higher education (OECD average 83%), and 99.1% of basic and secondary education expenditure, private funding (by private bodies and households) is significant in higher education, amounting to 22% in 2012. This share is similar to the average of the 21 EU countries that are members of the OECD, but lower than the OECD average (30%). Since 2013/14, studying full-time on programmes where the tuition language is Estonian is free of charge both in state-owned institutions of higher education as well as in public universities (OECD, 2015).

The MER is responsible for ensuring the quality of the educational institutions and for external evaluation, which is preceded by internal evaluation. The staff, students and external stakeholders (e.g., alumni, employers, in the case of general education also the parents) participate in the evaluation. The experts and students involved in the process of external education, and in case of vocational training institutions, assessors and employers, are selected via a public procurement procedure. The results of the external evaluation form a basis for assessing the sustainability of the educational establishment or the curriculum. At gymnasiums the results of the internal evaluation are taken into account in the elaboration of the development plan (MER, 2016b).

Extensive use of outcome-based principles is applied in curricula development, implementation, elaboration and evaluation. The right to provide instruction is granted to the educational establishment through the accreditation of the curriculum groups. In the course of compiling a report for the internal performance review every school analyses the sustainability of its curricula. An independent external assessment committee conducts the external evaluation or accreditation, and, based on their report, makes their proposal about the accreditation to the Estonian Quality Agency for Higher and Vocational Education (EKKA). The Assessment Council of EKKA uses this proposal for decision-making. The results of the assessment of all educational institutions and curriculum groups are available on the EKKA database (EKKA, 2016a).

Overall performance

Business leaders rank Estonia above the OECD average in terms of the quality of higher education and on-the-job-training (Figure 5.9). The quantity of education, as measured by an index of secondary and tertiary education enrolment rates, scores very high, as in most OECD countries.

Figure 5.9. Global Competitiveness Index: Higher Education and Training, 2016-17

Scale 1 to 7 (best)

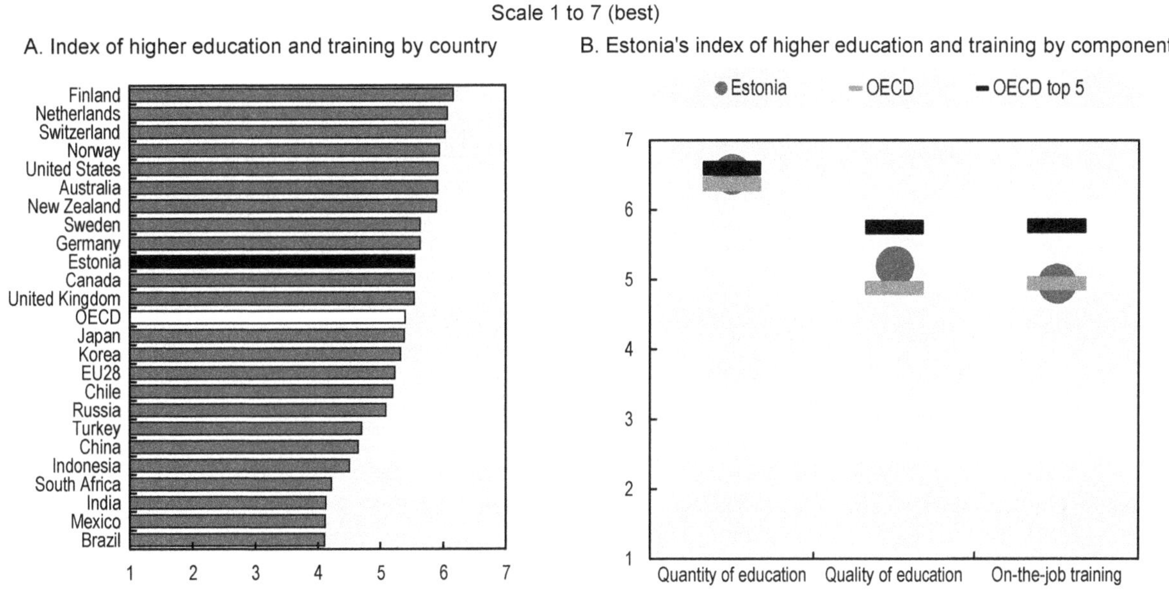

Indices for EU28 and OECD are the simple average of member-country indices.

OECD top 5 refers to the average of the scores for the top 5 performers among OECD countries (Finland, Netherlands, Switzerland, Belgium and Denmark). The quantity of education index is based on secondary and tertiary education enrolment rates from UNESCO Institute for Statistics. The quality of education index is based on responses from a WEF Executive Opinion Survey on "How well does the educational system meet the needs of a competitive economy; Executives' assessment of the quality of math and science education in schools and the quality of business schools; and on how widespread is Internet access in schools. The on-the-job-training index is based on survey responses on the availability of high-quality, specialised training services and the extent to which companies invest in training and employee development.

Source: World Economic Forum (2016), *The Global Competitiveness Report 2016-2017: Full data Edition*, Geneva 2016. http://reports.weforum.org/global-competitiveness-index/.

StatLink http://dx.doi.org/10.1787/888933654560

Educational attainment

Estonia has a long tradition of higher education and educational attainment is above the OECD and EU average (Figure 5.10). As in other Baltic countries, the share of the population with at least upper secondary education is among the highest in OECD countries: over 90% of 25-64 year-olds had attained at least upper secondary education in 2015, compared to the OECD average of 78%.

The shares of population with secondary and/or vocational education or second-tier education are practically equal in rural and urban settlements, whereas the proportion with only primary or basic education is higher in rural areas (EMÜ, 2011).

Figure 5.10. Upper secondary and tertiary attainment for 25-64 year-olds, 2016

Percentage of the population aged 25-64

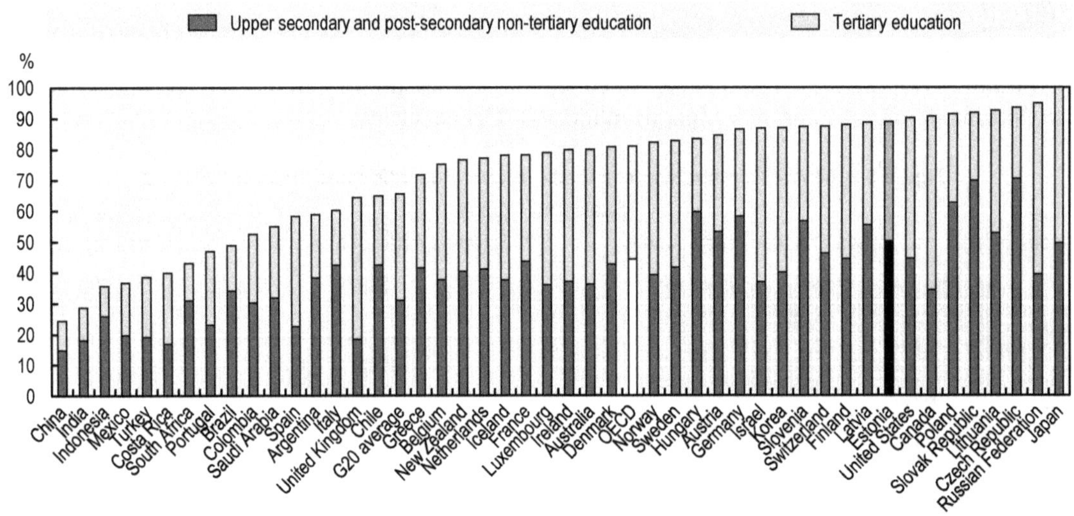

Source: OECD (2017b), *Education at a Glance 2017: OECD Indicators*, http://dx.doi.org/10.1787/eag-2017-en.

StatLink http://dx.doi.org/10.1787/888933654579

At tertiary level, Estonia's attainment rates are below those of top OECD performers. The share of the Estonian population aged 25-64 with tertiary education has gained 9 percentage points between 2000 and 2015 to reach 38%. However, this share is above 40% in a significant number of OECD countries such as Australia, Canada, Finland, Korea, Norway, the United Kingdom and the United States.

Increasing the number of doctoral graduates remains a real challenge for research in Estonia. According to the Innovation Union Scoreboard 2013, there were 0.9 new doctorate holders per 1 000 inhabitants in the 25-34 age group in Estonia in 2010 compared to 1.5 on average in the European Union (MER, 2014a). The Innovation Union Scoreboard 2017 reports higher numbers in 2015: 1.08 and 1.8 new doctorate holders respectively in Estonia and the European Union. In 2010-15, the number of doctoral graduates fluctuated between 175 and 250, whereas the target to be reached by 2020 laid down in the Estonian Lifelong Learning Strategy is 300 graduates a year.

According to the "Study of effectiveness of doctoral programmes in Estonia" (Eamets et al., 2011), the number of applicants to doctoral studies may decrease in the coming 5-6 years, due to the demographic trends in Estonia and a decrease in the number of externally financed doctoral study places after the introduction of the requirement to pay support to all doctoral students. The analysis also revealed that the prospective career path is not an essential motivator for PhD candidates. On the one hand wages in the academic sector are no longer competitive on the labour market, and, on the other hand, employers in the private sector do not attach any value to a doctoral degree. There are not enough large companies in Estonia with the need and the opportunity to recruit PhD students and specialists with a PhD. Only 1% of the adult respondents with higher education participating in the OECD Programme for the International Assessment of Adult Competencies (PIAAC) study said that they would have required a doctoral degree to get the job, which is two times less than the total of the 24 PIAAC participant countries and, for example, five times less than in Finland.

Education enrolment trends

The education system is faced with a long-term decline in the number of students, reflecting demographic trends depicting an ageing population and a declining number of births. In general education, the number of students has decreased by about 40% in the past 17 years. Over the last decade, the number of students enrolled in full-time general education has dropped by approximately 14%, and the number of schools by 11%.

Despite the overall decrease in the number of students, the number of adult learners (30 years and older) in higher education has remained relatively stable, and the number of adult learners in vocational education has increased, reflecting their willingness to upgrade practical skills and increase their competitiveness in the labour market. As a result, close to half of students in vocational education were over 20 years old in 20013/14, compared to less than 40% in 2009/10. Similar trends are found in universities. They pose challenges to study programmes and teaching methods, as mature students have very different backgrounds and expect a more individual approach from teachers.

There is a significant proportion of adults in Estonia who continue acquiring basic or secondary education in different flexible forms of non-stationary programmes, where they can study single specific subjects or take the final exams as external students. The share of adults participating in formal education or training in Estonia has doubled between 2005 and 2011 to reach about 12%, while in the European Union, it has fluctuated around 10% between 2005 and 2014.

Skills and competences

The quality of education in Estonia is reflected in the high scores obtained by students and adults for their skills and competences in international surveys. Two OECD programmes, the PISA (Programme for International Student Assessment) and the PIAAC (Programme for the International Assessment of Adult Competencies), include surveys measuring basic competences. Estonia participated in the PISA survey four times (in 2006, 2009, 2012 and 2015), and in the PIAAC survey for the first time in 2011/12. The results of the study showed that Estonia was among the top performers in reading, mathematics and science in PISA 2015.[4] Performance in mathematics and science has been stable since 2006, and has improved in reading. The impact of socio-economic status on student performance is below the OECD average. At the same time, equity between boys and girls is greater than the OECD average, and stable since 2006.

According to the PIAAC survey, Estonian adults (16-65 year-olds) performed well above the OECD average in literacy and numeracy, but below the average in problem solving in technology-rich environments (OECD, 2016b, Table 1.1). However, the problem-solving performance of young adults (16-29 year-olds) reaches the average.

The Estonian population is also highly skilled in languages. This facilitates cross-country co-operation and social innovation. According to an EU survey of Europeans and their languages, 87% of Estonian respondents said they were able to speak at least one other language besides their mother tongue (compared to 54% at the EU level), and 52% have practical skills in at least two foreign languages (25% at the EU level). Russian was the most commonly spoken of these foreign languages (by 56% of respondent) but has lost of lot of ground. English is increasingly used, every or almost every day by 28% of Estonian respondents (European Commission, 2012).

PIAAC and other surveys outline the discrepancy between supply and demand for skills in the Estonian labour market. In particular, a significant share of employees is overqualified and underemployed (Box 5.4).

Box 5.4. Unbalance between supply and demand for skills

The Estonian labour market does not offer enough jobs to match the qualification of the labour force. According to the last PIAAC survey, 26.5% of employees in the sample were overeducated and 12.2% underemployed, compared to 21.5% and 12.8% respectively for the OECD average (OECD, 2016c).[1] In addition, 35.3% of Estonian surveyed employees reported a field of-study mismatch, which is slightly lower than the OECD average of 39.6%.[2]

The likelihood of over-education is greater among the elderly and those with higher education. As to the fields of activity concerning over-education, agriculture, hunting, forestry and fishing, manufacturing, construction, accommodation and catering are affected the most. Those in the fields of education, professional education, research and technological activities, public administration and defence, health- and social care activities, are less affected. Underemployment is lowest among graduates of agriculture, engineering, manufacturing and construction, and services, as well as graduates of higher education institutions (MER, 2015b). Field-of-study mismatch appeared particularly high in agriculture and veterinary, compared with other fields, with 75.8% of Estonian employees reporting mismatch, and higher than the average of country covered in the survey for this field (70.9%) (OECD, 2016c).

A survey carried out among the alumni in Estonia in 2015 showed that only 50% of respondents felt that their current position required higher education, 11% thought that their job required professional education, 11% thought secondary education was sufficient and 15% of the respondents stated that the level of education was not important in their profession. This can partly be attributed to not being able to find a professional job (Laan et al., 2015).

Since 1989, considerable changes can be identified in the structure of employment: the share of skill-intensive positions has increased from 35% to 42.7% in 2014, and the trend towards more complex positions continues. However, Estonian entrepreneurs and foreign investors consider the shortage of adequately trained personnel a key challenge in the local economic development.

In Estonia, graduates' skills in the fields of teacher training, engineering, manufacturing and construction present the biggest problems, while those in the fields of natural science and engineering, as well as humanities and social sciences are at a higher level. In comparison with other EU countries, the problem-solving skills of Estonians employed in the manufacturing and processing industry are by far the weakest, and the use of computers at their workplace the second weakest. In Estonia both the levels of computer skills and the frequency of computer use are comparatively low, the exception being in the agricultural sector, where skilled workers use computers at work and in quite a number of different ways. For example, 37% of Estonian skilled workers in the sector use computers for work-related purposes, whereas the number of such users in Finland is 24%, in the Czech Republic 23% and for other countries this figure is even smaller (MER, 2015b).

PIACC results show that computer literacy is often required in some occupations in Estonia, but the computer skills of the employees do not meet the contemporary requirements and are limited to specific activities only. In this regard the personnel at Estonian educational institutions stand out. Their problem-solving skills in technology-rich environments are almost the lowest, while the frequency of computer use at work is still among the average. The survey also revealed that a significant number of young people (up to 24 years of age), who have good computer and problem-solving skills and use computers in everyday life are currently holding such jobs where computer skills are not needed (mainly in hotel and catering services) (Pruulmann-Vengerfeldt et al., 2015).

1. All those whose highest level of education attained exceeds the level that would be required for their employment are considered overeducated and those whose highest educational attainment is below the level of education that would require them to obtain work are underemployed.

2. Field-of-study mismatch occurs when a worker has a qualification in a different field than required for his/her job.

At the same time, a low level of education and lack of professional skills are the main obstacles to finding a job, both in urban and rural areas. The unemployment rate is highest among adults without secondary education (13.3% of the 15-74 year-olds in 2015) and their wages are also the lowest. In 2015, only a third of people with basic education had a job, whereas the employment rate for people with higher education was 78% and for vocational education 67-72% (MRA, 2016b). The employment rate in rural areas has grown annually from 53.7% in 2009 to 65.3% in 2015, but the problem lies in the lower level of education of the rural working age population, which considerably limits their competitiveness in the labour market.

Programmes promoting life-long skills development and re-training

At the European level the strategic objectives of co-operation in education and training have been laid down in the Education and Training 2010 work programme. At the national level, the Estonian Lifelong Learning Strategy 2014-20 is the key strategy guiding the most important developments in the educational sector. Several sub-programmes have been devised for 2016-19 to implement the strategy, including: general, vocational, higher education and adult education programmes; competent and motivated teachers and school leadership education programme; digital turn programme; study and career counselling programme; labour market and education co-operation programme; and school network programme.

Each programme has its objective and as a rule the objectives are intertwined. To achieve the objectives, specific activities have been planned and respective indicators and targets set. The objectives set for 2020 are close to being achieved in a number of areas (Box 5.5).

Box 5.5. Estonian Lifelong Learning Strategy 2014-20 achievements by 2016

- The share of 30-34 year-olds with higher education has increased, exceeding 40% of this age group, the target of Estonia 2020 and Europe 2020.
- The share of graduates from higher educational institutions in natural and exact sciences, technology, engineering, manufacturing and construction in 2013-14 has been above 24%, which is close to the 2020 target of 25%.
- The unemployment rate among young people, aged 15-24 years, has more than halved (from 33% to 15%) in the past five years (2009-14), which is mainly attributable to an improved labour market situation. The target for 2020 is 10%. In 2014, the difference between the employment rate of young adults, aged 15-26, in urban and rural settlement differed by 7.8 percentage points (in urban settlements 50.3% and in rural settlements 42.3%), and has shown a slow but steady decline over the past 10 years from 11.5 percentage points in 2005 (Eesti Noorsootöö Keskus, 2016). In 2010-13 the employment rate was lowest in the rural population with basic education (23.2%, 26.2% and 28.2% and 32%, respectively), followed by those with secondary education (58.4%, 63%, 64.9% and 64.9%). Rural population with tertiary education had the highest employment rate (75.4%, 77.6%, 77.7% and 77.2%) (MRA, 2014a).
- The share of adults (aged 25-64) with no professional or vocational training was less than 30% in 2014, which is one of the goals of Estonia 2020.
- The proportion of 25 year-olds and older learners has increased in vocational education.
- The share of youth with a lower level of education and not involved in education (18-24 year-olds) dropped below 10% for the first time in 2013, however, by 2014 it was back to 11.6%. The target of the lifelong learning strategy is to decrease this figure to under 9%. The percentage of people with a lower level of education among the working-age population in rural settlements was higher than that in towns (e.g., 13.7% of the working age population in 2011 and 13.2% in 2013) (MRA, 2014a). The education level of the working age population in Estonia differs also by regions (e.g., 7.9% in North-Estonia and 16% in Central Estonia, in 2011) (MRA, 2014b).

A number of activities have been planned within the education system (MER, 2015b):

- In 2015, a total of 56 accreditations were carried out in 13 study programme groups.
- A network of communication specialists in vocational education has been launched to raise the reputation of vocational education. It offers training to that regard. A collection of success stories and study opportunities in vocational education "Help for decision-making-Vocational Training Opportunities in 2016/2017" has been published. In order to work out a practical training system in vocational education, a network of traineeship co-ordinators has been set up. Several network meetings and information days have been organised.
- A number of new curricula that could not have been opened at this level have been launched. For example, it is at present possible to acquire vocational secondary education in the fields of dairy, meat, fish, vegetables and beverages technology. Basic education grants access to food processing studies, which last for 3-4 years. Students are admitted to specific training in food technology on the basis of secondary education which last for 2-2.5 years. The qualifications can be acquired in two vocational education centres — the Olustvere School of Service and Rural Economics (www.olustvere.edu.ee) and the Tartu Vocational Education Centre (www.khk.ee).
- The number of interruption cases or early leaving of studies has generally declined, especially in vocational secondary education. The employment indicator of vocational school graduates is also on the rise.
- In recent years, the number of dropout cases in full-time general education has decreased and stabilised at a relatively low level of 0.5-0.6% in the third level of basic school and 0.9-1.1% in the

first year of secondary school. One of the expected results of the general education programme is a decline in the proportion of non-studying young people with a low level of education.

- There are advisory panels offering career guidance in all counties and a nationwide vocational counselling and placement centre.
- The number of young people registered as unemployed in the course of the 12 months following graduation has dropped, whereas the income earned by young people who earned income was higher than the median income or return from business activities.
- The programme called OSKA, "A system of labour market monitoring and future skills forecasting", which is funded by the European Social Fund, has been launched. The programme includes applied research surveys on sectoral needs for labour and skills necessary for the economic development of Estonia. The results of the analyses and forecasts feed the qualification and career guidance systems, curriculum development at educational institutions, and provide input to different agencies and authorities. The analysis of forestry and the timber industry was performed in 2016, and that of agriculture and the food industry sector will be performed in 2017, with a report published in November 2017. The programme aims to build platforms of co-operation between employers and education providers, analyse the development opportunities and needs of different sectors of the Estonian economy, prepare labour market training requirements based on various activities or professions to facilitate the planning of education provision at different levels of education and by types of school as well as in the fields of retraining and in-service training (OSKA, 2016).

Agricultural education

Availability of agriculture-related education programmes

Agricultural education is available in Estonia both through higher and vocational education programmes. Four higher educational institutions (among 24 in 2015/16) and 14 vocational education establishments (among 39) teach agricultural and food processing. There is only one higher educational institution specialising directly in agriculture (the Estonian University of Life Sciences, EMÜ) and three vocational education institutions, including one specialised in horticulture (Chapter 7).

EMÜ is specialised in agricultural higher education and research. The University promotes six focal areas – agriculture, environment, forestry, food and health, technology and engineering, and rural economy. It plays a key role in providing qualified workforce with the necessary competencies in the use of sustainable technologies and improves attitudes towards more sustainable professional work that is less harmful to the environment (EMÜ, 2016a). According to QS World University Rankings by Subject (2016), the Estonian University of Life Sciences is one of the top 100 universities in the world in the field of agriculture and forestry, ranked 51st. The university also belongs to the top 1% most cited research facilities in the world.

It is also possible to study agriculture, fisheries, forestry, life sciences, manufacturing and processing, and environmental sciences at the University of Tartu (TU), Tallinn University and Tallinn Technical University (TUT). At the vocational education level, however, only two vocational education institutions specialise directly in agriculture, most of the other twelve offer courses in food processing. In addition, the use of natural resources, sustainable agriculture, environmental protection and climate change-related disciplines are taught at Bachelor, Master and Doctoral levels.

Agriculture enrolment trends

As in the whole education system, the number of students enrolled at the EMÜ has decreased between 2013 and 2016, in particular at Bachelor level (-32%) (Figure 5.11). The number of students studying biosciences, environmental sciences and veterinary medicine has remained comparatively stable or even grown a little. The largest fall in student numbers can be observed in the fields of agriculture, forestry and fishery, and engineering, manufacturing and technology (Figure 5.12).

Overall, the number of university students enrolled in the curricula in veterinary medicine, engineering, manufacturing and technology has remained relatively stable in recent years, while the decline has been the steepest in the study programme group "business and administration", where EMÜ has one bachelor level curriculum — Agricultural Economics and Rural Entrepreneurship, and two master level curricula — Accounting and Financial Management; and Economics and Entrepreneurship.

Figure 5.11. Number of students at the EMÜ[1], by education level, 2013 and 2016

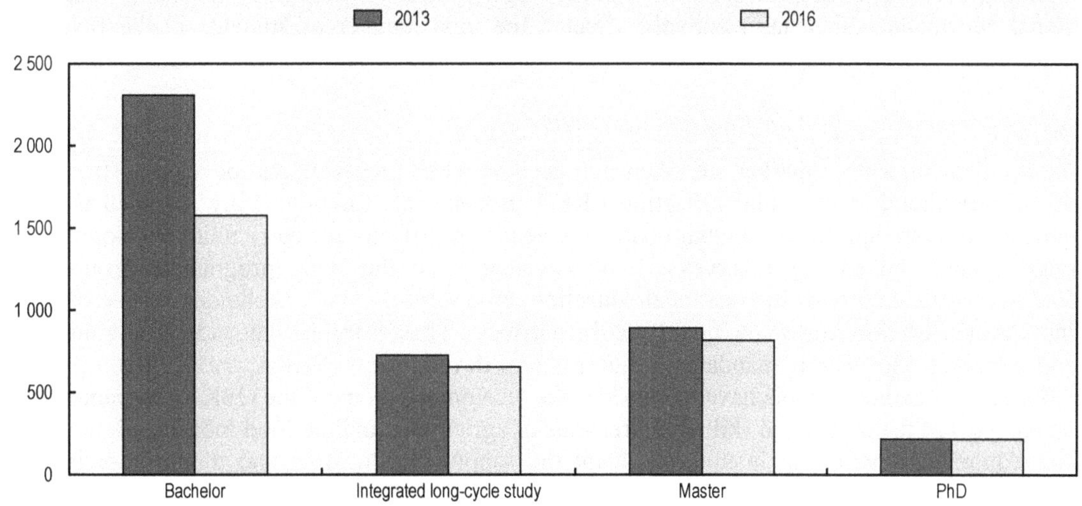

1. EMÜ: Estonian University of Life Sciences, as of 2 June 2016.

Source: EMÜ (2016b), http://stats.emu.ee/ (accessed 18 October 2016).

StatLink http://dx.doi.org/10.1787/888933654598

Figure 5.12. Number of university students, by field of study, 2013 and 2016

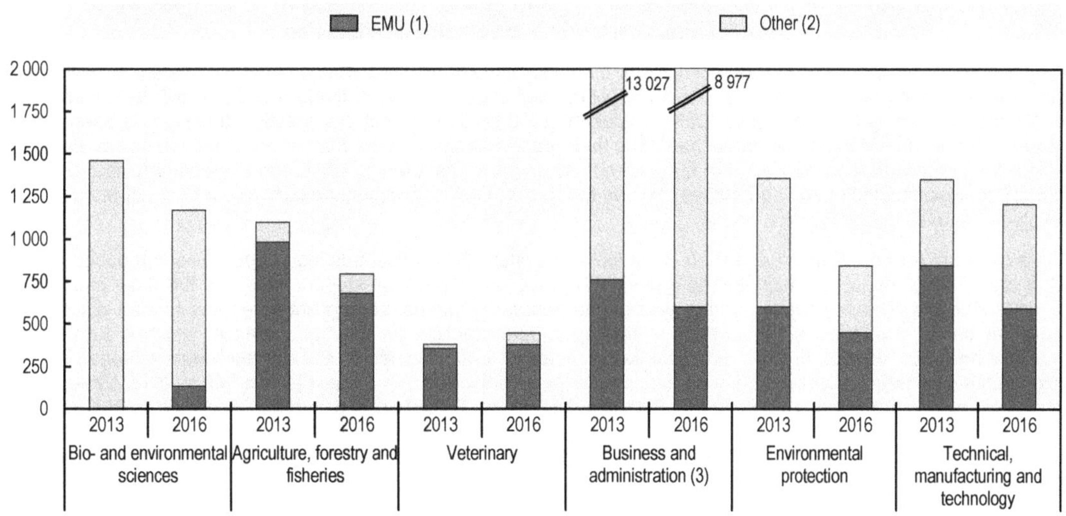

1. EMÜ: Estonian University of life sciences, as of 15 November 2016.
2. 2013 refers to 2012/13; 2016 refers to 2015/16.
3. Curricula in agricultural economics and rural entrepreneurship are taught at the EMÜ only.

Source: EMÜ (2016b), http://stats.emu.ee/ (accessed 18 October 2016); EHIS (2016a), www.hm.ee/ehis/statistika.html.

StatLink http://dx.doi.org/10.1787/888933654617

In vocational education, students' interest in agricultural specialties has increased over the past decade. Over the period 2004-14, the number of students on agriculture-related curricula increased by approximately 8%, while the total number of students in vocational education decreased by about 14% and the number of students in social sciences, business and law, engineering, manufacturing and building dropped by about 30% (EHIS, 2016a). Among agriculture-related curricula, the number of students in environment, agriculture, veterinary medicine, and manufacturing and processing has remained relatively stable. An increase can be observed in the fields of agriculture, forestry and fishery, whereas the number of students in manufacturing and processing suffered a marginal decline. In 2012, a new specialty – veterinary assistant – was opened in professional education, which has positively affected the total number of students in the fields of study analysed.

Meeting labour market needs in the food and agriculture sector

The needs of the labour market are taken into account when preparing and developing the curricula in the field of agriculture, in particular reflecting EKKA assessments. Employers are involved in curriculum development, both through the curriculum boards convened specifically for curriculum development, as well as through alumni and employer surveys. In the evaluation of the study programme groups in higher education, and curricula groups in vocational education, co-operation with stakeholders is one of the criteria taken into account when assessing the quality of the curricula. Thus, bringing the study programmes into line with labour market relevance is mandatory in curriculum development (EKKA, 2012, 2016b). From 2017, universities and vocational schools have to consider the recommendations of the OSKA programme, resulting from the analyses of the labour and skills requirements of agriculture and the food industry. Better knowledge of future requirements will help institutions adapt the supply of education and training services (OSKA, 2016).

In quantitative terms, the main challenges are to meet an increasing demand for agricultural specialists in a context of a decreasing number of students, attract students in vocational education where unfilled demand is greater, and retain workers in the sector. In qualitative terms, evaluations point to the need to develop student social skills and practical training in curricula (Box 5.6).

Box 5.6. Practical training in agricultural education

Concerning higher education in rural economics, the importance of practical work experience in student development has been stressed, especially by the employers. Graduates of the higher educational institutions of 2009 and 2012 identified the low amount of practical training as a deficiency. Only 56% of the 2009 graduates said that practical training had been a mandatory part of the curriculum, 9% of the respondents had done their practical training in the framework of an optional or elective course, and 35% of the respondents pointed out that they did not do any practical training within the curriculum (Eamets et al., 2011). Only 31% of the respondents of 2012 graduates claimed that the curriculum contained a sufficient amount of practical training in the workplace (Laan et al., 2015).

As a measure for improving students' practical skills, a system of practical training support was introduced in 2005. The support is specifically meant for such entrepreneurs who take on a pupil or student studying full time and whose main occupation is studying. The introduction of this system has generated interest among entrepreneurs to offer placements. As a result, the number of opportunities for students to find up-to-date practical training will increase, which in turn will raise the quality of training (MRA, 2016c). In 2013, practical training support was allocated to 115 entrepreneurs engaged in agricultural production or the processing of agricultural products. The respective figure in 2014 was 111 and 145 in 2015. Enterprises submit applications for practical training support to the Estonian Agricultural Registers and Information Board (ARIB) every year (in September-October). In 2013 and 2014, EUR 200 000 was earmarked for agriculture-related practice payments, the budget for 2015 was EUR 150 000 and EUR 160 000 for 2016. The number of trainees is not limited, but the supervisor is allowed to simultaneously oversee two trainees (ARIB, 2016).

New initiatives aiming to increase the importance of practical training and to help students find practical training positions in companies started in 2017. They are implemented in cooperation with the Estonian Chamber of Agriculture and Commerce.

Vocational schools and higher education institutions have difficulties attracting enough students to meet labour market expectations. Since 2003, one of the measures for increasing the number of applicants for agriculture and rural economics related curricula was the introduction of study allowances for the respective students at vocational education institutes.

The "Survey on Competence Level and Educational Development Needs in Agricultural Food and Forestry Sectors" commissioned by the Ministry of Agriculture in 2010 showed that regardless of the size of the company, the demand for skilled staff (in 50% of the enterprises) and managers/specialists (in 17% of the enterprises) in the canvassed sectors will increase. In the food industry, 60% of the respondents pointed out that they would require almost all specialists with professional higher or vocational education, whereas the need for unskilled labour and "all-in-one" staff is anticipated to decline. The biggest problem in the rural sector in Estonia, however, is the ageing of the work-force. The study also revealed that a significant number of posts are unoccupied in the agricultural sector, mainly for agronomists, mechanics, livestock engineers, veterinarians and milkers. As to food industry, the positions of technologists, product developers, but also skilled and unskilled jobs, as well as management positions were mentioned as having vacant positions. Most respondents expressed their concern about the shortage of skilled workers (automatician, technician), product developers, technologists and masters. The biggest problems in finding skilled staff included the attitude of the candidates, qualifications and salary expectations (Jalak, 2010).

Jalak (2010) found that agricultural and horticultural enterprises would like to recruit people with vocational education, but often they are not to found. This sector is not very attractive for young people, and many of the employers are located in rural areas, which makes finding suitable people even more difficult. That is why enterprises have been training their workforce themselves. In contrast to agricultural and horticultural enterprises, forestry companies hold vocational training in high esteem because the machine fleet of logging enterprises is very expensive and handling the machinery needs good training.

The survey conducted in 2016 exposed similar problems in the agricultural sector, which still suffers from the shortage of professionals and skilled workers. The migration of young people, in the age range of 25-29, from rural areas also causes problems (Kurvits, 2016).

The survey conducted among the alumni of the Estonian universities in 2015 showed that in 2012 about 48% of graduates in agriculture related specialties did not practice their profession, which is about 17% more than in 2009. Nearly 25% continued their formal studies and another 11% combined work and study. In 2012, the number of unemployed graduates was about 2%. (Laan et al., 2015). According to the alumni survey carried out in 2011, about 28% of the 2009 graduates of agricultural curricula did not work in their acquired specialty. Approximately 80% of the Bachelor-level graduates continued their studies at the Master level and 15% of Master graduates continued on to doctoral level. In 2009, the number of unemployed graduates was about 7% (Eamets et al., 2011). According to findings of the 2011 and 2015 surveys, the main reason for the graduates of agricultural higher education to continue their studies was to pursue an academic career, earn a better salary or get an appropriate job (alumni who graduated from the higher education institution three years previously constituted the sample).

The reasons for not practising their profession were not finding a professional job, including not finding a professional job in the region of residence, and giving preference to the salary and working conditions in other fields. The employer survey gave the same reasons for the shortage of skilled workers in the agricultural sector (Jalak, 2010). Average gross wages in the agriculture, forestry and fishing sectors are smaller than the average gross salary (Figure 5.6). At the same time, the average wages in agriculture grew faster than the national average (9.3% and 5.9% in 2013-14, 7.1% and 6.9% in 2014-15 and 10.5% and 7.6% in 2015-16, respectively). Wages in Estonia are also lower in rural areas.

The survey carried out among Estonian vocational school graduates in 2012 (the survey covered the 2008-10 graduates, who were interviewed half a year after their graduation) shows that the employment rate of graduates in the field of agriculture is higher than that of vocational school graduates from other areas. Analysts explain the higher employment rate by the graduates' age, which is on average higher (30+) than that of other graduates and the fact that many graduates of agriculture were already working during their studies. According to the survey, 72% of the 2008 and 2010 graduates worked during their studies. Unlike graduates from higher education institutions, vocational graduates in the field of agriculture were more satisfied with the profession acquired, ranking their satisfaction rate higher (4.8 points out of 5) (Nestor, 2012). In the survey of higher education graduates of 2012 and 2009, on average about only 50% of respondents admitted that the studies met their expectations (mainly on the grounds that the objectives and learning outcomes of the curricula were not clear and the graduates were dissatisfied with the volume of practical training in the curriculum) (Eamets et al., 2011).

According to a survey of vocational school alumni, graduates of agricultural specialties acknowledge the benefits of their acquired knowledge in the field of entrepreneurship, i.e. almost as highly as graduates of the business and management curriculum group (3.6 and 3.9 points in the 5-point system). At the same time, similarly to graduates of higher agricultural institutions, the share of vocational education graduates not practising their profession was the highest compared to graduates of other curricula. The 2015 survey revealed that the proportion of such university graduates was about 48%, and the number of vocational school graduates even lower at 30%. The given result cannot, however, be regarded as statistically reliable as the number of respondents to this question was too small. However, graduates of vocational education considered their professional prospects truly viable (4.2 points on a 5-point scale) (Nestor, 2012).

In addition to general mechanisms, agriculture-specific measures are available to support agricultural education and training:

- To increase the number of applicants for agricultural curricula, vocational education students on the curricula related to agriculture and rural economy are paid a study allowance from the education allowance measure by the Estonian Rural Development Foundation (MRA, 2016c).
- In order to improve the practical skills of agricultural students, practice support measures are implemented. They partly compensate for the supervision and organisation costs related to the practical training of students specialising in agriculture and rural economy, incurred by the farmers or processors of agricultural products.
- The Estonian RDP 2014-20 supports farmers' access to training and advisory services (See Chapters 6 and 7).

Science and environment awareness in education and society

Education has an important role in spreading awareness of the potential benefits of innovation in enhancing productivity and sustainability, and promoting sustainable development. A high level of general and scientific education facilitates acceptance of technological innovation by society. Popularising science in education is to generate interest towards research and technology, improve the attractiveness of research and engineering careers, and ensure the spread of a scientific world-view in the society. Environmental education is expected, in the long term, to lead to sustainable use of natural resources, lower pollution and reduced environment-related health risks, by influencing the impact of human activities on the environment through behavioural changes. In addition, these fields of science affect the ability of the agricultural sector to innovate, through the generation of new technologies with agriculture and food related applications.

Science

The fields of science and engineering have progressed the most in Estonian higher education, presenting, unlike for the OECD average, an equal interest to both male and female students. In Estonia, on average every third, and in the OECD countries every fifth, graduate obtained their Master's degrees in science or engineering, manufacturing and construction, and more than a half of doctoral graduates acquired their degree in science and engineering (OECD, 2015). There might, however, be an issue at earlier stages of education.

Experts think that Estonia lacks a system for the fruitful introduction of science into formal education (Kirss et al., 2013). The survey carried out by the Centre for Policy Studies Praxis in 2013 "Study on various activities for popularising science and technology" outlined, among other things, that the present formal education system does not help link knowledge and life, and does not show the necessity of science and technology in social development. Science popularisation activities are started too late, when most of the students have made their (professional) choices for the future already. The lack of co-operation between the people involved in the popularisation of science and relying only on their personal experience may also cause a problem.

Environment

Environment has been an integral theme of the Estonian national curriculum for the last two decades. First incorporated into the national curriculum in 1996, the environment theme was extended in 2002 to cover sustainable development issues. Sustainable development was also one of the eight themes of the new national curricula for basic and secondary schools adopted in 2011. Environmental issues are also addressed at the pre-school level in Estonia: the national pre-school curriculum includes the topic "Me and the environment" to help develop children's cognitive skills (such as the ability to watch nature), as well as their practical skills and values (for example, giving value to a healthy and safe way of life) (Aria et al., 2012).

The Ministry of the Environment, together with the Environmental Board, the State Forest Management Centre and the Estonian Museum of Natural History that are under its governance, are responsible for raising the environmental awareness of the Estonian population. Their action lines are the following (MoE, 2015):

- **Supporting the inclusion of environmental education in the national curricula, primarily in general education (including pre-school) programmes.** The themes of the study programmes include Estonian nature, nature conservation, forestry, water management, waste management, use of mineral resources, etc. Environment and sustainable development are set out as a recurring theme in the national curricula on the primary, basic and secondary school levels.
- **Developing specific awareness-raising and outreach activities**. Such activities aim to support the objectives of environmental and nature conservation, and typically target specific groups. For example, programmes include informing land owners of protected areas about nature conservation principles and practices, communicating environmental requirements to entrepreneurs, informing visitors of protected areas of the natural values, explaining rules on movement in nature, spreading public information on sustainable consumption, and informing private forest owners about sustainable forest management and forest heritage objects, etc.
- **Organising passive environmental education to support independent learning about nature and the environment.** This includes putting up information boards for hikers and travellers in nature, marking hiking and study trails and building resting places and camp sites, promoting hiking in nature and presenting good practices in hiking, and presenting natural values on the internet, online and through other e-solutions, etc.

Information on climate change and its impact is shared by a broad range of institutions. The Development Plan on Adaptation to Climate Change 2030 aims to raise the willingness and ability of society to adapt to the impacts of climate change at the national, regional and local levels. To this end, support is provided to pre-school, general education establishments and hobby groups, environmental education centres and vocational training institutions in adapting to the impacts of climate change. The availability of up-to-date and comprehensive information on climate change to these institutions is ensured by supporting the development of training materials, capacity building activities for teachers and educational specialists on climate and climate change adaptation; the development and implementation of climate change-related study programmes; climate research; and the participation of Estonian scientists in international climate change-related research programmes and co-operation initiatives (MoE, 2016a).

The Environmental Awareness Index, based on a biennial survey, indicates a growing awareness about environmental issues among Estonians. Carried out since 2010, these studies focus on Estonia's current environmental status and main challenges; reliability of environmental institutions and the image of the Ministry of the Environment; perceptions of environmental protection in Estonia; attitudes towards different energy sources; environmentally friendly behaviour; environmental awareness and sources of information; awareness about eco-labels and attitudes towards climate change. The Environmental Awareness Index was higher in 2016 (42.0 points) than in 2014 (37.5 points) and 2012 (37.9 points). The attitudes of the respondents from Ida-Viru County differed from the others, standing out for their markedly pessimistic undertone. They rated the status of the environment in Estonia as a whole, as well as the situation in individual areas, lower than the average. Availability of environmental information also causes problems, which might also explain the lower confidence of the inhabitants in the opinion leaders and in different environmental institutions in the region. Research has shown that young people aged 15-19 are the best informed about the topic of climate change. Over the four-year period (2012-16) the views on certain sectors have generally improved. Considerable improvement is founded in reducing industrial pollution from large enterprises, eco-friendly construction, mining, ambient air quality and accessibility to clean drinking water (MoE, 2016b).

The Environmental Board (EB) also promotes environmental education for school children. EB has developed more than 100 different environmental academic programmes, which help to tie in the knowledge and skills acquired at school. These programmes are in line with most of the topics in the natural sciences curricula and are built on the principles of active learning – the students gain knowledge and experience through practice. To this end, the EB maintains nature centres and environmental education support points all over Estonia. There are nine nature centres with comprehensive permanent exhibitions introducing the nature and cultural heritage of the area and facilities for carrying out environmental education programmes. The mobile centre - in the form of an environmental education bus - offers additional possibilities for environmental training in the Harju, Järva and Rapla counties. Moreover, the EB is currently developing programmes that can be carried out in schools, in the vicinity of schools or at environment-related enterprises (waste collection points, landfills, water treatment plants). These programmes will focus on issues such as waste management, mining, fishing, hunting, water protection, air protection, and protection from radiation) (Environmental Board, 2016).

According to a 2012 study "Education for Sustainable Development and Its Promotion", sustainable development is well covered in the Estonian national curriculum for basic education, though certain related issues remain wanting. In particular, sustainability, sustainable development and the stock of natural resources are covered extensively in the curriculum. Some attention is also paid to biodiversity. Less consideration is devoted, however, to agriculture, natural disasters, climate change, air quality, development of rural areas and exhaustion of the planet's natural resources. Moreover, the approach to sustainable development in the national curricula is relatively one-sided, without facilitating a comprehensive understanding. The skills and values promoting sustainable development in the curricula are not addressed in an integrated way; only a few key aspects (such as understanding the complexity of the world, respect and responsibility) are highlighted, while change management, co-operation skills and basic science skills are ignored (Aria et al., 2012).

5.4. Summary

- The physical infrastructure in Estonia is comparable to the average of all OECD countries, with significant differences among type of infrastructure and in some cases regions. There are in particular some problems with the availability and quality of transport infrastructure in rural areas, where agricultural and agri-food activities are located to a large extent.
- High prices for grid connection and electricity capacity upgrading are the main general problems. Since electricity grid connection is expensive, the Estonian electricity network company considers using off-grid solutions or stand-alone power systems for sparsely populated regions.
- Among transportation modes, port infrastructure is considered very good, thus facilitating international trade. Limited capacity of air and rail transport infrastructure mainly affects passengers, not freight. Most main-line railways have been upgraded to enable faster speed, and renovation is progressing. More frequent and faster trains would increase opportunities for diversified marketing of agri-food products and tourism activities. The quality of road infrastructure is unequal: main roads are mostly in a good or very good condition, and basic roads in a satisfactory condition, but the secondary and local roads need improvement as acknowledged in the Transport Development Plan 2014-2020, which aims at reducing the proportion of secondary and local roads in poor and very poor condition.
- Agricultural land improvement infrastructure in Estonia mainly consists in drainage systems that cover more than half of the utilised agricultural area. Upgrading the drainage systems, which are mostly over thirty years old, would raise agricultural productivity and sustainability.

- Estonia invested successfully in ICT and continues to do so: scores for mobile telephone subscriptions are very high and for internet use relatively high (80% of individuals use internet). Almost all companies use computers and almost all enterprises have broadband Internet connections. Since 2010, Estonia has been rapidly developing the basic broadband infrastructure (passive optical network) with the EU support. The problem lies in making high-speed broadband access to the Internet network accessible to the end users, resulting in low use of capacity (10%).

- To develop the technical infrastructure EU structural funds support is used, with the exception of electrical grid infrastructure, which is financed from electricity transmission charges. PPP is not applied in the development of technical infrastructure.

- Urbanisation and population concentration in Tallinn and the surrounding municipalities has led to the aggregation of public and private services to the regional centres, leading to a deterioration of the physical accessibility and the quality of services in rural areas, with adverse consequences on the labour market. On the other hand, the volume of certain physical public services has decreased with the spread of internet, improvement of computer skills and the development of public e-services.

- Despite this constraint, the Estonian labour market is considered as one of the most efficient among OECD countries. It stands out for employment flexibility and the high proportion of women in the labour market, but attracting and retaining talent is a serious issue as salaries are relatively low. A significant share of employees is considered overqualified or underemployed.

- The extent to which labour costs reflect labour productivity, a determinant of companies' competitiveness, places Estonia around the average of OECD countries. Unit labour costs increased faster than labour productivity, in particular during the periods of high economic growth 2006-08 and 2012-16.

- The quality of the Estonian education and training system is reflected in the high scores of students and adults in international surveys. Strengths include high educational attainment, interest in sciences and technology, and gender equity.

- A challenge is the decline in the number of students related to demographic trends. At the same time, the share of adult learners entering vocational education is increasing, reflecting their willingness to adapt their skills to market requirements.

- Estonian rural areas face labour shortages, in particular in agriculture. Estonian agriculture offers seasonal jobs, which could attract workers from non-EU countries given the remuneration is relatively low for Estonians and other EU citizens. However, the terms for recruiting temporary seasonal workers from non-EU countries are very restrictive, creating competitiveness problems, in particular for horticulture, which is a very labour intensive branch of agriculture. Regulatory changes recently implemented are expected to facilitate non-EU employment.

- Meeting the growing labour market demand for agricultural specialists is a challenge for the education system in a context of an overall decreasing number of students. In higher education, the number of students enrolled in agriculture has declined over the past decade. In vocational education, however, the decline does not affect agricultural sciences, in which student enrolment has increased in recent years. Another challenge is retaining workers in the sector — a growing share of the university graduates of agriculture-related specialties (almost half in 2015) do not practice their profession, either because they continue their studies or because they find employment in other sectors.

- To increase motivation, study allowances are paid to students on the agriculture-related curricula in vocational education and specialisation scholarships are available for students in higher education while practical training support helps to improve students' practical skills. More general efforts to guide skills development include the establishment of a system to monitor and forecast labour market future skills requirements, using the information to adapt curriculum development.

- Science and engineering attract an increasing share of students in higher education, both male and female, but science and technology is not introduced early enough in general education.
- A number of actions promote environmental and sustainable development education at every level, and measures have been recently introduced to raise awareness of climate change.

Notes

1. Labour costs consist of wage and non-wage costs, such as employers' social contributions. In Estonia, wage costs make up about three-quarters of labour costs, as they do on average in the EU28 and the OECD area.

2. In 2015 and 2016, the migration balance has been slightly positive, but it is too early to identify a change in trend.

3. The periods prescribed for their implementation are not over yet, thus their impact cannot be assessed. The transposition date for the 2014/36 is 30 September 2016 and for 2014/66 29 November 2016.

4. PISA website: www.compareyourcountry.org/pisa/country/EST.

References

Aria, K., L. Cherry, and K. Peterson (2012), Säästvat arengut toetav haridus ja selle edendamisvõimalused Eestis [education for sustainable development], www.praxis.ee/fileadmin/tarmo/Projektid/Haridus/HP_ESDPI/ENJOINED_praxis_briif_1-2012_web.pdf (accessed 18 October 2016).

ARIB (2016), Nõuanne, koolitus, arendamine [Advice, training, development], www.pria.ee/et/toetused/valdkond/nouanne_koolitus_arendamine (accessed 18 October 2016).

Bringing talent home (2016), Talendid koju [Bringing talent home], www.talendidkoju.ee/projektist (accessed 1 June 2016).

Eamets, R., K. Krillin, and A. Themas (2011), Estonian universities' alumni study 2009, http://skytte.ut.ee/sites/default/files/ec_files/Vilistlasuuring%202009_0.pdf (accessed 18 October 2016).

Eesti Noorsootöö Keskus (2016), *Noorteseire* [Youth observatory], www.noorteseire.ee/indicators/370# (accessed 18 October 2016).

EHIS (2016), *Õppeasutuste ja õppurite kohta käiv statistika* [Statistics on educational institutions and students], www.hm.ee/ehis/statistika.html (accessed 17 October 2016).

ELASA (Eesti Lairiba Arenduse Sihtasutus) (2017), EstWin arvudes, Estonian Broadband Development Foundation, www.elasa.ee/index.php?page=171 (accessed 2017).

EKKA (2016a), Otsing: Õppeasutus [Search: Education], https://wd.archimedes.ee/?page=ekka_search_dynobj&tid=94722&u=20150610134521&desktop=10016 (accessed 18 October 2016).

EKKA (2016b), Procedure for accreditation of curriculum groups of vocational education and training, http://ekka.archimedes.ee/wp-content/uploads/Procedure-for-accreditation-of-curriculum-groups-for-vocational-education-and-training.pdf (accessed 18 October 2016).

EKKA (2012), Quality Assessment of Study Programme Groups in the First and Second Cycles of Higher Education, http://ekka.archimedes.ee/wp-content/uploads/Guidelines_SPG_07.08.12_ENG.pdf (accessed 18 October 2016).

EMÜ (Estonian University of Life Science) (2016a), Development plan of Estonian University of Life Sciences until 2025, www.emu.ee/ylikoolist/yldinfo/arengukavad-ja-strateegiad/ (accessed 18 October 2016).

EMÜ (2016b), University in figures, Database of EMÜ students http://stats.emu.ee/ (accessed 18 October 2016).

EMÜ (2012), Uuring "Maapiirkonna ettevõtjate olukord, arengutrendid ning toetusvajadus". Uuringu lõpparuanne. ["The situation of rural enterprises, development trends and the need for support." Final report], Tartu.

EMÜ (2011), Maaelu arengu aruanne 2011 [Rural Development Report 2011], https://vana.emu.ee/userfiles/Maaelu_arengu_aruanne_2011FINAL.pdf (accessed 18 October 2016).

Environmental Board (2016), Keskkonnaharidus [Environmental education], www.keskkonnaamet.ee/teenused/keskkonnaharidus-2/ (accessed 18 October 2016).

European Commission (2012), "Europeans and their languages", *Special Eurobarometer 386*, June. http://ec.europa.eu/public_opinion/archives/ebs/ebs_386_en.pdf.

Eurostat (2017), Labour cost levels by NACE Rev. 2 activity, http://ec.europa.eu/eurostat/data/database (accessed 30 June 2017).

EUSAE (European Union Structural Assistance to Estonia) (2016), Euroopa Liidu struktuuritoetus. www.struktuurifondid.ee/et/ (accessed 18 May 2016).

Gardening people (2014), Aiandusrahvas tahab võõrtööliste palkamiseks leebemaid nõudeid [The gardener wants less stringent requirements for hiring migrant workers], www.saartehaal.ee/2014/10/11/aiandusrahvas-tahab-voortooliste-palkamiseks-leebemaid-noudeid/ (accessed 2 June 2016).

Jalak, K. (2010), Tööjõu kompetentside ja oskuste taseme ning tööturu vajaduste väljaselgitamine põllumajandus-, toidu- ja metsandussektoris: Uuringu aruanne [Labour competencies and skill levels of the labour market and the needs of the agricultural, food and forestry sectors: survey report], hwww.kutsekoda.ee/fwk/contenthelper/10373139/10373141 (accessed 18 October 2016).

Kirss, L., H.-S. Haaristo, M. Nestor, and E. Mikko (2013), Teadust ja tehnoloogiat populariseerivad tegevused Eestis. Uuringuaruanne [Popularising science and technology activities in Estonia. Report], Praxis, www.etag.ee/wp-content/uploads/2012/05/Praxis-2013-web.pdf (accessed 29 January 2016).

Kurvits, K. (2016), Põllumajandusettevõtete töötajate kvalifikatsioon ja personalivärbamise meetodid, Magistritöö. Eesti Maaülikool, majandus- ja sotsiaalinstituut [Farm workers' qualifications and recruitment methods, Master's thesis, Estonian University of Life Sciences, Institute of Economic and Social Sciences], https://dspace.emu.ee/xmlui/bitstream/handle/10492/2520/Ketlin_Kurvits_MA2016.pdf?sequence=1&isAllowed=y (accessed 18 October 2016).

Laan, M., A. Kuusk, H. Sunts, and J. Urb (2015), Eesti kõrgkoolide 2012, Aasta vilistlaste uuring. Lõpparuanne. Tartu: Haridus- ja Teadusministeerium, www.hm.ee/sites/default/files/2012._a_vilistlaste_uuring.pdf (accessed 17 October 2016).

Masso, M., J. Järve, K. Nurmela, S. Anspal, M.L. Räis, K. Uudeküll, and L. Osila (2013), *Töölepingu seaduse uuring* [Study of the Contracts Act], Tallinn: Poliitikauuringute Keskus Praxis [Praxis Center for Policy Studies], www.sm.ee/sites/default/files/content-editors/Ministeerium_kontaktid/Uuringu_ja_analuusid/Toovaldkond/tls_uuring_raport_uus.pdf (accessed 2 June 2016)

MEAC (Ministry of Economic Affairs and Communications) (2016), *Arengukavad* [Development Plans], www.mkm.ee/et/arengukavad (accessed 17 May 2016).

MEAC (2013a), Transpordi arengukava 2014-2020 [Transport Development Plans], www.mkm.ee/sites/default/files/transpordi_arengukava.pdf (accessed 17 May 2016).

MEAC (2013b), Eesti infoühiskonna arengukava 2020 [Estonian Development Plans for an Information Society], www.mkm.ee/sites/default/files/elfinder/article_files/eesti_infouhiskonna_arengukava.pdf (accessed 31 January 2016).

MEAC (2013c), Energiamajanduse riiklik arengukava aastani 2020 [National Energy Sector Development Plan], www.mkm.ee/sites/default/files/elfinder/article_files/energiamajanduse_arengukava_2020.pdf (accessed 18 May 2016).

MEAC (2012), *Eesti merenduspoliitika 2012-2020* [Estonian Maritime Policy], www.mkm.ee/sites/default/files/merenduspoliitika.pdf (accessed 19 May 2016).

MEAC (2010), *Eesti taastuvenergia tegevuskava aastani 2020* [Estonian National Renewable Energy Action Plan], www.mkm.ee/sites/default/files/taastuvenergia_tegevuskava.pdf (accessed 1 April 2016).

MER (Ministry of Education and Research) (2016a), *2015/2016 õppeaasta arvudes* [20015/16 academic year in figures], www.hm.ee/sites/default/files/2015-2016-oppeaasta_arvudes.pdf (accessed 17 October 2016).

MER (2016b), Välishindamine [External evaluation], www.hm.ee/et/valishindamine (accessed 18 October 2016).

MER (2015a), Haridus- ja Teadusministeeriumi aasta-analüüs 2015: Kokkuvõte [Annual Analysis of the Ministry of Education and Research 2015: Conclusion], www.hm.ee/sites/default/files/aastaanalyys2015_kokkuvote_16sept.pdf (accessed 18 October 2016).

MER (2015b), *Haridus- ja Teadusministeeriumi aasta-analüüs 2015: Kokkuvõte* [Development plan of the Ministry of Education and Science: Summary], www.hm.ee/sites/default/files/aastaanalyys2015_kokkuvote_16sept.pdf (accessed 18 October 2016).

MER (2014a), Haridus- ja Teadusministeeriumi valitsemisala arengukava "TARK ja TEGUS RAHVAS" 2015-2018 [Development plan of the Ministry of Education and Science "smart and active people"], www.hm.ee/sites/default/files/tark_ja_tegus_rahvas_2015_2018_final.pdf (accessed 17 October 2016).

MER (2014b), *Eesti elukestva õppe strateegia 2020* [Estonian Lifelong Learning Strategy 2020], www.hm.ee/index.php?popup=download&id=12568 (accessed 31 January 2016).

Mertsina, T, and T. Jänes (2012), *Tööjõu ühikukulu majanduse konkurentsivõime näitajana* [Unit labour cost as an indicator of the competitiveness of the economy], www.stat.ee/dokumendid/67463 (accessed 1 June 2016).

MoE (2016a), Kliimamuutustega kohanemise arengukava aastani 2030 [Climate Change Adaptation Plan 2030], www.envir.ee/sites/default/files/kliimamuutustega_kohanemise_arengukava_aastani_2030.pdf (accessed 18 October 2016).

MoE (2016b), Eesti elanike keskkonnateadlikkus: Elanikkonna küsitlusuuring [Estonian residents environmental awareness in the population survey project], www.envir.ee/sites/default/files/eesti_elanike_keskkonnateadlikkuse_uuringu_raport.pdf (accessed 18 October 2016).

MoE (2015), Fifth National Report to the Convention of Biological Diversity; Ministry of Environment, Tallinn, www.cbd.int/doc/world/ee/ee-nr-04-en.pdf.

MRA (Ministry of Rural Affairs) (2016a), Estonian Rural Development Plan 2014-2020, www.agri.ee/et/eesmargid-tegevused/eesti-maaelu-arengukava-mak-2014-2020 (accessed 29 January 2016).

MRA (2016b), Maa-asulate 15-74-aastaste tööhõive ülevaade, 2009–2015 [Rural situation of 15-74-year-olds: Employment overview], www.agri.ee/sites/default/files/content/uuringud/2016/uuring-2016-toohoive-ulevaade-2009-2015.pdf (accessed 18 October 2016).

MRA (2016c), Teadusnõukogud ja -komiteed [Scientific Council and Committee], www.agri.ee/et/eesmargid-tegevused/teadus-arendus-ja-nouanne/teadus-ja-arendustegevus#noukogud (accessed 3 February 2016).

MRA (2014a), *Maa-asulate tööturu ülevaade, 2007–2014 III kv*. [Labour market review of rural settlements], www.agri.ee/sites/default/files/content/uuringud/2014/uuring-2014-tooturu-ulevaade-2014-03.pdf (accessed 18 October 2016).

MRA (2014b), Regionaalne SKP piirkondade ja majandussektorite järgi [Regional GDP in the regions and economic sectors], www.agri.ee/sites/default/files/content/uuringud/2014/uuring-2014-regionaalne-skp.doc (accessed 18 October 2016).

National Audit Office (2014), *The Impact of innovation support measures on the Competitiveness of Companies*, Report to the Estonian Parliament (Riigikogu), Tallinn, 1 December, www.riigikontroll.ee/DesktopModules/DigiDetail/FileDownloader.aspx?FileId=13243&AuditId=2340 (accessed 11 February 2016).

Nestor, M. (2012), Kutseõppeasutuste vilistlaste uuring [Study on the graduates of vocational schools], www.kutsekoda.ee/fwk/contenthelper/10373139/10431393/kutse6ppeasutuste_vilistlaste_uuring.pdf (accessed 18 October 2016).

OECD (2017a), Productivity and unit labour cost by main economic activity (ISIC Rev 4), OECD database, http://dotstat.oecd.org/?lang=en.

OECD (2017b), *Education at a Glance 2017: OECD Indicators*, OECD Publishing, Paris, http://dx.doi.org/10.1787/eag-2017-en.

OECD (2016a), Employment Protection Database, www.oecd.org/employment/protection.

OECD (2016b), *Education policy outlook: Estonia*, www.oecd.org/estonia/Education-Policy-Outlook-Country-Profile-Estonia.pdf (accessed 17 October 2016).

OECD (2016c), *Skills Matter: Further Results from the Survey of Adult Skills*, OECD Skills Studies, OECD Publishing, Paris, http://dx.doi.org/10.1787/9789264258051-en.

OECD (2015), "Analysing Policies to improve agricultural productivity growth, sustainably: Revised framework", www.oecd.org/tad/agricultural-policies/Analysing-policies-improve-agricultural-productivity-growth-sustainably-december-2014.pdf.

OSKA (2016), OSKA sectors, http://oska.kutsekoda.ee/oska-valdkonnad/ (accessed 18 October 2016).

Pruulmann-Vengerfeldt, P., A. Roots, T., Strenze, and M. Ainsaar (2015), Tehnoloogiarikkas keskkonnas probleemilahendusoskuse tase ja ikt kasutus eesti elanike hulgas. PIAAC uuringu temaatiline aruanne nr 5. http://dspace.ut.ee/bitstream/handle/10062/46965/IKT_ARUANNE.pdf?sequence=1 (accessed 17 October 2015).

Recruiting from abroad (2016), Värbamine välismaalt ja töölubade taotlemine [Recruiting from abroad and applying for work permits] , www.eesti.ee/est/varbamine_valismaalt_ja_toolubade_taotlemine (accessed 1 June 2016).

Road Administration (2016), Maanteehoiu majanduslik taust [Road of savings and economic background], www.mnt.ee/index.php?id=10802 (accessed 18 May 2016).

Soosaar, O. (2015), Labour market review, Bank of Estonia, www.eestipank.ee/en/publication/labour-market-review/2015/labour-market-review-22015 (accessed 29 March 2016).

Statistics Estonia (2017), Online statistical database: www.stat.ee (accessed September 2017).

Timm, M. (2016), "Päike teeb elektriliinidele tuule alla" [The sun makes the wind power lines down], *Maaleht*, 28 July.

Unemployment Insurance Fund (2016), Töötukassa koolitused [Unemployment Insurance Training], www.tootukassa.ee/content/teenused/koolitused (accessed 6 June 2016).

Uus, M., M. Tatar, and R. Vinni (2014), *Avalike teenuste delegeerimine vabaühendustele 2014* [Delegation of public services to NGOs], Tallinn: Poliitikauuringute Keskus Praxis [Praxis Center for Policy Studies], www.praxis.ee/wp-content/uploads/2014/12/teenuste-delegeerimine.pdf (accessed 19 May 2016).

WEF (World Economic Forum) (2016), *The Global Competitiveness Report 2016-2017: Full data Edition*, Geneva, http://reports.weforum.org/global-competitiveness-index/.

Chapter 6

Agricultural policy in Estonia

This chapter provides an overview of the agricultural policy framework and instruments, focusing on EU Common Agricultural Policy (CAP) measures and their implementation in Estonia. It also reports trends on the level and composition of payments to producers and expenditure on general services to the sector. Finally, it discusses the likely policy impact on structural change, innovation, productivity growth and sustainability performance.

6.1. Agricultural policy framework

Estonia is a member state of the European Union (EU) since 2004. Therefore, the main agricultural policy framework is strongly related to the EU Common Agricultural Policy (CAP). Numerous agricultural and food sector and sub-sector strategies have been used in setting policy priorities regarding the implementation of CAP measures for 2014-20, given the flexibility offered by the CAP framework.

CAP programmes and funding are laid out in two pillars. Pillar 1, which is funded by the European Agricultural Guarantee Fund (EAGF), includes market measures under the common market organisation (CMO), and Direct Payments.[1] Pillar 2 includes rural development support which is implemented according to the national Rural Development Programme (RDP) for Estonia.[2] This plan defines Estonia's choice of measures addressing different objectives and funding levels, within the EU framework. Estonia elaborated a national RDP. Pillar 2 measures are co-financed by the European Agricultural Fund for Rural Development (EAFRD) and EU member states. In addition to the RDP, EU and national measures are mobilised in Estonia under various national development plans and strategies to address specific issues (Box 6.1).

For the 2014-20 programming period,[3] the National ceiling of Direct Payments in Estonia is EUR 897.2 million (Table 6.1). Estonia decided to transfer funds from Pillar 1 to Pillar 2, up to the maximum allowed by the EU framework.[4] [5] The remaining Pillar 1 Direct Payment budget is about EUR 800 million, while the indicative budget of the Estonian RDP in 2014-20, which includes both EU and national co-financing, is about EUR 993 million. Thus, Estonia is one of the few member states where Pillar 1 payments account for a smaller share of total EU and national CAP funding — 45% versus 61% on average (Figure 6.1). This reflects Estonia's choice to transfer funds from Pillar 1 to Pillar 2, but also lower Direct Payments compared to the EU28 average.

Within Pillar 2 funding, national payments in Estonia account for a small share — less than 10% — of total CAP and national co-financing, compared to 14% for the EU28 average. This reflects higher EU co-financing rates in "less-developed regions" such as Estonia, but also the fact that the funds transferred from Pillar 1 to Pillar 2 do not require any national co-financing. Logically, EU co-financing of Pillar 2 accounts for a larger share of all payments than the EU28 average — 46% versus 24% (Figure 6.1).

When the sum of EU and national funding for Direct Payment and RDP measures over 2014-20 is divided by the number of years (seven) and by the Utilised agricultural Area (UAA) in 2015, the average annual payment rate in Estonia is lower than the EU28 average (Figure 6.2), however it is close to that in other Baltic countries, Bulgaria, Romania, but also the United Kingdom and Spain. It should be noted, however, that according to the convergence provision, annual payments increase gradually in Estonia over the period 2014-20.

On the other hand, when annual CAP and national support over 2014-20 is related to the value of agricultural output in 2014-16, it is higher in Estonia (33%) than the EU28 average of 16%, but lower than in Finland (close to 50%), as farmers receive additional regional payments, and in Latvia (38%) (OECD, 2017a, Figure 2.2).

Figure 6.1. Share of CAP and national payments by EU member state, 2014-20

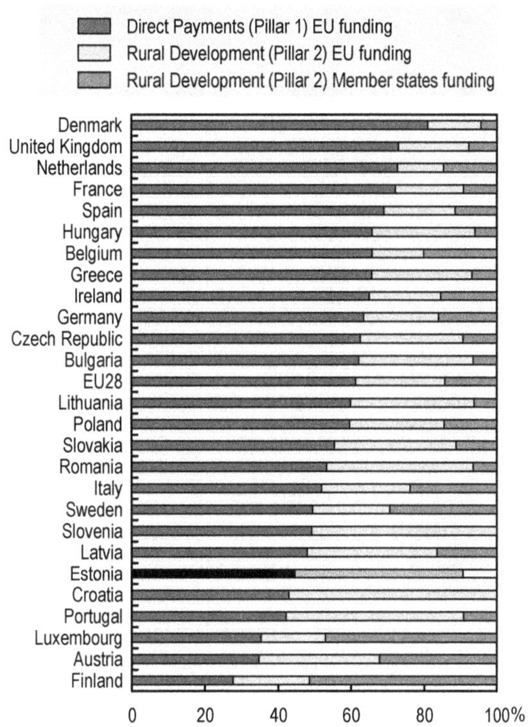

Countries are ranked according to Direct Payments (Pillar 1) EU funding levels.

Source: Figure 2.1 in OECD (2017a), *Evaluation of Agricultural Policy Reforms in the European Union: The Common Agricultural Policy 2014-20*, http://dx.doi.org/10.1787/9789264278783.

StatLink http://dx.doi.org/10.1787/888933654636

Figure 6.2. Average annual payment rate per ha over 2014-20

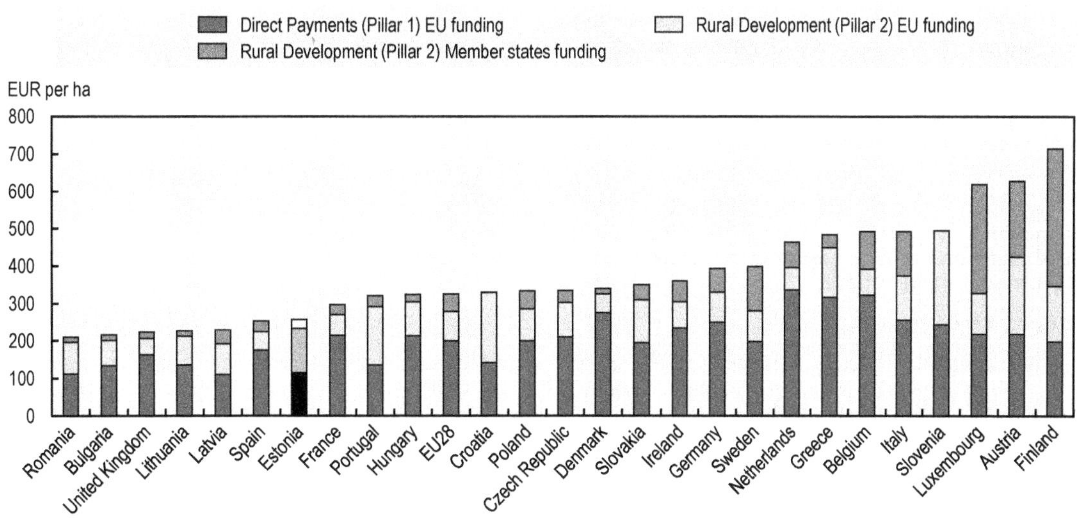

Source: Budget data calculated in OECD (2017a), http://dx.doi.org/10.1787/9789264278783, divided by the number of hectares of utilised agricultural area from Eurostat.

StatLink http://dx.doi.org/10.1787/888933654655

Box 6.1. Sectoral development plans and climate change strategy

Sectoral plans

The Estonian Dairy Strategy 2012–20 is the first strategic approach covering the whole dairy chain that was initiated by dairy sector representatives already in 2009. The strategy was issued in 2012 and it consists in analysing the situation in the Estonian dairy sector, outlining problems and identifying measures and actions to address these problems. The main goals of the strategy are to increase the volume of dairy production (to at least 1 million tonnes) and processing, to ensure the developmental capabilities of the Estonian dairy sector, to increase: dairy products export value (especially value-added products), small-scale dairy production and processing preservation; organic production, joint promotion activities, and dairy consumption. The strategy was an important input for Estonian RDP 2014–20.

The **Estonian Organic Farming Development Plan 2014–20** covers production, processing, catering, distribution and consumption, scientific studies and applied research, training, consulting and dissemination of information and legislation and supervision. The strategic goal is to improve the competitiveness of organic farming and to promote the consumption of local organic food. The plan also includes operational goals in every domain and a list of measures and actions to reach them. The main goals are to increase the net value added per labour unit in organic farming from EUR 12 400 in 2013 to EUR 20 500 by 2020, and to increase the proportion of regular (weekly) organic food consumers in Estonia from 8% in 2013 to 20% by 2020. Organic agricultural area is expected to increase from 153 400 hectares in 2013 to 180 000 hectares by 2020 and the number of organic processing facilities from 90 in 2013 to 220 by 2020. By 2016, the area of organic land had already reached 185 000 hectares and there were 1 753 organic farms in Estonia. There were 314 registered organic processing and marketing enterprises in Estonia, and about half of them were food processors.

The **Development Plan of Seed Business 2014–20** aims to increase the competitiveness of the seed and seed potato sector and to increase the use of certified seeds. Some activities are financed by the Ministry of Rural Affairs (MRA) and others by the seed sector, in addition to CAP and other measures.

The **Estonian Cereal Sector Development Plan 2014–20** covers Estonian cereals, oilseeds and legume plants. It assesses the sector's current situation and lays down the measures and actions to be taken to fulfil the established objectives for further development of the sector. The main objective of the development plan is to increase and maintain cereal production at a minimum of 1.5 million tonnes a year by rising yields to 4.5 tonnes per hectare in 2020, which will increase production and is expected to double the volume of Estonian grain exports.

The Estonian Development Plan of the Horticultural Sector for 2015–20 aims to increase the level of self-sufficiency of vegetables grown in Estonia from 58% to 75%, and the fruits and berries self-sufficiency level from 10% to 15% by 2020. It also aims to increase value-added and the share of the horticultural products of Estonian origin in consumers' food baskets and to broaden the horticultural sector. The development plan provides several actions to contribute to the long-term sustainability of Estonian horticultural sector. The main ones are to provide advice to producers and conduct surveys.

The **national development plan Estonian Food** has been implemented since 2016 to increase the competitiveness of local food products and to promote the Estonian food industry. The strategic document **Estonian Food 2015–20** was signed in December 2014. The aim of the programme is to create and develop the image of Estonian Food both in Estonia and abroad, to enhance the co-operation of food sector parties and to develop new export opportunities for Estonian food sector enterprises. Activities cover both Estonian and foreign markets. Pre-school and school children are also considered as an important target group. Projects are financed from the state budget. Activities (mostly organised through procurements) are related to food culture and improving the image of Estonian food. They include the creation of the webpage (www.estonianfood.eu) as a part of improving the image of Estonian food; the participation in international fairs, the organisation of the Estonian Food Month (in September), and other events.

The **Vision paper for Estonian beef sector 2016-20** was jointly developed by representatives from the Estonian beef sector and the Ministry of Rural Affairs (MRA). The main jointly-agreed goals are to promote export sales, achieve a uniform quality of beef meat, increase beef meat consumption, increase the involvement of research and development institutions and promotion in cooperative activities.

Climate change strategy

In addition to other sectors, **international and the EU climate change** policies and targets also cover agriculture. For instance, Estonia, as a member of the European Union, has taken a commitment to reduce greenhouse gas (GHG) emissions. Regarding Decision (EC) No 406/2009 of the European Parliament and of the Council on the effort of member states to reduce their GHG emissions, Estonia has undertaken an obligation to keep the increase of GHG emissions from non-Emission-Trading-System (ETS) sectors (including agriculture) below 11% of 2005 emissions. According to the 2030 policy framework for climate and energy, Estonia has to reduce its GHG emissions from non-ETS sectors at least by 10% from the 2005 level by the year 2030. Estonia also subscribes to the **adaptation** objectives initiated by the European Commission in 2009.

Estonia also has several **national policies** to lay out climate change priorities. In 2016, two strategic documents related to climate change were adopted in Estonia: **General Principles of Estonian Climate Policy till 2050**, which focuses primarily on climate change mitigation, and **Estonian Climate Change Adaptation Development Plan 2030**. Key measures in reducing the GHG emissions from agriculture are the following: manure management, biogas and biomass production, efficient use of fertilisers, management of peat lands and increasing carbon stock in soils. The main adaptation measures are consulting and information distribution, plant breeding, mitigation of changes in water regimes, insurance against damages caused by climate change, observation of the spread of pests, plant and animal diseases and implementation of necessary protection measures.

6.2. Broad-based measures

Pillar 1 Direct Payments are broad-based as they apply to all hectares or animals when they are specific to some sectors. In Estonia, 96% of Direct Payments are paid as a flat-rate per-hectare payment. As in the rest of the European Union, recipients need to be active farmers but except for a small share of payments for specific commodities, they are not required to actually produce to receive payments. Payments are, however, conditional on the respect of regulations and the adoption of specific farm practices. Pillar 1 payments include:

- The basic payment is implemented in Estonia as a flat-rate per hectare payment under the Single Area Payment Scheme (SAPS) and comprises the main part (65.5%) of Pillar 1 Direct Payment budget (Table 6.1). It is conditional on maintaining agricultural land in good agricultural and environmental conditions (See Box 6.2 on cross compliance conditions).
- The greening payment, which accounts for 30% of Pillar 1 Direct Payments, rewards agricultural practices beneficial for the climate and environment and is also implemented as a flat rate payment per hectare. The greening farming practices are annual measures that go beyond cross-compliance and are based on crop diversification, maintenance of permanent grassland and the establishment of ecological focus areas (Box 6.2).
- Voluntary Coupled Support (VCS), which can be granted to specific sectors or regions, accounted for 3% of Pillar 1 in 2015 and 2016, and benefited dairy, beef, sheep meat, and fruit and vegetable producers. VCS accounted for 5% of Pillar 1 in 2017, and from 2017, they only concern the dairy, and fruits and vegetable sectors.
- The Young Farmers' Scheme (YFS), which is a top-up payment for young farmers, accounts for the remainder (Table 6.1). The annual payment for young farmers is calculated as 25% of the per-hectare payment multiplied by the number of eligible hectares, limited to 39 ha (Parliament of Estonia, 2014).

Table 6.1. Breakdown of CAP Pillar 1 Estonian National ceiling, 2014-20

EUR million

	2015	2016	2017	2018	2019	2020	Total 2014-20	
							Amount	% of Pillar 1
Basic payment (SAPS)	75.5	75.6	80	87.2	94.2	111.9	524.3	65.5
Greening	34.3	34.4	37.1	40.2	43.2	50.8	240	30.0
Voluntary coupled support (VCS)	4.2	4.2	6.1	6.1	6.1	6.1	33	4.1
Young farmers' scheme (YSF)	0.3	0.3	0.4	0.4	0.5	0.6	2.6	0.3
Total Pillar 1 direct payments	114.3	114.5	123.6	133.9	144	169.4	799.9	100.0
Transfer to Pillar 2	7.5	19.1	21.8	23.5	25.4	0	97.3	
National ceiling	121.9	133.7	145.5	157.4	169.4	169.4	897.2	

Source: compiled on the basis of Regulation (EU) No 1307/2013, European Parliament (2015), and communication from MRA.

In 2015-16, VCS in Estonia was paid to farm households with a maximum of 100 dairy cows; for those with a maximum of 25 suckler cows and heifers of up to 8 months of age; for ewes and sheep in herds with 10-100 ewes or she-goats that are at least one year old; and for growing fruits and vegetables on at least 1 ha of land (MRA, 2015a).[6] The support rates of direct payments are relatively modest by EU standards (Table 6.2; Figure 6.2).

Within the EU framework, due to the difficult situation in the milk farming sector, the MRA increased the payment rate for farm households that have a maximum of 100 dairy cows for the period 2017-20, and to introduce a payment for those that have between 100 and 400 cows. VCS for suckler cows and heifers, and for ewes and sheep were abolished in 2017 (MRA, 2016b).

Estonia is one of the EU member states allowed to pay transitional national aid (TNA) in addition to the EU National ceiling. However, in 2014-16, the Government decided not to utilise this opportunity. The new government that took office in November 2016 paid TNA in the maximum amount, starting from 2017 (Government, 2016).

Table 6.2. Support rates of direct payments, 2015 and 2016

Direct payment scheme	Unit	2015	2016	% change
Single area payment scheme (SAPS)	EUR/ha	79.00	79.64	0.8
Payment for agricultural practices beneficial for the climate and environment (greening)	EUR/ha	36.14	36.20	0.2
Young farmers scheme (YFS)[1]	EUR/ha	19.87	19.91	0.2
VCS[2] for growing fruits and vegetables	EUR/ha	572.86	526.97	-8.0
VCS for dairy cows	EUR/cow	130.80	123.19	-5.8
VCS for suckler cows	EUR/cow	91.32	75.90	-16.9
VCS for ewes and goats	EUR/animal	15.88	14.13	-11.0

1. Limited to 25% of the SAPS on the first 38 ha. 2. Voluntary Coupled Support

Source: ARIB (2015), www.pria.ee/et/toetused/valdkond/taimekasvatus/pindalatoetused_yld_2015/; ARIB (2017), www.pria.ee/et/toetused/valdkond/taimekasvatus/pindalatoetused_yld_2016/.

Box 6.2. Conditions for receiving CAP support

Most CAP payments are conditional on the respect of **cross-compliance** requirements, which include:

- Statutory Management Requirements (SMR), related to the respect of EU regulations, including prevention of nitrate pollution in a nitrate-sensitive area; conservation of wild birds, natural habitats, fauna and flora; food and feed safety, the use of hormones in livestock farming, animal identification and registration; transmissible spongiform encephalopathy (TSE), use of plant protection products, minimum standards for the protection of calves, minimum standards for the protection of pigs, the protection of livestock; and
- Good Agricultural and Environmental Conditions (GAEC), including water protection, soil and carbon conservation, preservation of landscape features and minimum level of maintenance.

Moreover, since 2015, Estonian farmers claiming support under the single area payment scheme (SAPS) have to meet additional 'greening' conditions, attached to the greening top-up payment that makes 30% of Direct Payments.[1] These requirements cover agricultural practices related to crop diversification, the maintenance of permanent grassland and the establishment of ecological focus areas, which are beneficial for the climate and the environment. The regulation foresees that if the greening payment conditions are not fulfilled the green payment is disrupted and penalties may apply).

1. All EU member states implement the Greening payment, whether they receive the Basic Payment Scheme, or the SAPS like Estonia.

Direct payments to Estonian farmers increased over the period 2004-12, as EU payments gradually increased during the transition period following accession, and with the introduction of complementary national direct payments in 2004 (Figure 6.3). In 2009, however, when economic recession was deepest, the amount of direct payments was lower than in the two previous years. Between 2012 and 2015, the annual amount of total EU and national direct payments decreased and fell below the 2007 level in real terms in 2014 and 2015. It was first due to lower complementary national direct payments in 2013. From 2014, the main reason was the government's decision not to pay TNA, and to transfer some funds from Pillar 1 to Pillar 2 from 2015. However, direct payments increased again in 2016 as planned by the EU external convergence mechanism under which payment differences between member states will gradually narrow over 2014-20. The value of Pillar 1 direct payments as a percentage of agricultural output (in current prices) has declined from 18.2% in 2008 to 11.6% in 2015, and increased again to 16.3% in 2016 (Figure 6.3). The amount of direct payments received by Estonian farmers will increase further with convergence and with the introduction, from 2017, of TNA up to the maximum amount allowed (Government, 2016).

Figure 6.3. Developments in direct payments in Estonia, 2004 to 2016

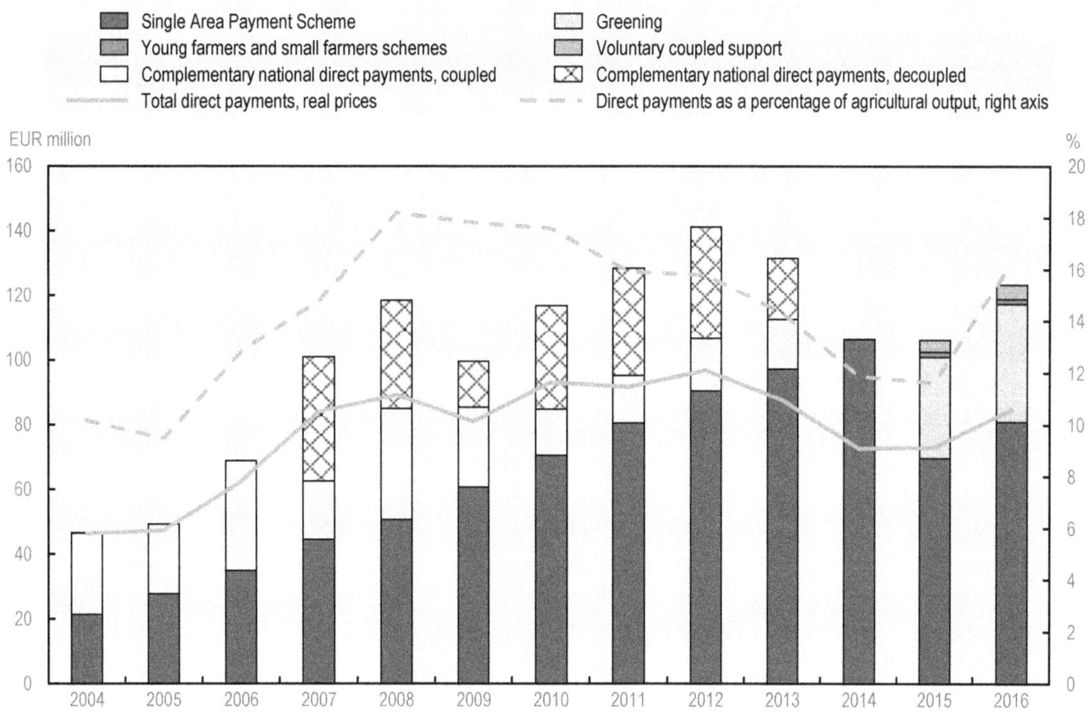

Source: Communication from MRA, Statistics Estonia (2017), www.stat.ee.

StatLink http://dx.doi.org/10.1787/888933654674

Pillar 1 also includes funding for market support measures. The following EU market regulation measures were applied in Estonia in 2016 (MRA, 2017):

- School milk support scheme — Estonia started subsidising milk for school children in 2001 before it implemented the EU scheme after accession in 2004. Expenditures for this programme in Estonia increased from EUR 1.52 million in 2015 to EUR 1.65 million in 2016, of which EUR 0.86 million national co-financing and EUR 0.79 million EU funding).
- School fruit and vegetables scheme — the EU scheme provides support to fruits and vegetables for schools with 10% national co-financing. Since implementation in 2009/10, the scope of the programme has expanded and expenditures in Estonia reached EUR 0.98 million in 2015/16.
- EU intervention mechanisms remain for some cereals and dairy products — while in 2014/15, no purchase of cereal or dairy products were made for intervention storage, the mechanisms were triggered the following year for dairy products as producer prices fell below intervention prices leading to the purchase of 672 tonnes of skimmed milk powder for a monetary value of EUR 1.18 million between February and July 2016.
- EU private storage aid — as EU average market prices for pig meat fell below the reference threshold, the temporary removal of pig meat was supported for a few months in both 2015 and 2016. The total amount of private storage aid for pig meat in Estonia was EUR 0.16 million in 2015 and EUR 22 million in 2016.
- Export refunds — in 2015 and 2016, no export refunds were paid in the European Union.
- A specific programme for honey production and market development is co-financed by EU funds. It supports technical assistance to beekeepers, measures for combating beehive invaders, and measures to support laboratories for the analysis of apiculture products.

- A number of programmes fund information provision and agricultural products promotion measures for Estonian fresh fruits and vegetables, dairy products and grass-fed beef, under Pillar 1. In 2015 and 2016, expenditures amounted to less than EUR 0.5 million annually.
- Production quotas — since the EU milk quotas expired on 31 March 2015, no production restrictions apply, as Estonia does not produce wine or sugar.
- Exceptional aid to milk producers and the pig sector — with the deterioration of market conditions starting from 2014, the European Commission granted EUR 7.6 million exceptional aid to Estonian dairy and pig meat producers in October 2015, which was complemented by EUR 7 million of national support. An exceptional adjustment aid of EUR 16.2 million was paid in 2017, co-financed 50-50 by EU and national funds.
- The EU milk production reduction scheme was launched by the European Commission in July 2016 in response to the milk crisis. By March 2017, EUR 0.57 million were granted to Estonian milk producers agreeing to voluntarily reduce their production in the last quarter of 2016 and in January 2017.
- Exceptional aid to the horticulture sector — since the beginning of the Russian Federation ban in August 2014, the European Commission granted a series of exceptional support measures to producers of certain fruits and vegetables, which included Estonian beneficiaries. They include market withdrawals, notably for free distribution, and compensation for non-harvesting and green harvesting. Expenditures for this programme are very small.

6.3. Domestic measures targeting specific issues

General characteristics of the Estonian RDP

Measures under successive RDPs respond to priority areas defined at the EU level. The four thematic axes guiding the implementation of the RDP for 2007-13 have been replaced by six priority areas for the period 2014-20:

1. Fostering knowledge transfer and innovation;
2. Enhancing competitiveness of all types of agriculture and the sustainable management of forests;
3. Promoting food chain organisation, including processing and marketing, and risk management;
4. Restoring, preserving and enhancing ecosystems;
5. Promoting resource efficiency and the transition to a low-carbon economy; and
6. Promoting social inclusion, poverty reduction and economic development in rural areas.[7]

The EUR 992.8 million planned budget for the Estonian RDP over 2014-20 was allocated to these priorities through the implementation of 14 measures, as indicated in Table 6.3. Investment support (Measure 04) is related to all RDP priorities and comprises close to 30% of the Estonian RDP budget. Environmental measures (Measures 10), which is related to the Ecosystem management priority 4 accounts for about a quarter of the total. The third measure receiving the highest funding (12.3%) is measure 06: Farm development, which is related to several priorities: Competitiveness, Resource efficiency and climate change, and Social inclusion and local development. It is followed by the LEADER measures addressing social inclusion and local development in general (9%).

Regarding allocation by priority, Ecosystem management comes first with close to 37% of total funds, as support for organic farming and Natura 2000 areas are expected to contribute to this priority in addition to agri-environment and climate measures. The competitiveness priority follows with close to 30% of total RDP funds.

Table 6.3. Indicative budget of Estonian RDP, 2014-20

	Priorities[1]								
Measures	1. Knowledge transfer and innovation[1]	2. Competitiveness	3. Food chain	4. Ecosystem management	5. Resource efficiency and climate change	6. Social inclusion and local development	Technical assistance	Total	% of total
01 Knowledge		2.3	3.2	4.6	1.9			12.0	1.2
02 Advisory		5.4	0.2	0.7	0.4	2		8.7	0.9
03 Quality schemes			1.0					1.0	0.1
04 Investments		212.0	50.0	2.5	8.0	17		289.5	29.2
06 Farm development		52.1			3.0	67		122.1	12.3
08 Forest				1.0	9.0			10.0	1.0
09 Producer groups			6.0					6.0	0.6
10 Environment				244.9				244.9	24.7
11 Organic				77.7				77.7	7.8
12 Natura				32.7				32.7	3.3
14 Animal welfare			40.6					40.6	4.1
16 Cooperation		11.7	4.0	1.5	1.5			18.7	1.9
19 LEADER						90		90.0	9.1
20 Technical assistance							38.9	38.9	3.9
Total		**283.5**	**105.0**	**365.6**	**23.8**	**176**	**38.9**	**992.8**	
% of total		28.6	10.6	36.8	2.4	17.7	3.9		

1. Priority 1 is attributed throughout all priorities.

Source: European Commission (2015), http://ec.europa.eu/agriculture/rural-development-2014-2020/country-files/ee/factsheet_en.pdf.

Compared to the EU28 average, Estonia's RDP includes a higher share of funds for investment, reflecting needs for further modernisation to improve competitiveness, and efficient use of resources at the farm level and in the whole food chain (Figure 6.4). Forestry investments are also included, but in Estonia they are minor compared to agro-food ones. The share of payments for improving sustainability (Measures 10 to 13) through better ecosystem management is lower than the EU28 average, but is close to that in other Baltic countries. In many other EU member states, payments for the environment include specific payments for areas facing natural constraints, which can be high in some countries, but which Estonia did not include in its RDP.

The results of various analysis and impact assessments were considered in developing the Estonian RDP 2014-20 (Box 6.3). For example, it includes sub-measures 'Innovation clusters' and 'Long-term programmes of knowledge transfer' where applicants should form a consortium consisting multiple partners from Research and Development (R&D) institutions, agricultural producers, food processors, advisory system, vocational education institutions and other stakeholders. In addition, the advisory system was reformed, and the coordination role was given to the Rural Development Foundation. Young farmers are now supported from both CAP pillars 1 and 2, and measures that target the food processing industry receive larger funding than in the previous RDP.

Figure 6.4. RDP 2014-20 choices by selected EU member states

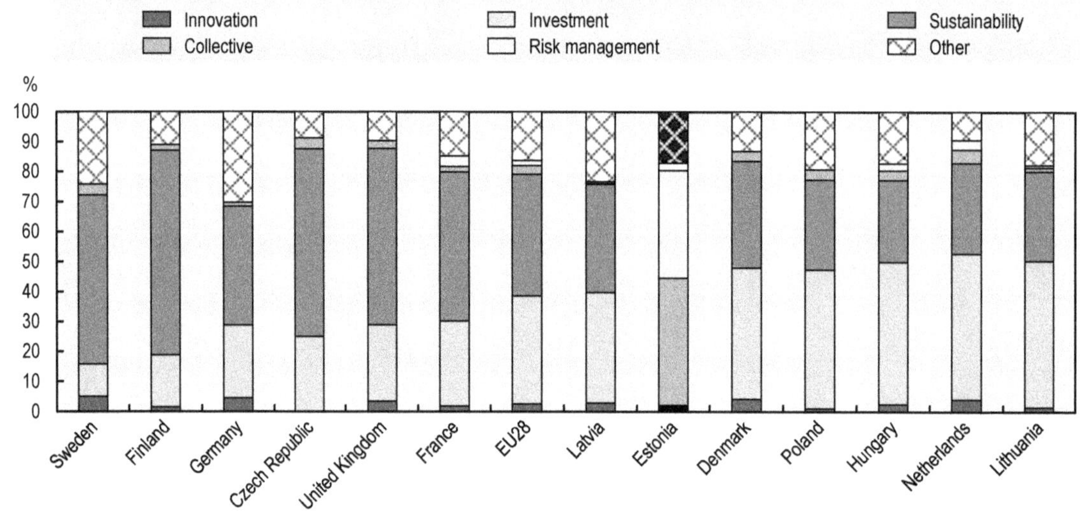

Countries are ranked according to Investment levels.

Innovation includes Measures 01 and 02; Investment is the sum of Measures 04, 05, 06 and 08; sustainability is the sum of Measures 10, 11, 12, 13 and 15; Measures supporting collective actions are 09 and 16; and risk management is Measure 17.

Source: European Commission (2015), http://ec.europa.eu/agriculture/rural-development-2014-2020/country-files/ee/factsheet_en.pdf.

StatLink http://dx.doi.org/10.1787/888933654693

Box 6.3. Evaluation of RDP agricultural policy measures

During the programming period of the Estonian RDP 2007-13, an ongoing evaluation was carried out for the first time. It provided analyses and feedback on the implementation and results of the RDP. During the development of the Estonian RDP 2014-20, an *ex ante* evaluation was carried out, as planned by EU procedures. In parallel, a strategic environmental evaluation was done. Several recommendations of the strategic environmental evaluation were implemented in designing the measures of the RDP 2014-20. The results of the ongoing evaluation were used as input in the process of *ex ante* evaluation. The monitoring and evaluation system of the RDP will be explained in Chapter 7.

In the SWOT analysis section of the RDP 2014-20, among others, the following conclusions were drawn in relation to innovation, structural change and sustainable use of resources:

- During the period 2005-12, labour productivity increased markedly in primary agriculture, by 53.3%. This growth was mainly due to structural changes, improvement in efficiency and intensification of production.
- Insufficient communication of R&D results and lack of cooperation between different parties in innovation activities hinder knowledge transfer from science to practice, as well as awareness of scientists of the practical problems of enterprises. In the longer term, this could hinder the competitiveness of agriculture. Therefore, promotion of cooperation between research groups, agricultural producers, entrepreneurs and advisors is needed.
- In the fields of agriculture and the rural economy, various training and knowledge transfer activities should include, among others, the themes related to management, maintenance of agricultural land, and agri-environment. In the programming period 2007-13, there were not enough training activities on themes important to the state, such as climate change and water protection.
- In developing the advisory system, the advisory centres should increase cooperation between themselves, and with the coordinating centre, R&D institutions and various specialty organisations.
- Hiring and training of new advisors is necessary, especially in the fields of adaptation to climate change and innovation.
- In terms of land improvement, efficient use of 55% of the agricultural area requires well-functioning drainage systems. Most of the drainage systems are more than 30 years old and require renovation and reconstruction. Over 2004-13, 15% of required reconstruction and 25% of required renovation was done with support from RDP funds.
- Considering the positive results of support measures for young farmers, but acknowledging the insufficient share of young farmers, the entry of qualified and experienced (in agriculture) younger farm managers' generation should be supported (from both Pillar 1 and Pillar 2 measures).

Box 6.3. Evaluation of RDP agricultural policy measures (cont.)

- While organic production has developed and 15% of agricultural land is organic,[1] more attention should be paid to developing the supply chain to ensure that more correctly labelled organic products reach final consumers.
- The food processing industry needs to reduce exports of raw materials or low value added products and increase exports of high value added products. The range of export partners should be expanded in order to reduce risks.
- In addition to insufficient investments into fixed assets, the Estonian food processing industry lacks the capacity to make the production process more knowledge intensive.
- Several recommendations have been made in relation to biodiversity and landscapes (farmland birds, landscape elements, local breeds and varieties, semi-natural habitats, Natura 2000 agricultural land, high nature value agricultural land), water protection and management (use of pesticides, nutrient leaching, manure storage and spreading, manure spreading equipment, nitrate vulnerable zone, organic production), soils (loss of organic matter, low K and P reserves in soils, reduction of cultivation on peat soils, liming of soils, water erosion), energy efficiency (more efficient use of motor fuels), renewable energy and use of residues, reduction of GHG emissions (biogas production, more efficient use of Nitrogen fertilisers, climate-friendly cultivation techniques, environmentally friendly management of peat soils, manure storage and application, improve CO_2 sequestration).
- Availability and quality of high speed internet connection should be improved in rural areas.

1. Agricultural land under organic practices further increased to 18% in 2015.

Source: MRA (2015b), www.agri.ee/sites/default/files/content/arengukavad/mak-2014/mak-2014-kommunikatsioonistrateegia.pdf.

Detailed RDP measures

Box 6.4 provides the list of detailed measures implemented under the 13 EU measures retained in the Estonian RDP. These measures are implemented gradually. In 2016, EUR 187.29 million was committed and in total EUR 115.04 million was paid out.

Box 6.4. Detailed 2014-20 RDP measures in Estonia

1. Knowledge transfer and information actions

1.1 Arrangement of training activities

1.2 Arrangement of demonstration and information activities

1.3 Arrangement of visits to enterprises and study groups

1.4 Long-term programmes

2. Advisory services, farm management and farm relief services

2.1 Support to individual advisory services

2.3 Support for training of advisors

3. Quality schemes for agricultural products, and foodstuffs

3.2 Information and promotion activities of products produced in the framework of Union and nationally recognised quality schemes

3.3.1 Support to bioenergy

4. Investments in physical assets

4.1 Investment in improving the performance of farm holdings

4.2 Investments into processing and marketing of agricultural products

4.3 Investments into development and maintenance of agricultural and forestry infrastructure

4.4 Support for the restoration of stonewalls

5. Restoring agricultural production potential damaged by natural disasters and catastrophic events and introduction of appropriate prevention actions

5.2 Restoration of the agricultural production potential damaged by harmful plant pests and animal diseases

Box 6.4. Detailed 2014-20 RDP measures in Estonia (cont.)

6. Farm and business development

- 6.1 Setting up of young farmers
- 6.3 Development of small farms
- 6.4 Support for the diversification of rural economy towards non-agricultural activities

8. Investments in forest area development and improvement of the viability of forests

- 8.3 Prevention and elimination of damages to forests and restoration of damaged forests
- 8.6 Improving the viability and economic value of forests

9. Setting up of producer groups and organisations

10. Agri-environment-climate

- 10.1.1 Support for environmentally friendly management
- 10.1.3 Regional soil protection support
- 10.1.4 Support for environmentally friendly horticulture
- 10.1.5 Support for growing plants of local varieties
- 10.1.6 Support for keeping animals of local endangered breeds
- 10.1.7 Support for the maintenance of semi-natural habitats

11. Organic farming

- 11.1 Conversion to organic farming
- 11.2 Maintaining of organic farming

12. Natura 2000 and Water Framework Directive payments

- 12.1 Natura 2000 support for agricultural land
- 12.2 Natura 2000 support for private forest land

14. Animal welfare

16. Cooperation

- 16.0 Innovation clusters
- 16.2 Development of new products, processes and technologies
- 16.4 Short supply chains and the development of local markets

19. Support for LEADER local development

- 19.2 Implementation of local development strategies
- 19.3 Cooperation
- 19.4 Animation of the territory and operation of local action groups

Source: MRA (2017), Communication to OECD on agricultural policy implemented in Estonia in 2016.

Measures for improving adoption of innovation

Adoption of new technologies is supported through investment support in RDP measures 4 and 6. In addition to enhancing productivity and income, investment support is also used *inter alia* to purchase technology enabling more efficient use of farm inputs, including natural resources, and management of livestock manure, leading to improved sustainability performance. Both measures support investment for adding value along the food chain and for the diversification of activities on the farm, which can contribute to more optimal allocation of farm household labour and thus higher farm labour productivity.

Measures 1 and 2, which support technology transfer and advisory services, aim to facilitate the diffusion of new knowledge and practices (Chapter 7). Moreover, innovation is the focus of RDP measure 16 that supports cooperation activities in innovation clusters; the development short supply chains and local markets; and the development of new products, practices, processes and technologies. These measures aim to support the cooperation of farms, food processing industry, R&D institutions and other actors in finding innovative solutions relevant for the whole agricultural and food sector or sub-sector, or individual enterprise or group of enterprises.

Instruments for supporting variable input use

As part of State Aid measures,[8] the main instrument related to variable input use in Estonia is a fuel excise tax exemption for agricultural producers for using diesel fuel in the machinery used in the process of agricultural production. The exemption amounted to EUR 48 million in 2016 (Chapter 4).

A subsidised insurance programme was introduced in 2008, also as a State Aid measure. The subsidy covers 65% of insurance premiums for agricultural crops, agricultural animals, poultry and bees in small and medium sized agricultural enterprises (SMEs). The purpose is to offer a sustainable solution to agricultural producers to manage the losses caused by adverse weather conditions, climate disasters and animal and plant diseases or pest infestations. The total amount of support paid in 2015 and 2016 was EUR 0.01 million. In practice, only insurance products covering animal diseases were offered. The regulations also allow support to crop insurance schemes but there are no crop insurance products on the market in Estonia.

Measures facilitating structural adjustment in the food and agricultural sector

In the farming sector, the main measure facilitating structural adjustment is support to young farmers, both under Pillar 1, and under RDP measure 6.1, which provides investment support to young farmers, with the aim to facilitate the transfer of farm management to younger and well-prepared managers.

In the food sector, the creation of producer groups is supported via RDP measure 9. In addition, the RDP includes support to large projects, i.e. large-scale investment (with support EUR 2-15 million) in processing facilities. This measure is only eligible to applicants, in which producer cooperatives own a majority of shares.

The clarification of property rights during the transition period also facilitated land transfers and investment.

Agri-environmental measures

Under Estonia's RDP, Estonian farmers are eligible for payment for **voluntary** agri-environmental commitments. As environmental protection for water, soil and biodiversity are key priorities of the RDP, voluntary commitments have a strong environmental emphasis. In particular, the RDP supports sustainable agriculture in Estonia through the environmentally friendly management (EFM) scheme, now under Measure 10: agri-environment and climatic measures (AECM). In 2016 the EFM scheme covered 447 065 ha, or close to 45% of agricultural land in Estonia (ARC, 2016).

The EFM basic scheme requirements are as follows (ARIB, 2016a).

- To ensure crop rotation, the same crop or vegetable is grown in the same field for up to two consecutive years (for cereals, up to three consecutive years; for cruciferous crops, every fourth year).
- Leguminous crops are grown on at least 15% of the land subject to support either in pure culture, in a mixture with gramineous grasses, or in a mixture with other agricultural crops used as green fertilisers. Under-sowing of legumes is allowed.
- At least 30% of the land subject to support is under winter vegetation from 1 November to 31 March the following year.
- At least 15% of cereal crops are sown with certified seed (in spring and winter in total).
- The application of glyphosates is prohibited from the time of emergence and planting of cultivated plants and vegetables until harvesting. It is also prohibited on green fallows and grasslands used as green manures and on fields where the pastures for bees are established with the help of EFM support.

- The applicant arranges the collection of soil samples at least once during the obligation period and sends the soil samples to an accredited laboratory.
- The applicant draws up a fertilisation plan by 15 June for the whole UAA.
- The applicant or his/her representative must participate in the EFM basic training by 1 December of the first year of the obligation period and in an EFM extension training by 15 June of the fifth year of the obligation period.
- If the area of arable land (under crops or vegetables or unplanted fallow) is larger than 20 ha and borders with a public road, the applicant must leave or establish a 2–5 metre wide grassland strip with perennial vegetation or other kind of landscape element between the field and public road.

The **EFM support rate** varies according to measures undertaken. The basic requirements package is EUR 50/ha. Additional support for implementing additional water protection activities and for creating "bee pastures" is also provided (ARIB, 2016b; ARIB, 2016c). Since 2015, support for soil protection has also been offered to encourage the sustainable usage of eroded and peaty soils on the fields that are not covered with other area payments under RDP support.

Farms in Natura 2000 areas receive a subsidy of EUR 27/ha under Measure 12 in an effort to compensate the additional costs incurred or income not received due to restrictions (RT I, 26.04.2016, 13).

Support to organic farming

Support is available in the form of payments per hectare of agricultural area to farmers who convert to, or maintain, on a voluntary basis, organic farming practices and methods defined in Council Regulation EC No 834/2007. Payments aim to compensate for all or part of the loss of income and the additional costs associated with the implementation of organic practices and methods. Payment rates depend on agricultural land use and range from EUR 25/ha to EUR 660/ha in Estonia. Payments for organic farming are also part of a wider plan to develop the Estonian organic agro-food sector (Box 6.1).

The number of Estonian enterprises engaged in organic production, the area under organic practices and the size of organic farms have increased in the last decade (Box 2.1). As the number of hectares under organic practices rose from 46 000 ha in 2004 to 171 000 ha in 2015 and 185 000 ha in 2016, support to organic farming increased from EUR 3.2 million in 2004 to EUR 12.9 million in 2015 and EUR 13.3 million in 2016.

The number of organic enterprises increased to 1 629 in 2015 (and 1 753 in 2016), and the number of organic support recipients increased from 1 335in 2014 to 1 450 in 2015 (ARIB, 2016a). This would indicate that some producers farm organically without support.

FADN data show that the value of organic crop production increased over the period 2010-14, while organic livestock production remained rather stable. Although the land productivity of organic farming has improved over the past five years, the value of livestock production per livestock unit has declined (FADN, 2016).

General services to the food and agriculture sector

The food and agricultural sector also benefits from general services, which are mainly supported by the Estonian budget. According to the OECD General Services Support Estimate (GSSE), total spending on general services to food and agriculture amounted to EUR 54 million in 2014-16. This represents a quarter of payments to farmers (Figure 6.5). Of these total expenditures, the agricultural knowledge and innovation system and inspection and control services accounted for most funding, with 36% of the total each. The development and maintenance of infrastructure accounted for 18% of all expenditures on general services, marketing and promotion for 10% and public stockholding for less than 1%. All these expenditures are expected to facilitate innovation for improved productivity, safety, and sustainability performance.

Figure 6.5. Composition of support to food and agriculture, 2014-16

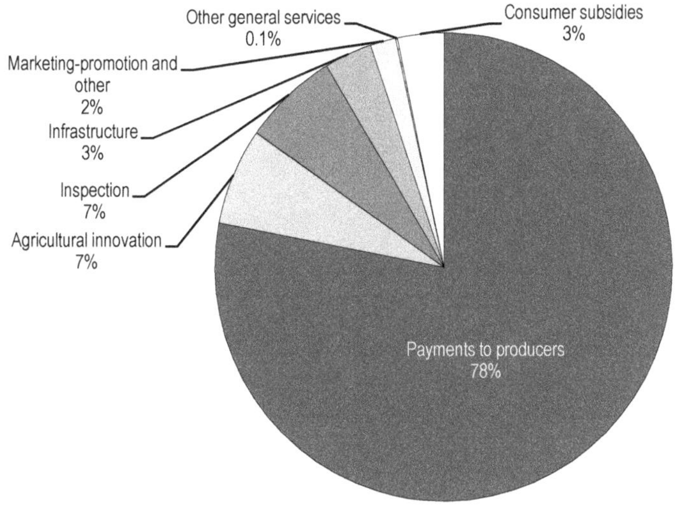

Source: MRA (2017), Communication to the OECD of EU and national expenditures in Estonia.

StatLink http://dx.doi.org/10.1787/888933654712

6.4. Developments in agricultural support

Since Estonia became an EU member state in 2004, payments to farmers almost doubled to reach EUR 248 million in 2016. At the same time payments have become increasingly decoupled over time, with the share of payments based on fixed parameters representing almost two-thirds of payments in 2016 (Figure 6.6). Payments based on current parameters, mainly hectares and animal numbers, have been relatively stable until they started to decline in 2014, when Estonia decided not to grant additional payments to specific sectors. Developments in payments based on variable input use mainly reflect the recent increase in the fuel tax rebate reflecting higher general tax levels. Investment support, classified as payments based on fixed capital formation, has decreased in recent years, but that may reflect delays in implementing the recent RDP.

Expenditures on general services to food and agriculture have been multiplied by 3.5 over the period 2004-16, which partly reflects a methodology change in 2013 (Figure 6.7). As a result, they were equivalent to 22% of payments to producers in 2016, compared to 12% in 2004. The highest increase was for innovation-related expenditures on research and development, extension and agricultural education, which increased ten-fold. Support for the marketing and promotion of agricultural products, which benefit from EU support, also increased strongly. Support to inspection services for pest and disease control and farm inputs was also reinforced.

Figure 6.6. Developments in payments to producers, 2004 to 2016

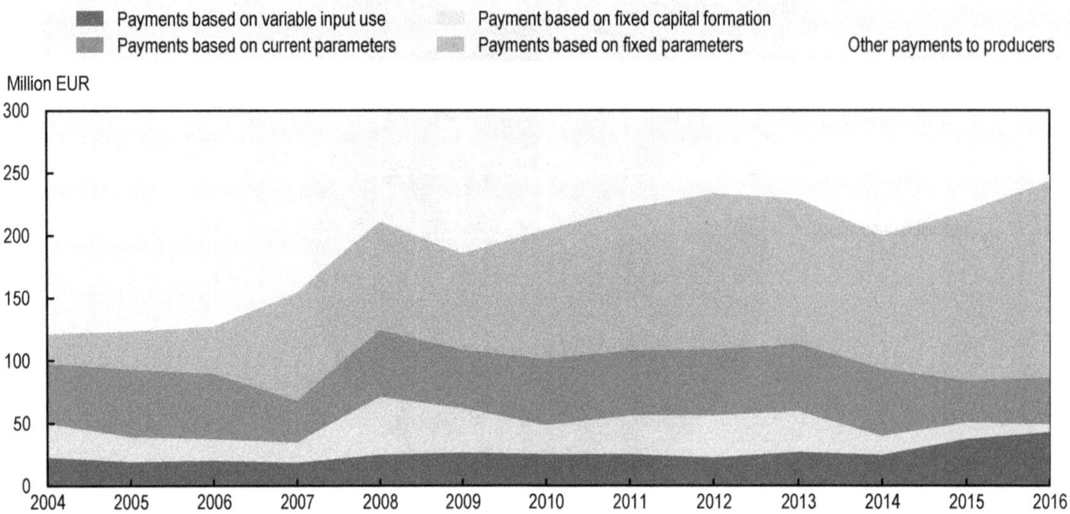

Source: MRA (2017), Communication to the OECD of EU and national expenditures in Estonia.

StatLink http://dx.doi.org/10.1787/888933654731

Figure 6.7. Developments in Estonian agriculture-related expenditure on general services, 2004 to 2016

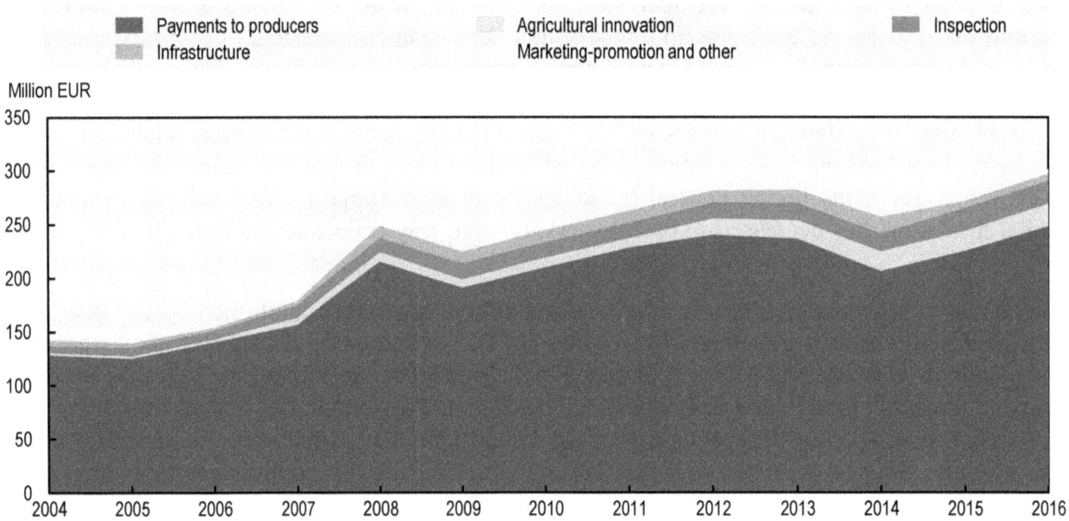

Source: MRA (2017), Communication to the OECD of EU and national expenditures in Estonia.

StatLink http://dx.doi.org/10.1787/888933654750

6.5. Extent to which agricultural policies are supportive of productivity growth, sustainably

Agricultural policy measures affect farm investments and practices through a variety of instruments, with different intended and unintended impacts on structural change, natural resource use and innovation. A policy instrument will affect business decisions by changing the relative prices of inputs and outputs. For example, investment support lowers the price of land and capital and could thus facilitate structural change and investment in new technologies. The path of productivity growth and sustainability outcomes will then depend on both market and other policy incentives and disincentives.

Sustainability outcomes are linked to the way natural capital, which is the source of service flows entering the production process, or ecosystem services, is being priced and used. In cases where public policy is deficient to address these market failures in pricing natural assets, which often have a common pool, externality or public good characteristics, there is a risk that innovation systems and productivity growth in agriculture follow a non-sustainable pathway, leading to progressive depletion of natural assets, which may not be substituted by other forms of capital or by labour. In such cases, there would be a trade-off between productivity growth in the short- and long-term.

Estonia being an EU member state, EU border protection, and market price support (MPS) mechanisms apply. When they maintain domestic prices above world prices, these measures distort markets and reduce producers' incentives to use production factors more productively. As such, they hinder structural adjustment and discourage producers to innovate to become more competitive. These distorting measures can maintain resources in the sector that would otherwise be reallocated to more productive uses; they can encourage more intensive production, sometimes on marginal or fragile land; and they can encourage production practices that do not always take adequate consideration of longer term environmental sustainability. In the European Union in general, and thus in Estonia, the support they generate has decreased over time, although some commodities continue to receive significant MPS (OECD, 2017b, Chapter 2.8). In the Estonian case, MPS concerns mainly beef, and poultry meat, as Estonia does not produce any rice or sugar.

Since the EU milk quotas expired in 2015, production restrictions no longer apply in Estonia, which does not produce any wine or sugar. According to Viira et al. (2015), the withdrawal of EU milk quotas, which was announced in 2008, led to a 7% increase in EU production volumes from 2008 to 2014. Although production quotas restricted dairy production, farm consolidation resulted in significant resource reallocation in dairy farms, leading to higher productivity (Kimura and Sauer, 2015).

Support to variable input use may encourage intensive and unsustainable production practices by lowering farm input costs, such as energy, fertiliser and pesticides. In Estonia, the only distorting measure is the fuel excise tax exemption for agricultural producers, which pay about 27% of the full tax. As it lowers fuel cost, tax exemption does not encourage a reduction in fuel consumption, which would benefit the environment.

A large share of support to producers is granted as a broad-based payment per hectare mostly decoupled from commodity production. This is a more effective way to transfer income to producers and thus increase their capacity to invest and innovate. It also leaves more flexibility to producers to undertake new activities and switch to new products. However, even if decoupled from production choices, as most Pillar 1 payments in Estonia, broad-based income support slows the structural adjustment needed to facilitate economies of scale, attract new entrants and thus foster innovation and productivity growth. As payments are conditional on the adoption of environmentally-friendly practices, they are expected to ensure a minimum degree of sustainability in resource use on a broad-scale. However, as environmental problems vary locally, they are unlikely to be best fitted in all situations. In addition, one of the greening conditions, which requires maintaining the permanent grassland area, may not be adapted to the situation of Estonia. The large areas under grassland do not reflect an economic or environmental optimum, but result in part from past history. In the 1990s, support to agricultural producers was very low if not negative, and large areas of agricultural land were idle. After the implementation of the SAPS in 2004, parts of this idle land have been put into use – some for crop production, some as permanent pasture kept in GAEC.

In transition economies, agricultural producers often faced budget constraints that hindered the investment for farm modernisation. In Estonia, agricultural, land and ownership reforms were carried out in the beginning of the 1990s. At the same time, a liberal trade policy with zero tariffs was applied. This opened the Estonian market to cheap imports and led to low farm-gate prices and negative market price support for a short period (Viira, 2014). It was thus difficult and expensive for agricultural producers to obtain credit in the 1990s, which resulted in low investments in the agricultural sector. Direct payments were first implemented in 1998, capital (credit) subsidies at the end of the 1990s. To compensate for the "lost decade in agricultural investments", agricultural policy in Estonia has paid attention to supporting investments in modernisation of agricultural holdings. The EU pre-accession programme SAPARD launched in 2001, and successive RDPs

2004-06, 2007-13, and 2014-20 included a significant amount of investment support to agricultural producers for modernisation of their technologies. Figure 6.8 shows that, according to the classification of the economic accounts of agriculture (EAA), investment grants, subsidies on products and other subsidies have clearly affected investments (gross and net capital formation) into agricultural holdings.[9] As discussed in Chapter 2, the agricultural production indices have significantly increased since the beginning of the 2000s, suggesting that the policy decisions and farm investments have markedly affected the production and (partial) productivity development.

Investment support has also greatly contributed to adjustment, by facilitating investment in modern technology or additional inputs needed to increase economies of scale, and thus productivity. While it is not specifically targeted to the purchase of innovative or more sustainable technologies in Estonia, market and policy incentives, including compliance to EU regulations, guided investment in these areas. An area for further investment identified in RDP evaluation, however, is the upgrading of drainage systems (Box 6.3). If done in a sustainable way, this is expected to improve long-term land productivity.

Figure 6.8. Investments, subsidies and credits in Estonian agriculture, 1995 to 2016

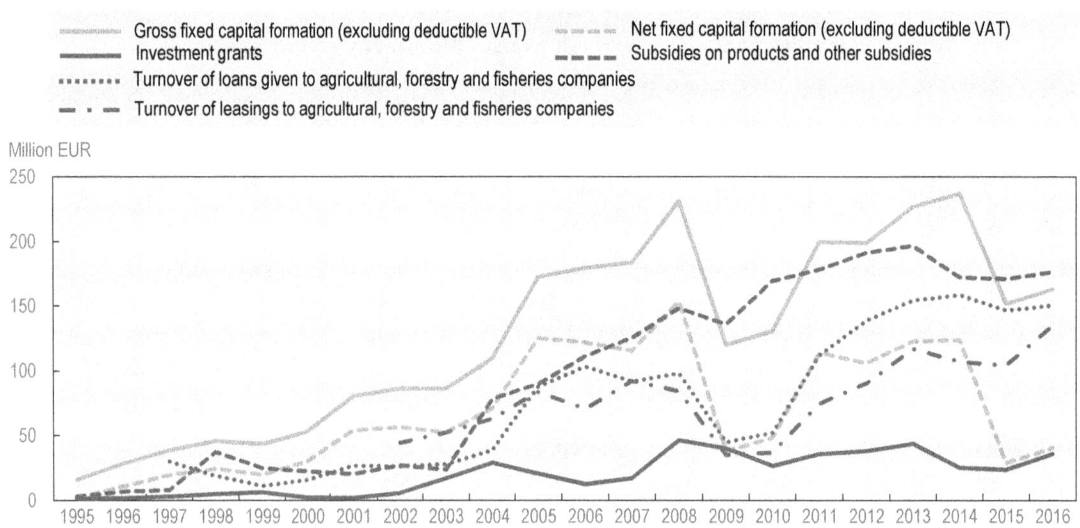

Source: Statistics Estonia (2017), Economic Accounts of Agriculture, www.stat.ee; Bank of Estonia (2016), www.eestipank.ee/en/publication/estonian-competitiveness-report/2016/estonian-competitiveness-report-2016.

StatLink http://dx.doi.org/10.1787/888933654769

Some agricultural policy measures aim to facilitate resource allocation within and across sectors. In response to the recommendations drawn from the evaluation of former measures, Estonia chose to boost support to new entrants using Pillar 1 payments and investment support from Pillar 2. It is important to attract a new generation of well-trained managers in the sector. Investment support also contributed to farm consolidation and the diversification of on-farm activities.

Agricultural producers face risks, which result in variation in outcomes. Support for risk management can be considered as reducing the cost of risk for farmers. Risk management is essential to improve adoption of innovation and more sustainable practices that could increase risk exposure. In the European Union, trade protection and CMO measures for some products act as a safety net by limiting price falls. Pest and disease control measures, including compensations for the culling of animals, contribute to limiting pest and disease risks. Livestock farmers can use a subsidised insurance scheme to manage some risks, but it is hardly being used, and Estonia did not take advantage of EU RDP funds to develop risk management instruments. Rather *ad hoc* support compensates farmers for income losses. It should also be noted that Direct Payments provide income support that cushions market-based income variations. The need for targeted risk management tools should be explored, when investigating the failing of the insurance scheme.

Agricultural measures that **support innovation** directly are likely to create stronger incentives and capacity for innovation among agricultural producers and will help structural change. In addition to funding agricultural research, development and education, a number of RDP measures support innovation in Estonia. These include investment support, which facilitate the adoption of new technologies in farms and food processing industries, but also new support to national technology transfer and advisory activities and services, aiming to facilitate the diffusion of new technologies and practices. The strengthening of advisory systems was a recommendation from the evaluation of the previous RDP. Moreover, RDP support to cooperation activities facilitates the cooperation of farms, food processing industry, R&D institutions and other actors in finding innovative solutions for the food and agricultural sector. Sectoral and strategic development plans include support for the development or the diffusion of innovation with a view to reaching the objectives (Box 6.3). The seed development plan in particular aims to improve the competitiveness of Estonian seed companies and increase the use of certified seeds, with enhanced performance.

Agricultural policy instruments that support explicitly the adoption of more sustainable technologies or practices (agri-environmental measures) or measures to adapt and mitigate climate change, are often associated with regulation and market-based mechanisms. They are likely to steer farmers towards innovative sustainable practices more effectively. In the long-term, they are also likely to guide the content of innovation in the direction of sustainability. Estonian farmers and food industries have to comply with EU environmental regulation. Investment in technology needed to comply can be supported by EU and national funding. Farmers also have to respect cross-compliance conditions for receiving EU support (Box 6.2). In addition, support is available for farmers, who engage in voluntary environmentally-friendly practices.

Current support schemes are associated with several positive trends in environmental impacts and farm management practices. For instance, the risk of point source pollution from farms has decreased as a result of subsidy-supported investments into manure storages and other farm technologies, as well as the establishment of an integrated environmental permit system. Moreover, the 2011 ARC survey revealed that 77% of farmers applying for the RDP support followed all of the Codes of Good Agricultural Practice, compared to 57% of farmers who were getting only SAPS payments (ENR, 2016). Changes in the soil fertility indicators of EFM and SAPS producers indicate that more attention has also been paid to achieving the nutrient balance through a variety of agro-technological methods (crop rotation, fertilisation). As fulfilling GAEC and environmental regulations is a pre-requisite for receiving direct payments, the incentives to comply are high. Still, the ongoing education of producers is necessary to ensure proper implementation. For instance, the results of inventories have revealed shortcomings of silage storages, as well as waste water handling, especially in farms with older technological systems (ENR, 2016).

The Estonian organic farming development plan aims to increase the production and consumption of organic products. The target for increasing the organically-farmed area by 2020 has been reached. However, the productivity of organic livestock farming remains low. While this does not affect sustainability through land use changes in Estonia, where land is relatively abundant, care should be taken that organic livestock farms manage manure in a sustainable way.

Overall, within the EU CAP framework that allows EU member states some flexibility in implementing payments, Estonia made choices that limit market distortions across commodities, and traditionally placed strong priority to investing in modern technology, upgrading facilities in farming and agri-food companies, and facilitating structural adjustment. More recently, more emphasis was given to attracting new entrants, improving advisory services, and responding to agri-environmental and climate change challenges.

6.6. Summary

- The EU Common agricultural policy provides most of the support to Estonian farmers. Unlike most EU member states, Pillar 2 funding exceeds Pillar 1, and the national contribution to Pillar 2 is lower than EU average.
- Most Pillar 1 Direct Payments are implemented as flat-rate per-ha payment (SAPS and greening). This ensures there is no distortion among commodities, but may reduce incentives to productivity.

Commodity-specific payments are limited to less than 5% of the total envelope. Payment rates are lower than in most EU member states, although they are expected to increase with convergence and the introduction of a national complement (the Transitional National Aid, TNA), after two years without TNA. This will increase farmers' income but may give them the wrong signals about the long-term profitability of their operations.

- Cross-compliance ensures minimal requirements on sustainable farm practices covering all agricultural land. The greening requirement constraining the conversion of grass land into crop production, may prevent moving to more efficient production, without significant benefits for the environment, as grassland is already abundant for non-agronomic reasons and crop production is extensive in Estonia.
- Market measures such as intervention purchase were used to limit price declines during the recent dairy crisis, thus acting as a safety net. Milk quotas no longer restrict production choices.
- Policies provide support for a range of risk management tools but there has not been widespread uptake. First, the offer of insurance products on the market is limited to coverage of animal disease risk, second the annual budget for insurance schemes is rather small (EUR 10 000). The need for targeted risk management tools should be explored.
- RDP choices reflect the traditional government emphasis on investment support in food and agriculture since the beginning of the transition period, where it was most important to acquire up-to-date technology, leading to sustainable productivity growth. Investment support also facilitated farm consolidation and the emergence of technically efficient farms. It is also expected to attract a new generation of well-trained managers. Regarding infrastructure investment needs, upgrading on-farm drainage systems sustainably would help increase further productivity and profitability.
- Support for organic farming and market signals have contributed to the expansion of land farmed organically and organic production over the last decade.
- Estonia relies on a number of domestic policy instruments to encourage sustainable technologies and practices; preliminary evidence suggests positive impacts on agri-environmental indicators in recent years. For instance, environmental taxes are used to encourage the efficient use of environmental resources and pollution reduction in Estonia. Moreover, Pillar 1 Direct Payments are subject to cross-compliance requirements and greening. Under Estonia's RDP, Estonian farmers are also eligible to receive payments for voluntary agri-environmental commitments. Current support schemes are associated with several positive trends in environmental impacts (such as point source pollution, soil fertility) and the adoption of good agricultural practices.

Notes

1. At the EU level, CMO measures account for about 4% of all CAP funding for the period 2014-20 (OECD, 2017a).

2. Some EU member states chose to develop regional RDPs.

3. Most CAP 2014-20 measures started to be implemented in 2015.

4. Transfers from Pillar 1 to Pillar 2 vary over time as a percentage of the national ceiling: 0% in 2014/15, 6.1% in 2015/16, 14.3% in 2016/17, 15.0% in 2017/18, 14.9% in 2018/19 and 15% in 2019/20. They represent 10.8% of the National Ceiling on average over the period.

5. EU member states below 90% average Pillar 1 payments/ha may transfer up to 25% of their RDP envelope from Pillar 2 to Pillar 1, http://ec.europa.eu/agriculture/sites/agriculture/files/direct-support/direct-payments/docs/direct-paymenst-financial-mechanisms_en.pdf.

6. RT I, 22.04.2015, 30; RT I, 22.04.2016, 2

7. This last priority is also identified as LEADER (from the French Liaison Entre Actions de Développement de l'Économie Rurale).

8. Article 107 of the Treaty on the Functioning of the European Union (TFEU), defines State aid as "any aid granted by a Member State or through State resources in any form whatsoever which distorts or threatens to distort competition by favouring certain undertakings or the production of certain goods [...], in so far as it affects trade between Member States" (OJ, 2012). For more information on state aid in the agricultural sector, see Box 2.1 in (OECD, 2017a).

9. However, as shown in Figure 6.2, the gross capital formation declined significantly in 2015, compared to 2014. This decline is related to the crisis in milk (Russian import ban, withdrawal of EU milk quotas) and pig (outbreak of ASF) sectors, as well as a decline in the total amount of direct payment rates in 2014 and 2015.

References

ARC (Agricultural Research Centre) (2016), Eesti maaelu arengukava 2014-2020 4. Ja 5. Prioriteedi meetmete; 3. Prioriteedi loomade heaolu meetme ja 2. Prioriteedi tegevuse "kiviaia taastamine" püsihindamisaruanne 2016. Aasta kohta [Estonian Rural Development Plan 2014-2020: priority actions 4 and 5; Priority 5 animal welfare measures and priority action 2 Restoring the "stonewall" in 2016], http://pmk.agri.ee/mak/wp-content/uploads/sites/2/2017/04/PMK_aruanne_meetmed_HK_18_04_2017.pdf.

ARIB (2017), Pindalatoetused 2016 ÜLDINFO [General information on area payments], http://www.pria.ee/et/toetused/valdkond/taimekasvatus/pindalatoetused_yld_2016/ (accessed 30 June 2017).

ARIB (2016a), Infoleht "Keskkonnasõbraliku majandamise toetus", Estonian Agricultural Registers and Information Board, www.pria.ee/docs/resources/9587.rtf (accessed 9 June 2016).

ARIB (2016b), Keskkonnasõbraliku majandamise toetus (MAK 2014-2020 meede 10.1.1) 2016, Estonian Agricultural Registers and Information Board, www.pria.ee/et/toetused/valdkond/taimekasvatus/ksm_2016/ (accessed 6 June 2016).

ARIB (2016c), Mahepõllumajandusele ülemineku toetus ja mahepõllumajandusega jätkamise toetus (MAK 2014-2020 meede 11) 2016, Estonian Agricultural Registers and Information Board, www.pria.ee/et/toetused/valdkond/taimekasvatus/mahe_toetus_uus_2016/ (accessed 6 June 2016).

ARIB (2015), Pindalatoetused. Üldinfo [General information on area payments]. www.pria.ee/et/toetused/valdkond/taimekasvatus/pindalatoetused_yld_2015/ (accessed 18 August 2016).

Bank of Estonia (2016), Estonian Competitiveness Report, www.eestipank.ee/en/publication/estonian-competitiveness-report/2016/estonian-competitiveness-report-2016 (accessed 29 March 2016).

ENR (2016), Estonian Nitrate Report 2016. Nõukogu direktiivi 91/676/EMÜ, veekogude kaitsmise kohta põllumajandusest lähtuva nitraadireostuse eest, täitmine Eestis 2012-2015, www.envir.ee/sites/default/files/nitrate_report_2016_estonia.pdf (accessed 17 October 2016).

European Commission (2015), Factsheet on 2014-2020 Rural Development Programme for ESTONIA, http://ec.europa.eu/agriculture/rural-development-2014-2020/country-files/ee/factsheet_en.pdf (accessed 17 August 2016).

European Parliament (2015), Implementation of the first pillar of the CAP 2014 – 2020 in the EU member states, Study requested by the European Parliament's Committee on Agriculture and Rural Development.

FADN (2016), Standard results of Estonian FADN farms, online database, http://maainfo.ee/standardtulemused/ (accessed 5 June 2016).

Government (Republic of Estonia Government) (2016), Objectives and activities — Rural Life. https://valitsus.ee/en/rural-life-0 (accessed 4 December 2016).

Kimura, S. and J. Sauer (2015), "Dynamics of dairy farm productivity growth: Cross-country comparison", *OECD Food, Agriculture and Fisheries Papers*, No. 87, OECD Publishing, Paris. http://dx.doi.org/10.1787/5jrw8ffbzf7l-en.

MRA (2017), Communication to the OECD of EU and national expenditures in Estonia.

MRA (2016a), Tootmiskohustusega seotud otsetoetused alates 2017, Aastast [Coupled Direct Payments from 2017], 8 June, www.agri.ee/sites/default/files/content/komisjonid/pman/pman-2016-06-08-talvik-01.pdf (accessed 18 October 2016).

MRA (2016b), Estonian Rural Development Plan 2014-2020, www.agri.ee/et/eesmargid-tegevused/eesti-maaelu-arengukava-mak-2014-2020 (accessed 29 January 2016).

MRA (2015a), Otsetoetused: toetusõiguslikkuse ja rohestamise nõuded [Direct payments: eligibility criteria and greening], PowerPoint slides from 9 April 2015, www.agri.ee/sites/default/files/content/arengukavad/mak-2014/infopaevad-2014-otsetoetused.pdf.

MRA (2015b), Eesti maaelu arengukava 2014-2020 kommunikatsioonistrateegia [Estonian Rural Development Plan 2014-2020 Communication Strategy]. www.agri.ee/sites/default/files/content/arengukavad/mak-2014/mak-2014-kommunikatsioonistrateegia.pdf (accessed 31 January 2016).

OECD (2017a), *Evaluation of Agricultural Policy Reforms in the European Union: The Common Agricultural Policy 2014-20,* OECD Publishing, Paris, http://dx.doi.org/10.1787/9789264278783-en.

OECD (2017b), *OECD Economic Surveys: Estonia 2017*, OECD Publishing, Paris, http://dx.doi.org/10.1787/eco_surveys-est-2017-en.

OJ (Official Journal) (2012), Official Journal C 326 , 26 October 2012, pp.0001–0390, http://eur-lex.europa.eu/legal-content/EN/TXT/?uri=celex%3A12012E%2FTXT.

Statistics Estonia (2017), Online statistical database, www.stat.ee (accessed June 2017).

Viira, A.-H., R. Omel, R. Värnik, H. Luik, B. Maasing, and R. Põldaru (2015), “Competitiveness of the Estonian dairy sector, 1994–2014”, *Agraarteadus: Journal of Agricultural Science*, Vol. 24, No. 2, pp. 84–104.

Viira, A.-H. (2014), *Structural Adjustment of Estonian Agriculture – The Role of Institutional Changes and Socioeconomic Factors of Farm Growth, Decline and Exit,* PhD thesis, Estonian University of Life Sciences.

Chapter 7

The Estonian agricultural innovation system

This chapter describes the Estonian Agricultural Innovation System and outlines recent changes. It provides an overview of the general innovation system; describes agricultural innovation actors and their roles in the system. It then describes main trends in public and private investments in R&D, mechanisms of funding and mechanisms to foster knowledge markets and networks. It presents mechanisms to facilitate the transmission of knowledge, outlining developments in farm advisory services. The last section outlines the participation of agricultural R&D actors in regional and international co-operation.

7.1. General innovation profile

This section provides an overview of the economy-wide environment for science, technology, and innovation as it determines the underlying incentives and dis-incentives in all sectors. Moreover, agricultural innovation systems (AIS)[1] are increasingly driven, in particular by economy-wide process and organisational innovations, new developments in Information and Communications Technology (ICT), and the bio-economy. A thriving innovation profile will ensure that general knowledge and specific knowledge in other fields (needed to develop and implement agriculture innovation) are available, and that economic actors and society in general share an innovation culture (OECD, 2015).

General innovation framework

The Estonian Government is a major actor in the national innovation systems,[2] providing economic incentives to innovation through innovation policy. The current focus of public research and development (R&D) activities is placed on areas with greatest growth potential, in compliance with competitiveness objectives based on smart specialisation (Kalvet et al., 2010; OECD, 2014).

In Estonia, innovation policy is included in all policy areas, and contributes to innovation largely through achieving the agreed wider economic objectives. National and sectoral objectives, in turn, contribute to reaching the European-wide economic objectives, as depicted in Figure 7.1. This means that food and agriculture is fully integrated in the general policy and the innovation system.

Sectoral development plans are usually prepared for seven years. Sectoral strategies are in line with the country's budgeting strategy, which is drawn up for four years and updated annually. This ensures the medium-term plans are constantly adapted in response to the changes in economy, fiscal and sectoral environment (MoF, 2015). Main governance mechanisms for national and sectoral policies, including food and agriculture related policies, are presented in Annex 7.A1

Two national horizontal strategies cover innovation, entrepreneurship and sustainable development concerns:

- **Sustainable Estonia 21** is the most general overarching guidance document, covering many areas under the responsibility of different ministries. Completed in 2005, it devises broad sustainable development objectives running to 2030. The implementation of the strategy is monitored on the basis of sustainable development indicators presented in bi-annual reports (Linnas, 2007).
- **Estonia 2020** describes the objectives and activities needed to improve competitiveness, the two central objectives being to increase productivity and employment. The development plan serves as an important basis for targeting national investments as well as the use of EU funds in Estonia (Government Office, 2014). In compliance with the EU's Smart Specialisation Platform, it focuses on growth areas and value chains with greatest growth potential. Priority growth areas are: 1) ICT, horizontally through all sectors; 2) health technologies and services, and; 3) more efficient use of resources. Key sectors are: programming, telecommunications, electronics, logistics, valorisation of wood, machine building and food industry. They were selected on the basis of their role and development potential over the period of 2014-20, in terms of value added, export volume and intensity, and number of employees in the Estonian economy, as well as on developments in Europe and in the world (EDF, 2013; Kaarna et al., 2015). Moreover, energy, sustainable development and environmental issues are increasingly important government priorities (OECD, 2017a).

At the sectoral and sub-sectoral level, the main strategy document guiding the development of Estonia's research, development and innovation (RDI) policy is **Knowledge-based Estonia**, compiled by the Ministry of Education and Research (MER), and the Ministry of Economic Affairs and Communications (MEAC). Covering 2014-20, it is the third consecutive strategic document in this area. This strategy is closely related to the **Estonian Entrepreneurship Growth Strategy for 2014-20.**[3] The underlying principle in the division of labour in RDI between the MEAC and the MER is that the MEAC is responsible for offering support to innovation, including product and service innovation and capital inflow to enterprises. The MER oversees international cooperation in R&D, guaranteeing a high level in R&D activities and supporting universities, and public research institutions. Both ministries are accountable for supporting cooperation between enterprises and research institutions in accordance to the division above.

Figure 7.1. Framework for EU, national and sectoral innovation

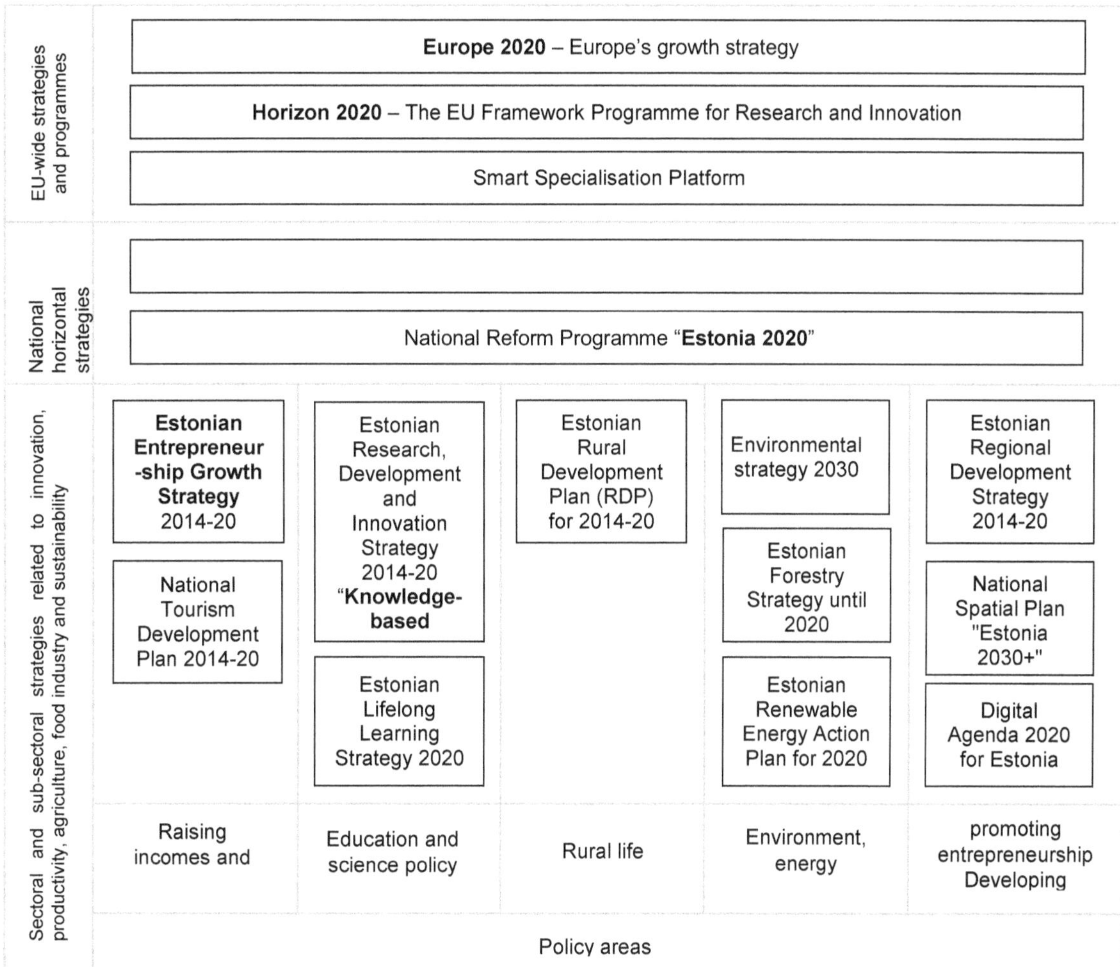

Source: Compiled by authors on the basis of Christensen et al. (2012) www.hm.ee/index.php?popup=download&id=11652, and Government (2016), https://valitsus.ee/en.

In addition to its own resources, Estonia is using EU structural funds[4] to facilitate economic development, thus the investments are related to the long-term objectives of the European Union (MoF, 2014a). In the previous programming periods, the priorities and measures of Estonia's development plans were related to the renewal of infrastructure. In particular, a significant part of the EU Structural Funds has been invested into the development of R&D infrastructure, human capital and entrepreneurship (MER, 2014a). In the current period, the EU and Estonian priorities and measures are aimed at economic growth, increasing people's well-being, as well as the quality of work and life, which is closely related to innovation in products, services, processes and organisations (EUSAE, 2015). In particular, the EU focus is on the implementation of its smart specialisation platform.

The development of the 2014-20 plan reflected experience from the implementation of previous plans. For example, ministries, including the Ministry of Rural Affairs (MRA) were more proactive in providing substantive input to RDI policy pursuant to their priorities and needs. They were given greater responsibility in developing networks supporting policy-making in their sectors. By organising sectoral debates social partners were better involved in the process of developing sectoral programmes and measures (MoF, 2014b).

General innovation performance

According to the *OECD Science, Technology and Innovation (STI) Outlooks* (OECD, 2014, 2017a), the strengths of the Estonian innovation system are the conducive business environment (Chapter 4), government strategy integrating innovation and economic growth objectives, and investing in smart specialisation high-growth areas, including Information and Communication Technology (ICT), the relatively strong public research system, with high level of public Research and Development (R&D) expenditure and strong performance in journal publication and international cooperation, and good skills base in the population, in particular young performers in science (Figure 7.2). Shortcomings are mainly related to low R&D and innovation in firms, which, in part is due to the relatively small size of Estonian companies.[5] In particular, industry-science linkages are not strongly developed, although programmes have been developed facilitate public-private cooperation in R&D and to connect better education and skills need to labour-market needs. Moreover, despite recent progress, Estonia still lags behind the OECD average with the doctoral graduate rate in science and engineering, and top adult performers in technology problem solving (Chapter 5). This indicates shortcomings in knowledge transfer from high level R&D groups to the education system.

Regarding the overall effectiveness of the innovation policy so far, R&D activities in Estonia have perked up over the past decade, which has boosted productivity growth. Overall, enterprises in Estonia can be regarded as innovative, as reflected in their willingness to experiment with new products, services and solutions, and introduce innovative products (see for example Box 7.1 on innovation in food and drink processing companies). The innovative character of Estonian organisations is close to the EU average, both in product and process innovation, as well as in organisational and marketing innovation (Statistics Estonia, 2015a).

As to agriculture, in 2009-13 most of the applications for innovation (investment) support asked financing for the purchase of modern equipment, whereas in food production and forest enterprises support was predominantly requested for new product development (EMÜ, 2015a). However, the results of the survey "Innovation in Estonian enterprises and innovation support schemes" conducted under the aegis of the MEAC showed that the added value created by the low-tech enterprise sector has so far been higher than that of the high-tech enterprises. For example, based on the data of the first three quarters of 2015, beverage production ranked among the first in producing the highest added value per employee. The added value per employee in the timber industry was almost one and a half times higher than the corresponding figure for the furniture industry. Some very complex products are produced in Estonia, but units responsible for their technological solutions, marketing and sales are located elsewhere. The timber industry, on the other hand, is dominated by a number of companies based on national capital that control the entire value chain and, therefore, the added value remaining in Estonia is higher. There are a number of very successful and innovative enterprises in Estonia (for example, Estonia is the biggest exporter of wooden houses, and Europe's largest wood pellet producer is located in Estonia), but their impact on the Estonian economy as a whole has so far been modest (Kaarna et al., 2015).

According to MER (2014a), the aspect calling for development in the innovation system is the cooperation in R&D between enterprises and universities, especially in the light of demand-driven innovation policy development. It is also necessary to develop communication between the public sector (as to long-term strategic plans) and the private sector (as to innovation capacity). Estonian enterprises need a new qualitative leap in the highly competitive and global production and innovation networks. This requires enterprises to have greater capacity and skills to make progress in value chains.

Figure 7.2. Science and innovation in Estonia, 2016

Comparative performance of national science and innovation systems

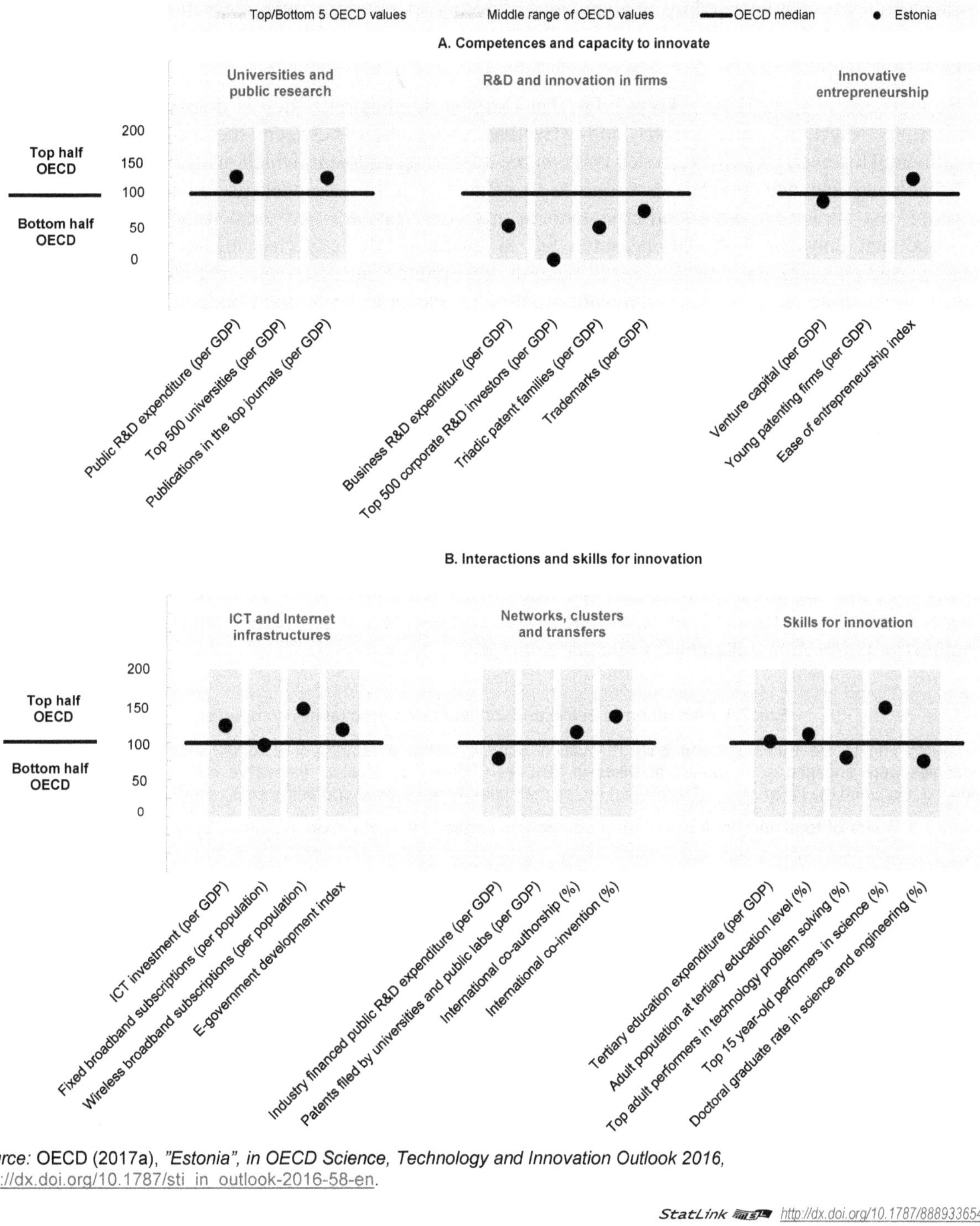

Source: OECD (2017a), *"Estonia", in OECD Science, Technology and Innovation Outlook 2016*, http://dx.doi.org/10.1787/sti_in_outlook-2016-58-en.

StatLink http://dx.doi.org/10.1787/888933654788

Investigating the feasibility of implementing demand-side innovation policy instruments in Estonia, Romanainen et al. (2014a) also call for improvements in co-operation between various parties, including the meaningful involvement of stakeholders. Although stakeholder involvement in the design and implementation of innovation policy in Estonia has gained momentum, their involvement is mostly restricted to participation in discussions with sectoral umbrella organisations and universities. Among activities that call for further development, they also include the implementation of horizontal innovation policy in the country as a whole, and the management of risks relating to the implementation or purchase of innovation. They find that Estonian innovation policy is characterised by an abundance of policy documents, strategies, action plans, programmes and projects, which inter-connectedness is difficult to identify. According to some experts, this may be considered a problem.

Romananien et al. (2014a) acknowledge that Estonian innovation policy is objective-based, with clear prioritisation, selectivity mechanisms and effective cooperation between the stakeholders in policy development. However, it is characterised by resource-based management, which primarily focuses on how to use the existing and new purchased resources to achieve a lasting competitive advantage. Demand side innovation[6] has attracted more attention in Estonia in recent years for two main reasons. First, it has been understood that only supply-based measures fail to guarantee the expected results in the promotion of innovation and economic growth in general. Second, the country must find new and more effective ways to continue to elaborate on the existing innovation policy measures in the limited budgetary conditions. Public procurement has so far been the most frequently used demand-side tool with the highest impact.

According to recent analyses of Estonian innovation policy (Karo et al., 2014a; 2014b), there are comparatively asymmetric and fragmented RDI networks in Estonia that do not facilitate cooperation between the various parties, and the holistic management of innovation ecosystem. So far, the implementation of RDI policy at the measures, regulations, indicators level has been based on the linear understanding that innovation begins with basic research, which is followed by applied research and by the implementation of the new practical solutions in industry and the economy. The persistence of this linear approach in Estonia can be explained by the relatively limited understanding of the role of the government in science and innovation, which finds expression in low-intervention and high-tech centred RDI policy affecting mainly the framework conditions for the economic environment, and where the main feedback mechanisms of innovation policies are general statistics on the developments in the research systems and corporate financial indicators, such as the number of publications and added value per employee.

Box 7.1. Innovation in Estonian food and drink processing companies

According to the Eurostat Community Innovation Survey,[1] about a quarter of Estonian food and drink processing companies were engaged in innovation activities in 2012-14 (Figure 7.3). Most of innovative companies were engaged in product design, and the introduction of innovation on the market and two-thirds in upgrading equipment.

Figure 7.3. Share of food and drink processing companies engaged in innovation activities, by type of activity, 2012-14

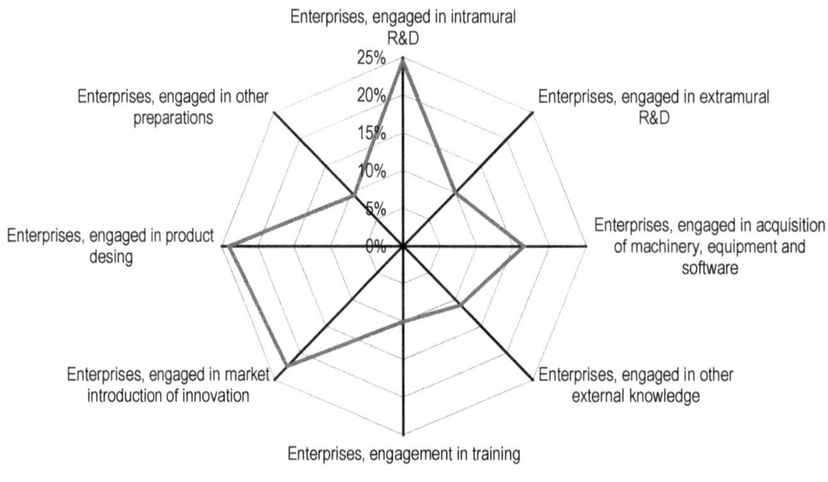

Source: Statistics Estonia (2015a), Table RDI1227: Technologically innovative enterprises by type of innovation activity engaged during 2012-2014 and economic activity, 2014, www.stat.ee; Calculations Estonian University of Life Sciences.

StatLink http://dx.doi.org/10.1787/888933654807

Box 7.1. Innovation in Estonian food and drink processing companies (cont.)

Collaboration of food and drink processing companies[2] is mainly with equipment, materials, components, and software vendors (about a quarter of the cooperating companies), and with other enterprises within the enterprise group (21%) but significantly less with universities and other institutions of higher education (12%) (Figure 7.4).

Figure 7.4. Share of food and drink processing companies that collaborate in product and process innovation with other companies or organisations, by origin, 2012-14

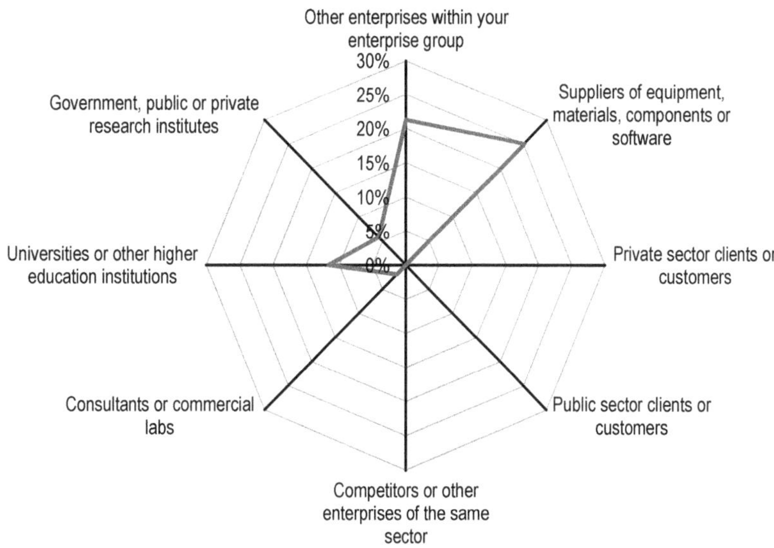

Source: Statistics Estonia (2015a), Table RDI1247: Technologically innovative enterprises finding partner most valuable during 2012-2014 by type of partner and economic activity, 2014, www.stat.ee; Calculations Estonian University of Life Sciences.

StatLink http://dx.doi.org/10.1787/888933654826

1. The statistical survey "Innovation Survey of Enterprises" is the implementation of the European Community Innovation Survey (CIS) in Estonia. The survey is carried out every two years in all European Union member and candidate states simultaneously. The frame of the survey covered all enterprises with at least ten employees in industry and selected economic activities in services. To evaluate an enterprise's innovativeness, it was asked about its activities in 2012–14. If an enterprise did not introduce during this period any innovations or did not engage in any innovative activities, it was considered non-innovative (Statistics Estonia, 2015a).

2. An enterprise that, during the years under consideration, introduced a product innovation to the market or implemented a process innovation or was involved in some other innovation activity (in connection with abandoned or ongoing innovation projects; also, research and development can be the main or secondary activity of the enterprise).

Government's communication with citizens on science

Estonian society is favourable to science and technology. The Eurobarometer 2015 survey shows that, compared to the EU average, Estonians consider innovation as a positive phenomenon that provides a number of benefits, including the overall increase in the quality of life, environmental sustainability (such as the introduction of electric cars), medical technology and the positive impact of pharmaceutical industry developments on medical services and drug efficacy, easier and faster access to the necessary information, e-services, including time-saving by means of digital signing and e-commerce, positive change in planning of working time and form (work from home, virtual meetings). However, such developments also pose threats, including a decline in social skills, data security, privacy loss, and manpower being replaced with machinery (Eurobarometer Qualitative Study, 2015).

During the period 2007-12, various activities for the popularisation of science were tested and developed, but the government did not offer a clear strategic approach (Kirss et al., 2013). A Research and Technology Pact was signed in 2015 between the government, municipalities, business, education and the tertiary sector, to provide joint support in the fields of science, technology and engineering for the implementation of the innovation strategies for 2020. One of the aims of the Pact is to popularise science, technology and engineering in the society. Activities include research competitions for schoolchildren and students under the leadership of the Estonian Research Council (ERC), and ERC annual research conferences, which primarily target students in general education (ERC, 2015a). Since 2006, Estonia acknowledges remarkable individuals and bodies with the national science communication award to value science communication.

TeaMe+ is an ERDF financed programme for popularising science, technology, engineering and math (STEM) education fields introduced in 2009. Introducing scientific topics in the mass media, developing science journalism and promoting an open dialogue between scientists and society are among its objectives. The programme has supported the public broadcast of two science programmes. "At the Top of the Pyramid" (Püramiidi tipus) aimed at the public, and adventurous science gameshow "Rocket 69" (Rakett 69) for the young. The latter was selected by the European Broadcasting Union as the best educational programme of 2012 (ERC, 2015b).

Initiated by Enterprise Estonia (EE), the largest competition of business ideas called *Ajujaht* (Brain Hunt) has been organised since 2007. Several times, the winners of the event have come from the primary sector related ideas (including a sensor-backed fish farming system, an automatic irrigation system for household plants, a web environment that allows people not having a household plot to purchase horticultural produce, a sensing device that makes it possible to measure the number and diameter of logs accurately and quickly, etc.). The competition is mainly targeted at professionals who want a career change, and students who want to create start-ups (Ajujaht, 2016).

The universities also support the popularisation of science. For example, the Estonian University of Life Sciences (EMÜ) organises applied science prize competitions designed to encourage scientists and working groups to find effective ways of cooperation with the end-users of research results, to introduce innovative ideas into practice, and contribute to an increase in the applied research capacity and volume of external financing at the University (EMÜ, 2013a). The University of Tartu (TU) is engaged in popularising science among the people of different ages interested in the research. The activities of TU Sciences School are targeted at young people in particular, and in cooperation with the Estonian Physical Society, the University launched science bus, where schoolchildren with a deeper interest in science have the opportunity to broaden and extend their knowledge. To introduce science to a wider public the TU cooperates with the Science Centre AHHAA[7] and administers the science news portal "Novaator" (TU, 2015).

The EU Framework Programme for Research and Innovation, Horizon 2020, pays more attention to social problems that affect people's lives, such as improving health services, environment-friendly transport, and food and energy security. It includes a separate activity "Science with and for society", which focuses on the integration of scientific and technological achievements into the society. In addition, Horizon 2020 introduces the endeavours in research and technology among young people.[8]

7.2. Actors, institutions and governance of agricultural innovation systems

Agricultural innovation systems (AIS) involve a wide range of actors who enable, guide, fund, perform, implement, inform and facilitate innovation. The key players include policy-makers, researchers, teachers, advisors, farmers, private companies and consumers. A well-functioning innovation system can help ensure good use of public funds, improved collaboration between public and private participants, including across national borders, and a more demand driven system that is responsive to the needs of "innovation consumers" (OECD, 2015).

In Estonia, the **Government** plays a central role in the governance of the AIS, by setting the policy, monitoring the implementation of programmes and evaluating policies and institutions (Figure 7.1). The MRA is responsible for planning, coordination and implementation of R&D activities related to agriculture (for more information on AIS governance, see Annex 7.A1). To this end, the MRA has drawn applied research programmes since 2004 (MRA, 2016a). The MRA is responsible for extension services and R&D institutions, except the universities, and finances applied research, knowledge transfer and innovation in agriculture, food and fisheries sector through national programmes. The European Union plays a growing role in the orientation and financing of Estonian national programmes and research collaboration between EU member states, including in the agri-food area.

Some organisations support the MRA in implementing policies. The Estonian Agricultural Registers and Information Board (ARIB) is a paying agency administrating agricultural policy measures. The Council of Agricultural Sciences advises the MRA on RDI issues under their authority, observes the implementation of RDI measures funded by the MRA and, on this basis, proposes improvements.

Regarding **R&D organisations**, the EMÜ carries out the largest part of agriculture-related research in Estonia, covering animal husbandry, veterinary, agricultural economics, rural sociology, environment, plant sciences, and food sciences. The TU carries out research in environmental sciences, and the Tallinn University of Technology (TUT) in biotechnology and food sciences. A research organisation specialised in crop research, the Estonian Crop Research Institute (ECRI), is under MRA umbrella (Figure 7.5). Previous research institutes have been integrated in universities (Box 7.2).

The Agricultural Research Centre (ARC) is mainly carrying field tests and experiments, laboratory analyses, preparing liming and fertilising maps, good agricultural practices and agro-chemistry research, evaluation of agri-environmental measures, and horticultural testing activities.

Higher **education** in agriculture-related fields is mainly in the EMÜ. At the vocational level, there are nine vocational schools in different regions. Three are specialised in Rural Economics and Service, Forestry, and Horticulture, respectively.[9]

Box 7.2. Merger of Estonian agriculture research organisations in the 1990s

Up to 1994, agriculture research institutes were under the jurisdiction of the Ministry of Agriculture (MoA). In 1993, they started being integrated into the universities. By 2001, five research institutes had been merged with the EMÜ. In 2003-06, faculties were restructured into institutes. By 2016, there was only one R&D institute under the umbrella of the MRA: the Estonian Crop Research Institute (Table 7.1)

Table 7.1. Merger of agriculture research institutes over 1993-2013

Research institutes	Year	Merger and other restructuration
Institute for Rural Development	1993	
Estonian Research Institute of Animal Breeding and Veterinary Science (ELVI)	1994	
Estonian Forest Research Institute	1996	Merged with the Estonian Agricultural University
Institute of Zoology and Botany, Institute of Experimental Biology, Estonian Plant Biotechnical Research Centre EVIKA	1997	
Estonian Agrobiocentre	2001	
Estonian Institute of Agrarian Economics	2001	Merged with Jäneda Training and Advisory Centre
Estonian Institute of Agricultural Engineering	2002	Merged with Estonian Research Institute of Agriculture
Jäneda Training and Advisory Centre	2006	renamed Rural Economy Research Centre
Jõgeva Plant Breeding Institute and Estonian Research Institute of Agriculture	2013	Merged into the Estonian Crop Research Institute, which remains under the Ministry of Rural Affairs

Source: compiled by the authors, based on EMÜ (2016a) and (MRA, 2005).

The research carried out in the research institutes under the jurisdiction of the Ministry of Agriculture was mainly applied research by nature. It concerned for example the development of new varieties, biological medicinal products, and technologies (MRA, 1999).

The Rural Development Foundation (RDF) is responsible for the elaboration of the **advisory system** for Estonian agricultural and rural enterprises and guaranteeing them access to high-quality consulting services. The Rural Economy and Agricultural Advisory Service is a registered trademark belonging to the RDF, which offers advisory services in agriculture and rural economy and brings together advisers who pass on advice to farmers and rural entrepreneurs. Farmers can also seek advice from Estonian and foreign input suppliers, cooperatives, and web-based providers.

The **private sector** is an important partner in the Estonian AIS, mainly as a user of innovation. Estonian enterprises are mostly small and they often lack resources for research-intensive activities. Therefore, competence centres, funded by Enterprise Estonia, were created to develop innovative solutions, in cooperation with enterprises in a specific field, universities and research institutes. Over 2014-20, six state-supported competence centres will operate in Estonia, two of them in the field of food technology and one in biomedicine (EE, 2016a).

Figure 7.5. Overview of the Estonia's research system's governance structure

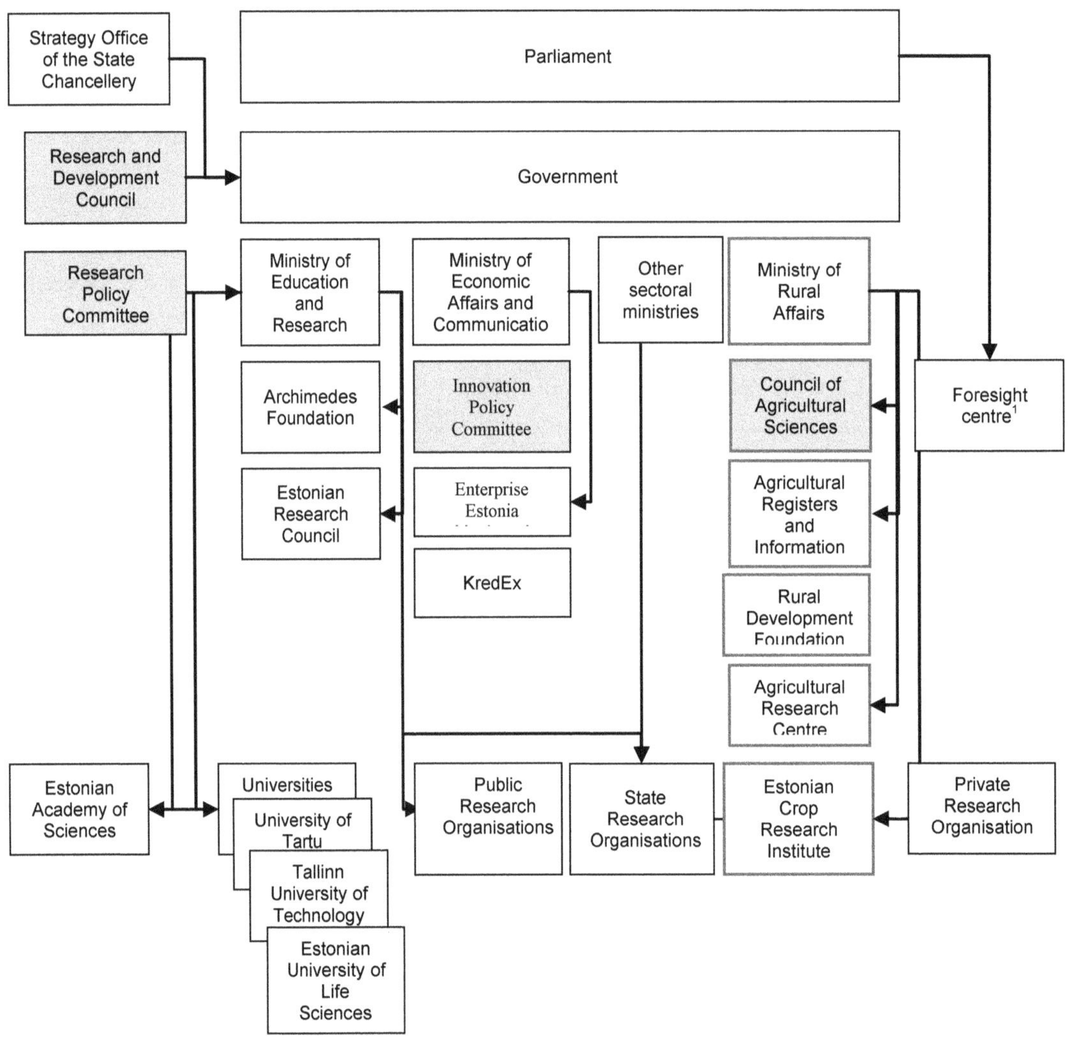

1. In April 2016, the Estonian Development Fund (EDF) was abolished. An independent unit (the Foresight Centre) with its own budget and competence for decisions was set up under the Estonian Parliament to carry out EDF monitoring activities (www.riigikogu.ee/en/foresight/), whereas the responsibility for EDF investment activities were transferred to KredEx.

Source: Christensen et al. (2012), www.hm.ee/index.php?popup=download&id=11652, elaborated in EMÜ (2017).

7.3. Public and private investments in agricultural R&D

In most countries, the public sector is the main source of funding for agriculture R&D, whether performed in public or private organisations. A wide variety of funding mechanisms are used from direct spending on research projects. Business investment in R&D is normally driven by market demand, but governments also provide different kinds of incentives. Knowledge infrastructure is a public good that can enable innovation; it includes ICT infrastructure and general purpose technologies as well as specific knowledge infrastructure such as databases and institutions (OECD, 2015).

Priorities for agriculture research, development and knowledge transfer

In Estonia, the general priorities for public research in agriculture stem from the EU level, national horizontal and sectoral strategies (Figure 7.6). The overall priorities and measures for Estonian R&D policy are defined in Knowledge-based Estonia (MER, 2013).

The specific aims for agricultural research in Estonia are: 1) Competent scientific support for designing and implementing the Common Agricultural Policy (CAP) and the fisheries policy; 2) Competent scientific support for the agriculture, food and fisheries sector; 3) Sustainability of scientific community; 4) State-of-the-art facilities and infrastructure; 5) Estonian researchers participation in international research cooperation; 6) Plant and animal breeding; plant genetic resources *ex situ* conservation and collection; and 7) Effective knowledge transfer, including between R&D organisations and agricultural producers (MRA, 2016b).

The MRA funds applied research, knowledge transfer and innovation in agriculture, food and fisheries through various national and EU programmes as shown in Figure 7.6. The three national programmes below are included in the framework for research and knowledge transfer in Estonian agriculture, food and fisheries sciences and fund applied research, while the main source for supporting knowledge transfer and innovation is the Estonian RDP through specific measures (Chapter 6):

- **Agricultural Applied Research and Development for 2015-21** aims to provide science-based input to the MRA for policy making, law making and monitoring; and to coordinate and to finance participation in international research cooperation (MRA, 2016a). The programme covers the following activities to pursue specific objectives:
  - Food safety, animal welfare and health; plant health and quality of production input: to ensure the safety of food produced and consumed in Estonia; to ensure animal welfare and animal and plant health; to ensure quality and safety of agricultural production inputs.
  - Rural life, agriculture and food industry: to ensure sustainable food production; to maintain traditional agricultural landscapes, a clean environment and biodiversity; to ensure balanced development of agricultural regions and improvement of rural living environment.
  - Fishing industry: to ensure competitive and sustainable fishing industry.[10]
- **Collection and Conservation of Plant Genetic Resources for Food and Agriculture for2014-20**[11] addresses the commitments that Estonia has taken with international agreements, such as the Convention on Biological Diversity, the Second Global Plan of Action for Plant Genetic Resources for Food and Agriculture, and the International Treaty on Plant Genetic Resources for Food and Agriculture. The main aims are to ensure the collection and conservation, evaluation of plant genetic resources for food and agriculture, and the wider utilisation and availability of plant genetic resources for research and study, plant breeding and to other non-profit users. The programme serves as a basis for "National Programme for Plant Breeding 2009-19" as well as contributes to overall goals of sustainable development of plant breeding and conservation in Estonia, healthy and safe food, the sustainable use of natural resources, the maintenance of genetic and landscape diversity, and the reduction of climate change hazards (MRA, 2013a).

- **National Programme for Plant Breeding for 2009-19** mainly aims to ensure the sustainable development of Estonian plant breeding and to preserve existing varieties; to breed varieties that help to increase the competitiveness of agricultural sectors; healthy and safe food; sustainable use of natural and environmental resources and the preservation of genetic and landscape diversity; and reduce the threats of climate change (MRA, 2008).

The **Estonian agriculture, food and fisheries science and knowledge transfer development plan for 2015-21** (MRA, 2016b) is a framework document that sets the objectives for research and knowledge transfer in MRA's governance area and directions for planning and coordinating different research measures in order to achieve their cohesiveness, including with EU and national horizontal and sectoral strategies, and the Rural Development Programme (RDP) 2014-20 (Figure 7.A1.1). The development plan addresses research in veterinary medicine; food technologies and food safety; animal production, including animal breeding; crop production, including plant breeding; horticulture (berries, fruits, ornamental horticulture); fisheries science, including aquaculture; and rural economics. The priority fields for agricultural sciences (stemming from Europe 2020) are climate change and resource efficiency, food safety, health care and aging, environmentally friendly production methods and land use (MRA, 2016c).

Figure 7.6. Main funders and programmes for agriculture-related research, 2017[1]

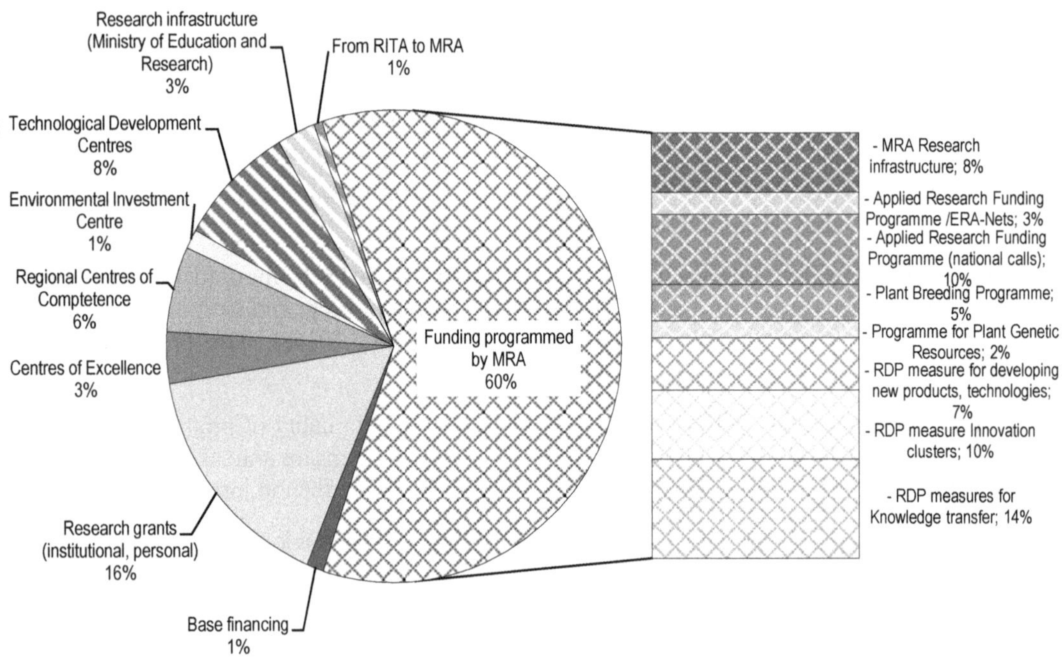

1. 2017 or annual average of programme period.

RITA: a programme that has been developed for 2014-20 to support more efficient collaboration between public sector decision makers and R&D institutions.

Numbers may not add up due to rounding.

Source: Communication from MRA.

StatLink http://dx.doi.org/10.1787/888933654845

Research funding instruments

The MEAC and the MER are responsible for most of the public research funding streams and horizontal policies as they design the policy and research funding instruments, distribute funds to their implementing agencies (Enterprise Estonia, Kredex for MEAC; ERC, Archimedes Foundations for MER), and distribute certain funds directly (ERC, 2013). The MER is counselled by the Research Policy Committee that also makes proposals on policy, R&D financing principles and strategies (MER, 2015a). The MRA is responsible for supporting research in agriculture-related areas, programming 60% of funds (Figure 7.6).

The main research funding instruments financed from the Estonian state budget are: block funding; grant research funding — institutional research grants and personal research grants; national R&D programmes; financing of centres of excellence and doctoral schools; and covering the expenses of R&D infrastructure (MER, 2015a).

The majority of public research funding in Estonia is project-based and is distributed through competitive calls in which applicants are evaluated by peer-review. Table 7.2 summarises the main research funding instruments funded through the MER, MEAC and MRA.

In addition, RDP funds are increasingly used to finance knowledge transfer. The Estonian RDP 2014-20 allocates 3.9% (4.0%) of total expenditure to three measures that can fund knowledge transfer: Knowledge transfer and information; Advisory services, farm management and farm relief services; and Cooperation, compared to 1.5% for knowledge transfer in the RDP 2007-13 (MRA, 2016d) (Chapter 6). This is still lower than the EU average of 4.9%, but higher than in other Baltic countries.

Trends in expenditures on R&D

Estonian gross domestic expenditure on R&D (GERD)[12] grew rapidly in the 2000s, increasing ten times in ten years. Fast growth can be partially attributed to the very low level of expenditure on R&D in the beginning of this period. Estonian GERD accounted for 0.6% of GDP in 2000, compared to 2.1% on average in OECD countries. While expenditure on R&D in government and higher education grew steadily during the 2000s, the most spectacular increase was in business enterprise R&D. The significant spike of R&D investments in 2010-12 was caused by a one-time large investment in oil shale industry (Statistics Estonia, 2015b). With those investments, GERD briefly reached 2.3% of GDP, but declined from 2012 to 1.5% in 2015, remaining below the OECD and EU28 averages of respectively 2.4% and 2% (Figure 7.7).

Estonia has set the target to increase R&D investments to 3% of GDP in 2020. Estonia 2020 estimates that this would mean quadrupling of R&D spending compared to 2009 (Government Office, 2014). The target of 2% of GDP for 2015 was not met, raising doubts about meeting the 2020 target.

Table 7.2. Most relevant funding measures for agricultural innovation

Types of funding/programmes	Purpose	Financing/ connection with AIS	Evaluation of applications
Block funding	To provide funding for organisations to attain their strategic development goals, for co-financing foreign and domestic projects and for opening up new research directions	2005-15: EUR 77.7 million Agricultural sciences[1] EUR 1.46 million	Main institutional, non-competitive instrument, distributed by the decision of the minister. The funds allocated for block financing from the state budget are provided to applicants based on the results of their R&D activities in previous three years (publications, patents, R&D funding, PhD defences).
Institutional research grants (replacing the previous target financing)	To finance high-level R&D, and related activities (research themes) of an institution to ensure the consistency of the R&D and to supplement and maintain the necessary infrastructure	Most sizeable research support measure. 2007-15: EUR 207.2 million (including target financing). Agricultural sciences: EUR 13.5 million	Competitive, project-based. Applications are evaluated by committee of national and international experts
Personal research grants	Innovative or high-risk research projects carried out by researchers or small research groups	2009-15 EUR 53.5 million (including ERC grants) Agricultural sciences: EUR 1.7 million	Competitive, project-based. Applications are evaluated by committee of national and international experts

Table 7.2. Most relevant funding measures for agricultural innovation (cont.)

Types of funding/programmes	Purpose	Financing/ connection with AIS	Evaluation of applications
Centres of Scientific Excellence	Formation of consortium by internationally recognised research groups to improve the quality and efficiency of scientific research through cooperation	2008-15: EUR 44.7 million; max. amount per project EUR 7.7 million, at least 5% co-financing requirement Centre of Excellence in Environmental Adaptation ENVIRON coordinated by EMÜ is one of the 12 centres created; funding EUR 3.0 million	Applications evaluated by committee of national and international experts
Competence centre programme	Formation of competence centre by consortium of enterprises and R&D institutions for innovative product development and cooperation	2014-20: EUR 40 million, maximum amount EUR 7 million per centre; at least 40% of financing from the consortium partners Out of the 8 centres established, three are related to AIS: The Centre of Food and Fermentation Technologies (TFTAK); The Competence Centre on Health Technologies (CCHT); and The Bio-Competence Centre of Healthy Dairy Products LLC (BioCC)	Applications are evaluated by committee of national and international experts
Regional Competence Centres	Support to regional entrepreneurship and labour market through cooperation between enterprises and R&D institutions to create knowledge intensive entrepreneurship (outside largest cities Tallinn and Tartu)	2014-20: EUR 14 million Maximum support per centre EUR 0.7 million; at least 15% self-financing from partners. In 2009-14 maximum support per centre EUR 3.19 million Out of six centres established since 2009, one is part of AIS: The Competence Centre for Knowledge-Based Health Goods and Natural Products	Application are evaluated at first by two appointed experts; followed by evaluation by a committee formed by EE.
Agricultural Applied Research and Development for 2015-21	Competent scientific input for agricultural policy and law making and monitoring; and coordination and financing of participation in international research cooperation	2015-21: EUR 9.61 million (2009-14: EUR 7.4 million)	Competitive, project-based. Steering committee decides on project calls and ordering of ongoing expert opinions and participation in international network projects.
Collection and Conservation of Plant Genetic Resources for Food and Agriculture for 2014–20	Collection, conservation, evaluation, and wider utilisation and availability of plant genetic resources for food and agriculture	2014-20: EUR 1.76 million (2007-13: EUR 1.35 million)	Non-competitive; but applications are evaluated by different departments of the MRA
National Programme for Plant Breeding for 2009–19	To ensure the sustainability of Estonian plant breeding and to preserve existing and breed new varieties	2009-12: EUR 3.6 million	

1. Frascati Manual classification, where agricultural sciences includes agriculture, forestry, fisheries and allied sciences (agronomy, animal husbandry, fisheries, forestry, horticulture, other allied subjects); and veterinary medicine.

Sources: compiled using MER-ERC (2014, 2015c, 2016a), EE (2016a, b); Etis (2016); MER (2015a); MRA (2013b, 2016c, 2016d).

Figure 7.7. Gross domestic expenditure on R&D as a percentage of GDP, 2000 to 2015

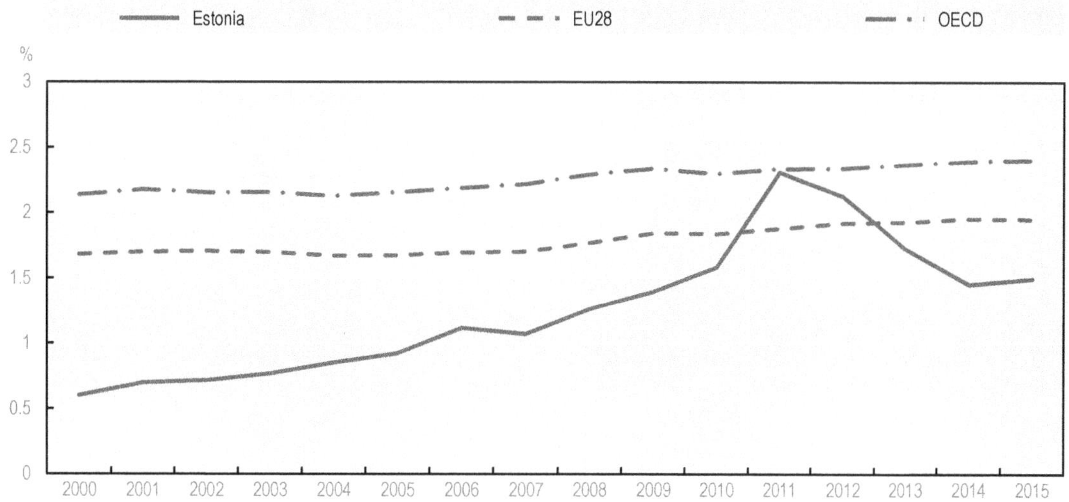

Source: OECD (2017b), *Main Science and Technology Indicators*, http://dx.doi.org/10.1787/msti-v2016-2-en.

StatLink http://dx.doi.org/10.1787/888933654864

Trends in public expenditures on agricultural R&D

Most agricultural R&D in Estonia is conducted in government and higher education organisations. GERD for agriculture in Estonia includes national estimates of expenditure on R&D performed in business enterprises, accounting for less than 1% of the total. GERD for agricultural sciences is only available for R&D conducted in government and higher education organisation. It is about 80% the equivalent GERD for agriculture as a socio-economic objective, illustrating that the sector relies on more than agricultural sciences. Budget appropriations are also used to have a broader picture of public investment in agricultural R&D, in particular for comparison purpose.

Public expenditure on agricultural R&D as a share of agricultural value added (research intensity) has increased rapidly between 2002 and 2012, with variations partly due to programming cycles (Figure 7.8.A). Research intensity more than doubled to reach 2.8% in 2012, but following a sharp decline, it settled at about 1.5% in 2014-15. The rapid increase in research intensity is mainly because R&D expenditure grew at a considerably higher rate than agricultural value-added. Public expenditure on agricultural R&D in real terms increased by 11% per year from 2003-05 to 2013-15, one of the highest growth rates among OECD countries in the last decade, together with Germany (13%), Mexico (10%), Korea (9%) and Norway (9%).

GERD for agriculture, which is mainly conducted in government and higher education organisation, whatever the source of funding, also reached a peak of 3% of agricultural value added in 2012, to be scaled back to 1.5% in 2015 (Figure 7.8.B).

Figure 7.8. Developments in agriculture and economy-wide R&D intensity in Estonia, 2000 to 2015

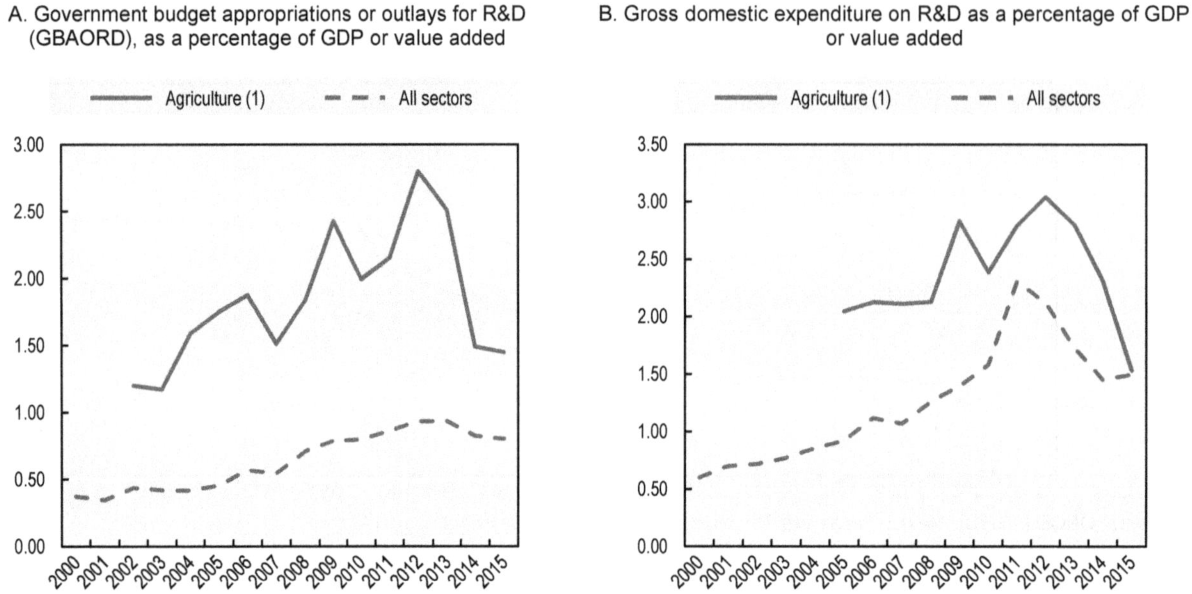

1. Agriculture as a socioeconomic objective in NABS2007.

Source: OECD (2017c), OECD statistics [Research and Development, OECD National Accounts], http://stats.oecd.org/ (accessed June 2017).

StatLink http://dx.doi.org/10.1787/888933654883

While in 2012-13, Estonia was among the countries with relatively high agricultural research intensity comparable to that in Denmark and Finland, by 2015 it was in the middle pack (Figure 7.9).

The intensity of public expenditure on R&D for agriculture is well above economy-wide R&D intensity, except in 2015 when agriculture is aligned with all socio-economic objectives (Figure 7.8). Public institutions play a larger role in R&D for agriculture than on average with less than 1% of R&D taking place in business enterprises compared to 40-60% overall.

While as a share of agricultural value-added, public expenditure on agricultural sciences increased, the share of agricultural sciences in total GERD decreased. With strong fluctuations in some years, Estonian (GERD) expenditures on agricultural sciences increased more slowly than in other sciences. In 2000, agricultural sciences accounted for 9.6% of all R&D expenditures in higher education and 15.4% in the government sector, but by 2015, their share had decreased to 4.1% in higher education and 6.6% in the government sector (Figure 7.10).

Figure 7.9. Share of budget expenditures on agriculture R&D as a percentage of agricultural value-added, 2000 and 2015

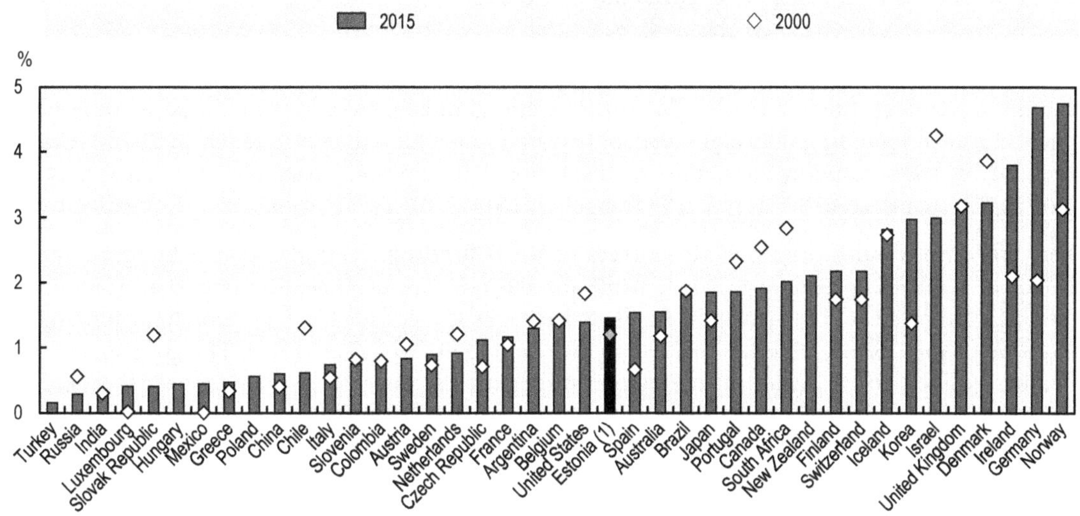

1. For Estonia, 2002 data are used for 2000.

Source: OECD (2017c), OECD statistics [Research and Development, OECD National Accounts], http://stats.oecd.org/; and ASTI (2017) for Argentina, Brazil, Chile, China, Colombia and South Africa (accessed June 2017).

StatLink http://dx.doi.org/10.1787/888933654902

Figure 7.10. Public expenditure on R&D for agricultural sciences, 2000 to 2015

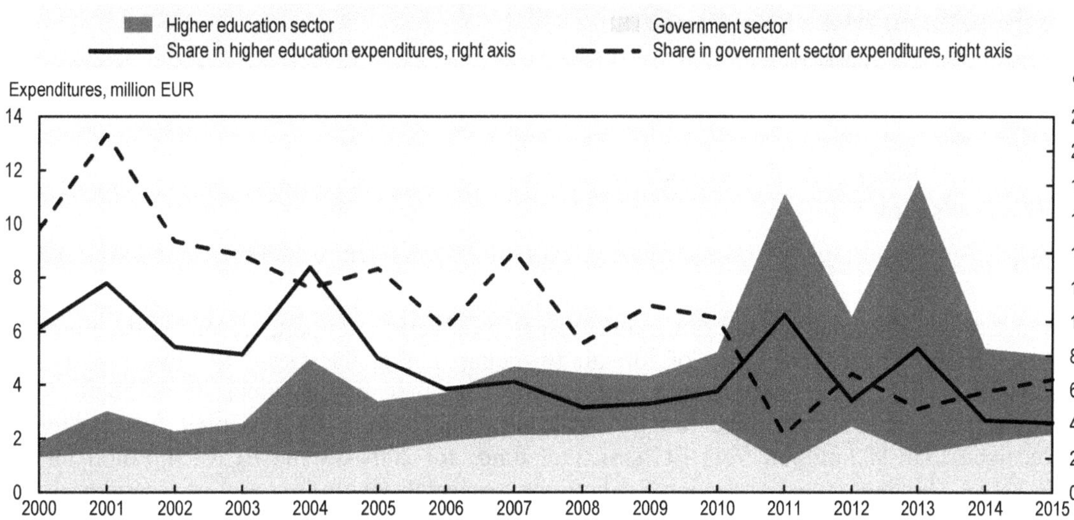

Source: Statistics Estonia (2017), on-line statistical database, www.stat.ee/en (accessed 13 June 2017).

StatLink http://dx.doi.org/10.1787/888933654921

Funding mechanisms and sources

The share of **project-based funding** of Estonian R&D is extremely high. Estimates for 2014 indicate that around 80% of R&D funding was project-based on average, over 90% in all public universities and 100% in some R&D institutes. This raises growing concerns for long-term strategic planning and sustainability of R&D institutions (Ukrainski et al., 2015b). The main funding measures are all project-based and competitive (Table 7.2). Block funding is the main non-competitive instrument. Its share in the total funding of R&D institutions was relatively small in 2005-13, remaining between 4% and 6% in most of the institutions (MER-

ERC, 2014). This information is not available by field of science, but as agriculture is integrated in the general system, this structure is likely to apply to agricultural sciences.

Following suggestions from the RDC, the Estonian Government plans considerable changes in research financing instruments. These include a significant increase in the share of block funding in order to achieve more stability in research funding (MER, 2015b). The aim is to achieve a 50:50 ratio between project-based funding (institutional funding grants and personal research grants) and block funding. In 2016 block funding was increased by 50%, resulting in a ratio of institutional funding and personal research grants to block funding of 73:27, compared to 80:20 in 2015 (Koppel, 2016).

There are various **public and private sources of R&D funding**. Overall, the state budget contributed to close to half of total R&D funding in 2014, while the business sector played an important role (41% of all R&D funding), followed by EU structural funds and foreign sources (Table 7.3). Structural funding through MER and foreign sources accounted for half of public funding in 2014 (Table 7.3). The government's share of R&D funding is likely to be higher for agriculture research as is the case in many countries where data are available, in particular given the low capacity of Estonian agri-food enterprises.

Table 7.3. Sources of R&D funding, 2010 and 2015

	Share in total funding (%)		Share in public funding (%)	
Sources	2010	2015	2010	2015
Business sector	41	39		
Personal research grants/Estonian Science Foundation grants	3	3	5	5
Institutional research grants/target financing	9	9	16	1
Block funding	3	3	5	5
Co-financing of structural funds and other R&D expenditures	11	7	18	12
Ministry of Economic Affairs and Communication	8	3	14	5
Other ministries	4	7	6	12
Foreign and EU sources	11	12	18	19
Structural funding through Ministry of Education and Research	7	17	13	27
Research infrastructure supports	3	0	5	0

Source: ERC (2016b), www.etag.ee/tegevused/uuringud-ja-statistika/statistika/teadus-ja-arendustegevuse-rahastamine-eestis.

The high share of foreign sources in Estonian research reflects the importance of EU structural funds in the national budget. The overall share of foreign financing in Estonia started to grow rapidly with the implementation of EU pre-accession programmes at the beginning of the 2000s. Over 2000-13, Estonia received more than EUR 5.4 billion in foreign assistance, mainly from EU structural funds (MoF, 2016). Estonia received EUR 802 million from EU structural funds for 2004-06 and EUR 3.4 billion for 2007-13 (EUSAE, 2015). The importance of foreign funding grew especially with the onset of recession in 2009, as this funding became the main source for financing public investments (Varblane, 2014). From 2009, the share of foreign support in the annual state budget has fluctuated between 11.2% and 13.8%; in 2015, foreign support amounted to EUR 1 billion and accounted for 11.8% of state budget expenditures (MoF, 2015).

For the programming period 2014-20 Estonia will receive EUR 4.4 billion from the five EU structural and investment funds. That includes EUR 725.8 million allocated to the development of the agricultural sector and rural areas from EAFRD, and EUR 100.8 million for the fisheries and maritime sector from EMFF (EC, 2014). Estonian research and higher education will receive EUR 359 million from structural funds over 2014-20 (MER, 2016a).

Support to knowledge infrastructure

Core infrastructure refers to infrastructures belonging to the R&D institutions, and which have been established in the public interest for the purpose of pursuing research themes, and can be used by other persons on the terms and conditions established by the owner institution (MER, 2015b). It includes high-class research equipment or technologies and a highly qualified workforce, which assist researchers, R&D teams, and the business sector by making expertise and analytical resources available.

General maintenance and funding of Estonian research infrastructure is addressed through a variety of instruments: the covering of infrastructure costs, the research infrastructure roadmap, core infrastructure supports, supports to scientific collections, and research libraries (MER, 2016b).

The infrastructure costs of public R&D institutions are funded from the budget of the umbrella ministry, mainly the MER. Private R&D institutions use private sources to cover infrastructure costs, although they may receive earmarked support from state budget and local government (Masso and Ukrainski, 2008). In 2012, research infrastructure support accounted for 5% of total government spending on R&D (ERC, 2016b). Since 2013, infrastructure costs are part of institutional and personal research grants (ERC, 2013).

In 2010, Estonia prepared the first research infrastructure roadmap, which is used as a long-term planning tool for investment decisions (MER, 2016b). The roadmap identifies the infrastructure items of national importance that are new or require modernisation (ERC, 2016c). The list is updated every three years. In 2014, the roadmap contained 18 items. EMÜ is a partner in four: Natural History Archives and Information Network (NATARC); Plant Biology Infrastructure — from Molecules to Crops; National Centre for Translational and Clinical Research (SIME); and Estonian Environmental Observatory (MER, 2016b). Estonia also participates in several international research infrastructures, including six European Strategy Forum on Research Infrastructures (ESFRI) items (ERC, 2016c).

Applications for core infrastructure support are submitted through institutional research grants (MER, 2015a). In the 2013 call for funds, the budget for core infrastructure support was EUR 0.5 million (ERC, 2016c).

From 1990 to the mid-2000s, Estonian R&D infrastructure suffered from underinvestment. Research infrastructure has been one of the main targets of EU structural funding (Christensen et al., 2012; Ruttas-Küttim, 2014). Over 2007-13 EUR 29 million from structural funds were invested for supporting research infrastructure of national importance (MER, 2016b). On the basis of the roadmap, for 2014-20 ERC administers EUR 30.9 million in support of investment plans for research infrastructures of national importance (ERC, 2016c). Overall, recent infrastructure investments have been generally sufficient to cover the previous underinvestment, but care should be taken to ensure the future sustainability of research infrastructure (Ruttas-Küttim, 2014).

R&D infrastructure improvement needs will also be addressed by a new programme –"Institutional development programme for R&D and higher education institutions" (ASTRA), which allocates EUR 122 million — one of the largest investments from EU structural funds in 2014-20 — for the construction of research and teaching facilities in R&D institutions, facilitating structural reorganising, improvement of quality and efficiency of teaching and research quality, modernising infrastructure, and for internationalisation, and increased cooperation, including between businesses and higher education institutions (MER, 2016a).

Regarding AIS institutions, MRA and EU structural and investment funding have modernised R&D infrastructure, but some laboratories and buildings remain outdated rendering them uncompetitive and unable to provide scientific support for the public and private sectors. EMÜ provides R&D infrastructure and competence for veterinary medicine, animal breeding, food science and technologies, and plant breeding, aquaculture and rural economics. Some of the facilities for food technology and product development for meat and fish products, bakery products, beverages, nature and plant products; aquaculture, and experimental stations need modernisation or expansion. The renovation of certain EMÜ buildings to establish a food centre with necessary laboratories and facilities for research on food technologies is in progress. Research in food technologies, including food safety, and development of products with high export potential, is also supported by some of the established competence centres. The Bio-Competence Centre of Healthy Dairy Products, the Centre of Food and Fermentation Technologies, and the regional Competence Centre for Knowledge-Based Health Goods and Natural Products Research have modernised facilities. In plant breeding, ECRI has facilities and suitable test fields, however, test apparatus and laboratories are in urgent need of modernisation (MRA, 2016b).

MER funds the maintenance of scientific collections that have passed evaluations with approximately EUR 0.8 million per year. EMÜ has the following scientific collections: The Estonian soil museum, mycological collection, botanical collection, and zoological collection that are part of the larger national collections (MER, 2016b).

The EMÜ library is one of the six research libraries responsible for the collection, preservation and processing of scientific information, and for making such information available to the public (MER, 2016b). The libraries are also financed from the MER budget.

Trends in funding and structure of agricultural knowledge institutions

The budget of R&D institutions reflects the strong fluctuations in research funding, due to the high contribution of EU funding, which follow programming period cycles.

The Estonian University of Life-Sciences (EMÜ) is the main institution in Estonia carrying out agricultural research and providing higher education in agriculture. EMÜ's budget has increased from EUR 17.3 million in 2007 to EUR 27.1 million in 2017 (Figure 7.11). Government financing for teaching undergraduate and graduate students, which accounts for half of the university's budget, has been steadily increasing. The research budget, however, has been fluctuating strongly. The disbursements from structural funds and foreign contracts at the end of the EU seven-year budget cycle 2007-13 sharply increased the EMÜ research budget from EUR 7.5 million in 2011 to EUR 14.2 million in 2013. But the disbursements fell back to 2011 levels in 2015 and 2016 due to delays in the implementation of measures for 2014-20, and started to increase again to EUR 10.7 million in 2017.[13] Structural funds were mostly used for investments, including in infrastructure.

One of the distinctive features of research funding in EMÜ is the high share of national contracts in research budget, which represented around 40% of annual research funding over 2007-15. In comparison, national contracts accounted for around 10% of the research budget of the TU in 2014 and 2015 (TU, 2016).

The Estonian Crop Research Institute, ECRI, specialises in applied and basic research for the development and upgrade of agrotechnologies, improvements in yield and quality of used varieties and agrotechnologies; and on plant protection, plant health, agrochemistry, fertilisation, and agrometeorology. The institute also breeds new varieties of agricultural crops, is responsible for the maintenance breeding of registered varieties and preservation of plant genetic resources, and produces and distributes certified seeds of various agricultural crops (ECRI, 2015).

Figure 7.11. EMÜ budget, 2007 to 2017

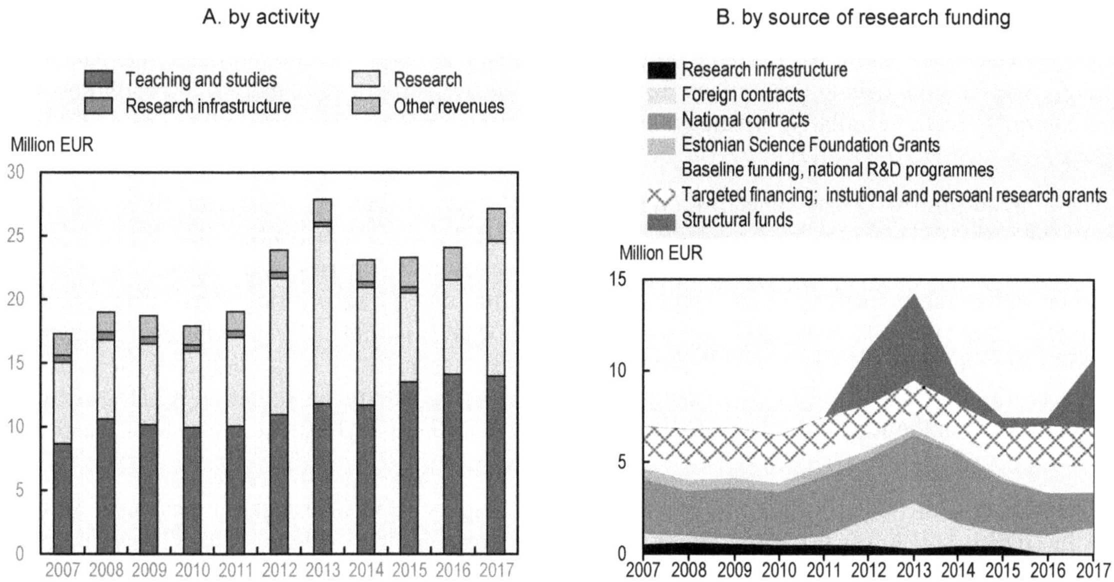

Source: Update from EMÜ (2015b), www.emu.ee/ylikoolist/yldinfo/eelarve/.

StatLink http://dx.doi.org/10.1787/888933654940

ECRI results from the merging of the Jõgeva Plant Breeding Institute and the Estonian Research Institute of Agriculture in 2013 (ECRI, 2015). The aim of the merger was to improve cooperation and efficiency, but it also allowed reducing costs (Figure 7.12). Around half of ECRI's revenues come from economic activities, including seed sales, different contracts and training. The research revenues are dominated by the MRA's applied science programmes and allocations from the state budget for research infrastructure (Figure 7.12).

Figure 7.12. ECRI budget, 2009 to 2017

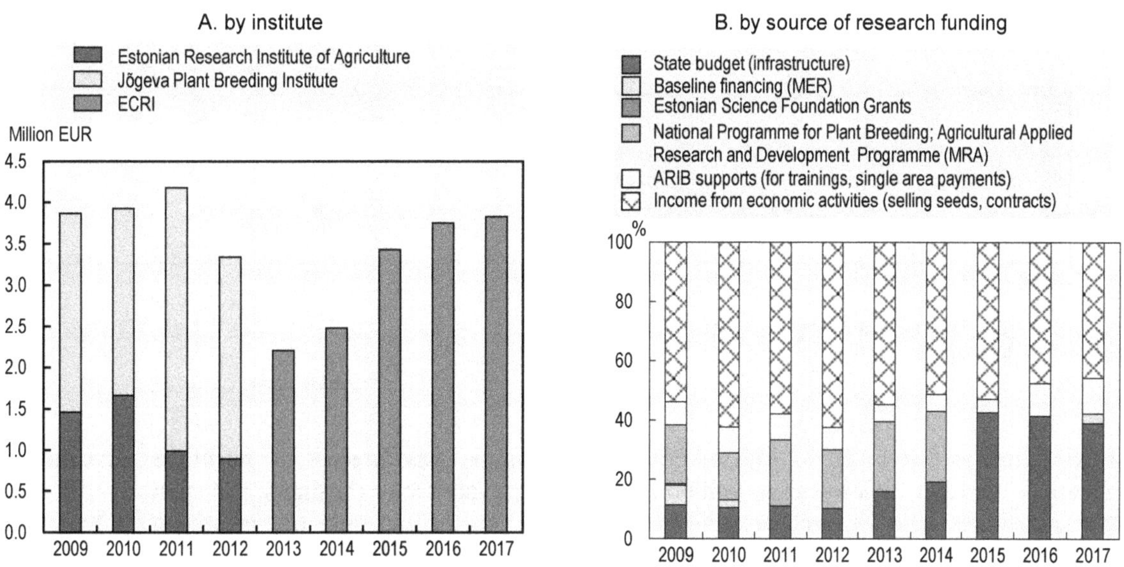

2009-13 Jõgeva Plant Breeding Institute; 2014 ECRI.

Source: Based on MRA (2016c), www.agri.ee/et/ministeerium-kontakt/majandusteave, and ECRI (2017).

StatLink http://dx.doi.org/10.1787/888933654959

Trends in private expenditures on R&D

Estimates of Estonian R&D expenditures in the business enterprise sector for enterprises in the field of agriculture, forestry and fishing are available only for some years. In 2007 and 2008 intramural expenditure of agriculture, forestry and fishing enterprises accounted for less than 1% of the total expenditures in the business enterprise sector. Similarly, private companies are estimated to account for a minor share of R&D for agriculture (less than 1% of GERD).

General trends in BERD may concern food processing companies. Data on GERD and BERD come from surveys of enterprises. The number of enterprises reporting R&D expenditures to Statistics Estonia is small. There is no enterprise whose main activity is agriculture, forestry and fisheries, and statistics on their R&D activities on agricultural sciences is not available. Among the enterprises making R&D investments, the 50 largest enterprises made 85% of R&D investments (Varblane and Ukrainski, 2016). Out of 259 enterprises, 43% were manufacturing enterprises, followed by enterprises specialised in professional, scientific and technical activities (21%) and ICT (16%). Among the manufacturing enterprises reporting R&D expenditures, 17 enterprises were in the food industry (6.5% of enterprises reporting R&D expenditures) (Mürk and Kalvet 2015).

Starting from a low level, BERD as a percentage of GDP grew rapidly throughout the 2000s. However, its share in GDP is still lower than the OECD and EU28 average in 2015 (Figure 7.13). The peak in 2011 reflects the one-time investment in the shale oil industry, which also shows in GERD development (Figure 7.7).

Figure 7.13. Business enterprise expenditure on R&D (BERD) as a percentage of GDP, 2000 to 2015

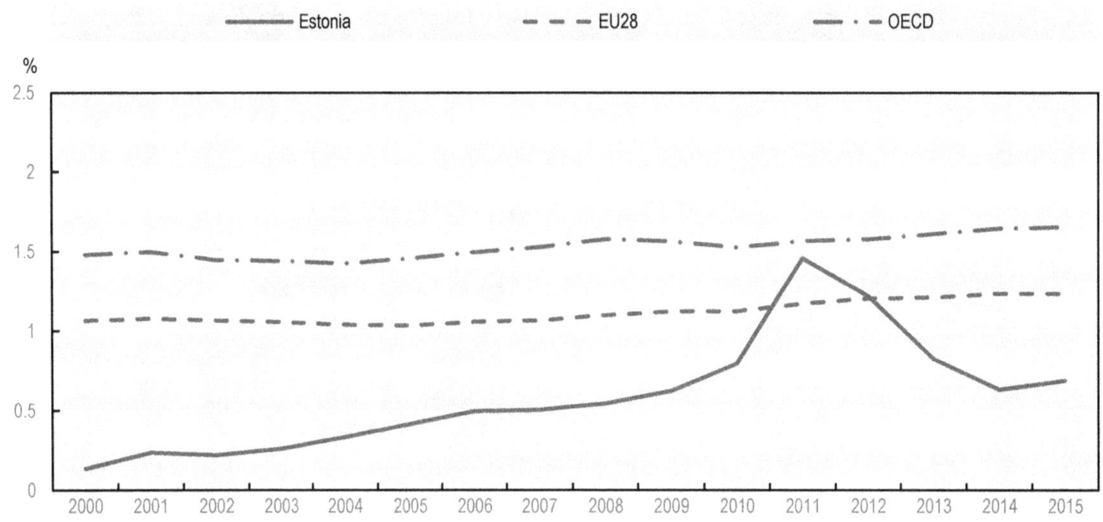

Source: OECD (2017b), main science and technology indicators, http://stats.oecd.org/Index.aspx?DataSetCode=MSTI_PUB (accessed on 16 June 2017).

StatLink http://dx.doi.org/10.1787/888933654978

ERC estimates that in 2014, 90% of government funding was directed to the higher education and government sectors and 10% was used to fund R&D in the private sector (business, private non-profit). Most private expenditures fund research activities in the private sector and only 6% is used to procure R&D services from universities and public research institutions (Koppel, 2016).

As the Estonian economy is dominated by microenterprises and with low industrial concentration in most sectors, the majority of firms lack the capacity to finance or perform R&D. The Estonian R&D system is more dependent on public funds than the OECD or EU average. However, as BERD increased in the last decade, the percentage of Estonian GERD financed by the industry increased from 24% in 2000 to 41% in

2015 (Figure 7.14.A). The growing importance of the role of businesses in the Estonian R&D system can be observed also from the increasing share of R&D carried out in business enterprises. In the early 2000s, 22.5% of expenditures concerned R&D in businesses, while higher education counted for over half of GERD (Figure 7.14.B). In over a decade, the share of expenditures on R&D made in the business sector almost doubled to reach 46% in 2016.

Figure 7.14. Estonian GERD financing by source and sector of performance, selected years

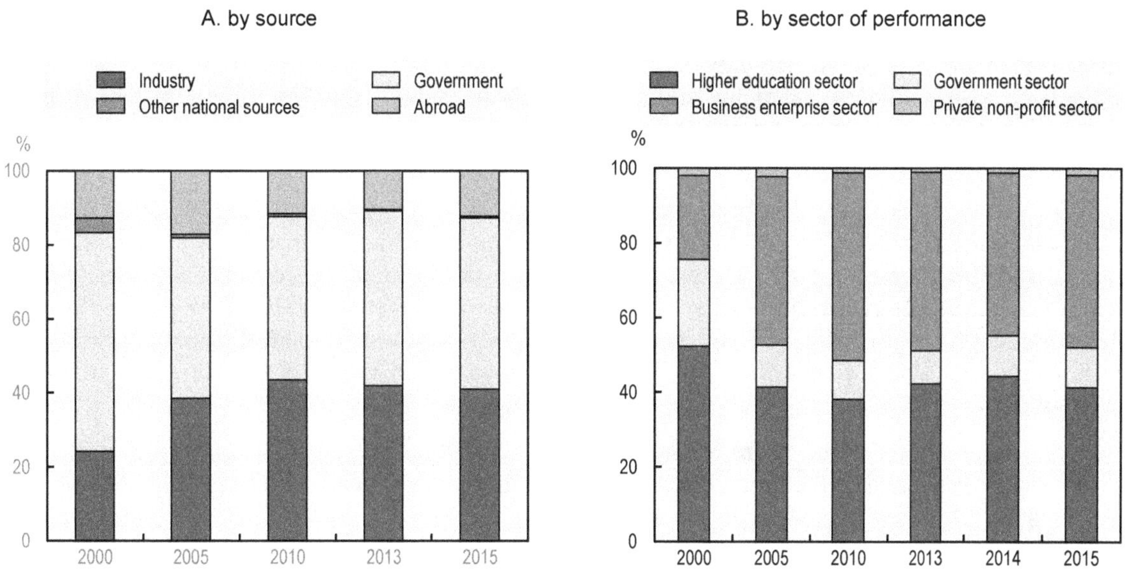

Source: OECD (2017b), Main science and technology indicators, http://stats.oecd.org/Index.aspx?DataSetCode=MSTI_PUB (accessed 16 June 2017).

StatLink http://dx.doi.org/10.1787/888933654997

Public incentives to private investment in agricultural R&D

In Estonia, the main incentives for private investments in R&D are different research grants and supports for innovation. Smart specialisation growth areas are prioritised in innovation support measures (e.g. competence centres, applied research in smart specialisation growth areas, applied research in smart specialisation growth areas).

Different tax incentives are common instruments for encouraging R&D investments. Most commonly used R&D tax incentives aim at reducing corporate income tax liability of the company incurring R&D expenses, and labour tax incentives (Staehr, 2010). Estonia does not employ tax incentives specifically directed at R&D, and thus 100% of government support to BERD is direct funding. However, although the measure is not specifically aimed at R&D investments, they are supported by the exemption from taxation of all reinvested business profits since 2000. Business profits are taxed when they are distributed (e.g. as dividends) or transferred abroad (Sepp and Wrobel, 2011). On the negative side, there is no incentive to invest in R&D as opposed to any other investment opportunity that may provide faster profits (Staehr, 2010).

Role of public procurement and other "pull mechanisms" in research funding

Pull-mechanisms, such as innovation prizes, reward research output tax credits on sales, or patent buyouts, reward successful innovations *ex post*, while push mechanisms fund potential innovations *ex ante* (OECD, 2013; Rietzke, 2015).

Estonian innovation policy has so far used mostly supply-side policy instruments or "push mechanisms" in the form of research and innovation grants (Romanainen et al., 2014b). The main focus of RDI policy has been on strengthening the systemic linkages by focusing on supply-side measures, such as R&D

infrastructure, support to Competence Centres and centres of excellence and provision of R&D grants (Lember and Kalvet, 2014).

The previous Estonian RDI strategy Knowledge-based Estonia 2007-13 (MER, 2007) emphasised that the state must be "a role model and a competent innovation consumer, whose procurements significantly emphasise innovativeness, quality and good design". It also outlined the need for public procurements to be more diversified, and the importance of the participation of enterprise offering innovative products and services. The importance of the public sector as "a smart customer, ensuring that in public procurements as much freedom as possible is left for offering innovation solutions" is also one of the principles for the development of information society expressed in the Estonian Information Society Strategy 2013 (MEAC, 2006) as well as the follow-up strategy Digital Agenda 2020 (MEAC, 2013b). However, those ideas have been mostly left unimplemented and public procurements have not been systematically used for facilitating innovation (Lember and Kalvet, 2012).

So far public procurement has been successfully applied in ICT and moderately in the defence sector (Lember and Kalvet, 2014). There are also some examples of innovation procurement initiatives supporting usage of local energy resources and waste collection; however, these mostly reflect the impact of EU-level policies (Roolaht, 2012). A feasibility study for smart procurement ordered by MEAC recommended focusing on e-government (ICT), e-health (ICT and health technologies) and construction (efficient use of resources) as there is already sufficient competence, readiness and knowledge in these sectors for stimulating demand (Eljas-Taal, 2014).

Estonian public procurements are registered in the Public Procurement Registry. However, the registry does not distinguish whether the procurement was innovative or not, and this makes it impossible to track procurement of innovation (Romanainen et al., 2014b).

A specific support measure for smart procurement to support innovation has been planned for the period 2014-20, and will be managed by Enterprise Estonia. EUR 20 million are budgeted, with a maximum of EUR 500 000 per application and 50% of self-financing (EE, 2016b). The measure is targeted to the public sector organising tenders and to enterprises offering innovative solutions. The aim is to improve the public sectors' ability for procuring innovative solutions as well as to support enterprises' abilities to develop new products and services (EE, 2016c).

7.4. Creating knowledge markets and networks

Intellectual property rights (IPRs), knowledge networks, and knowledge markets are of growing importance in fostering innovation. Reinforcing linkages across participants in the AIS (researchers, educators, extension services, farmers, industry, NGOs, consumers and others) can help match the supply of research to demand, facilitate technology transfer, and increase the impact of public and private investments. Partnerships can also facilitate multi-disciplinary approaches that can generate innovative solutions to some problems (OECD, 2015).

Policy regarding access to knowledge

Public access to scientific information is not a new phenomenon in Estonia. For example, the majority of Estonian scientific journals have been *de facto* open to the public since the electronic versions of articles emerged more than ten years ago. Research libraries have actively promoted open-access by organising traditional workshops and information days in the framework of the international Open Access Week.

Estonia is following the concept of the European Research Area (ERA), for which ensuring open access to knowledge, optimal knowledge circulation and transfer through the application of digital ERA is a priority. The underlying principle is to make research data, created or obtained with public funding publicly accessible. Plans related to the creation, preservation and dissemination are becoming an integral part of research projects (ERC, 2015c).

Estonia is preparing policy recommendations on open science, with a view to create a common framework for handling open science in Estonia. The document will define the strategic objectives until 2025, setting separate objectives for scientific publications and research data:

- Open access to scientific publications: The research community knows and accepts the principles of open science and open access. Scientific articles published with the help of national funding are freely accessible to the public one year after their first publication at the latest, whereas at least half of the articles become immediately and permanently available. All publicly funded scientific journals, and scientific journals published in Estonia, adhere to the principles of open access and a free content license.

- Open access to research data: The research community knows and accepts the principles of open science and open access. Research data resulting from nationally supported research are freely accessible and reusable. Research data are stored in trusted and open repositories and are made available as soon as possible (ERC, 2015c).

Farmers have free access to research information on the website of the Estonian Agricultural and Rural Advisory Service (www.pikk.ee). This page includes agriculture-related applied research reports, collections of national variety tests, publications, articles, presentations, dissertations, defended theses and project descriptions issued by different agriculture-related R&D institutions.

Access to R&D material

From 2013 onwards, a prerequisite for receiving competitive research funding in Estonia — institutional research funding (IRF) and personal research funding (PRF) — is open access. Both IRF and PRF allow to cover the article processing charges of the open-access articles form the grant budget, but this practice is so far not very widely spread (ERC, 2015c).

In the last decade Estonian scientists have published articles in more than 4 200 different journals, 355 of which (8%) are the so-called gold open access.[14] As of the end of 2015, Estonian scientific publishers issued 46 peer-reviewed scientific journals and nearly three-quarters of them are *de facto* gold open access. Out of the 11 Estonian scientific journals, which are listed in the Thomson Reuters Web of Science, nine are open access journals. Only part of the Estonian open-access journals have clearly defined copyright ownership and licensing conditions, and not all of them are properly reflected in the Directory of Open Access Journals (DOAJ) list and the SHERPA/ROMEO register (ERC, 2015c).

The status of research data has not been legally regulated in Estonia. The MEAC has compiled the first nation-wide policy document on open data, "The Green Paper on Open Data". However, in this document the topics related to research data remain in the background. Infrastructure for the preservation of scientific data and for making them available have already been or are still being created, including the "Natural History Archives and Information Network (NATARC)", the Estonian Language Resource Centre, the Estonian Biocentre, the Estonian e-Repository and the Conservation of Collections (ERC, 2015c).

In 2014, Estonia joined the international consortium DataCite under the research infrastructures roadmap initiative. The consortium DataCite Estonia, which has the right to assign unique scientific data identifiers (DOI), was launched at the beginning of 2015. DataCite ensures the visibility and usability of the high-quality research resources created by affiliated research institutions. To date, a number of professional interfaces have been worked out and more than 500 000 data sets in Estonia have been allocated a DOI identifier, most of them via the biodiversity database PlutoF and research infrastructure roadmap NATARC. The Estonian State and the national research institutions are actively collaborating with a number of pan-European research infrastructures (ERC, 2015c).

In order to preserve biodiversity and promote sustainable agricultural production, genetic resources of agricultural crops are collected and preserved. Since 1999, Estonia has participated in the European Cooperative Programme for Plant Genetic Resources (ECPGR) as a full member (MRA, 2013a). In Estonia genetic resources of agricultural crops are collected and preserved by the following institutions:

- The Gene bank of the Estonian Crop Research Institute collects and preserves the genetic resources of cereals, legumes, oil crops, grasses and legumes, as well as vegetable genetic resources outside their natural habitat (seeds in *ex situ* gene bank). 2 800 accessions of 57 species are deposited in the gene bank.
- The Department of Biotechnology of the ECRI manages the collection of different potato and horticultural plant varieties and breeds and the conservation of their genetic resources as meristem plants in test tubes (*in vitro*). The collection includes 490 potato and 118 horticultural and decorative plant accessions.
- The Polli Horticultural Research Centre of the EMÜ collects and preserves genetic diversity and cultivar resources of fruit and berry crops of Estonian origin. The collection includes 1 145 items of 17 plant species, including 136 varieties bred in Estonia.
- The Botanical Gardens of the TU preserve medicinal herbs, aromatic and ornamental plants in *ex situ* collections. The collection contains 387 varieties of ornamental plants originating from Estonia, and 55 species of medicinal plants and herbs.
- The Department of Gene Technology of the TUT studies and describes plant material using molecular biology techniques.
- The Non-Governmental Organisation (NGO) Maadjas collects, preserves and exchanges threatened native breeds, plant seeds and plant material.

Intellectual property protection

Intellectual property rights (IPR) in the Estonian agricultural and food sector are related to industrial property, which includes: the rights to patent protected inventions, useful models, trademarks, the use of geographical indications and new plant varieties.

These IPRs are regulated by various laws.[15] The most important treaties are the Paris Convention for the Protection of Industrial Property (1883), the TRIPS Agreement, and the European Patent Convention (1973). Estonia has also joined the Madrid Agreement Concerning the International Registration of Marks Protocol (1989) and the Hague Agreement Concerning the International Registration of Industrial Designs (1925) (Hanson et al., 2015).

Protection documents valid in Estonia are patent certificates for invention and trademark registration certificates for utility models or geographical indication.

Patents

The Estonian Patent Office (EPO) is a government agency that operates in the Ministry of Justice and provides legal protection to patents, trademarks, utility models, industrial designs, geographical indications and topology of micro-switches (EPO, 2016). The Estonian Intellectual Property and Technology Transfer Centre (EIPTTC) offers a wide variety of intellectual property (IP) and technology transfer support services. For example, it performs IP studies, advises enterprises on IP issues, and provides training and education. EIPTTC conducts research on a variety of patent related issues, supports trademark and design search, and helps the entrepreneurs to make right decisions in the development and creation of IP in their enterprise (EIPTTC, 2016). In addition, patent attorneys provide legal services in the field of industrial property.

There are two important issues concerning IPR: time and territoriality. A registered trademark is valid for 10 years, a patent and a utility model for 20 years and the protection of geographical indications is perpetual. Territoriality is an important principle, which means that a patent registered in Estonia does not confer any rights in other countries (Hanson et al., 2015).

Over 1994-2013, 3.1% of registered patent and utility model applications submitted in Estonia were in the agricultural sector (mainly patents in plant breeding) and 2.9% in the food sector.

According to Patent Co-operation Treaty (PCT) statistics[16] during the period 2006-11, the number of patent applications from the Estonian agricultural sector was 31, accounting for a very small fraction of the global PCT patent applications. However, the PCT patent applications in agriculture and food sciences comprised 12% of Estonia's total patent applications, which is double the OECD average (Table 7.6). Most of these (10.3% of total Estonian applications) were in food sciences.

The total number of food and agriculture patents developed in cooperation with foreign partners was 15 in 2006-11, accounting for 0.039% of the total world agricultural joint patents. Joint food patents applications comprised 13.8% of the national total joint patents, and there were no joint patent applications in agricultural sciences. These figures were significantly below the OECD average (Table 7.7).

In addition to the size of the country, other reasons explain the relatively low number of patents in Estonia:

- Holding a patent requires large investments from the patent holder over a long period of time.
- After patenting, the patent holder has to see to the issues of marketing and selling (commercialisation), but the research community lacks adequate experience and knowledge, as well as the human, time and financial resources.
- The patent value of an invention is changing. The present trend is that inventions are immediately geared to production and, for example, high-tech inventions are patented.

In summary, an IPR system is in place in Estonia that ensures IP protection, although the number of Estonian agricultural patent applications is modest. According to the Intellectual Property Protection Index estimated by WEF, IP protection has increased in Estonia over the last decade, and is equivalent to the average of OECD countries and slightly higher than the average of EU28 countries (Figure 7.15).

Figure 7.15. WEF Intellectual Property Protection Index, 2007-08 and 2016-17

Score 1-7 (best)

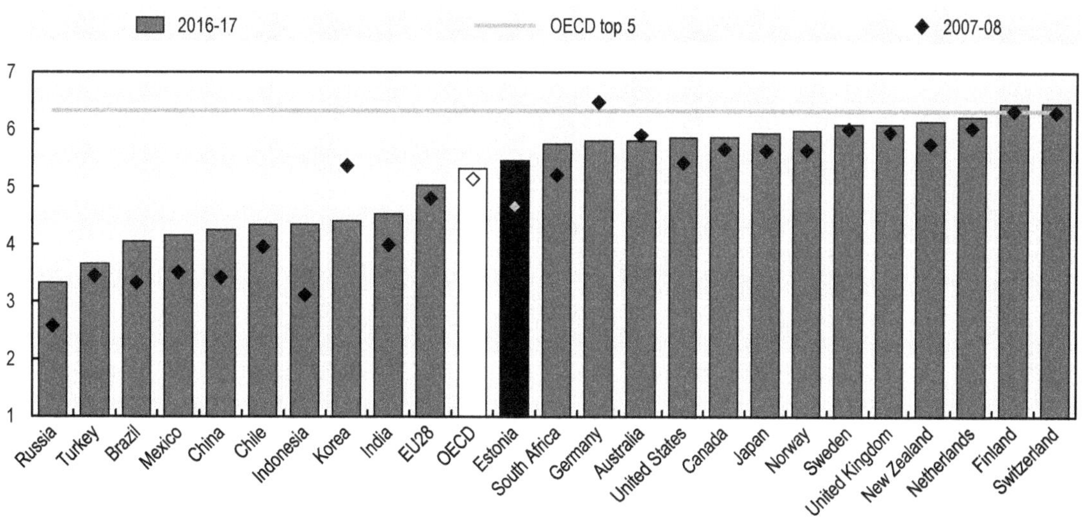

Countries are ranked according to 2016-17 levels.
OECD top 5 refers to the average of the scores for the top 5 performers among OECD countries (Switzerland, Finland, Luxembourg, Netherlands and New Zealand) for 2016-17.
Indices for EU28 and OECD are the simple average of member-country indices.

Source: World Economic Forum (2016), *The Global Competitiveness Report 2016-2017: Full data Edition*, www.weforum.org/reports/the-global-competitiveness-report-2016-2017-1.

StatLink http://dx.doi.org/10.1787/888933655016

Plant breeding and IPR

The Estonian plant variety protection system was introduced in 1994. Plant breeding is regulated by the Plant Propagation and Plant Variety Rights Act and the Regulation of the MRA on the list of plant species the seed and propagating material of protected varieties of which may be grown in small quantities. Plant varieties entered in the Register of Plant Variety Rights remain under protection for 25 years, with the exception of vines and tree crops which remain under protection for 30 years (EIPTTC, 2016).

The principles for the EU plant variety protection system are laid down in Council Regulation (EC) No. 2100/94 on Community plant variety rights, and the EU and the EC Regulation No. 1768/95 on agricultural exemption (Rand and Ardel, 2010).

Estonia became a member of the International Union for the Protection of New Varieties of Plants (UPOV), which offers strengthened protection and improves the plant breeders' ability to recover their initial costs of variety breeding and development, and generate the funds necessary for further re-investment in this activity by signing the UPOV Convention 1991 Act in 2000 (UPOV, 2016). The Plant Variety Protection Index of Estonia is lower than in Finland and the Netherlands, mainly reflecting more recent participation (Figure 7.15).

Estonia is a member of the OECD Schemes for the Varietal Certification of Seed Moving in International Trade, which promotes the use of agriculture seed of consistently high quality. The OECD certification provides for official recognition of "quality-guaranteed" seed, thus facilitating international trade and contributing to the removal of technical trade barriers.[17]

Figure 7.16. Plant Variety Protection Index

Score 1-5 (best)

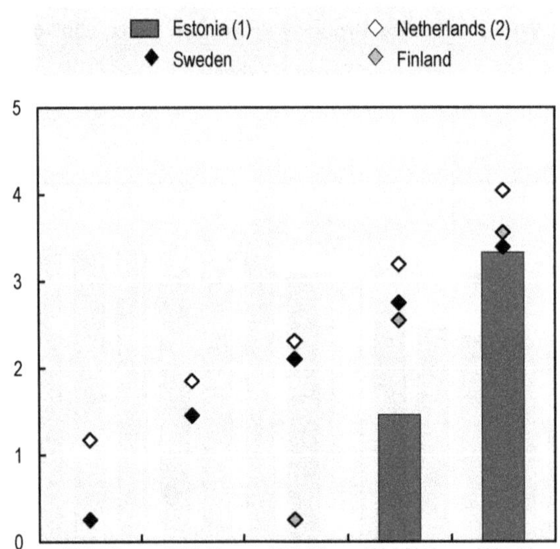

1. For Estonia, data prior to 1991 are not available.
2. For Finland, data prior to 1981 are not available.

Source: Campi and Nuvolari (2013), "Intellectual property protection in plan varieties: A new worldwide index (1961-2011)", http://hdl.handle.net/10419/89567.

StatLink http://dx.doi.org/10.1787/888933655035

The registration and cataloguing of varieties, and organising their protection are the responsibilities of the Agricultural Board (AB, 2015). The AB keeps a record of the varieties under protection in a catalogue, which is publicly available on the AB website (Rand and Ardel, 2010).

The programme "Genetic Resources for Food and Agriculture 2014-20" has been introduced, whose main objective is to grant the collection, preservation and study of the plant genetic resources for food and agriculture of Estonian origin as a fund for variety and species diversity, thereby creating conditions for sustainable development. The key activities for achieving the objectives include the collection of genetic resources of agricultural and food crops, management of collections, international cooperation, promotion, organisation and communication (MRA, 2008).

Co-operation between public and private actors

Investments in R&D have created a modern and attractive environment for research in Estonia and have strengthened the research community. Cooperation between R&D organisations is comparatively good, but collaboration between private companies and R&D institutions is low, as pointed out in current and previous national R&D strategies.[18] Lack of public-private collaboration can be explained by the low research capacity of Estonian SMEs and the disproportionate public funding of basic research compared to applied research and technological development. In addition, there are a few domestic capital-based industries in Estonia and as to product development, branches of foreign companies predominantly get their R&D support from the parent company (Vooremäe, 2011). The fact that most support for conducting studies and trials (product development), carrying out analysis, as well as providing consulting services and training, is project based may also cause problems for cooperation between academia and enterprises (EMÜ, 2010). Lack of public-private collaboration has not facilitated the emergence of economically viable end-results of research projects (MER, 2014b). As indicated below, efforts were made for the 2014-20 programming period to improve the situation (MRA, 2015a).

The main form of collaboration is through participation of private sector representatives in the different advisory councils that contribute to the formulation of financing policies in Estonia, for example in RDC and the Research Policy Committee. The Council of Agricultural Sciences at the MRA includes representatives of farmers' organisations. At present, out of 14 members (including chair and vice-chair) of the Council of Agricultural Sciences, three members are representatives of the sector (representing the Estonian Chamber of Agriculture and Commerce, the Central Union of Estonian Farmers, and the Estonian Farmers Federation); one represents the advisory system (RDF); four represent the MRA, and six represent R&D institutions (MRA, 2016a).

Different financing measures are available in Estonia to facilitate research collaboration between public and private actors, including centres of excellence, competence centres, regional competence centres, clusters, innovation and development vouchers; as well as applied research programmes on smart specialisation growth areas. They also facilitate international cooperation.

The **Competence Centre** (CC) programme administered and supported by Enterprise Estonia was launched in 2004 to create a link between research and entrepreneurship. In addition, Enterprise Estonia administers a separate programme for **regional competence centres** since 2009 (Box 7.3).

At present, there are six CCs in Estonia, including three in the agricultural and food sector (MRA, 2016e). There is also a regional CC and a Centre of Excellence with activities related to plants:

- The Competence Centre of Food and Fermentation Technologies,[19] deals mainly with research on the metabolism of lactic acid bacteria and yeasts.
- The Bio-Competence Centre of Healthy Dairy Products, LLC[20] has five partners and its activities encompass the whole chain, from cattle breeding, nutrition and dairy technology to functional food. In cooperation with universities (EMÜ, TU), the CC has registered 14 patents.
- The Competence Centre on Health Technologies[21] is a research and technology organisation focused on applied research and product development in personalised medicine, drug development and reproductive medicine, both in human and veterinary medicine.
- PlantValor is a regional Competence Centre for Knowledge-Based Health Goods and Natural Products that belongs to the EMÜ. The Centre focuses on the sustainable use of plant material in

food and non-food products by raising the quality, functionality and storing properties of the plant material (PlantValor, 2016).

- The Centre of Excellence ENVIRON is a consortium led by the EMÜ, bringing together five leading research groups from the EMÜ, TU and TUT. The interdisciplinary research goal of ENVIRON is to study how plants and ecosystems cope with and adjust to stress induced by changing environmental conditions. The research results form a basis for the sustainable management of Estonian natural resources in forestry crop production in view of the future climate.

Box 7.3. Competence Centres in Estonia

Competence Centres (CCs) are private entities established by a consortium of R&D institutions and enterprises. CCs are research institutions oriented at long-term cooperation between academia, industry and the public sector, and focusing on applied research (Arnold et al., 2008). They can be regarded to some extent as public-private Partnerships (PPPs).

CCs are involved in multiple activities: pooling of knowledge, creation of new knowledge by performing different types of research, training and dissemination of knowledge and networking. CCs are involved in developing new technologies and looking for new and innovative technological solutions in the partners' key areas. Some CCs are also related to innovation clusters and the European Innovation Partnerships (EIP).

In addition to supporting research for the development of new and high value-added products, services and technologies, the measure promotes technology transfer and mobility of researchers among research and private business organisations and provides research opportunities for graduate students (MER, 2013). From 2007-13 CCs created 350 jobs (Pakkas, 2014). However, research jobs in CCs were often part-time and in some centres, teams were fragmented across high number of part-time contributors (Arnold et al., 2008).

The CC programme implemented by Enterprise Estonia was launched in 2004 and is directed at cooperation in the fields of smart specialisation. The maximum share of public support for the period 2014-20 is 60% and EUR 7 million per centre (EE, 2016a). The total budget for CCs over 2015-22 is EUR 40 million and six centres have received funding from Enterprise Estonia during this period, including three agriculture-related ones (EE, 2016a). In comparison, five CCs received a total of EUR 11.8 million of public support in 2004-08, and in 2009-15 eight CCs received EUR 57.7 million (Pakkas, 2014). After the 2014-20 programming period, Enterprise Estonia will no longer support CCs, which will have to find their own resources.

The CC programme has provided an overall positive experience for increasing R&D collaboration between private enterprises and public organisations. While the first financing period of 2004-08 was a first learning experience for establishing common interests and long-term cooperation; the second period of 2009-15 was characterised by the development of human resources, facilities and organisational structures; and a considerable increase in the number of private partners as well as their growing capacities and funding resources for implementing the R&D results (Pakkas, 2014). The number of private businesses participating as partners grew from 27 in 2004-08 to 100 in 2009-15, while their financial contribution increased from EUR 5.8 million to EUR 25.4 million (Pakkas, 2014). The programme strengthened links between universities and industry, encouraged concentration of research and educational resources in the smart specialisation growth areas, and increased the research output and R&D capabilities of partners (Arnold et al., 2008).

Enterprise Estonia also administers a separate programme for regional competence centres since 2009. The aim of the regional centres is to support regional entrepreneurship and labour market development through cooperation between enterprises and R&D institutions and to create conditions for knowledge-intensive entrepreneurship outside the areas of two largest cities in order to increase regional competitiveness (EE, 2016a). The maximum support per centre for 2009-14 was EUR 3.2 million and the maximum share of public subsidy for an application was 85% of eligible costs (EE, 2016a).

Issues with CC implementation included the bureaucracy, shortcomings in inter-ministerial coordination regarding the monitoring of the CCs, and conflicts over ownership of results (Huisman et al., 2007). The latter issue has been amplified by the fact that many employees worked part-time in university and part-time in CC. In addition, centres research output remained below the level initially expected (Arnold et al., 2008).

The sustainability of the CCs may cause problems as CCs do not have enough projects to cover their fixed costs and funding is not stable. Applied research can be financed from two sources: contributions from businesses, and support from various support measures, which require the recipient's own contributions. Corporate-funded R&D activities are primarily carried out in global corporate groups. It is very difficult for domestically owned companies to get funding. It has been suggested that an outreaching CC-wide organisation could offer CCs marketing and generic services. The overall objective is that the competence centres receiving support in the period of 2015-22 should grow strong enough to manage without public support from EE after the end of the programming period (Pakkas, 2014).

The objective of these centres is, by integrating the knowledge and experience of enterprises and R&D institutions, to create new food- and feedstuffs with high export potential, to improve the quality, functionality and storage characteristics of food and to develop new technologies. One of the aims of applying the research in practice is to make the production and processing of raw materials more efficient. To achieve this, R&D activities cover the whole food chain: from animal breeding, feeding and keeping, to the creation of health promoting food products and conducting clinical and physiological trials to prove their health promoting qualities (BioCC, 2016; TBP, 2015a).

The **Innovation voucher** programme provides SMEs with grants (maximum EUR 4 000, maximum share of support 80%) for cooperating with a higher education institute, test laboratory, or intellectual property experts to develop innovative solutions for development obstacles, carry out tests with new materials, gather knowledge on technologies, and conduct studies in intellectual property databases (EE, 2016b). 884 innovation vouchers were financed with the total amount of EUR 4.55 million in the period 2008-12 (MER, 2013). At present, the data on the funded innovation vouchers does not specify the field of activity; and so it is not possible to distinguish the number of innovation vouchers connected with the AIS without a separate survey.

The total budget for this programme increased to EUR 10 million for the 2014-20 period, and an additional measure was introduced offering larger grants for preliminary research in SMEs, whose development ideas need advanced professional know-how (EE, 2016c, OECD, 2017a): **Development vouchers** offer grants of maximum EUR 20 000 per voucher, maximum share of support 70% of total costs. Four enterprises out of the first 26, who received first development vouchers in 2015 (EE, 2016d), are connected with food and agricultural technologies, and vouchers are used for developing malt processing technology, food packaging designs, developing greenhouse and smart gardening technologies.

The application of innovation vouchers has contributed to enhanced cooperation between academia (including the EMÜ) and industry in terms of putting knowledge and know-how into practice. Innovation vouchers give SMEs access to research and innovation services. They can, in collaboration with universities, testing laboratories and intellectual property experts, develop innovative solutions to obstacles, experiment with new materials, gathering information on innovative technologies, and research intellectual property databases. According to a recent evaluation, the innovation voucher scheme has proved successful and, as an independent measure, received relatively positive feedback. However, only in a few cases has this short-term and small-scale scheme developed into a longer-term and more systematic collaboration with universities (Lember et al., 2015).

Enterprise Estonia also implements a **cluster programme**, under which 20 clusters and 49 pre-projects for preparation for establishing a cluster received a total of EUR 10.4 million during the period of 2008-12 (Mihkelson et al., 2013). The maximum share of public financing was respectively 70% and 75% of total project costs. The EMÜ is one of the partners of the Estonian Waste Recycling Cluster (Jäätmete Taaskasutusklaster 2016) and the pre-project for establishing Estonian Organic clusters (Eesti Maheklaster 2016). Other projects connected food and agriculture were pre-projects for a milk cluster, a soy cluster, and a food cluster in southern Estonia (EE, 2016d).

Agricultural enterprises were not eligible for subsidies under this cluster programme implemented by Enterprise Estonia, but they are under the cooperation measure of the Estonian RDP 2014-20 (see below).

In the programming period 2014-20, Estonia has developed additional measures specifically addressing cooperation between R&D institutions and enterprises in the smart specialisation growth areas. Those include:

- **NUTIKAS**, a measure for applied research in smart specialisation growth areas. The funding of EUR 41 million is allocated to businesses for commissioning necessary applied research or product development projects from R&D institutions (ERC, 2016d). The self-financing rate depends on the size of enterprise. In applied research, the maximum public support is 70% of eligible costs for small enterprises, 60% for medium-sized enterprises and 50% for large enterprises. For product development, public support rates are 45%, 35% and 25% respectively (SA Archimedes 2016).

- **NUTIPRO** with EUR 10 million specifically addressing large-scale projects. The programme supports R&D initiatives with large-scale impact and coordination of applied research projects and targets R&D institutions and enterprises (MER, 2016a).

A separate programme, **RITA**, has also been developed for 2014-20 to support more efficient collaboration between public sector decision makers and R&D institutions. EUR 28.1 million will be allocated to support the government in strategic management of research and the capacity of R&D institutions in carrying out social- relevant research (MER, 2016a; ERC, 2016e). The ministries will select topics for applied research on the basis of needs of their governance area. The applied research will be carried out by R&D institutions (ERC, 2016e). This programme will finance a study on the prospects of the bioeconomy in Estonia

EU programmes also emphasise research collaboration as Estonian national horizontal and sectoral strategies and plans. Horizon 2020, previous **EU Framework Programmes for Research**, other EU programmes as well as specific programmes provide a variety of measures open to researchers in the private and public sectors (described also in the sub-chapter on International cooperation). Foreign contracts have been also an important source of financing.

In the EU 7th Framework Programme (FP7) 2007-13, there were 541 Estonian participants in 451 successful applications receiving EUR 88.6 million. The EMÜ took part in 12 projects (in thematic areas "Food, agriculture and fisheries, biotechnology" and "Environment"), and the Estonian Crop Breeding Institute in two projects. Twenty-nine successful projects with 30 Estonian participants belonged to the FP7 thematic areas "Food, agriculture and fisheries, biotechnology" (6.4% of successful applications). Out of those 30 participants eight were higher and secondary education institutes; eight private for profit organisations, six public bodies, four research organisations, four other organisations. The successful applications received EUR 2.6 million and the success rate of applications was 25%. The eight private for profit organisations were all SMEs participating in 26.7% of all successful projects in "Food, agriculture and fisheries, biotechnology". SME's overall participation rate in successful projects was 33%, however, it varied strongly by area, for example, SMEs participated in 8.7% of successful projects in the area of "Environment". The MRA was the most active participant among the Estonian public bodies (ERA-NET projects), followed by the MER (mostly research infrastructure projects). The EMÜ was the most active Estonian participant in "Food, agriculture and fisheries, biotechnology" (Must et al., 2014). Moreover, out of three European Research Council individual grants received by Estonian researchers, one — "Stress-Induced Plant Volatiles in Biosphere-Atmosphere System" (EUR 2.26 million for 2013-18) — was awarded to EMÜ's Professor Ülo Niinemets (EC, 2016).

As of October 2016, Estonia participated in 170 successful applications in Horizon 2020 (ERC, 2016e). Fifteen successful applications (9% of Estonian successful applications so far) belong to the thematic section "Food Security, Sustainable Agriculture and Forestry, Marine, Maritime and Inland Water Research and the Bioeconomy". The successful participants included five private sector enterprises, five universities, the MRA, a state agency, two non-profit organisations; the total amount of EU funding for those successful Estonian applicants was EUR 2.6 million.

While both private and public actors can participate jointly to projects funded by EU Framework programmes for research, European Union has also developed programmes that encourage research partnerships more specifically. **EU Joint Programming Initiatives (JPI)** fund partnerships between public and private researchers, with one being dedicated to Agriculture, Food Security and Climate Change (JPI-FACCE). The MRA represents Estonia at the FACCE-JPI, that sets the strategic priorities for trans-disciplinary and innovative European research on agriculture, food security and climate change (MRA, 2016b). The FACCE-JPI provides a framework for the alignment of national programmes and joint research efforts, under five core themes: sustainable food security under climate change; environmentally sustainable growth and intensification of agricultural systems under current and future climate and resource availability; assessing and reducing trade-offs between food production, biodiversity and ecosystem services; adaptation to climate change; greenhouse gas mitigation (FACCE-JPI, 2016).

The European Innovation Partnerships (EIP) bring together all relevant actors across the whole research and innovation chain, at EU, national and regional levels, in order to: 1) step up research and development efforts; 2) coordinate investments in demonstration and pilots; 3) anticipate and fast-track any necessary regulation and standards; and 4) mobilise "demand" in particular through better coordinated public procurement to ensure that any breakthroughs are quickly brought to market. One of the EIPs concerns agricultural sustainability and productivity (EIP-AGRI). The RDP measure "Co-operation" (16) can fund its networking activities (Box 6.4). It includes the sub-measure "Development of new products, processes and technologies", which provides support to innovation cooperation, such as EIP operational groups; as of 2017, 22 cooperation projects were being funded. Innovation cooperation is supported also by another RDP sub-measure – the Innovation clusters sub-measure. By June 2017 six innovation clusters had been approved for financing (ARIB, 2017):

- Dairy Cluster.
- Estonian Field Crops Innovation Cluster.
- Horticulture Cluster.
- Organic Farming Cluster.
- NGO Liivimaa Lihaveis (Beef Cattle Cluster).
- Field Crops Cluster.

Agriculture-specific measures facilitating cooperation and knowledge flow

Some agricultural policy measures support specifically research cooperation and knowledge transfer in the food, agriculture and forestry sector. Innovation is an important priority of the Estonian RDP 2014-20. One of its objectives — functioning cooperation, timely research and development, and knowledge transfer between the manufacturer, the processor, the adviser and the researcher — is also aimed at innovation. The main focus is to enhance cooperation between the various parties (producers, consultants, academics), and thus applying the research results into practice. Three measures in particular contribute to this objective: knowledge transfer and information (budget of EUR 12 million), extension services (budget of EUR 8.6 million) and cooperation (budget of EUR 18.7 million) (MRA, 2016d).

The measure "Knowledge transfer and information actions" offers support for:

- The organisation of one- or multi-day training sessions allowing the acquisition and upgrading of vocational, occupational or professional knowledge and skills, as well as retraining;
- The organisation of presentation and outreach activities introducing already existing innovative technologies and modes of action or production. Outreach activities arranged to inform target groups on the topics relevant to their work are also supported;
- The organisation of visits to companies and workshops focusing on raising environmental awareness in agriculture and forestry, production methods or technologies, the diversification of agricultural production, and short supply chains;
- The publication of training and teaching materials;
- The organisation of long-term training programmes (duration of up to seven years), which combines all the above-mentioned activities; and
- The following long-term training programmes are being prepared: plant cultivation, livestock farming, organic farming, horticulture, food safety, cooperation and agricultural policy (MRA, 2015b).

The measure "Advisory services, farm management and farm relief services" offers support to farm advisory services for delivering individual advice in various areas including sustainable plant protection and household or enterprise management, and for cooperation, governance of business processes or technologies, management structure, market analyses or work organisation analysis, strategic planning and consultancy on the introduction of amendments. The Estonian advisory system is described in the following section on innovation adoption.

The "Co-operation" measure supports co-operation approaches among different actors in the union agriculture sector, forestry sector and food chain and with other actors that contribute to achieving the objectives and priorities of rural development policy, including producer groups, cooperatives and inter-branch organisations. The measure supports:

- Innovation clusters: the clusters that have drawn up a four-year action plan for the development of new products, processes or technology, small business collaboration, diversification of agricultural activities, collaboration between small-scale enterprises, etc. are supported. The action plan includes the division of tasks concerning fostering innovation between the members of the cluster. The activities in the action plan must be geared towards the practical needs of the company.
- Short supply chains and the development of local markets: promotion activities such as the organisation and participation in exhibitions, competitions, fairs, investments into equipment necessary for product distribution, Information Technology (IT) solutions, etc. are supported.
- The development of new products, practices, processes and technologies: the aim is to support individual projects, which promote cooperation and develop innovation, especially in the agriculture, food and forestry sectors, and solve specific producer- and processor-related challenges (MRA, 2015b). These projects can be developed as part of the EIP-AGRI, the measure supporting the activities of EIP Operational Groups.[22]

The interest for the sub-measure of innovation clusters has been high: ten action plans for the total sum of EUR 7.5 million were submitted in the first call in 2015. Those include three for crop production and processing clusters, two for meat production and processing, and two for organic production and processing clusters; one application for horticultural production and processing; milk production and processing; and other agricultural activities each (ARIB, 2016). However, only two applications — for a milk and a crop production and processing cluster — received financing. Competition for the sub-measure "Development of new products, processes and technologies" has also been very high.

Investment measures, which support different technologies, contribute to innovation indirectly, thereby facilitating the introduction of different innovation into production. Innovation is at the heart of LEADER 'local development' measure (CLLD), which endeavours to foster finding innovative solutions and their application. To this end, the local action groups should also describe innovative elements in the strategies they are compiling. In addition to that, the LEADER programme focuses on how to take advantage of local resources for the development of the local business and social environment, with an emphasis on innovative solutions (MRA, 2016d).

7.5. Facilitating the adoption of innovation in food and agriculture

The potential benefits of innovations are only realised if effectively implemented. Policy incentives for the adoption of innovation include a wide range of regulatory and financial approaches, including business investment support, and support to public-private co-operation arrangements and participation in networks. In primary agriculture, training, extension and advisory services can facilitate the transfer and successful adoption of innovation. These services are critical to facilitate farmers' access to technology and knowledge and contribute to facilitate farmers' effective participation in innovation networks and ability to formulate their specific demands. It is also important to support the diffusion of innovation in small agri-food firms (OECD, 2015).

Knowledge transfer and advisory system

Several organisations provide policy advice and monitor developments in knowledge transfer and advisory services in the field of agriculture:

- **Council of Agricultural Sciences.** The Council advises the Minister of Rural Affairs on RDI activities within the scope of the MRA, and monitors the implementation of the RDI measures funded by the MRA.

- **Advisory Board of EMÜ.** The EMÜ Advisory Board links the university and society, whose members are appointed by the Council of the EMÜ, after hearing the opinion of the University. The term of office of the members of the Advisory Board is three years (EMÜ, 2016a).
- **Knowledge Transfer Council.** The Knowledge Transfer Council monitors the development of agricultural sciences, knowledge transfer and advisory services with regard to the producers' needs and environmental awareness. In addition, the Council keeps account of the implementation of the priorities of relevant national strategy documents and makes recommendations concerning the implementation of the Estonian RDP 2014-20 knowledge transfer and consultancy measures. The Council comprises of representatives of the MRA and the MER, farmers' associations and agricultural producers and farmers (MRA, 2016c).
- **The Consultative Council of the Rural Development Foundation** (RDF). The RDF Consultative Council is an advisory body to the RDF in all matters concerning advisory services. The representatives of farmers, processors of agricultural products, research and development institutions and the MRA belong to the Council. The activities of the Council are aimed at attaining the overall objective of advisory services, which is to develop a sustainable agricultural and rural economy in Estonia through providing advice (RDF, 2016).

Education institutions offer co-ordinated and regulated knowledge transfer and promotion services, including training. These institutions may be universities, vocational schools, or associations of producers. In 2007-13, universities and R&D organisations that had their own knowledge and/or technology transfer departments, played a more active role in knowledge production and they were highly ranked among the farmers and food processors (EMÜ, 2012). The EMÜ, the ARC (mainly environmental-education training) and the ECRI have been among the most active trainers in agriculture and the food industry and they have provided training all over Estonia. Producer associations have also played a significant role in knowledge transfer by arranging training activities at the municipal and county levels.

The **Advisory Centre of RDF** also provides co-ordinated and regulated advisory services to farmers and rural entrepreneurs. Local contact points of the Advisory Centre are located in every county of Estonia, which give free information on the consultancy services on offer. It is also possible to order advisory services.

In the last 25 years, the advisory system has been reformed and has changed hands several times, which has hindered the natural development of the system (Box 7.4). The performance of advisory centres in 2007-14 indicated that cooperation between the coordinating advisory centre and research and development organisations was chaotic. It was difficult for individual advisory centres to employ advisors in the new fields that are important for the state, and regions where the number of agricultural producers are small. Therefore, the aim of the recent reform was to create a common countrywide agricultural and rural economy advisory organisation that would assure coordination of information and cooperation with interested parties, supportive services to advisors, and that would take care of more even workload of individual advisors. The development of services is also concentrating on facilitating access to advice by the target group, improving the relevance of advice.

Public funding for the Estonian advisory system is increasingly channelled through RDP measures (Figure 7.17). Significant changes were introduced for the programming period 2014-20, as outlined in Table 7.4. They include the introduction of differentiated support rates by type of advice, higher annual support for RDP measures, and advisory services development being funded by own revenues rather than the State Budget. Moreover, a new measure "Improving knowledge transfer and innovation in the agricultural and forestry sector and rural areas" offers support to farm advisory services for the delivery of advice to farmers and for advisors to acquire and develop new vocational, occupational and/or professional knowledge, skills and competences, as well as for retraining. The measure supports the services of a consultant or a mentor, as well as meeting costs (MRA, 2016c). A farmer may be supported with extension services for up to EUR 3 000 per calendar year (MRA, 2016d).

The farmers who applied for support from the sub-measures of the Estonian RDP 2007-13 Environmentally friendly management, Organic farming and Maintenance of semi-natural habitats, were obliged, dependent on the sub-measure, to go through a certain number of seminars and training sessions regarding the environmentally friendly management, organic production or maintenance of semi-natural habitats, respectively. The same system is followed in the RDP 2014-20. Since horticultural enterprises were added to the list of businesses eligible for support for environmentally friendly management, it is compulsory for the horticultural entrepreneurs to undergo training on environmentally friendly management as well.

Large-scale farmers approach researchers directly. Constructive advice can also be obtained from farm inputs providers, but commercial interest may lead producers to pay unnecessary costs and result in an excessive burden on the environment. Larger cooperatives have their own advisers who try to generate more interest for advice among producers.

In addition, RDF local advisory centres, start-ups and operating businesses may get free advice from municipal development centres. The centres share information on funding opportunities and entrepreneurship. Novice entrepreneurs are supported in starting a business and compiling a business plan. Municipal development centres operate as a network in every county. Enterprise Estonia coordinates the activities of the network (CDCIS, 2016).

Table 7.4. Measures supporting the advisory system in the Estonian RDPs 2007-13 and 2014-20

2016 (Estonian RDP 2014-20)	2013 (Estonian RDP 2007-13)
The Estonian RDP 2014-20 introduced different support rates depending on the type of advice: Support for most advisory services, covering animal and plant production, and organic farming for example, covers 90% of the total fee (farmers and producers paying 10%); Support for advice on management issues and drawing up a business plan covers 50% of the total fee and support for mentoring covers the total cost (RDF, 2016).	In the Estonian RDP 2007-13, support covered 75-80% of the total cost of receiving advisory services.
For the period 2014-20, the government signed a contract with the RDF for delivering advisory services. RDF has 54 certified advisors.	The supported advisory services were provided by recognised advisory centres.
For the period 2014-20, support amounts to up to EUR 8.2 million, i.e. around EUR 1 million a year, depending on the amount of advisory services provided.	Annual RDP support amounted to around EUR 770 000.
The aim is to reach 1 000 advisory contracts a year (in 2016 the number of advisory contracts was 699). In case the number of advisory contracts is less than 90% of the set target, the amount of support will be decreased by 3%.	The number of advisory contracts varied between 950 and 1 050 per year.
The development of the advisory system will be covered by revenues from advisory activities (at least 10.1% will be used for developing the system and at least 72.1% will be paid to advisors).	For the development of the advisory system, EUR 547 000 were allocated annually from the state budget, including for covering information requests in regional centres (EUR 157 000), administration, costs of internet portal pikk.ee (EUR 158 000), marketing, development of advisory products, procurement of tools, start-up support for new advisors and internship (EUR 97 500).
A new RDP measure with a budget of EUR 400 000 supports the training of advisors. The number of certified advisors is 153, including 45 forestry advisors. Procurement for training will be carried out by ARIB.	EUR 50-65 000 per year were allocated in the State budget for the training of advisors and extension officers.
From 2014, advisors will mentor clients on the use of ARIB e-services. In 2016, 3 714 clients received mentoring, and 3 657 submitted application using ARIB e-services. Provision of advice on African Swine Fever continued (each pig farmer was directly contacted). End of the year, unused funds were directed to internship support for advisors.	EUR 50-70 000 per year (without administration expenses) were allocated in the state budget for short term consultations during the application period of area payments.

Source: MRA (2013b, 2016d).

As a supporting structure, the Estonian National Rural Network (NRN) also contributes to the knowledge and innovation transfer (RERC, 2016), including the promotion of innovation in agriculture. In order to achieve the set objectives, the NRN collects, aggregates and disseminates best practices, examples of networking and innovative approaches, helps to find partners (also for innovation clusters) and participates in the work of the Innovation Network. In 2012, the NRN issued the publication "Take notice of innovative agriculture" (NRN, 2013). In the framework of the activities of the NRN, the Agricultural Innovation Network (AIN) was established in 2014. AIN fosters co-operation between the manufacturer, processor, adviser and researcher and the implementation of the European Innovation Partnership (EIP) operational groups' action plans and information clusters. The latter encourages a faster and wider transposition of innovative solutions into practice and contributes to the product, market, operational, organisational or personnel innovation is rural economy.

Particular attention should be paid to training, extension and advisory services that can facilitate the transfer and successful adoption of innovation. The potential benefits of innovations are only realised if effectively implemented.

Figure 7.17. Funding of advisory activities, 2013 and 2016

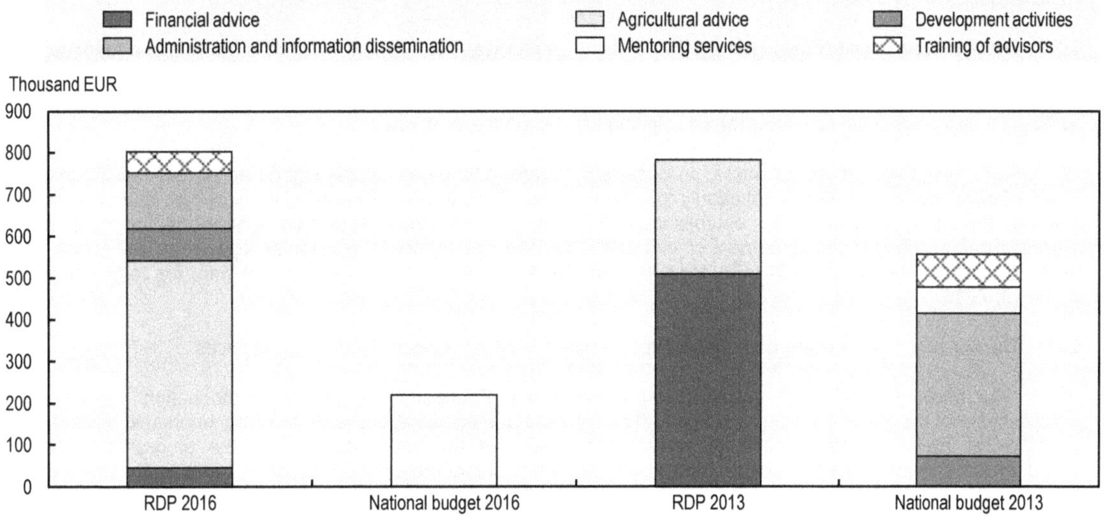

Source: MRA (2017), Compiled by MRA from various sources.

StatLink http://dx.doi.org/10.1787/888933655054

Box 7.4. Main steps in the development of the Estonian farm advisory system

- 1991: The creation of the first advisory services system, the Estonian Farmers' Federation (EFF), under the aegis of a project. The system joined the advisory stations of regional farmers' unions, two training centres working at the farmers' unions (Harju and Viljandi) and the Jäneda Training and Advisory Centre.
- 1993: A cooperation project between the Estonian Farmers' Federation and the Danish Agricultural Advisory Centre was launched to build up an advisory system based on the farmers' associations. The structure of the advisory system was interfaced to the structure of the farmers' union.
- 1994: Advisory unions were formed in Viljandi, Tartu, Jõgeva and Järva Counties with the financial support of the mentorship programmes run by the German and Estonian Ministries of Agriculture. The Estonian Association of Rural Consultants (Eesti Konsulentide Ühing) was founded.
- 1995: National advisory programme was launched. The foundation was laid for the contractual relationships between the consultant and the producer.
- 1997: On the initiative of the Estonian Association of Rural Consultants, a system for the certification of the rural consultants was worked out, which aimed to raise the quality of advice through checking the qualifications of the consultants.
- 2000: The "Rural Development and Agricultural Market Regulation Act" that defined such terms as "advisory support", "advisory support recipient" and "requirements set for the adviser and their attestation" was adopted.
- 2002: By means of public procurement information dissemination centres are opened by the farmers' or producers' associations at the county-levels. Rural Development Foundation (RDF) took over the information dissemination programme.

Box 7.4. Main steps in the development of the Estonian farm advisory system (cont.)

- 2003: The Estonian Chamber of Agriculture and Commerce took over from RDF the activities related to the dissemination of information (Agricultural Knowledge and Information System - AKIS).
- 2005: The Minister recognises the need to have advisory centres in every county, and they are used simultaneously as information dissemination centres. The Estonian Chamber of Agriculture and Commerce is held responsible for the harmonisation of the level of information offered by the advisory centres, for the training and continuing education of advisers and for the producers' needs analysis. Regular training and development activities are introduced.
- 2006: The Ministry of Agriculture in collaboration with the Estonian Chamber of Agriculture and Commerce start the reorganisation of the agricultural advisory system to simplify administration and make the provision of extension services more flexible.
- 2007: The Agricultural and Rural Advisory Coordinating Centre was established, which has the role of a mediator between the Ministry of Agriculture and the advisory centres and the advisers.
- 2010: RDF will once again take over the coordination of the advisory services.
- 2011: RDF recognised advisory centres, producer and professional organisations signed an Agreement for Joint Activity. The parties joined the agreement voluntarily to combine their efforts to ensure the availability of high-quality advice and act towards the common goal – the establishment of a nationwide single extension system by the year 2013. The organisations acceded to the agreement of joint action devised and adopted the Estonian agriculture and forestry advisory system development plan for 2012–20, together with the Action Plan for 2012–20. Agreement for Joint Activity ceased activity in 2013.
- 2014: The Ministry of Agriculture procured a public tender to find a provider of extension services
- 2015: The Ministry of Agriculture and Rural Development Foundation signed an authorisation agreement, which establishes that the Rural Development Foundation will offer subsidised agricultural and rural economic advisory services in 2015-21. The estimated volume of extension services for the entire duration of the programme (2015-21) is 1 000 advisory cases and 1 800 unique clients per year. The value of the contract is EUR 8.2 million. Provision of advisory services is financed from the budget of the Estonian RDP 2014-20. The Advisory Council is an integral part of the RDF and comprises of the representatives of farming and processing industry, research and development institutions and the Ministry of Rural Affairs. The activities of the Advisory Council are targeted at attaining the objectives of extension services, i.e. to develop sustainable agriculture and rural economy in Estonia. The structure of the advisory services is made up of the Estonian Agricultural and Rural Advisory Service (coordinator of the advisory system, support structure for advisers and mentors) and local contact points in every county, where free-of-charge information on the advisory services and the range, nature and price list of the advisory products can be found. It is also possible to order advisory services.

Source: Advisory service of the Rural Development Foundation, www.pikk.ee/.

Availability and use of extension services

One of the most important roles of the advisory services is the communication of research information to the manufacturer. In this area, the activities of the R&D organisations overlap, in part, with those of the advisory system, but these organisations have no direct links with advisory centres. Estonia is characterised by an open extension service market and today there is a wide range of extension services operating in Estonia, whereas each of them has their own peculiarities and target audience. Part of the research activities are carried out as direct contacts between companies and researchers and are not reflected in the statistics concerning agriculture (Vooremäe, 2011).

During the period 2008-15, 2 671 farmers used the supported extension service (CAP pillar 2 measure 114, Advisory services). The number of agricultural holdings totalled 19 186 in 2013, and a total of EUR 5.4 million was spent on extension. Entrepreneurs covered 25% of the sum, the rest constituted the EAFRD and the State's contribution. Advice on financial economics ranked first (Figure 7.18), but the advice was used to compile investment applications. In 2014–20, the emphasis is placed on principal production-related advice.

Figure 7.18. Supported advisory service capacity, 2008-15

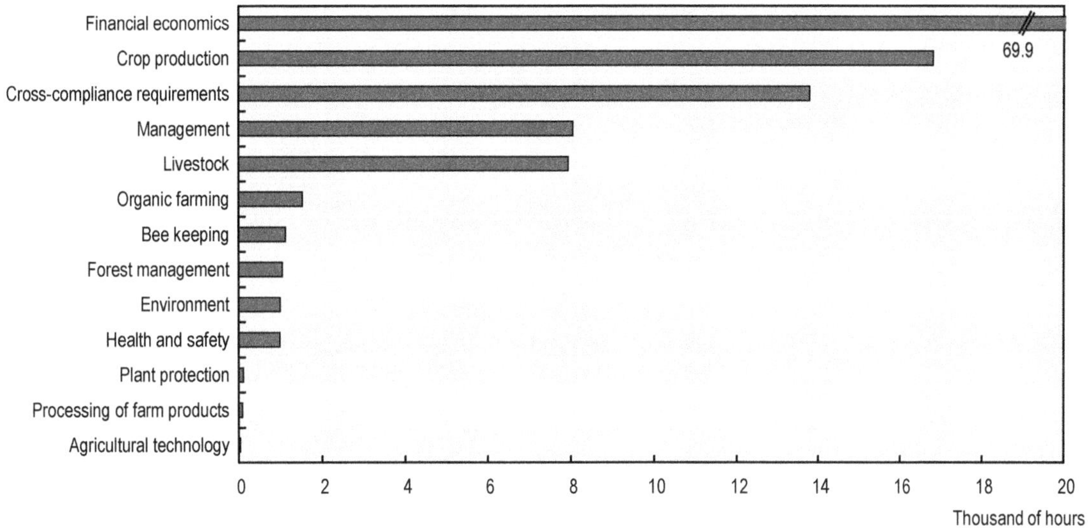

Source: ARIB (2015), Estonian Agricultural Registers and Information Board (ARIB), www.pria.ee.

StatLink http://dx.doi.org/10.1787/888933655073

The reasons why so few farmers have used advisory services may be rooted in the bureaucracy related to the advisory support and the cost of the products and services. The farmer was paid the advisory support only after having received the service and submitting the corresponding application for payment to the paying agency (ARIB).

Dependent on their financial situation, the farmers and food processors may self-finance their training, or receive training from input salesmen, raw material suppliers or purchasing agents, whose activities are tied to the economic interests, or have received free training as supported from other EU and Estonian state funds. Farmers and food processors have been offered regulated training, dissemination and outreach activities in the Estonian RDP 2007-13 measure 111 (vocational training and information actions). This training measure was based on the initiative of trainers and sector representative organisations, thus it was a supply-side measure. The implementation of the measure can be considered very important for agricultural producers and food processors, as the training was in most cases free of charge, or training on a given topic was not provided elsewhere (EMÜ, 2012). With support from EAFRD and from the State budget in the amount of EUR 3.4 million, courses that were not part of regular agricultural education programmes were organised in 2008-15. The provided training courses were primarily meant for agricultural producers (Figure 7.19). Training was provided in other areas, such as livestock farming, organic farming, food hygiene and crop-production (EMÜ, 2013b).

In 2010-15, on average 21% of all persons employed in agriculture attended the training courses organised in the framework of measure 111, while the average participation rate in the food industry was around 3% of the employed sector (Figure 7.20).

Figure 7.19. Number of participants in training, 2008-15

Estonian RDP 2007-13, measure 111

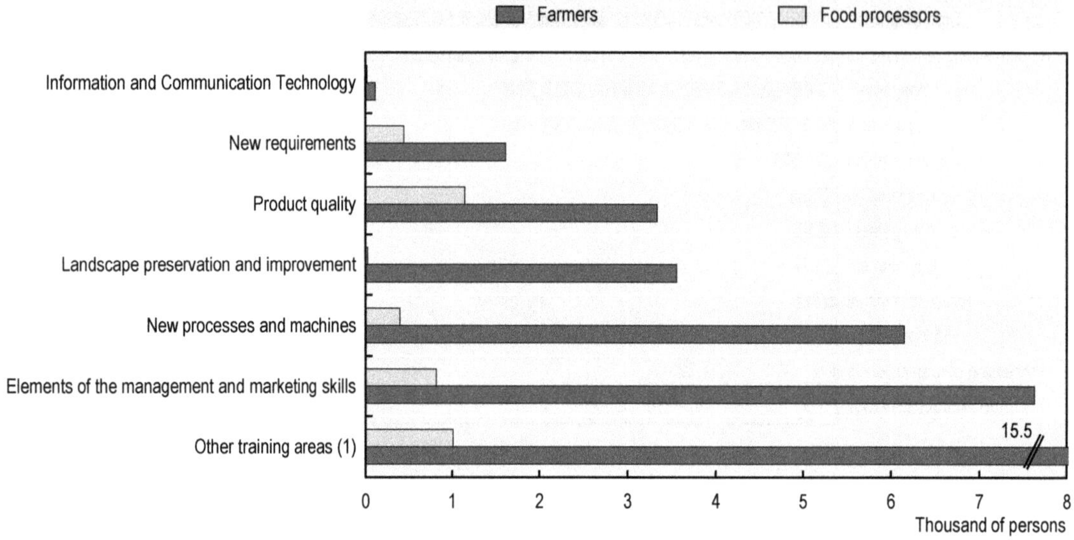

1. Other training areas include livestock farming, organic farming, food hygiene and crop-production.

Source: Estonian Agricultural Registers and Information Board (ARIB), 2015, http://www.pria.ee/.

StatLink http://dx.doi.org/10.1787/888933655092

Figure 7.20. Participants' share in the sector, 2008 to 2015

Estonian RDP 2007-13, measure 111

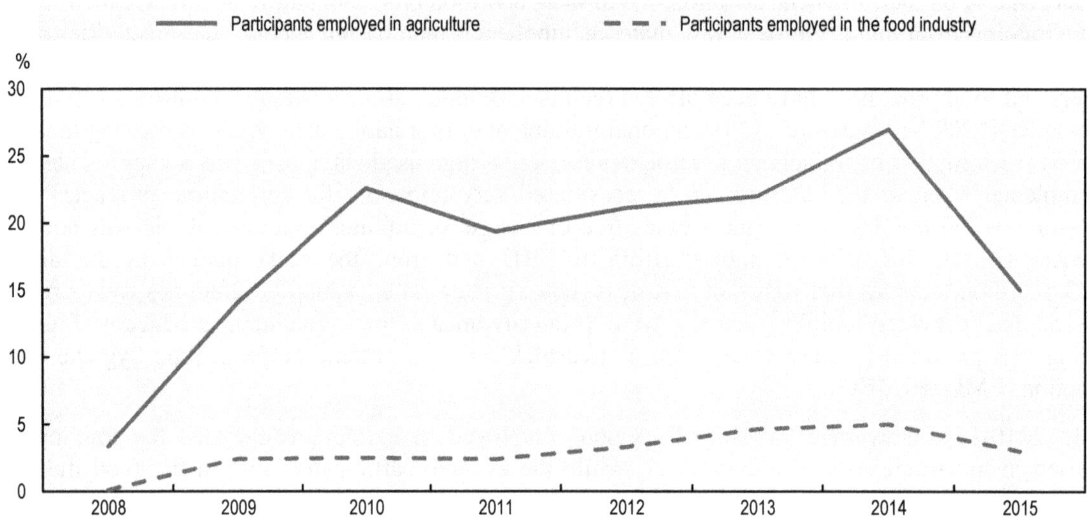

Source: EMÜ (2016c).

StatLink http://dx.doi.org/10.1787/888933655111

Programmes promoting the adoption of specific innovations

Strategic development documents handle innovation at a more general level. However, in a sense the implementation of the Estonian RDP 2007-13 within Pillar 2 of the CAP can be regarded as a programme fostering innovation. This programme offered training and advice for the agri-food industry sector. The investment measures of the same programme contributed to innovation, by supporting a variety of technologies, thereby enabling the application of a variety of innovations into production or the production of new products.

Three investment measures in the same programme contributed directly to the implementation of environmentally friendly technologies (EMÜ, 2016b):

- "Bioenergy production" which the farmers used to purchase machinery or equipment for energy crops cultivation, biomass procession and bio-energy production. Preference was given to applications whose results promised a bigger effect on reducing CO_2 emissions. In the framework of this project, 79 enterprises invested EUR 17 million in bioenergy production.
- "Processing of agricultural products"[23] that food processors and feed manufacturers used mainly for the purchase, installation and application of equipment and technology necessary in food and feed production. In the application evaluation, higher scores were given for investment in environmental sustainability and innovativeness of the investment. Ninety-five companies used the support to invest a total of EUR 88 million into industry, almost all of whom launched a new product to market or introduced a new technology.
- "Livestock facilities". Preference was given to applicants who planned a bioenergy installation next to the livestock housing. These measures helped 269 farmers to invest EUR 182 million in livestock facilities.

In addition to RDP 2014-20 measures supporting innovation, a business development programme was launched in 2015, with the help of the Enterprise Estonia. It supports the elaborated development of the enterprise, better planning of activities, introduction of innovation and product development. Each company participating in the programme will launch new products and services that guarantee higher profitability. At least three-year-old enterprises with at least eight employees specialising in industrial or smart specialisation areas are eligible for the grant. The budget of the programme amounts to EUR 73 million, which come from the State and the ERDF (EE, 2016a).

7.6. R&D outcomes

Overall progress to create and adopt relevant innovations can be usefully monitored. Proxy measures, such as the number of patents of bibliographic citations, is available from international databases, including for primary agriculture and for upstream and downstream industries, and by type of innovation (OECD, 2015).

The number of patents is not a comprehensive indicator of the outcomes of the innovation system, as not all innovations are patented, not all patents are used, other IPR systems exist for plant varieties, and trade secrets, rather than patents, are frequently used for food processing innovations. In addition, numbers should be complemented with indicators of patent quality, which are being developed at OECD (2013). This is, however, an informative proxy. Estonia's patent results are discussed in the section on IP protection.

Estonia has a very small share in the world's agri-food publications, remaining below 0.2% (Table 7.5).

Based on the Scopus journal classifications Estonia's share of agricultural science publications amounted to 13.7% of all science publications and agricultural publications to 12.8% of all agricultural publications in 2007-12, which is significantly higher than the OECD average. However, in a global context and given the small size of Estonia, agricultural science publications and agricultural publications make up a very small share.

Scopus journal classifications show that Estonia's share of agricultural science citations amounted to 14% of all science citations and agricultural citations to 13.1% of all agricultural citations in 2007-12, which is significantly higher than the OECD countries' average (Table 7.5). However, in view of the small size of Estonia, Estonia's agricultural science citations and agricultural citations make up a very small share from the global perspective (0.9%).

Table 7.5. Agriculture and food R&D outcomes, 2007-12

	Denmark	**Estonia**	EU15 average	Finland	Germany	Latvia	Nether-lands	Sweden	**OECD average**
Agro-food specialisation: Agro-food science outputs as a share of country's total (%)									
Patents	11.3	**12.0**	6.9	3.4	4.4	3.1	8.8	3.6	**5.6**
Publications	10.2	**13.7**	8.4	9.7	6.4	6.9	6.9	7.9	**9.4**
Citations	8.7	**14.0**	10.8	9.3	16.9	8.3	6.4	20.4	**11.9**
Country's contribution to world agro-food science output (%)									
Patents	0.5	**0.02**	0.6	0.2	2.7	0.03	1.0	0.4	**0.7**
Publications	0.9	**0.13**	1.9	0.75	4.5	0.03	1.6	1.2	**2.0**
Citations	1.1	**1.0**	2.4	0.8	5.7	0.02	2.8	1.4	**2.4**

Source: OECD Patent Database, January 2014; SCImago. (2007). SJR — SCImago Journal & Country Rank, www.scimagojr.com (accessed 19 March 2014).

7.7. International co-operation in agricultural R&D

International co-operation on agricultural research and development offers universal benefits. While this is generally true given the public good nature of many innovations in agriculture, it is particularly the case where global challenges are being confronted (as in the case of responding to climate change) and when initial investments are exceptionally high. The benefits of international co-operation for national systems stem from the specialisation it allows and from international spill-overs. In countries with limited research capacity, scarce resources could then focus on better taking into account local specificities (OECD, 2015).

Mechanisms used to encourage cross-country, international collaboration

Estonia's agricultural innovation programmes include objectives regarding international co-operation and associated funding. The applied R&D Programme of the MRA for 2015-21 dedicates EUR 2.6 million (27.2% of the programme budget) for international research projects over the period. The programme states that international research collaboration and participation in international networks gives researchers (and through that to agricultural producers, food processors and advisors) experience and knowledge necessary for professional development and improves research quality. The priorities are related to the international networks and co-operation that the MRA is participating in: EU Joint Programming Activities, ERA-Net projects, and other international collaborative research projects. The programme is expected to result in increased number of international research projects and scientific publications in which Estonian researchers contribute to (MRA, 2016f).

Estonia's "Agriculture, Food and Fisheries Science and Knowledge Transfer Development Plan for the Period 2015-21" aims to increase the number of international collaborative research projects by 50% by 2021 compared to 2014. It is expected that in 2021, there will be 45 collaborative projects, of which 4 in veterinary medicine, 3 in food technology and safety, 3 in animal husbandry and breeding, 18 in crop production and plant breeding, 8 in horticulture (berries, fruits, landscape gardening), 6 in fisheries and aquaculture, and 3 in rural economics (MRA, 2016g).

In some cases, if the research topic requires cross-country comparisons (as in the case of agricultural and rural development policy analyses), the call for tenders for some specific applied research project (for example by the Standing Committee of Rural Affairs of the Parliament of Estonia) encourages international collaboration by giving additional evaluation points if foreign experts are involved in the project.

More generally, collaboration with international peers in evaluating applications in different R&D measures is general practice in Estonia. For example, the applications of the main research financing instruments — personal and institutional research grants — are first assessed by international peers, and then by a panel of Estonian scientists with the final decision made by an evaluation committee of renowned scientists (ERC, 2016b).

Policy efforts regarding exchange of staff, domestically or internationally

Exchange of research staff and students across countries provides opportunities for cross-country collaboration with long-term benefits (OECD, 2015). In Estonia, participation in EU networks and mobility programmes facilitate cross-country exchanges and collaboration.

In Estonia, international staff exchange is facilitated via various programmes. In particular, ERC provides mobility grants and scholarships for Estonian and foreign researchers to carry out research in a new research environment and exchange experience, expand their co-operation networks and obtain new skills:

- The research mobility funding programme **Mobilitas Pluss**,[24] with a budget of EUR 35.4 million over 2016-21, 83.5% of which is covered by the ERDF. The programme aims to improve the international visibility of Estonian research, business and higher education and Estonia's attractiveness as a destination country for study and research; support opportunities for Estonian R&D institutions and companies to collaborate with transnational research organisations and networks, including through synergy with Horizon 2020 actions; and expand international collaboration and professional development opportunities. Mobility support schemes in Mobilitas Pluss programme include:
  - Mobilitas Pluss post-doctoral grant– support for researchers coming to Estonia to carry out their research projects. The support is aimed at researchers who have defended their doctoral degrees abroad.
  - Returning researcher grant– support for researchers who have carried out their post-doctoral research (or research at least at the same level) abroad and return to continue their research in Estonia.
  - Top researcher grant– support for top researchers who come from abroad to work in an Estonian R&D institution and to establish their own research group.
  - Support for study visits and training abroad– support for researchers working at Estonian R&D institutions to participate in training and study-visits.
- **Post-doctoral research funding**: the aim of postdoctoral grants is to support researchers with an Estonian PhD degree or those with equivalent international research qualifications to continue their independent research careers in strong collaborative research groups for up to two years. Researchers who have received their doctorate in Estonia cannot apply for a postdoctoral project at an Estonian R&D institution.
- During 2010-15, the postdoctoral research grant programme **ERMOS** (Estonian Research Mobility Scheme) was applied to develop and diversify Estonian research potential through the mobility of researchers and exchange of experience. This was expected to strengthen international exchange of knowledge and support the career development of young researchers. The grants were co-financed through the FP7 Marie Curie COFUND the "People" Programme (ERC, 2016e).

Development plans of several Estonian research organisations (for example EMÜ) foresee that members of academic staff should participate in teaching, research or training in research institutions abroad. In addition, international competition for academic posts is fostered (EMÜ, 2016c).

The start-up research grant conditions of ERC require that a principal investigator of a start-up research grant can be a researcher who has been awarded the first doctorate or equivalent qualification at least two years before and no more than seven years prior to the call, and has completed postdoctoral studies (preferably abroad) after receiving a doctorate or equivalent qualification. The evaluation committee may, where justified, consider eligible a person who has not completed postdoctoral studies but has comparable research experience (preferably abroad) (ERC, 2016c). Therefore, the experience of working as a postdoctoral researcher in international research groups (for which the mobility programme is available) can be regarded as a precondition of starting up an individual researcher career.

In addition, Estonia participates in the EURAXESS, which is an EU wide network for researchers in motion, providing a one-stop shop for researchers seeking to advance their careers and personal development by moving to other countries (ERC, 2015c).

Participation in international and regional networks

The MRA participates in the co-ordination of several international scientific networks and joint initiatives with an aim to increase the competitiveness of Estonian researchers and develop respective scientific disciplines in Estonia (MRA, 2015c). The MRA also contribute as a funder of research.

The MRA represents Estonia in the following EU Joint Programming Initiatives (JPIs) (MRA, 2015c):

- The Joint Programming Initiative on Agriculture, Food Security and Climate Change (FACCE-JPI). Estonia was part of the first project launched in 2012.
- The Joint Programming Initiative Healthy and Productive Seas and Oceans (JPI Oceans).
- The Joint Programming Initiative on Antimicrobial Resistance (JPIAMR).

The MRA participates in the following ERA-Net co-operation networks (MRA, 2015c):

- ERA-Net SUSFOOD — SUStainable FOOD production and consumption;
- ERA-Net CORE Organic — Coordination of European Transnational Research in Organic Food and Farming Systems;
- ERA-Net C-IPM — Coordinated Integrated Pest Management in Europe;
- ERA-Net Plus Climate Smart Agriculture: adaption of agricultural systems in Europe;
- ERA-Net Cofund FACCE SURPLUS — Sustainable and Resilient agriculture for food and non-food systems;
- ERA-Net COFASP — Cooperation in Fisheries, Aquaculture and Seafood Processing;
- ERA-Net Cofund — European Research area on Sustainable Animal Production Systems

The MRA is planning to join the co-operation networks working on animal production, cereals production and Marine Biotechnology ERA-Net (MRA, 2015c).

The MRA participates in the following co-operations (MRA, 2015c):

- Euphresco — a network of organisations funding research projects and coordinating national research in the phytosanitary area.
- BONUS — the joint Baltic Sea research and development programme for years 2010-17;
- OECD Co-operative Research Programme on Biological Resource Management for Sustainable Agricultural Systems;
- Interreg Central Baltic Programme 2014-20.

In addition, Estonia participates in COST — European Cooperation in Science and Technology (ERC, 2015c).

ERC is a member of the European Science Foundation, where Estonia has its representatives (ERC, 2015c). Moreover, ERC is one of the founders of Science Europe, which promotes the collective interests of the Research Funding and Research Performing Organisations of Europe (ERC, 2015c).

Estonia has a liaison office of research and development in Brussels. This office is responsible for promotion of Estonian research and development activities, participating in the Informal Group of RTD

Liaison Offices, provides support for Estonian research and development organisations in organising events, and provides opportunities of internships in Brussels (ERC, 2015c).

Estonia is relatively well represented in various EU research co-operation networks by the ERC and the MRA. The limiting factor is the limited and uneven capacity of research organisations and research groups, and ability of scientists to actively participate and benefit from these networks. Therefore, in some disciplines the opportunities are successfully utilised while in other areas the ministry or research council level cooperation has not yet lead to research organisation, research group or scientist level co-operation.

Cooperation outcomes

The extent of international scientific collaboration can be measured by the percentage of documents with collaborating authors from a foreign country (Table 7.6). In Estonia, over 2007-12, 48.1% of all scientific output, and 47.3% of food and agriculture science output were published in collaboration with authors from foreign countries. OECD averages for all scientific output and agricultural science output were 45.6% and 50.8%, respectively. Therefore, the average of all scientific output in Estonia exceeds the OECD average by 2.5 percentage points, while the average of food and agricultural science output is 3.5 percentage points below the OECD average. In Scandinavian countries and the Netherlands, the share of all science and food and agricultural science output with collaborating countries in foreign countries was larger. In Latvia and Canada, this proportion was similar to the Estonian one, in Poland and the Czech Republic, it was markedly lower.

When considering annual data, the share of food and agricultural documents with foreign co-authors in Estonia has increased over the period, from 46% in 2007 to 54% in 2012. But it remains lower than in most Northern European countries at the end of the period.

Table 7.6. Agri-food R&D co-operation, 2007-12

Agri-food outputs with co-authors as a share of total agri-food outputs (%)

	Denmark	**Estonia**	EU15 average	Finland	Germany	Latvia	Nether-lands	Sweden	**OECD average**
Patents	22.1	**13.8**	17.0[1]	5.4	12.0	1.5	16.7	7.8	**12.7**
Publications	64.3	**47.3**	57.7	52.3	55.2	46.9	65.1	62.9	**50.8**

1. EU28.

Source: OECD Patent Database, January 2014; SCImago. (2007). SJR — SCImago Journal & Country Rank, www.scimagojr.com (accessed 19 March 2014).

Fostering international collaboration is one of the priorities of the applied R&D Programme of the MRA for 2015-21, and Estonia's Agriculture, Food and Fisheries Science and Knowledge Transfer Development Plan for the Period 2015-21. Considering that Estonia is a relatively small country with limited research capacity, expansion of co-operation in agricultural research could focus on research organisations in Scandinavian and other Northern European countries. The benefits stem from the culture of cross-border scientific collaboration in these countries, similar climate zones and agricultural production practices, and similarities in institutions and culture.

7.8. Summary

- The Estonian innovation system has many strengths: the conducive business environment; government strategy integrating innovation and economic growth objectives, with investments targeting smart specialisation high-growth areas; a relatively strong public research system, with a high level of public R&D expenditure and strong performance in journal publication and international cooperation; good skills base in the population, in particular young performers in science; and society's positive attitude to science and technology. Shortcomings are mainly related to low R&D and innovation in firms, partly linked to the relatively small size of Estonian companies. The most innovative companies in Estonia are the subsidiaries of foreign companies and foreign-owned companies.

- The strategic framework for innovation policy is clear, but there is an abundance of strategic documents, action plans, policies programmes and projects, which does not facilitate coherence. Innovation priorities have changed between 2004-14, where the focus was on infrastructure, capacity, entrepreneurship, and 2014-20, which emphasises horizontal innovation, risk and acceptance.
- Agricultural innovation strategy, as all sectoral innovation strategies, is fully integrated with the nation-wide strategy.
- Demand side innovation policy is widely discussed but supply side innovation dominates, in particular in agriculture, where the major part of innovation in Estonia and in other countries is facilitated by equipment and material suppliers.
- Public expenditure on agricultural research has increased since 2000, in particular as a share of agricultural value-added.
- The share of project-based research funding, including in food and agricultural areas, is very high at about 80% of total public funding. This share is planned to decrease to ensure more stability for research institutions.
- The Estonian University of life Sciences (EMÜ) carries out most agricultural-related research in Estonia, with two other universities being engaged in environmental sciences and biotechnology and food sciences, and the Estonian Crop Research Institute in crop sciences. The EMÜ research budget is variable, due to the dominance of project-based funding, and the dependence on EU sources, which follow programming cycles.
- Since 2010, research infrastructure roadmaps guide long-term investment decisions, identifying the infrastructure items of national importance that are new or require modernisation. The list is updated every three years. EU structural funds have greatly contributed to the modernisation of the Estonian research infrastructure, which was much needed. Some facilities still need upgrading and further investments from EU structural funds are planned for 2014-20.
- While Estonian agri-food companies are considered as innovative users, they have little capacity to carry out research activities and their contribution to the funding of agricultural research is estimated to be minimal. The most innovative companies in Estonia are foreign-owned companies or their subsidiaries, so research in done abroad.
- Intellectual Property Protection (IPP) is not a problem as an adequate IPR system is now in place in Estonia and the IPP Index increased over time to reach the OECD average level.
- Lack of collaboration between private companies and R&D institutions is a major concern. The most common form of collaboration is participation of representatives in steering committees and networks.
- Incentives are in place to facilitate public-private collaboration. Competence centres are an important source of collaborative innovation, but as private participation is generally from foreign companies, the focus is often on international issues as opposed to topics that can benefit the domestic agriculture sector.
- International cooperation is facilitated through participation in EU research programmes, projects and networks, and incentives for research mobility such as grants and conditions favouring international experience in project allocation and nominations.
- Open access to knowledge, optimal knowledge circulation and transfer through the application of digital European Research Area (ERA) is a priority of the ERA concept that Estonia follows. Farmers are granted free access to the research information on the website of the Estonian Agricultural and Rural Advisory Service.

- The advisory system is also expected to foster knowledge flows. A number of different Estonian organisations provide training and advisory services, including cooperatives, input providers, and education institutions. The Advisory Centre of RDF is currently in charge of the publically-funded advisory system, providing advice to farmers and rural entrepreneurs for a minimal fee.
- Innovation policy and the impact of other policies on innovation are evaluated. The evaluation of EU programmes is based on input and output indicators defined at the EU level, which describe and analyse the dynamics of the Estonian RDI system based on the framework of EU policies and objectives. The current use of indicators has thus been of a monitoring nature.

Notes

1. The term "Agricultural Knowledge and Innovation System (AKIS)" is used in the European Union to describe the features of systems producing agricultural innovation, with the same meaning as the term "Agricultural Innovation System" (AIS) used in the OECD and the World Bank for example.
2. The innovation systems approach highlights the importance of systemic links between scientific research, technological change, learning and innovation. The main focus is on the functioning of the system and the complex relationships that involve a variety of organisations and institutions within the system. At the same time, the focus is shifted away from the activities of individual and isolated parties (companies and consumers) (Chaminade and Edquist, 2005).
3. Innovation wise the **Estonian Entrepreneurship Growth Strategy for 2014-20** is expected to facilitate the achievement of the umbrella objectives within the Estonia 2020, thereby contributing directly to attaining the goal 'Growth of welfare' in the Sustainable Estonia 21 (MEAC, 2013a).
4. Over 2014-20, Estonia is allocated support from five EU structural and investment funds: 1) the European Regional Development Fund (ERDF); 2) the European Social Fund (ESF); 3) the Cohesion Fund (CF); 4) the European Agriculture Rural Development Fund (EAFRD); and 5) The European Maritime and Fisheries Fund (EMFF), which, in line with the Europe 2020 strategy, support economic development in all EU member states.
5. In Estonia, Business Expenditure on R&D (BERD) is concentrated in medium-high to low-technology manufacturing and services, and in a small number of firms (OECD, 2017a, Figure 6).
6. Demand side innovation activities include support for entering to new markets, establishment of quality requirements that initiate creation of new products. Respective policy instruments include regulations, public procurement, and support of private demand. Supply side innovation activities include provision of finances and services. In this case, the policy instruments include capital support, financial instruments, and support to public sector research, training and mobility support, and grants to R&D activities in processing industry (Paltser and Reiljan, 2015).
7. Science Centre AHHAA: www.ahhaa.ee/.
8. See Horizon 2020 web site: https://ec.europa.eu/programmes/horizon2020/.
9. Järvamaa Vocational Education Centre, Olustvere School of Rural Economics and Service, Luua Forestry School, Pärnumaa Vocational Education Centre, Hiiumaa Training Establishment, Räpina School of Horticulture, Väike-Maarja Vocational Education Centre, Viljandi Vocational Education Centre, Tartu Vocational Education Centre.
10. Agricultural Applied Research and Development for 2015-20 is the third programme of this type following the 2004–08 and 2009–14 programmes. However, the MRA has financed agricultural applied research for several decades. The main objective of the first national programme for 2004–08 was to contribute to raising the competitiveness of agricultural production and the processing of agricultural products, analysing the risks to the consumer and the environment arising from agricultural production of agricultural production, and developing solutions for minimising those risks in the whole production and processing chain (MRA, 2004). For the period 2009-14, the main aims were to increase competitiveness of agricultural production

and processing, to ensure its sustainability, analysis of risks associated with agricultural production and produce, and risk management solutions (MRA, 2016a).

11. The present programme is the third programme; previous ones covered 2002–06 and 2007–13.

12. GERD includes expenditure on R&D conducted in the country by Business enterprise; Government; Higher education; and Private non-profit sectors. All sources of funding are included.

13. For example, measures for 2014-20 administered by Enterprise Estonia were not fully implemented in 2015 as they were still in the process of being developed (EE, 2015).

14. Golden Open Access (Gold Open Access) means that the publication is immediately and permanently available free of charge for everyone on the publisher's website. The article publishing charge may be covered by the authors, their institutions or an organisation, such as a university or a professional association or the Academy of Sciences. Most of the scientific journals in Estonia use the latter model, and the authors do not have to pay the article publishing charge to the journals. The specific conditions for the gold open access publications are determined by a specific license. Most of the open-access articles use the so-called Creative Commons licenses. It is allowed to file away such publications oneself and store the copy in the institutional (for example, university digital archive), national (for example, the Estonian Research Information System, ETIS), or an international repository (for example, arXiv, PubMed Central).

15 Laws governing industrial property include: Legal Regulation of Industrial Property Act, Trade Marks Act, Patents Act, Utility Models Act, Geographical Indication Protection Act, Competition Act, Plant Propagation and Plant Variety Rights Act.

16. The PTC provides a unified procedure for filing patent applications to protect inventions in each of its contracting states. The Treaty makes it possible to seek patent protection for an invention simultaneously in each of a large number of countries by filing an "international" patent application. Patents can be then granted by national and regional authorities.

17. OECD seeds schemes web site: www.oecd.org/tad/code/abouttheoecdseedschemes.htm.

18. A 2006 study indicated that the private sector's participation in implementation and assessment of R&D policies was very limited in Estonia. Most common private collaboration is participation through industrial associations in steering committees, boards, and occasionally in networks (Inzelt, 2006).

19. Competence Centre of Food and Fermentation Technologies website: http://tftak.eu/et/.

20. LLC website: http://tptak.ee/.

21. Competence Centre on Health Technologies website: www.ccht.ee/.

22. A EIP-AGRI Regional Workshop on "Establishing Operational Groups under Rural Development Programmes" took place in Tallinn on 2-3 April 2014, https://ec.europa.eu/eip/agriculture/en/content/eip-agri-workshop-regional-workshop-establishing-operational-groups-under-rural-developmen-0.

23. Measure 1.7.1, Processing of agricultural products, was the predecessor of the current innovation cooperation support measure (M 16.2).

24. It replaces the project Mobilitas in place during the period 2008-15.

References

AB (Agricultural Board) (2016), www.pma.agri.ee/index.php?id=104&sub=128&sub2=296&sub3=297 (accessed 9 April 2016).

AB (2015), Põllumajandusameti tegevusülevaade 2014 [Agriculture Agency for review], www.pma.agri.ee/docs/pics/PMA_tegevusulevaade_2014_1(1).pdf (accessed 11 January 2016).

ARIB (2017), http://www.pria.ee/et/toetused/valdkond/taimekasvatus/innovatsiooniklastri_toetus_2015/; http://www.pria.ee/et/toetused/valdkond/taimekasvatus/innovatsiooniklaster/.

ARIB (2016) Innovatsiooniklastri toetus (MAK 2014-2020 meede 16) 2015 [Innovation support (RDP 2014-2020 Measure 16) 2015], www.pria.ee/et/toetused/valdkond/taimekasvatus/innovatsiooniklastri_toetus_2015/#maar (accessed 17 February 2016).

ARIB (2015), Estonian Agricultural Registers and Information Board (ARIB), www.pria.ee.

Ajujaht (2016), www.ajujaht.ee/ajujahist/ (accessed 15 March 2016).

Arnold, E., K. Männik, R. Rannala, A. Reid, B. Bayer, and S. Ljungström (2008), Mid-Term Evaluation of the Competence Centre Programme, Final report, Innovation Studies No. 12, www.mkm.ee/sites/default/files/is12_competence_center_programme_2008.pdf (accessed 16 February 2016).

ASTI (2016), database, http://asti.cgiar.org/.

BioCC (2016), Bio-Competence Centre of Healthy Dairy Products LLC (BioCC) webpage, http://tptak.ee/en (accessed 8 February 2016).

Campi, M. and A. Nuvolari (2013), *Intellectual property protection in plan varieties: A new worldwide index (1961-2011)*, LEM Working Paper Series, No. 2013/09, http://hdl.handle.net/10419/89567.

CDCIS (County Development Centres Information System) (2016), Maakondlikud arenduskeskused. http://old.arenduskeskused.ee/Maakondlikud-arenduskeskused.html (accessed 3 February 2016).

Chaminade, C., and C. Edquist (2005), "From theory to practice: the use of systems of innovation approach in innovation policy", CIRCLE, Lund University, *Electronic Working Paper Series*, Paper No. 2005/2.

Christensen, T.A., S. Freireich, J. Kolar, and P. Nyberg (2012), "Peer-Review of the Estonian Research and Innovation System. Steady Progress Towards Knowledge Society", *Innovation Studies*, No. 19, www.hm.ee/index.php?popup=download&id=11652 (accessed 7 February 2016).

Competence Centre for Knowledge-Based Health Goods and Natural Products (2016), Polli Horticultural Research Centre, http://pk.emu.ee/en/structure/polli/competence-centre-for-knowledge-based-health-goods-and-natural-products/ (accessed 4 April 2016).

EC (2016), Projects & Results, CORDIS, European Commission, http://cordis.europa.eu/project/rcn/106468_en.html (accessed 15 March 2016).

EC (European Commission) (2014), Summary of the Partnership Agreement for Estonia, 2014-2020. https://ec.europa.eu/info/sites/info/files/partnership-agreement-estonia-summary-jun2014_en.pdf (accessed 5 December 2017).

EC (2012), Elements of the Common Strategic Framework for the period 2014-2020, http://ec.europa.eu/esf/BlobServlet?docId=386&langId=en (accessed 11 February 2016).

ECRI (2017), Annual Financing of ECRI 2007-2017, Data provided by the Estonian Crop Research Institute.

ECRI (2015), Estonian Crop Research Institute, www.etki.ee/index.php/eng/ (accessed 12 February 2015).

EDF (2013), Nutikas spetsialiseerumine – kvalitatiivne analüüs, [Smart specialisation - Qualitative analysis], Eesti Arengufond [Estonian Development Fund], February, www.arengufond.ee/upload/Editor/Publikatsioonid/Nutikas%20spetsialiseerumine%2020_02_2013.pdf (accessed 15 March 2016).

EE (Enterprise Estonia) (2016a), Tehnoloogia Arenduskeskused [Technology Development Centres], www.eas.ee/teenus/tehnoloogia-arenduskeskused/ (accessed 31 January 2016).

EE (2016b), Development voucher, www.eas.ee/service/development-voucher/?lang=en (accessed 9 March 2016).

EE (2016c), Tark hankimine [Getting smart], www.eas.ee/teenus/tark-hankimine/ (accessed 6 April 2016).

EE (2016d), Toetatud projektide andmebaas [Supported project database], EAS, http://workestonia.eu/et/eas/sihtasutusest/toetatud-projektid/toetatud-projektid-alates-2004a-aprill (accessed 15 March 2016)

EE (2015), Ettevõtluse Arendamise Sihtasutuse 2015, aasta koondtegevuskava (Annual Activity Plan for the Entrepreneurship Development Foundation, 2015], www.eas.ee/wp-content/uploads/2015/11/koondtegevuskava_2015.pdf (accessed 19 February 2016).

EERC (Estonian Environmental Research Centre) (2016), Biomajandus [Bioeconomy], www.klab.ee/kohanemine/valdkonnad/biomajandus/ (accessed 9 April 2016).

EIC (2016), Environmental Investment Centre, www.kik.ee/et/kik/pohikiri (accessed 17 March 2016).

EIPTTC (2016), Intellectual Property, The Estonian Intellectual Property and Technology Transfer Centre, http://eitk.ee/intellektuaalomand/ (accessed 11 January 2016).

Eljas-Taal, K. (2014), Riik kui tark tellija ehk kuidas saab riik toetada turunõudlust innovatsiooni järele [Wise country if the customer or the state can support market demand for innovation], www.mkm.ee/sites/default/files/ds_uuringu_tutvustus_121114.pdf (accessed 4 April 2016).

EMÜ (2017), Background report for the OECD review on Estonian innovation policy and agricultural innovation system, January.

EMÜ (2016a), Kuratoorium [Board of Governors], www.emu.ee/ylikoolist/yldinfo/juhtimine/kuratoorium/ (accessed 3 February 2016).

EMÜ (2016b), Eesti maaelu arengukava 2007-2013 1., 3. ja 4. telje püsihindamise aruanne [Estonian Rural Development Plan 2007-2013, the first, third and fourth axis permanent evaluation report], 2015 year.

EMÜ (2016c), Development plan of Estonian University of Life Sciences until 2025, www.emu.ee/ylikoolist/yldinfo/arengukavad-ja-strateegiad/ (accessed 18 October 2016).

EMÜ (2015a), Eesti maaelu arengukava 2007-2013 1., 3. ja 4. telje püsihindamise aruanne [Estonian Rural Development Plan 2007-2013, the first, third and fourth axis permanent evaluation report], 2014.

EMÜ (2015b), Majandusaasta aruanded 2007-2015 [Annual Reports], www.emu.ee/ylikoolist/yldinfo/eelarve/ (accessed 5 December 2016).

EMÜ (2015c), Innovatsioonimõõdikud põllumajandussektori ja toiduainetööstuse ettevõtjate investeeringute ja konkurentsivõime analüüsimiseks [Indicators of innovation in the agricultural sector and the food industry and the competitiveness of enterprises to analyse investments], www.agri.ee/sites/default/files/content/uuringud/2015/uuring-2015-innovatsioonimoodikud.docx (accessed 11 February 2016).

EMÜ (2013a), Eesti Maaülikooli rakendusteaduse auhinna statuut [Estonian University of Life Science Award application statute], www.emu.ee/userfiles/Teadus/Oigusaktid/Rakendusteaduse%20auhinna%20statuut.pdf (accessed 29 January 2016).

EMÜ (2013b), Eesti maaelu arengukava 2007–2013 meetme 1.1 "Koolitus- ja teavitustegevused" rakendamistulemuste analüüs [Estonian Rural Development Plan 2007-2013, measure 1.1 "Training and Information Activities" Analysis of the implementation results], pp. 19.

EMÜ (2012), Koolitus- ja teavitustegevuste mõju põllumajandus-, toidu- ja metsandussektoris hõivatute konkurentsivõimele [Training and information activities impact on agriculture, food and forestry sector, the competitiveness of the employed].

EMÜ (2010), EMÜ tehnoloogiasiirde ja koostööpartnerite uuring: Lõpparuanne. B. I. A. [Technology transfer and cooperation partners in the study: final report].

EPO (2016), Patendiamet, The Estonian Patent Office, www.epa.ee/et/ametist/patendiamet (accessed 11 January 2016).

ERC (2016a), Keskkonnakaitse ja -tehnoloogia teadus- ja arendustegevuse programm KESTA [Environmental protection and technology R&D programme KESTA], www.etag.ee/rahastamine/programmid/loppenud-programmid/kesta/ (accessed 31 January 2016).

ERC (2016b), Teadus- ja arendustegevuse rahastamine Eestis [R&D funding in Estonia], www.etag.ee/tegevused/uuringud-ja-statistika/statistika/teadus-ja-arendustegevuse-rahastamine-eestis/ (accessed 30 January 2016).

ERC (2016c), Infrastructure Funding, www.etag.ee/en/funding/infrastructure-funding/ (accessed 15 February 2016).

ERC (2016d), Applied research in smart specialisation growth areas: NUTIKAS.

ERC (2016e), Valdkondliku TA tegevuse toetamine – RITA [TA support to sectoral activities], www.etag.ee/rahastamine/rakendusuuringute-toetused/rita-rakendusuuringud/ (accessed 7 April 2016).

ERC (2015a), Teaduse populariseerimine [Science popularisation], Estonian Research Council, www.etag.ee/tegevused/teadpop/ (accessed 29 January 2016).

ERC (2015b), TeaMe+ tegevused, www.etag.ee/tegevused/teadpop/teamepluss/ (accessed 29 January 2016).

ERC (2015c), Avatud teadus Eestis. Tööversioon [Open Science working draft], www.etag.ee/wp-content/uploads/2016/03/AT_soovitused_20160229.pdf (accessed 23 March 2016).

ERC (2013), Estonian R&D funding system (since 1 March 2012), www.etag.ee/wp.../SEV2013_ENERG_RD-system/ (accessed 13 December 2015).

Etis (2016), Eesti Teadusinfosüsteem: Projektid [Estonian Research: Projects], www.etis.ee/Portal/Projects/Index (accessed 30 January 2016).

Eurobarometer Qualitative Study (2015), Public Opinion On Future Innovations, Science and Technology Aggregate Report June, http://ec.europa.eu/public_opinion/archives/quali/ql_futureofscience_en.pdf (accessed 17 March 2016).

EUSAE (European Union Structural Assistance to Estonia) (2015), Webpage www.struktuurifondid.ee/en/ (accessed 29 January 2016).

FACCE-JPI (2016), What is FACCE-JPI? www.faccejpi.com/About-Us/What-is-FACCE-JPI (accessed 4 April 2016).

Government (Republic of Estonia Government) (2016), Objectives and activities, https://valitsus.ee/en (accessed 10 February 2016).

Government Office (2016), Research and Development Council, https://riigikantselei.ee/et/valitsuse-toetamine/teadus-ja-arendusnoukogu, 15 November.

Government Office (2014), National Reform Programme "ESTONIA 2020", (accessed 28 January 2016).

Hanson, M. Kuningas, T. Muuk-Adrat, R. Pohlak, and A. Urmet (2015), Intellektuaalomandi õppematerjal, Eesti Intellektuaalomandi ja Tehnoloogiasiirde Keskus [Intellectual property teaching material. Estonian Intellectual Property and Technology Transfer Centre, EIPTTC], pp 8.

Health promotion research programme TerVE (2016), www.etag.ee/en/funding/programmes/closed-programmes/health-promotion-research-programme-terve/ (accessed 18 March 2016).

Huisman, J., P. Santiago, P. Högselius, M.J. Lemaitre, and W. Thorn (2007), OECD reviews of tertiary education: Estonia, http://www.oecd.org/estonia/39261460.pdf (accessed 31 March 2016).

Inzelt, A. (2006), Private Sector Interaction in the Decision Making Processes of Public Research Policies. Country Profile: Estonia, http://ec.europa.eu/invest-in-research/pdf/download_en/psi_countryprofile_estonia.pdf (accessed 28 January 2016).

Jaaksoo, K., M. Kitsing, K. Lember, and T. Rebane (2012), "Ettevõtlus- ja innovatsioonipoliitika vahehindamine" [Interim evaluation of enterprise and innovation policy], *Innovation Studies*, No. 21, www.mkm.ee/sites/default/files/inno_21.pdf (accessed 31 January 2016).

Kaarna, K., K. Ojamäe, E. Welch, B. Fisher, and K. Lember (2015), Eesti ettevõtete uuendusmeelsus ja innovatsiooni toetamise võimalused [Estonia's support for innovation and innovation in business opportunities], *Innovation Studies*, No. 24, www.mkm.ee/sites/default/files/inno_24.pdf (accessed 28 January 2016).

Kaeramaa, M. (2014), Tõuaretus on tõstnud Eesti põllumajanduse konkurentsivõimet [Animal breeding has increased the competitiveness of Estonian agriculture], https://maablogi.wordpress.com/2014/09/18/touaretus-on-tostnud-eesti-pollumajanduse-konkurentsivoimet/ (accessed 11 February 2016).

Kalvet, T., E. Karo, and R. Kattel (2010), Eesti ettevõtete uued võimalused – ärimudelid, avatud innovatsioon ja riigi valikud [Estonian companies, new opportunities - business models for open innovation and public choices], *Innovation Studies* No. 14, www.arengufond.ee/upload/Editor/ettevotlus/Eesti%20ettev%C3%B5tete%20uued%20v%C3%B5imalused%20%E2%80%93%20%C3%A4rimudelid,%20avatud%20innovatsioni%20ja%20riigi%20valikud_2010.pdf (accessed 28 January 2016).

Karo, E., R. Kattel, V. Lember, K. Ukrainski, H. Kanep, nad U. Varblane (2014a), Nutika spetsialiseerumise võimalused ja väljakutsed Eestis teadus-, arendus- ja innovatsioonipoliitika kujundamisel ja juhtimisel 2014-2020, TIPS poliitikaanalüüs [Smart specialisation opportunities and challenges in the research, development and innovation in policy-making and leadership from 2014 to 2020, TIPS policy analysis], http://dspace.ut.ee/bitstream/handle/10062/40970/TIPS_NS_pol.analyys.pdf (accessed 11 February 2016).

Karo, E., R. Kattel, P. Tõnurist, K. Valdmaa, L. Looga, M. Kirs, P. Lumi, and M. Käger (2014b), Eesti teadusfinantseerimise instrumendid ja teaduse rakendatavus majanduses: poliitikaanalüüs tänase TAI süsteemi väljakutsetest ja võimalustest, TIPS uuringu 5.1 lõppraport [Estonian research funding instruments and scientific applicability in the economy: a policy analysis today TAI system challenges and opportunities, TIPS 5.1, Final report of the study], http://tips.ut.ee/index.php?module=32&op=1&id=3637 (accessed 11 February 2016).

Kirss, L., H.-S. Haaristo, M. Nestor, and E. Mikko (2013), Teadust ja tehnoloogiat populariseerivad tegevused Eestis. Uuringuaruanne. Praxis, [Popularising science and technology activities in Estonia: Study report], www.etag.ee/wp-content/uploads/2012/05/Praxis-2013-web.pdf (accessed 29 January 2016).

Koppel, A. (2016), Kulutused teadus- ja arendustegevusele: investeering tulevikku [Spending on research and development: investing in the future], Eesti teadus 2016, Tartu: Eesti Teadusagentuur, pp. 11-18, www.etag.ee/wp-content/uploads/2014/01/TA_teaduskogumik-2016-veeb.pdf (accessed 5 December 2016).

Lember, V., E. Karo, M. Kirs, P. Tõnurist, K. Valdmaa, R. Mäekivi, and R., Hanson (2015), Eesti teadussüsteemi ja majanduse seosed: juhtumianalüüsid avaliku ja erasektori nõudlusele vastamisest, TIPS uuringu 5.2 raport [Estonia's research system and economic relationships: the case studies of public and private sectors to meet demand, 5.2 TIPS study report], TTÜ Ragnar Nurkse innovatsiooni ja valitsemise instituut [University Nurkse Innovation and Governance Institute], Tallinn, pp. 29-30.

Lember, V. and T. Kalvet (2014), "Estonia: Public procurement, innovation and 'no policy' policy", in Lember, V., R. Kattel, and T. Kalvet (Ed.), *Public Procurement, Innovation and Policy: International Perspectives*, Heidelberg, Springer, pp. 127–149.

Lember, V. and T. Kalvet (2012), Riigihanked ja innovatsioon Eestis: milleks kulutada 11 miljonit päevas? [Public procurement and innovation in: Why spend 11 million a day?], Riigikogu Toimetised [Proceedings], Vol. 26, pp. 110–126.

Linnas, R. (2007), "Innovatsioonipoliitika kavandamisest Eesti [Innovation policy design Estonia]", *Riigikogu Toimetised* [Riigikogu Papers], No. 15, www.riigikogu.ee/rito/index.php?id=11572&op=archive2 (accessed 28 January 2016).

Masso, J., M. Liik, and K. Ukrainski (2013), Teaduse-arendustegevuse ja innovatsiooni indikaatorid Eesti innovatsiooni- ja teaduspoliitikas: senine praktika ja poliitikasoovitused, Uuringu 7.1, raport [R&D and innovation indicators of the Estonian innovation and research policy: current practice and policy recommendations, Study 7.1, Report], http://dspace.ut.ee/bitstream/handle/10062/40969/Indikaatorid_raport_Eesti.pdf (accessed 30 January 2016).

Masso, J. and K. Ukrainski (2008), Public Research Funding in Central and Eastern European Countries. Estonian Country Report, www.enid-europe.org/papers/research_funding_Estonia.pdf (accessed 15 March 2016).

MEAC (2013a), Estonian Entrepreneurship Growth Strategy 2014-2020, http://kasvustrateegia.mkm.ee/pdf/Estonian%20Entrepreneurship%20Growth%20Strategy%202014-2020.pdf (last accessed 28 January 2016).

MEAC (2013b), Digital Agenda 2020 for Estonia. www.mkm.ee/sites/default/files/digital_agenda_2020_estonia_engf.pdf (accessed 30 March 2016).

MEAC (2006), Eesti infoühiskonna arengukava 2013 [Estonian Information Society Strategy], www.riigikantselei.ee/valitsus/valitsus/et/valitsus/arengukavad/majandus-ja-kommunikatsiooniministeerium/T_iendatud_info_hiskonna_arengukava.pdf (accessed 23 March 2016).

MER (2016a), Teadusraha [Research funds], www.hm.ee/et/tegevused/teadus/teadusraha (accessed 4 April 2016).

MER (2016b), Financing of the infrastructure, https://hm.ee/en/activities/research-and-development/financing-infrastructure (accessed 17 February 2016).

MER (2015a), Infokiri teaduse rahastamisest 2016 Aastal [Newsletter science funding in 2016], www.etag.ee/wp-content/uploads/2016/01/HTM-infokiri-teaduse-rahastamine-2016-22.12.2016.pdf (accessed 22 October 2016)

MER (2015b), Research and Development, https://hm.ee/en/activities/research-and-development (accessed 14 December 2015).

MER (2014a), Eesti teadus- ja arendustegevuse ning innovatsiooni strateegia 2014–2020 "Teadmistepõhine Eesti" [Estonian Research and Development and Innovation Strategy 2014-2020 "Knowledge-based Estonia"], www.hm.ee/sites/default/files/59705_teadmistepohine_eesti_est.pdf (accessed 28 January 2016).

MER (2014b), Eesti elukestva õppe strateegia 2020 [Estonian Lifelong Learning Strategy 2020], www.hm.ee/index.php?popup=download&id=12568 (accessed 31 January 2016).

MER (2013), Eesti teadus- ja arendustegevuse ning innovatsiooni strateegia 2007-2013 "Teadmistepõhine Eesti": Aruanne strateegia eesmärkide ja rakendusplaani täitmisest 2012, aastal [Estonian Research and Development and Innovation Strategy 2007-2013 "Knowledge-based Estonia": Report on the objectives of the strategy and implementation plan of 2012, www.riigikantselei.ee/valitsus/valitsus/et/valitsus/arengukavad/haridus-ja-teadusministeerium/TAI%20aruanne%202012.pdf (accessed 30 January 2016).

MER (2007), Knowledge-Based Estonia: Estonian Research and Development and Innovation Strategy 2007-2013, http://cs.ioc.ee/excs/policy/teadm-pohine-eesti2-en.pdf (accessed 23 February 2016).

MER-ERC (2014), Haridus- ja Teadusministeerium, Eesti Teadusagentuur. Baasfinantseerimise kasutamise analüüs 2005-2013 [Ministry of Education and Research, Estonian Science Agency: Analysis of the use of basic financing 2005-2013], www.etag.ee/wp-content/uploads/2014/02/Baasfinantseerimise-kasutamise-analyys.pdf (accessed 30 January 2016).

Mihkelson, P., T. Rebane, M. Kitsing, and K. Lember (2014), Ettevõtlus- ja innovatsioonipoliitika vahehindamine [Interim evaluation of enterprise and innovation policy], www.eas.ee/images/doc/sihtasutusest/uuringud/ettevotlus/ettevotlustoetuste-vahehindamine-2014.pdf (accessed 11 February 2016).

Mihkelson, P., T. Rebane, E. Peters, and K. Lember (2013), Klastriprogrammi vahehindamine [Interim evaluation of the cluster], Tallinn, http://workestonia.eu/images/doc/sihtasutusest/uuringud/ettevotlus/klastriprogrammi-vahehindamine-2013.pdf (accessed 21 March 2016).

MoE (2016a), Kliimapoliitika põhialused aastani 2050, Põllumajanduse valdkonna mõjude hindamine [Climate Policy Fundamentals for 2050, agricultural impact assessment], http://envir.ee/sites/default/files/kpp_pillumajanduse_mijude_hindamise_seletuskiri_18.03.pdf (accessed 9 April 2016).

MoE (2016b), Studies and reports, www.envir.ee/et/eesmargid-tegevused/vesi/uuringud-ja-aruanded (accessed 3 October 2016).

MoF (2016), Välistoetused [Foreign Grants], www.fin.ee/valistoetused (accessed 11 February 2016).

MoF (2015), Riigi eelarvestrateegia 2016-2019 [State Budget Strategy], www.fin.ee/riigi-eelarvestrateegia (accessed 31 January 2016).

MoF (Ministry of Finance) (2014a), Ühtekuuluvuspoliitika fondide rakenduskava 2014-2020 [Cohesion Policy Funds Implementation], www.struktuurifondid.ee/public/Rakenduskava.pdf (accessed 29 January 2016).

MoF (2014b), Euroopa Liidu struktuuritoetus: Hindamine. [European Union's structural support: evaluation], www.struktuurifondid.ee/hindamine (accessed 30 January 2016).

MRA (2016a), Rakendusuuringud ja arendustegevus [Applied Research and Development], www.agri.ee/et/eesmargid-tegevused/teadus-arendus-ja-nouanne/teadus-ja-arendustegevus#rakendusuuringud-arendustegevus (accessed 31 January 2016).

MRA (2016b), Eesti põllumajandus-, toidu- ja kalamajandusteaduse ning teadmussiirde arengukava aastateks 2015–2021 [Estonian agriculture, food and fisheries economics of knowledge transfer Development Plan for 2015-2021], http://agri.ee/sites/default/files/content/arengukavad/arengukava-teadmussiire-2015-2021.pdf (accessed 10 February 2016).

MRA (2016c), Majandusaasta aruanded. Majandusteave [Annual budgets of MRA governance area, Economic Information], www.agri.ee/et/ministeerium-kontakt/majandusteave (accessed 30 March 2016).

MRA (2016d), Estonian Rural Development Plan 2014-2020, www.agri.ee/et/eesmargid-tegevused/eesti-maaelu-arengukava-mak-2014-2020 (accessed 29 January 2016).

MRA (2016e), Toiduainetööstus [food], www.agri.ee/et/eesmargid-tegevused/pollumajandus-ja-toiduturg/ulevaated/toiduainetoostus (accessed 30 January 2016).

MRA (2016f), Põllumajandusministeeriumi valitsemisala arengukava 2016-2019 [The Ministry of Agriculture Development Plan 2016-2019], www.agri.ee/sites/default/files/content/arengukavad/pollumajandusministeerium-vau-2016-2019.pdf (accessed 18 October 2016).

MRA (2016g), Applied Research and Development Programme of Ministry of Rural Affairs for 2015-2021, http://agri.ee/et/pollumajanduslikud-rakendusuuringud-ja-arendustegevus-aastatel-2015-2021 (accessed 11 February 2016).

MRA (2015a), Agricultural Applied Research and Development Activities 2015-2021, www.agri.ee/sites/default/files/content/.../arengukava-arendustegevus-2015-2021.odt (accessed 18 October 2016).

MRA (2015b), Eesti maaelu arengukava 2014-2020 kommunikatsioonistrateegia [Estonian Rural Development Plan 2014-2020 Communication Strategy], www.agri.ee/sites/default/files/content/arengukavad/mak-2014/mak-2014-kommunikatsioonistrateegia.pdf (accessed 31 January 2016).

MRA (2015c), International R&D Co-operation of MRA, http://agri.ee/et/ministeerium-kontakt/rahvusvaheline-koostoo/pollumajandusministeeriumi-rahvusvaheline-teadus-ja (accessed 11 February 2016).

MRA (2013a), Collection and Conservation of Plant Genetic Resources for Food and Agriculture in 2014-2020, www.agri.ee/sites/default/files/content/arengukavad/program-genetic-resources-2014-2020.pdf (accessed 5 February 2016).

MRA (2013b), Evaluation of the Rural Development Plan for the period 2007-2013, www.agri.ee/en/evaluation (accessed 30 January 2016).

MRA (2008), Riiklik programm "Sordiaretusprogramm aastatel 2009–2019". Põllumajandusministri 03.07.2008. käskkirja nr 152 lisa [The National Program "Plant breeding period 2009-2019" Minister of Agriculture 03.07.2008. Decree No. 152, www.agri.ee/sites/default/files/public/juurkataloog/TEADUS-ARENDUS/Ministri_kk_152_2008_2_sordiaretusprogramm.pdf (accessed 31 January 2016).

MRA (2005), Põllumajandus- ja maaelu areng. Ülevaated aastatest 1998-2005 [Agricultural and Rural Development. Overviews from 1998-2005], www.digar.ee/arhiiv/et/raamatud?id=7291 (accessed 4 April 2016).

MRA (2004), Põllumajanduslikud rakendusuuringud ja arendustegevus aastatel 2004–2008. [Agricultural Applied Research and Development 2004- 2008], www.agri.ee/sites/default/files/public/pllumajanduslikud_rakendusuuringud_ja_arendustegevus_aastatel_20042008.doc (accessed 27 April 2017).

MRA (1999), Põllumajandus ja maaelu areng, Ülevaade 1998. [Agricultural and Rural Development] Infotükk. Tallinn, 142 p.

Mürk, I., and T. Kalvet (2015), Teaduspõhiste ettevõtete roll Eesti T&A- ja innovatsioonisüsteemis – TIPS uuringu 4.3 lõppraport. Tallinn: TTÜ Ragnar Nurkse innovatsiooni ja valitsemise instituut [The role of science-based businesses in Estonian R&D and innovation system - 4.3 TIPS study final report. Tallinn: Tallinn University of Technology, Institute of Governance and Innovation Nurkse], https://energiatalgud.ee/img_auth.php/4/4a/Teadus-_ja_Innovatsioonipoliitika_Seire_Programm._Teadusp%C3%B5histe_ettev%C3%B5tete_roll_Eesti_T%26A-_ja_innovatsioonis%C3%BCsteemis._2015.pdf (accessed 28 November 2016).

Must, Ü., O. Otsus, A. Soon, M. Habicht, Ü. Napa, T. Tuisk, S. Lätt, R. Uus, and M. Lust (2014), Eesti Euroopa Liidu teadus- ja arendustegevuse 7. Raamprogrammis. Horizon 2020 [Estonia and the European Union research FP7 and Horizon 2020], www.horisont2020.ee/wp-content/uploads/2014/01/Eesti-EL-7.-raamprogrammis.pdf (accessed 5 February 2016).

NAO (National Audit Office) (2014), The Impact of innovation support measures on the Competitiveness of Companies. Report to the Estonian Parliament (Riigikogu), Tallinn, 1 December, www.riigikontroll.ee/DesktopModules/DigiDetail/FileDownloader.aspx?FileId=13243&AuditId=2340 (accessed 11 February 2016).

NRN (Estonian National Rural Network) (2013), Take notice of innovative agriculture, Publication, www.maainfo.ee/data/trykis/Notice_the_Innovative_Agriculture_eng_2013_WEB.pdf.

OECD (2017a), "Estonia", in *OECD Science, Technology and Innovation Outlook 2016*, OECD Publishing, Paris, http://dx.doi.org/10.1787/sti_in_outlook-2016-58-en.

OECD (2017b), *Main Science and Technology Indicators, Volume 2016 Issue 2*, OECD Publishing, Paris, http://dx.doi.org/10.1787/msti-v2016-2-en (last accessed in June 2017).

OECD (2017c), OECD statistics [Research and Development, OECD National Accounts], http://stats.oecd.org/ (last accessed in June 2017).

OECD (2015), "Analysing Policies to improve agricultural productivity growth, sustainably: Revised framework", www.oecd.org/tad/agricultural-policies/Analysing-policies-improve-agricultural-productivity-growth-sustainably-december-2014.pdf.

OECD (2014b), *OECD Science, Technology and Industry Outlook 2014*, OECD Publishing, Paris, http://dx.doi.org/10.1787/sti_outlook-2014-en.

OECD (2013), *Agricultural Innovation Systems: A Framework for Analysing the Role of the Government*, OECD Publishing, Paris, http://dx.doi.org/10.1787/9789264200593-en.

Pakkas, E. (2014), TAK programm täna ja homme : Mis hästi, mis halvasti? [TAK program today and tomorrow: As good as bad?] http://biopark.ee/wp-content/uploads/2014/12/28.11.2014_Eve-Pakkas.pdf (accessed 23 February 2016).

Paltser, I., and J. Reiljan (2015), Eesti rahvusvaheline positsioon innovatsioonipoliitika eri valdkondades [Estonia's international position in innovation policy in different areas], Riigikogu Toimetised [Proceedings of Riigikogu], Vol. 32, www.riigikogu.ee/rito/index.php?id=16015 (accessed 29 January 2016).

Parliament of Estonia (2016), Majanduskomisjon otsustas Arengufondi tegevuse lõpetada. Pressiteade. Majanduskomisjon [The Economic Development Fund has decided to terminate its activities, Press Release], www.riigikogu.ee/pressiteated/majanduskomisjon-et-et/majanduskomisjon-otsustas-arengufondi-tegevuse-lopetada/ (accessed 18 March 2016).

PlantValor (2016), Competence Centre for Knowledge-Based Health Goods and Natural Products, http://plantvalor.ee/index.php/home (accessed 4 April 2016).

Rand, L., and P. Ardel (2010), Seeme on saagi algus: Sertifitseeritud seemne eelistest ja sordikaitsest Eestis [The seed is the beginning of the harvest: Certified seed of the benefits and variety protection in Estonia], Põllumajandusministeerium [Ministry of Agriculture], www.agri.ee/sites/default/files/public/juurkataloog/TRUKISED/2010/trykis_seemesaagialus_2010.pdf (accessed 11 January 2016).

RDF (Rural Development Foundation) (2016), Nõuandekeskus [Advisory], www.mes.ee/nouandekeskus (accessed 31 January 2016).

RERC (Rural Economy Research Centre) (2016), Maaeluvõrgustik. Innovatsioonivõrgustik [Innovation Network], www.maainfo.ee/index.php?page=4& (accessed 1 February 2016).

Rietzke, D. (2015), "Push or Pull? Grants, Prizes and Information", Lancaster University Management School, *Economics Working Paper Series* 2015/011, www.lancaster.ac.uk/media/lancaster-university/content-assets/documents/lums/economics/working-papers/LancasterWP2015_011.pdf (accessed 4 April 2016).

Romanainen, J., K. Eljas-Taal, J. Rigby, J. Edler, P. Cunningham, K. Izsak, K. Männik, J. Angelis, K. Kosk, and J. Vallistu (2014a), "Teostatavusuuring innovatsioonipoliitika nõudluspoole meetmete väljatöötamiseks ja rakendamiseks Eestis. Uuringu II osa – poliitikasoovitused" [Feasibility study of innovation policy: Demand side measures for the development and implementation of Estonia. Part II of the study - the policy recommendations], *Innovation Studies* No. 23, www.mkm.ee/sites/default/files/inno_23_final.pdf (accessed 28 January 2016).

Romanainen, J., K. Eljas-Taal, J. Rigby, J. Edler, P. Cunningham, K. Izsak, K. Männik, J. Angelis, K. Kosk, and J. Vallistu (2014b), Feasibility Study for the Design and Implementation of Demand-side Innovation Policy Instruments in Estonia. Final report part 1 – Market Potential and International Experiences, Technopolis Group, www.mkm.ee/sites/default/files/final_report_part_1.pdf (accessed 1 March 2016).

Roolaht, T. (2012), "The problems of Estonian R&D and innovation strategy and the demand-side innovation policies", *Discussions on Estonian Economic Policy*, Vol. 1, pp. 186–203.

Ruttas-Küttim, R. (2014), ERAWATCH Country Reports 2013: Estonia, JRC Science and Policy Reports, https://rio.jrc.ec.europa.eu/en/library/erawatch-country-report-estonia-2013 (accessed 15 February 2016).

SCImago. (2007), SJR — SCImago Journal & Country Rank, Retrieved March 2014, from www.scimagojr.com.

Sepp, J., and R. Wrobel (2011), "The Double Challenge of Transformation and Integration: European Experiences and Consequences for Korea". Sepp, J.; Frear, D. (eds), *The Economy and Economics after Crisis,* Berliner Wissenschafts-Verlag, pp. 211–233.

State Journal (2005), Eesti säästva arengu riikliku strateegia "Säästev Eesti 21" heakskiitmine [Estonian national sustainable development strategy "Sustainable Estonia 21" approval], www.riigiteataja.ee/akt/940717 (accessed 30 January 2016).

Staehr, K. (2010), "An analysis of tax incentives to promote research and development in Estonia", KPMG Baltics AS, Praxis Center for Policy Studies, www.mkm.ee/public/TA-Maksuuuring-2010-01.pdf (accessed 3 March 2016).

Statistics Estonia (2017), Online statistical database, www.stat.ee (last accesssed 13 June 2017).

Statistics Estonia (2015a), Technologically innovative enterprises by type of innovation activity engaged during 2012-2014 and economic activity, 2014, www.stat.ee.

Statistics Estonia (2015b), Statistical Yearbook of Estonia, Statistics Estonia, Tallinn, www.stat.ee/en.

TBP (Tartu Biotechnology Park) (2015a), Toiduainetööstus muudab tooteid teadusega tervisele kasulikumaks [The food industry makes products more useful to health science], http://biopark.ee/uudised/toiduainetoostus-muudab-tooteid-teadusega-tervisele-kasulikumaks (accessed 29 January 2016).

TBP (2015b), Tallinna Teaduspargi Tehnopol ja Tartu Biotehnoloogia Pargi poolt juhitav tervisetehnoloogia klaster sai EAS-ilt 600 000 eurose toetuse [Tallinn Science Park Technopol and Tartu Biotechnology Park, operated by the Health Technology Cluster, received a EE 600 000 euro grant], http://biopark.ee/uudised/tallinna-teaduspargi-tehnopol-ja-tartu-biotehnoloogia-pargi-poolt-juhitav-tervisetehnoloogia-klaster-sai-eas-ilt-600-000-eurose-toetuse (accessed 29 January 2016).

TU (2016), Eelarved [Budget], www.ut.ee/et/ulikoolist/avalik-teave-ja-statistika/finantsstatistika/eelarved (accessed 23 February 2016).

TU (2015), Teaduse populariseerimine [Science popularisation], University of Tartu, www.ut.ee/et/teadus/populariseerimine (accessed 29 January 2016).

Ukrainski, K., T. Tänav, E. Karo, M. Kirs, V. Lember, T. Kalvet, A. Kelli, J. Vallistu, and U. Varblane (2015a), Eesti teadus- ja arendustegevuse ning innovatsiooni strateegia 2007-2013 täitmise analüüs, Lõpparuanne [Estonian Research and Development and Innovation Strategy 2007-2013 Analysis of performance, final report], https://dspace.ut.ee/bitstream/handle/10062/50390/TAI%20strateegia%202007_2013anal%C3%BC%C3%BCs.pdf?sequence=1&isAllowed=y (accessed 30 January 2016).

Ukrainski, K., H. Kanep, K. Timpmann, T. Tänav, T. Hirv, H. Kanep, and E.-L. Otsus (2015b), Eesti teaduse rahastamise seire, Uuring 2.2, lõppraport [Estonian research funding for monitoring, Study 2.2, Final report], http://tips.ut.ee/index.php?module=32&op=1&id=3697 (accessed 10 February 2016).

UPOV (2016), List of UPOV Members, International Union for the Protection of New Varieties of Plants, www.upov.int/members/en/ (accessed 29 January 2016).

Varblane, U., and K. Ukrainski (2016), Teadus- ja arendustegevus ja tootlikkus rahvusvahelises võrdluses, Tartu: Eesti Teadusagentuur, 31-42 [Research, development and productivity in international comparison, Tartu: Estonian Research Agency, pp. 31-42], www.etag.ee/wp-content/uploads/2014/01/TA_teaduskogumik-2016-veeb.pdf (accessed 5 December 2016).

Varblane, U. (2014), Euroopa raha võlu ja valu [The magic of money and pain], Riigikogu Toimetised [Proceedings], Vol. 29, pp. 25–39.

Vooremäe, A. (2011), Teadus- ja arendusstegevuse mõju põllumajandus- ja toidusektori arengule [Research and breeding impact on the agriculture and food sector], Põllumajandus ja maaelu 2011. Koosatnud: M. Aamissepp, E. Matveev, Maamajanduse Infokeskus, Jäneda.

World Economic Forum (2016), *The Global Competitiveness Report 2016-2017: Full data E*dition, Geneva 2015.

Annex 7.A1

Agricultural Innovation System governance mechanisms

Priority setting

Establishment and communication of priorities

Setting priorities in development strategies in Estonia is based on the goals of the Europe 2020 strategy. Achieving the objectives of innovation strategies — ensuring the sustainable development of society through RDI — is supported by Sustainable Estonia 21 and Estonia 2020.

To implement Estonia 2020, MEAC devises an annual roadmap, which is approved by the Government. The roadmap includes the list of planned activities together with the indicators, budgets and responsible parties. With each new action plan, the report for the previous period is submitted to the Government. The bodies involved in the development and implementation of innovation and entrepreneurship policies have the following roles (MEAC, 2013a):

- MEAC sets the strategic directions and formulates the application principles and distributes the roles between the implementing authorities.
- Innovation and Enterprise Policy Committee advises the Minister of Economic Affairs and Communications on key policy issues and assesses policy implementation.
- EDF organised the foresight activities necessary for long-term policy-making and made direct venture capital investments till the launch of the state venture capital fund, monitored and analysed international economic indexes and made policy suggestions on the basis thereof.
- KredEx supports business development through various financial instruments. KredEx portfolio includes loans, credit insurance and government-guaranteed securities. As a new direction KredEx will start to manage the venture capital fund.
- Enterprise Estonia (EE) helps to implement the innovation and entrepreneurship policy through various support schemes, advising and training. In 2014-20, the foundation puts more emphasis on the development of long-term partnerships with enterprises, and providing support through comprehensive development plans.

Figure 7.A1.1 describes the mechanism for the development of priority areas in agriculture.

Figure 7.A1.1. Mechanism for the development of priority areas

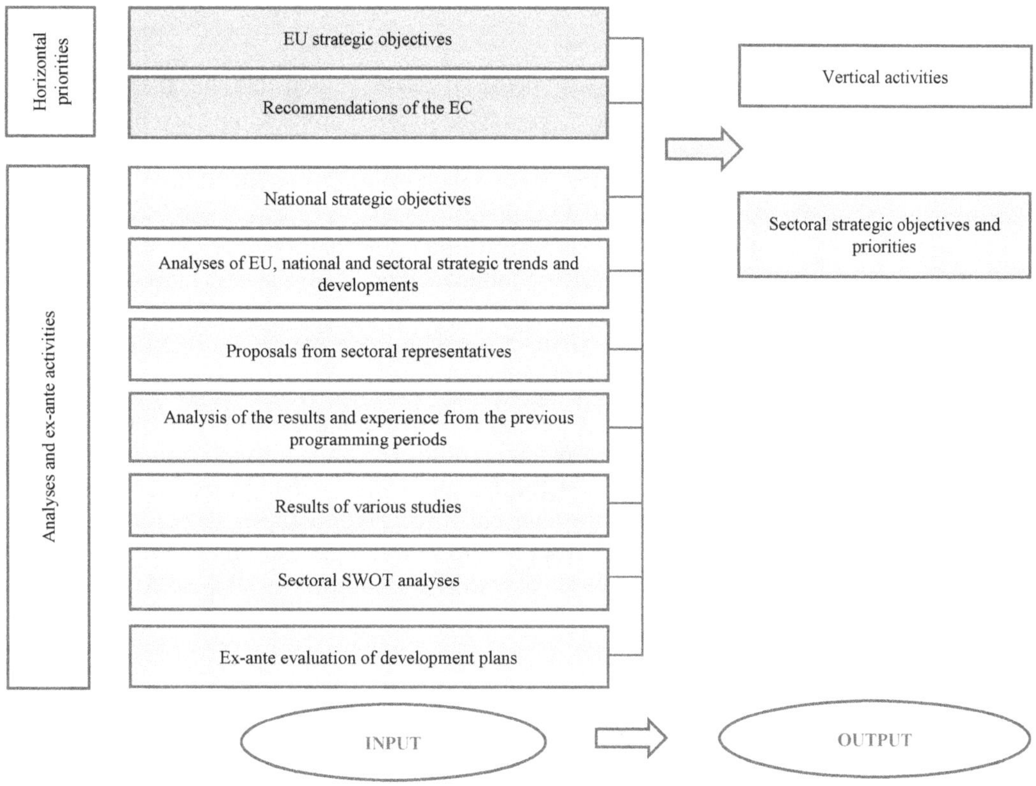

Source: EMÜ (2017).

The development plans are based on SWOT analyses, the analysis of the strategic documents of the EU, other countries and sectors, as well as the results and experience from previous development plans. According to the Regulation of the European Parliament and of the Council of the European Agricultural Fund for Rural Development (EAFRD) *ex ante* evaluation and SWOT analysis form a mandatory part of the development plan (Official Journal, 2014). The *ex ante* evaluation of the Estonian RDP is carried out by the procured enterprises, whereas the MRA and the permanent evaluators (from the EMÜ and the ARC) provide their input (MRA, 2016c).

During the *ex ante* evaluation, the evaluators conduct interviews with the representatives of the organisations responsible for the implementation and consult with the representatives of the Government Office and ministries, in order to take into account the developments in national policies. For example, when providing *ex ante* evaluation on the RDP 2014-20, the experts suggested that a greater emphasis should be placed on the dissemination of information in the field of RDI, as well as on enhancing cooperation between the different parties, including farmers, entrepreneurs and advisory services. A significant threat to the sustainability of agriculture is the insufficient spread of RDI information, and the lack of cooperation between different stakeholders in promoting innovation. The evaluators also state that offering multi-disciplinary solutions to agricultural producers and processors has taken a secondary place, as a result of which the actors have not received sufficient information on the entire production chain (MRA, 2016c).

Measurement and evaluation of performance

Framework for performance evaluation

Until March 2016 the Estonian Development Fund (EDF) was responsible for the monitoring and analysis of the growth areas, engaging entrepreneurs, researchers, and sectoral ministries, and, if necessary, other institutions or partners in the discussions on specific growth areas. Smart specialisation areas were controlled by a Steering Committee comprising the representatives from the MER, MEAC, Government Office, MoF and, if necessary, the representatives of other ministries and enterprises. The Steering Committee monitored the movement towards achieving the goals and fulfilment of the objectives and, when necessary, made proposals for changes in policies and activities, or initiated changes to the strategies (MEAC, 2013a). To continue the monitoring activities performed by the EDF, an independent unit with its own budget and competence for decisions will be set up under the Estonian Parliament, whereas the responsibility for EDF investment activities will be transferred to KredEx (Parliament of Estonia, 2016).

The priority of the Cohesion Policy Funds Operational Programme 2014-20 "Stimulating business growth supported by R&D" is related to economic growth and RDI. Performance indicators include the share of private spending on R&D activities in the public sector, Estonia's success rate in Horizon 2020, the scope of agreement of the obtained funding per capita, the share of R&D expenditure in the private sector (% of GDP), the share of enterprises cooperating for innovation with universities and other institutions of higher education as a percentage of total surveyed enterprises, and resource productivity attained through innovative solutions (MoF, 2014b).

Programmes are evaluated to find out how effective an action has been. To do this, data on the results and impact of the programmes, including the environment, agriculture and rural development as a whole, is collected and consistency with the set targets is assessed. As to the nature of their content, the evaluations are divided into evaluations of an operational nature, focusing on the functioning of the system, and evaluations of a strategic nature, focusing on the achievement of the objectives. Evaluation is carried out in three stages (MoF, 2014b):

1. *Ex ante* evaluation (including the *ex ante* evaluation of the EU and the European Cohesion Policy Funds operational programmes, as well as *ex ante* evaluation of sectoral development plans).
2. Evaluations undertaken during the programme period (typically carried out in two-year cycles, with the aim to assess the efficiency, effectiveness and impact of priority axes).
3. *Ex post* evaluations (evaluations carried out after the end of the period. These evaluations are performed by the EC in cooperation with the member states. Member states, including Estonia, can arrange additional needs based evaluations to identify the effects of subsidies).

The evaluation of the RDI system in Estonia as a whole was carried out over the period 2011-15 in the framework of a special monitoring programme "TIPS" for research and innovation policies, launched specially by the MER, where evaluations were carried out by researchers and scientists from the TU and TUT.

Since 2002, a series of studies and surveys "Innovation Studies", commissioned by the MEAC has been published. The series brings together studies, evaluations and analyses on the Estonian innovation system and innovation policy. The action is an attempt to raise awareness for innovation and promote knowledge-based innovation policy in Estonia.

Permanent evaluators participate in the evaluations, policy studies are conducted by Estonian and international bodies and the National Audit Office of Estonia also passes its judgement through audits.

Levels (project, programme, system) and frequency of performance evaluation

Estonia 2020 is reviewed annually and updated, if necessary. The upgrading process takes into account the statistics related to achieving the set objectives, the country-specific recommendations obtained during the European semester, discussions between ministries, strategy documentation on the use of support/investments for the EU budget period 2014-20, as well as the priorities of the new government coalition and the challenges specified in the talks between the prime minister and ministers (Government Office, 2014).

Statistics Estonia, acting under the leadership of the MOF, monitors the implementation of Sustainable Estonia 21. Statistics Estonia collects and analyses the statistics on sustainable development and every two years publishes the results of the statistics in the publication "Sustainable Development Indicators" (Statistics Estonia, 2015a).

The implementation of the RDI policy is monitored on an annual basis. MER is responsible for the implementation of the programme and reports the monitoring results to the Government every year. The evaluation of the strategic objectives is based mainly on official and internationally comparable statistics (Eurostat, Statistics Estonia, European Innovation Union Scoreboard, Europe 2020 implementation surveys, OECD databases, the Estonian Education Information System EHIS; Scopus/Science Metrics, Thompson Reuters Web of Science, the Horizon 2020 database). All these sources are used to check whether the target levels of the indicators have been reached. For some indicators, where drawing comparisons is not possible, a methodology for benchmarking is developed. The monitored indicators include the share of private investment (% of GDP), productivity per worker as of the EU27 average (%), Estonia's place in the Innovation Union Scoreboard, number of PhD defences in an academic year, the proportion of high-level Estonian scientific papers among the 10% of the world's most cited articles, the number of high-level Estonian scientific articles per one million inhabitants, the share of private sector investments into the R&D expenditure of the public sector, the share of expenditure earmarked for socio-economic applications (except academic studies) from the state budget R&D allocations, the share of high-tech products and services in exports (%), the share of high and medium-high-tech sector employment as of total employment (%), Estonia's success rate in obtaining funding from the Horizon 2020, including the volume of contracts per capita (% of the EU average), and the proportion of internationally coordinated research in state-funded R&D (MER, 2014a).

In the middle of the programme period, an interim report on the implementation of the R&D strategy will be compiled under the leadership of MER. Interim evaluations are carried out by the respective specialised research institutions. Both quantitative (databases, statistics, reports, etc.) and qualitative (interviews, panel of experts, etc.) methods are used in the evaluation. At the end of the programming period, the success of the strategy as a whole, as well as the effectiveness of the measures and the capabilities of the participants are analysed, and recommendations for the next period are made.

The current RDI programming period (2014-20) is the third one. At the end of the first period (2004-06), the evaluators assessing the implementation of the strategy pointed out that the RDI system in Estonia was more public sector (financing) centred than in the EU countries on average, whereas the final report for the second period (2007-13) stated that Estonia was moving towards a model dominated by enterprise and higher education institutions, characteristic of the Nordic countries. A problematic aspect highlighted at the beginning of the third programming period was high dependence on the R&D activities of enterprises and higher education institutions on public funding, and the non-compliance of some indicators to peculiarities of Estonia (e.g. patents as too narrow an indicator, or Estonia's place in the Innovation Union Scoreboard, which is measuring the R&D-based innovation, rather than the import of knowledge and its application for the benefit of the society, which is important from Estonia's point of view (Ukrainski et al., 2015a).

In the framework of Estonia 2020, MEAC is responsible for the implementation and monitoring of the entrepreneurship and innovation policy in Estonia. The entrepreneurship and innovation policy evaluation is designed to assess the impact, effectiveness and feasibility of the implemented measures. To implement the strategy, every year MEAC prepares an action plan (with the report on the previous action plan), which is approved by the government. The action plan lists the planned activities together with the indicators, budgets and responsible parties. Mid-term evaluations take place every two years and assess the impact of business supports and loans on enterprises. Enterprises that have used the respective services are compared to companies that have not used such services. The evaluators use both the corporate economic performance data, and interviews and surveys. Quantitative and qualitative combined research methods are used. Interim evaluations are commissioned and organised by the MEAC and conducted by MEAC in cooperation with EE and KredEx (Jaaksoo et al., 2012).

In addition, Estonia participates in the Community Innovation Survey (CIS) carried out by the European Union every two years. Establishments answer questions about product, processes, marketing and organisational innovation, as well as about the sources of innovation and cooperation and the distribution and volume of investments. Information on new products and non-domestic revenues is also collected. The aim of the CIS data analysis is to identify the barriers to the innovation process and find the biggest obstacles affecting the innovation system (Kaarna et al., 2015).

As to Smart Specialisation, monitoring activities were carried out by EDF. The intermediate and *ex post* evaluations are arranged by RDC. These reports compare the obtained results against the set objectives as well as to the world-class achievements (MER, 2014a).

Criteria of performance measurement

Since 2006, a common pan-EU evaluation process, the Common Monitoring and Evaluation Framework (CMEF), is used to assess Estonian RDP. The CMEF establishes agreed indicators for assessing the achievement of established results and impacts. In addition, the CMEF includes evaluation questions, which can be approached through additional national indicator analysis. In 2014, the common monitoring and evaluation system (CMES), which is a part of the CMEF was introduced.

The aim of the ongoing evaluation system is to monitor the results and impact of the Estonian RDP. In the course of the ongoing evaluation, the assessors, among other things, perform sectoral studies and analyses necessary for elaborating on the evaluation. ARC (agri-environmental measures) and the Department of Rural Economy Research of the Institute of Economic and Social Sciences of EMÜ (other rural development measures) are responsible for the ongoing evaluations. The aim is to identify and monitor the results and impacts across the RDP, including the impact of CAP Pillar 1 measures on the Estonian RDP, and vice versa, as well as to assess the impact of other horizontal issues (sustainable development, climate change and innovation) in the context of the Estonian RDP and the contribution of the Estonian RDP into the common strategic framework. The evaluators measure the output indicators once a year.

The evaluation (2014-20) is predominantly conducted along the priorities, measures, target areas and priorities of the projects. According to the CMEF, output indicators are set on the measures level, result indicators on the target area level and impact indicators on the priorities level. For the period 2007-13, the indicators were set at the measure level. The impact of the implementation of the Estonian RDP is assessed in four sections (Figure 7.A1.2).

Figure 7.A1.2. Monitoring and evaluation system of the Estonian RDP

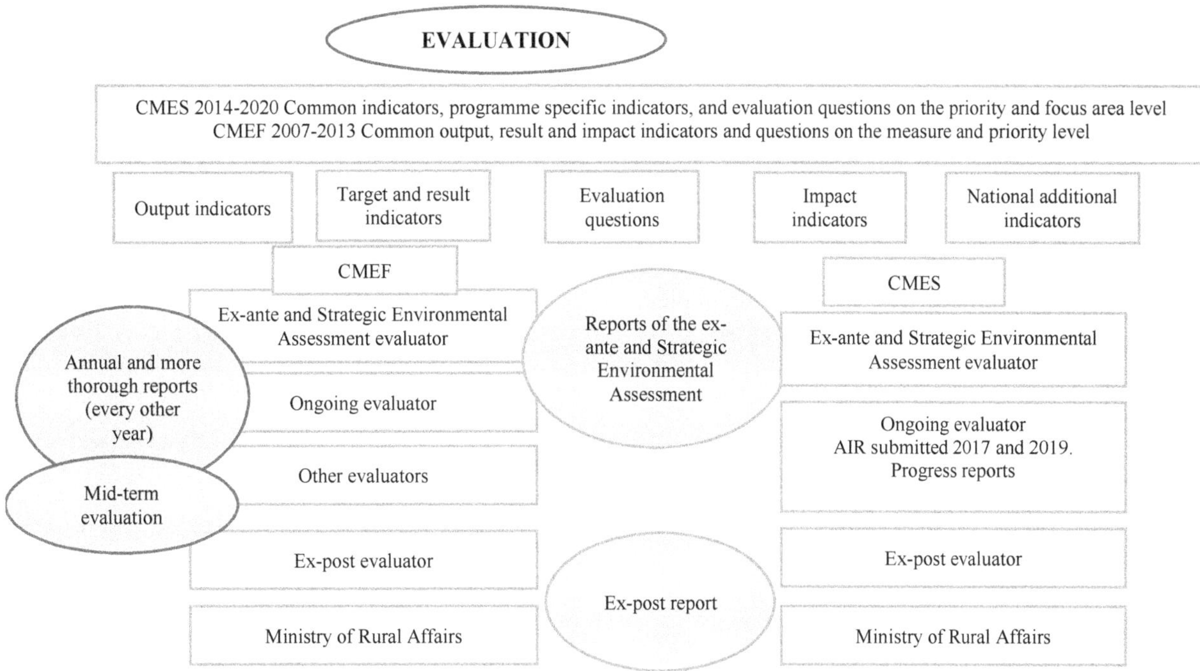

Source: Based on MRA (2016a).

Availability of input and output indicators

Different evaluations are carried out to identify the efficiency of the systems, programmes, measures, activities and projects. Indicators have been developed to measure the results, the changes as a result of the intervention and the performance of the participants. So far, the RDI indicators applied in Estonia have primarily been focused on the use of input and output indicators comparable to the EU that describe and analyse the dynamics of the RDI system based on the framework of EU policies and objectives. The current use of indicators has thus been of a monitoring nature. The development of more detailed indicators with intervention logic is carried out in the preparation phase of the specific operational plans and programmes (Karo et al., 2014b). The criteria used for the evaluation of indicators are in this case divided into three groups: validity (the indicator measures what needs to be measured) and reliability (replicability of results), efficiency (source data availability and processing costs), and quality (simplicity of use and impact). The indicators are assessed and the relevant recommendations are made by the expert analysts during the *ex ante* evaluation of the new strategy. Indicators are divided into input, output and performance indicators (Figure 7.A1.3) (Masso et al., 2013). Similar indicators are used in the field of agriculture and in the Monitoring and Evaluation System of the Estonian RDP.

Figure 7.A1.3. Types of indicators

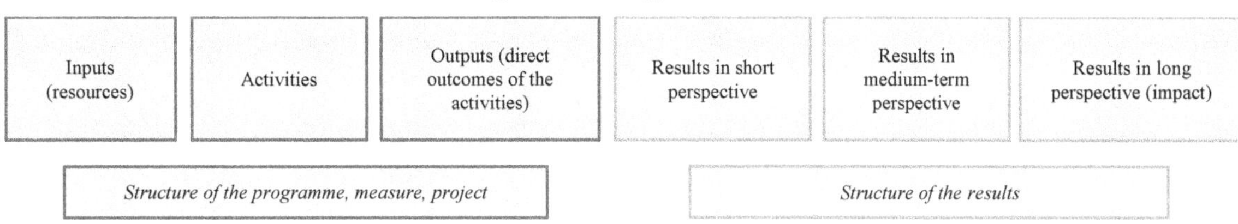

Source: Based on Masso et al. (2013).

At the measure level, monitoring data collection and reporting is carried out through ARIB and other relevant institutions, including the Foundation Private Forest Centre (PFC), LEADER local action groups and the RERC. Once a year ARIB prepares and submits an annual report to MRA on the basis of relevant information.

The innovation indicators for evaluating measures that support innovation in the Estonian RDPs for 2007-13 and 2014-20 are presented in Table 7.A1.1. In addition to indicators, the European Commission has developed common evaluation questions. Evaluation questions in the field of innovation in 2014-20 are quite similar to those used in 2007-13, although they are priority target areas based, rather than measure-based (Table 7.A1.2).

In addition to the evaluation of RDP implementation, the respective results achieved by agriculture-related companies/organisations are assessed in the course of the evaluation of all strategies listed in Table 7.A1.3, including RDI policy, Sectoral R&D activities and Entrepreneurship and innovation policy.

Table 7.A1.1. Indicators for the measures supporting innovation in RDPs 2007-13 and 2014-20

2007-13				**2014-20**			
Measures	Output indicator	Result indicator	Impact indicator	Focal sectors/measures	Target indicator	Output indicator	Result indicator
Priority: Improving the competitiveness of the agricultural and forestry sector				**Priority: Fostering knowledge transfer and innovation in agriculture, forestry, and rural areas**			
Training and information activities	Number of participants in training and information sessions; Number of training and information sessions a year	Number of successful completions	GVA changes per unit labour costs per year; Additional indicators: proportion of managers of agricultural holdings with basic and full education; proportion of adult population participating in life-long learning	Fostering innovation, cooperation, and the development of the knowledge base in rural areas Measures: - Knowledge transfer and information, - Advisory services, - Farm management and farm relief services, - Cooperation	Share of expenditure from the total Estonian RDP expenditure	Total public expenditure; total public expenditure on training and mobility and promotion schemes of agricultural enterprises	% of innovative projects out of all RDP supported projects; Number and types of partners involved in cooperation projects; Number of supported innovative actions implemented and disseminated by EIP operational groups
Support for advisory system and services	Number of agricultural producers and private forest owners supported Number of centres reformed	Increase in GVA of agricultural producers and private forest owners supported	GVA changes per unit labour costs per year	Strengthening the links between agriculture, food production and forestry and research and innovation, including for the purpose of improved environmental management and performance Measures: -Cooperation	Total number of cooperation projects (groups, networks/clusters, pilot projects, etc.) supported	Number of EIP working groups supported (creation and activity); Number of other cooperation projects (groups networks/clusters, pilot projects, etc.) supported	% of cooperation operations continuing after the RDP support including for the purpose of improved environmental management and performance Number and types of partners involved in cooperation projects

Table 7.A1.1. Indicators for the measures supporting innovation in RDPs 2007-13 and 2014-20 (cont.)

2007-13				**2014-20**			
Measures	Output indicator	Result indicator	Impact indicator	Focal sectors/measures	Target indicator	Output indicator	Result indicator
				Priority: Enhancing farm viability and competitiveness of all types of agriculture in all regions and promoting innovative farm technologies and the sustainable management of forests			
Modernisation of agricultural holdings	Number of agricultural entrepreneurs and producers supported; the volume of investments per programming period	Number of agricultural entrepreneurs and producers making innovative products or use innovative technologies per programming period; Increase in NVA by the end of the programming period	Growth in NVA and change in GVA per unit labour costs by the end of the programme	Improving the economic performance of all farms and facilitating farm restructuring and modernisation, notably with a view to increasing market participation and orientation as well as agricultural diversification Measures: -Knowledge transfer and information; -.Advisory services; - Farm management and farm relief services; - Investments into real property; - Development of agricultural; holdings and entrepreneurship; - Cooperation	The share of agricultural holdings receiving support for investments in the re-organisation and modernisation from the Estonian RDP	Number of participants in training; total public expenditure on education and skills acquisition actions, mobility and promotion in agricultural holdings; Number of beneficiaries receiving advice; Number of agricultural holdings receiving support for investing in agricultural holdings; total public expenditure on investments in infrastructure; Number of agricultural holdings receiving business start-up aid for setting up small-scale agricultural enterprises	% of agriculture holdings with RDP support for investments in restructuring or modernisation Complementary result indicator: Change in agricultural output on supported farms/AWU (Annual Work Units)

Table 7.A1.1. Indicators for the measures supporting innovation in RDPs 2007-13 and 2014-20 (cont.)

2007-13				**2014-20**			
Measures	Output indicator	Result indicator	Impact indicator	Focal sectors/measures	Target indicator	Output indicator	Result indicator
				Priority: Promoting food chain organisation, including processing and marketing of agricultural products, animal welfare and risk management in agriculture			
Improving the economic value of forests and adding value to forestry products	Number of properties supported; Total volume of investments Number of prevention and restoration actions	Boosting the production potential and value of forests; Number of micro-enterprises applying new products and innovative technologies		Improving competitiveness of primary producers by better integrating them into the agri-food chain through quality schemes, adding value to agricultural products, promotion in local markets and short supply circuits, producer groups and organisations and inter-branch organisations Measures: - Knowledge transfer and information; -.Advisory services; - Farm management and farm relief services; - Quality assurance schemes for agricultural and food products - Investments into real property; - Creation of producer groups and organisations -Cooperation	Share of agricultural holdings receiving support through quality assurance schemes, local markets and short supply chains, producer groups and organisations	Number of participants in training; total public expenditure on education and skills acquisition actions, mobility and promotion schemes in agricultural holdings; Number of beneficiaries receiving advice; Number of activities receiving support for investments; Number of activities receiving support for producer group creation; Number of agricultural holdings participating in activities of the supported producer groups; Number of agricultural holdings involved in the cooperation within the supply chain or promote cooperation on the local level	% of agricultural holdings receiving support for participating in quality schemes, local markets and short supply circuits, and producer groups/ organisations

Table 7.A1.1. Indicators for the measures supporting innovation in RDPs 2007-13 and 2014-20 (cont.)

2007-13				**2014-20**			
Measures	Output indicator	Result indicator	Impact indicator	Focal sectors/measures	Target indicator	Output indicator	Result indicator
Adding value to agricultural and non-wood forestry products	Number of enterprises and cooperative societies supported; total volume of investments	Number of enterprises and cooperative societies introducing new products and innovative technologies	Net value added expressed in purchasing power standard (PPS), (% of EU average); change in GVA per unit labour costs per year	Supporting farm risk prevention and management Measures: - Advisory services; - Farm management and farm relief services.	Number of agricultural enterprises participating in risk management schemes	Number of beneficiaries receiving advice; total public expenditure	% of farms participating in risk management schemes
Development of new products, processes and technologies in the sectors of agriculture, food and forestry	Number of cooperation projects supported	Number of entrepreneurs introducing new products and innovative technologies	Net value added expressed in purchasing power standard (PPS), (% of EU average); change in GVA per unit labour costs per year				

Sources: based on Estonian Rural development Plans for programming periods 2007-13 and 2014-20 and Common evaluation questions for rural development programmes 2014-20

Table 7.A1.2. Evaluation questions concerning innovation about the implementation and impact of the Estonian RDP 2007-13 and 2014-20

2007-13		**2014-20**		
Measure	Evaluation question	Priority	Focal sector	Evaluation questions
Training and information activities	To what extent have the training, information, knowledge and innovative practices dissemination activities improved labour productivity and/or other elements related to competitiveness in the agricultural, food and forestry sector? To what extent have the training activities contributed to improving sustainable land management, including sustainable use of natural resources? To what extent are the supported training courses in accordance with the actual needs and coherent with other measures of the programme?	Fostering knowledge transfer and innovation in agriculture, forestry, and rural areas	Fostering innovation, cooperation, and the development of the knowledge base in rural areas	To what extent have RDP interventions supported innovation, cooperation and the development of the knowledge base in rural areas? RDP projects have been innovative and based on developed knowledge • Operational groups have been created • Variety of partners involved in EIP operational groups • Innovative actions have been implemented and disseminated by the EIP operational groups
Support for advisory system and services	To what extent has the measure improved the management and economic performance of agricultural and forestry enterprises? Specify the following aspects: production techniques; quality standards: occupational safety; management of natural resources. To what extent has the measure contributed to improving the human potential in the agricultural sector? To what extent has the scheme contributed to improving the competitiveness of the agricultural sector?		Strengthening the links between agriculture, food production and forestry and research and innovation, including for the purpose of improved environmental management and performance	To what extent have RDP interventions supported the strengthening of links between agriculture, food production and forestry and research and innovation, including for the purpose of improved environmental management and performance? Long term collaboration between agriculture, food production and forestry entities and institutions for research and innovation has been established • Cooperation operations between agriculture, food production and forestry and research and innovation for the purpose of improved environmental management and performance have been implemented
Modernisation of agricultural holdings	To what extent have investment grants contributed to a better use of production factors in agricultural enterprises? Specifically, to what extent have investment grants facilitated the introduction of new technologies and innovation? To what extent have investment grants enhanced the market access and market share of agricultural enterprises? To what extent have investment grants contributed to long-term and sustainable activity of agricultural enterprises? To what extent have investment grants contributed to improving the competitiveness of the agricultural sector?	Enhancing farm viability and competitiveness of all types of agriculture in all regions and promoting innovative farm technologies and the sustainable management of forests	Improving the economic performance of all farms and facilitating farm restructuring and modernisation, notably with a view to increasing market participation and orientation as well as agricultural diversification	To what extent have RDP interventions contributed to improving the economic performance, restructuring and modernisation of supported farms in particular through increasing their market participation and agricultural diversification? Agricultural output per annual working unit of supported agricultural holdings has increased • Farms have been modernised • Farms have been restructured

Table 7.A1.2. Evaluation questions concerning innovation about the implementation and impact of the Estonian RDP 2007-13 and 2014-20 (cont.)

2007-13		2014-20		
Measure	Evaluation question	Priority	Focal sector	Evaluation questions
Improving the economic value of forests	To what extent have investment grants contributed to the diversification of the production of forest enterprises? To what extent have investment grants contributed to increasing the market share of forest enterprises, and improving market access in such sectors as renewable energy? To what extent have investment grants contributed maintaining or improving the sustainable management of forests? To what extent have investment grants contributed to increasing the competitiveness of forest holdings?	Promoting food chain organisation, including processing and marketing of agricultural products, animal welfare and risk management in agriculture	Improving competitiveness of primary producers by better integrating them into the agri-food chain through quality schemes, adding value to agricultural products, promotion in local markets and short supply circuits, producer groups and organisations and inter-branch organisations	To what extent have RDP interventions contributed to improving the competitiveness of supported primary producers by better integrating them into the agri-food chain through quality schemes, adding value to the agricultural products, promoting local markets and short supply circuits, producer groups and inter-branch organisation? Competitiveness of supported primary producers has improved • The share of the final price of agriculture products retained with primary producers has increased • The added value of agricultural products of primary producers has increased Implementation of quality schemes by primary producers has increased • Participation of primary producers in short circuit schemes, quality-oriented producer group and/or inter branch organisation has increased
Adding value to agricultural and forestry products	To what extent have investment grants contributed to introducing new technologies and innovation? To what extent have investment grants contributed to improving the quality of agricultural and forestry products? To what extent have investment grants contributed to improving the efficiency of agricultural and forestry product processing and marketing? To what extent have investment grants contributed to enhancing the market access and market share of agricultural enterprises and forest holdings, including in such sectors as renewable energy? To what extent have investment grants contributed to improving the competitiveness of the agricultural and forestry sector?		Supporting farm risk prevention and management	To what extent have RDP interventions supported farm risk prevention and management? Participation of farms in risk prevention and management schemes has increased
Cooperation in the sectors of agriculture, food and forestry to develop new products, processes and technologies	To what extent has the support enhanced the market access of primary agricultural and forestry products and the market share of innovative products, processes and technologies developed in cooperation between the participants in the production chain? To what extent has the support contributed to improving the competitiveness of agricultural, forestry and food sector?			

Sources: based on Guidelines for ongoing assessment, rural development programmes in 2007-13 and Common evaluation questions for rural development programmes 2014-20.

Table 7.A1.3. Innovation policy indicators in national strategies

Policy	Responsible institution	Evaluation frequency	Data sources	Submitted to:	Innovation indicators
RDI policy	Ministry of Education and Research *(sectoral RDI indicators are presented to MER by sectoral ministries, including MRA)*	Once a year	Eurostat; Statistics Estonia; Innovation Union Scoreboard; Surveys on Strategy "Europe 2020" implementation; OECD; Estonian Education Information System EHIS; Scopus/Science Metrics; Thompson Reuters Web of Science; Horizon 2020 database	National government	Proportion of RDI, including private investments, % GDP; *productivity per employee, % of the EU average, Place of Estonia in the European Innovation Scoreboard; Number of defended PhD theses in a study-year; Number of high-level articles belonging to the 10% of the most cited articles in the world; Number of high-level articles per one million inhabitant; Share of private investments in the RDI of the public sector; Share of financing earmarked for socio-economic activities (except academic research) in the RDI allocations in the state budget; Share of high-tech products and services in export, %; Employment in high-tech sector from total employment, %, Estonia's success in Horizon 2020, including the volume of financing received per inhabitant, % of EU average; Share of internationally coordinated research from the state supported R&D activities; Number of joint publications of public and private sector (Innovation Union Scoreboard)
Sectoral R&D activities	Sectoral ministries, including MRA	Once a year	Statistics Estonia	MER	Number of employees engaged in research and development; Internal and external expenditures on R&D of enterprises in entrepreneurship sector; Number of employees engaged in R&D activities in non-profit sectors Number of employees engaged in R&D activities in non-profit sectors by field of action; Expenditure on R&D by institutional sector and types of expenditure; Expenditure on R&D and their financing from the state and municipal budget
Entrepreneurship and innovation policy	MEAC	Once a year or every other year	Business register, Enterprise Estonia	National government	Number of enterprises cooperating in the field of innovation; R&D expenditures in enterprises; Added value per employee; Number of enterprises launching innovative products; Number of innovative ideas entering the market; Revenues from sales, including revenues from innovative products; Export income and net income of an enterprise.

Table 7.A1.3. Innovation policy indicators in national strategies (cont.)

Policy	Responsible institution	Evaluation frequency	Data sources	Submitted to:	Innovation indicators
Agricultural innovation policy (as expressed in the RDP)	MRA	Once a year	Statistics Estonia, ongoing evaluator, World Economic Forum	EC	Planned output indicators in 2014-20: Public sector expenditure on knowledge transfer and dissemination (including training, demonstration and dissemination activities, visits to enterprises, workshops); Number of participants in training; Public sector expenditure on advisory services (including individual advice and training of advisors) and agricultural enterprise management and replacement activities; Public sector expenditure on enhancing cooperation (including the development of innovation clusters, new products, practices, processes and technologies); Number of EIP working groups supported (launch and activity); Number of other cooperation projects (groups, networks, clusters, test projects, etc.): Additional indicator that were measured in 2007-13: Economic growth (measured through the net added value earned by the beneficiary (% of EU27 average); Productivity of labour; Competitiveness (better economic results, more efficient use of resources, etc. as compared to other enterprises); Labour efficiency and wages; Efficiency of production and marketing; Economic sustainability (expressed through financial ratios of beneficiaries).

Source: Based on MRA (2016a), MER (2014a), EMÜ (2015c), Mihkelson et al. (2014).

Benchmarking tools

In the course of the ongoing evaluation, the assessors analyse the implementation of the planned measures, as well as the fulfilment of the objectives set. The EMÜ and the ARC analyse the impact of the implementation of the agricultural innovation policy. ARIB registers, records of other pertaining institutions, research data on a sector basis, and various databases (Agricultural Board, Statistics Estonia, FADN, etc.) are used during the analysis.

In the assessment of the achievements in RDI, mainly official and internationally comparable statistics are used (Eurostat, Statistics Estonia; Innovation Union Scoreboard, Europe 2020 implementation surveys, the OECD, the Estonian Education Information System EHIS; Scopus/Science Metrics; Thompson Reuters Web of Science, the Horizon 2020 database), which the attained target objectives or levels are checked against.

The development of measures for the achievement of the objectives of the sector-specific development plans is preceded by an *ex ante* evaluation and a feasibility analysis, which include a comparative analysis of the objectives, the current situation and the context (necessary preconditions for the implementation of the instruments). The feasibility study also analyses similar experiences of other countries in implementing the measures (for example the development of demand-side measures for the innovation policy).

In the course of mid-term and *ex post* evaluations, experts compare the implementation results to the objectives set. Comparisons between the various sectors and performance within the sector are also carried out. The impact of support for entrepreneurship and innovation and loans on enterprises is also evaluated through comparative analysis. The enterprises granted the support are compared to businesses that have not used the support. The economic indicators of the company and surveys are used as data sources.

The effectiveness analysis comparing the implementation of innovation policy between the EU countries is conducted by the European Commission, which annually collects the necessary input data for the analysis from the member states.

Evaluation of economic, environmental and social impacts of innovation

For both the RDP 2007-13 and the RDP 2014-20, the impact of the innovation measures and innovation measures from other focal sectors on the economy, environment and the social sphere is assessed. These questions are reflected in the EC common evaluation questions for rural development. The results of the economic, environmental and social aspects are nationally assessed in the course of mid-term and *ex post* evaluations (in the new period during the compilation of the strategy report). Compared to the 2007-13 period, in the new period the above-mentioned aspects are evaluated horizontally, whereas in 2007-13 the results were assessed based both on the measure and through general evaluation questions horizontally. In both periods, assessing the outcome of the support interventions and the impact of innovation on economy has received the most attention. The impact of innovation on the environment and social aspects has been evaluated indirectly through the implementation of agricultural policy and support schemes earmarked for development. Tables 7.A1.2 and 7.A1.3 present the indicators reflecting the innovation performance on the economy, as well as the evaluation questions. Indirect effects of the innovation performance on the environment are assessed through the impact of investment grants on forest area management, preservation and improvement of biodiversity, ensuring animal welfare, developing farming systems, maintaining and improving water and soil quality, and mitigating the effect of climate change. The impact of innovation activities on the social aspects are assessed through the overall improvement in the quality of life in rural areas, an increase in employment growth and the promotion of entrepreneurship.

Evaluation methods and frequency

The impact of the RDI strategy on enterprises has been inclusively estimated in a number of studies (mainly in the framework of research and innovation monitoring programmes). Several measures have been studied in the 'analytical matching framework', where a control group was created. The control group was similar in all other characteristics, but did not receive the support. The performance of different groups was compared to identify the impact of the support. For example, in 2012, the Estonian Audit Office, which is also authorised to study the country-wide innovation impact on enterprise competitiveness, in collaboration with Statistics Estonia, carried out an 'analytical matching framework' study and survey into the impact of innovation support measures. To assess the impact of the innovation support measures, enterprises receiving subsidies for the years 2004-12 from EE were interviewed in 2012 and compared to enterprises not supported. The enterprises supported were asked how the received support affected the company's economic indicators (revenue, exports, value added), whether new products or services had been developed, etc. Enterprises not supported were asked to explain why they had not applied for support. Both groups of the enterprises were asked which kind of support companies should offer (NAO, 2014). TUT's researchers studying the same issue with a slightly different methodology than the Estonian Audit Office came to practically the same conclusions. Both studies showed that there were positive correlations with the company's turnover and number of employees, but the correlation with performance (productivity) could not be found, or a statistically significant negative correlation was detected. The general problem of the studies performed was that the time between receiving the grant and measuring the results was too short, which is the reason the results reflect the corporate profile of the companies receiving support rather than the effectiveness of the support (Ukrainski et al., 2015a).

The problem in assessing the success of the implementation of the programmes is a time-lag between the programme outcomes and their effects, which may take years. Usually the immediate control over the programme ends with the outputs. The changes induced by the outputs are affected by all sorts of external factors. The longer the delay between the output of the programme and the impact of the achieved output, the more uncontrollable factors intervene in the chain. However, this delayed impact is of real importance and should be evaluated (Masso et al., 2013).

Compared to the input and output indicators of the programmes, projects and activities, the use of result indicators has been limited despite the fact that performance indicators should make it clear what the actual impact of the intervention has been. The use of impact indicators in RDI fields, however, is difficult because the effects can be very versatile by nature (therefore, in recent assessments more and more attention is being paid to the so-called behavioural added value, where, for example the beneficiary of the supported R&D projects or research cooperation continues the use and expansion of the RDI network to meet the challenges facing them), and/or the impact of the specific intervention may manifest itself only after a longer period (Karo et al., 2014).

Use of evaluation results in priority setting and decision making

Thematic objectives and key actions have been agreed upon in the pan-European strategic coherence framework (EC, 2012). During the period 2014-20, the rural development policy is included in the common pan-European strategic frameworks of the ERDF, the European Social Fund, the Cohesion Fund and the European Maritime and Fisheries Fund. As part of the joint planning, a partnership agreement is negotiated and signed with the EC at the national level.

In setting long-term objectives, member states comply with the sectoral and cross-sectoral (including innovation) Europe-wide objectives, thereby contributing, through the implementation of the objectives, to the improved competitiveness on the European level. The member states also base their choice of measures for achieving the objectives on the key actions of the EU, taking into account national/regional specificities. The adoption of every new sectoral strategic plan is preceded by an *ex ante* evaluation, for which input includes results of the performance and impacts assessment of the previous programming period, as well as the analysis of economic trends and the international and national economic environment. Inputs are the basis for the formulation and development of the new economic and innovation policy. *Ex ante* evaluations usually take place in parallel with the elaboration of the development plans for the new period, which is why the inputs are up to date. *Ex ante*, mid-term and *ex post* evaluations are carried out by experts who give expert opinions and recommendations related to the goals and measures of the new period.

The Research and Development Council (RDC) advises the government in matters relating to the development of the national research, development and innovation system. The RDC advises the Government on the preparation of the draft state budget in respect to the amounts prescribed for research and development, on the establishment and reorganisation of research and development institutions and the termination of their activities and on establishing the conditions and procedures for the evaluation of research and development. The RDC also presents its opinion to the government on the national research and development programmes presented by the ministries and on the objectives of research and development policy for the forthcoming period (Government Office, 2016).

ORGANISATION FOR ECONOMIC CO-OPERATION AND DEVELOPMENT

The OECD is a unique forum where governments work together to address the economic, social and environmental challenges of globalisation. The OECD is also at the forefront of efforts to understand and to help governments respond to new developments and concerns, such as corporate governance, the information economy and the challenges of an ageing population. The Organisation provides a setting where governments can compare policy experiences, seek answers to common problems, identify good practice and work to co-ordinate domestic and international policies.

The OECD member countries are: Australia, Austria, Belgium, Canada, Chile, the Czech Republic, Denmark, Estonia, Finland, France, Germany, Greece, Hungary, Iceland, Ireland, Israel, Italy, Japan, Korea, Latvia, Luxembourg, Mexico, the Netherlands, New Zealand, Norway, Poland, Portugal, the Slovak Republic, Slovenia, Spain, Sweden, Switzerland, Turkey, the United Kingdom and the United States. The European Union takes part in the work of the OECD.

OECD Publishing disseminates widely the results of the Organisation's statistics gathering and research on economic, social and environmental issues, as well as the conventions, guidelines and standards agreed by its members.

OECD PUBLISHING, 2, rue André-Pascal, 75775 PARIS CEDEX 16
(51 2018 01 1 P) ISBN 978-92-64-28871-3 – 2018

www.ingramcontent.com/pod-product-compliance
Lightning Source LLC
Chambersburg PA
CBHW061207240926
51846CB00006B/1131